Influencer Marketing

This is one of the first textbooks to explore the phenomenon of Influencer Marketing and how it fits within marketing communications to build brands and their communities. Influencers – those who can impact a brand's marketing and advertising strategies as well as build brand communities – are making extensive use of the new digital and traditional communications platforms. Influencers offer brands the ability to deliver the "right" communication and marketing messages to a specific target audience.

Across four core sections, this book brings together the key theory and practical implications of this new marketing tool: how it works as part of communications campaigns, including how to select the right influencers and measure their success, the dark side of influencer marketing, and the legal and ethical framework. With contributions from authors across the globe, each chapter is also accompanied by an in-depth case study – from the Kardashians to Joe Wicks – that demonstrates how the theory translates to practice.

Influencer Marketing is important reading for advanced, postgraduate and executive education students of Marketing, Digital Marketing, Marketing Communications, Brand Management and Public Relations. With its accessible style and practical content, it is also highly valuable for Marketing Communications, Branding and PR specialists.

Sevil Yesiloglu Ph.D., is a senior lecturer in Advertising at London College of Communication, University of Art London, UK.

Joyce Costello Ph.D., is a Public Affairs Specialist for the US Army, and was previously a senior lecturer in Digital Marketing at Bournemouth University, UK.

Influencer Marketing

Building Brand Communities and Engagement

Edited by

Sevil Yesiloglu and Joyce Costello

Routledge
Taylor & Francis Group

LONDON AND NEW YORK

First published 2021
by Routledge
2 Park Square, Milton Park, Abingdon, Oxon OX14 4RN

and by Routledge
52 Vanderbilt Avenue, New York, NY 10017

Routledge is an imprint of the Taylor & Francis Group, an informa business

British Library Cataloguing-in-Publication Data
A catalogue record for this book is available from the British Library

Library of Congress Cataloging-in-Publication Data
Names: Yesiloglu, Sevil, editor. | Costello, Joyce, editor.
Title: Influencer marketing : building brand communities and engagement / edited by Sevil Yesiloglu and Joyce Costello.
Description: 1 Edition. | New York : Routledge, 2021. |
Includes bibliographical references and index.
Identifiers: LCCN 2020027019 (print) | LCCN 2020027020 (ebook) |
ISBN 9780367338664 (hardback) | ISBN 9780367338688 (paperback) |
ISBN 9780429322501 (ebook)
Subjects: LCSH: Marketing. | Influence (Psychology) | Social media. |
Communication in marketing. | Advertising–Planning,
Classification: LCC HF5415 .I5144 2021 (print) |
LCC HF5415 (ebook) | DDC 658.8–dc23
LC record available at https://lccn.loc.gov/2020027019
LC ebook record available at https://lccn.loc.gov/2020027020

ISBN: 978-0-367-33866-4 (hbk)
ISBN: 978-0-367-33868-8 (pbk)
ISBN: 978-0-429-32250-1 (ebk)

Typeset in Scala
by Newgen Publishing UK

Contents

Contributors

Adriana Arcuri is a senior marketing executive. She holds a master's degree at Fundação Getulio Vargas. Her research has been published in *Consumption, Markets & Culture*.

Laura Biondi is public relation executive at Gravity Global. She specializes in the business-to-business sector.

Hayleigh Bosher, Ph.D., is an internationally published legal academic, speaker and consultant specializing in intellectual property, media and entertainment law. She is a Lecturer in Intellectual Property Law at Brunel University London, Visiting Research Fellow at the Centre for Intellectual Property, Policy and Management, author and Book Review Editor for the specialist IP blog IPKat, and founder of the World IP Women (WIPW). She holds a Ph.D. in Copyright Law from Bournemouth University.

Antonella Capriello, Ph.D., is Associate Professor of Marketing at the University of Eastern Piedmont in Italy. Her research activities include studies on event management, networking processes in tourist destinations, social entrepreneurship, and franchising. She has published more than 60 research papers, including articles in the *Journal of Business Research* and *Tourism Management*.

Fiona Cownie, Ph.D., is Associate Professor within the Faculty of Media and Communication at Bournemouth University. Dr Cownie's research focus is a relational approach to HE and its implications for the student and alumni experience. Fiona is an experienced educator and her teaching lies within the areas of relationship marketing and word-of-mouth communication. She works hard to co-create with her students in the areas of education and research.

Simrit Gill, EMEA, is Corporate Analyst Graduate at JP Morgan Chase. She started a career in Investment Banking after studying for a BSc (Hons) in Marketing at Bournemouth University.

Scott Guthrie is an independent influencer marketing consultant, conference speaker, guest university lecturer, top 10 PR blogger, and media commentator. He is co-chair of the CIPR influencer marketing panel, a PRCA council member, a founding member of the BCMA influencer marketing steering group and an editorial board member of both Talking Influence and Influence publications. Scott has written chapters for four business books on the subject of progressive public relations and influencer marketing.

James Harrison is a Marketing Executive at Global, the Media and Entertainment Group. He studied Marketing and Communications at Bournemouth University and was awarded a prize for his research paper at the Promotional Communications Conference (2018).

Elina Kahri is a master's student of Marketing at Aalto University, Finland. Her research interests include consumer behavior in social media as well as influencer marketing.

Tytti Kirvesmies, MSc, is Junior Account Executive at Ogilvy, Germany. She has a master's degree in marketing from Tampere University, Finland. Her research interests include consumers' parasocial relationships in social media.

Marina Leban is a Ph.D., Candidate at the Department of Marketing, ESCP Business School, Denmark. Her research focuses on social media marketing and luxury consumption. She is particularly interested in new forms of luxury consumption practices in the context of visual social media such as Instagram. Her work has been published in the *Journal of Business Ethics* and the *Journal of Business Research*.

Eser Levi, Ph.D., works as an Assistant Professor at Istanbul Bilgi University, Faculty of Communication, Department of Communication Design and Management. She received both her Masters Degree and Ph.D. from Marmara University. Her research interests are predominantly in the area of Advertising, Branding, and Consumer Behavior. She teaches courses such as The Foundations of Advertising, Quantitative Reasoning, Advertising and Communication, and Copywriting. Levi has been the Head of Communication Design and Management Department since 2018.

Iain MacRury, Ph.D., is Professor of Media and Communication in the Department of Culture, Media and Communication at the University of Stirling. His publications in this field include *Advertising*, (Routledge, 2009) and contributions, as co-editor, to *The Advertising Handbook* (4th Edition), (Routledge, 2018). He teaches and researches communication in the context of culture, media and creative industry organizations.

Elina Närvänen, Ph.D., is Associate Professor of Services and Retailing at Tampere University, Finland. Her research focuses on consumer behavior, consumer communities, branding and sustainability. Her research has been published in several international journals, including *European Journal of Marketing, Journal of Consumer Behaviour* and *Journal of Service Management*.

Ayse Bengi Ozcelik, Ph.D., works as an Assistant Professor at Istanbul Bilgi University, Faculty of Communication, Department of Communication Design and Management. She holds a Ph.D degree in Marketing from Istanbul Technical University and an MA degree in Marketing Communications from Istanbul Bilgi University. Her research interests include digital marketing, customer experience, consumer behavior and consumer culture. She teaches courses such as Marketing and Advertising, Communication Design, Applied Entrepreneurship, and Marketing Research.

Irene Quintana Ramos, MA, is a Postgraduate in Media and Communication, with a background in Journalism. Her areas of interest lie within sustainability, with particular emphasis in veganism, and ecological lifestyle choices.

Sabina Riboldazzi, Ph.D., is Assistant Professor of Management at the University of Milan-Bicocca, Department of Economics, Management and Statistics, Milan. She graduated from the University of Eastern Piedmont and gained her Ph.D. in Marketing and Business Management from the University of Milan-Bicocca. She teaches global trade management and global marketing management. Her interests lie in global business management with particular reference to marketing channels, large-scale retailers, sustainability in retailing, and innovation in retailing.

Benjamin Rosenthal is Senior Lecturer at Fundação Getulio Vargas in São Paulo, Brazil. His research projects cover diverse topics such as consumption practices, brand communities, social movements, social media, and older consumers. His work has been published recently in *Business Horizons, Marketing Intelligence & Planning*, and *Research in Consumer Behavior*.

Raluca Rusoiu is a public relations specialist and social media manager for the global creative agency This Is Crowd. She enjoys working with fashion influencers and previously researched how the fashion industry is impacted by CGI models. She has a BA in Public Relations from Bournemouth University.

Klaudia Maria Urbanska is in Marketing Management at L'oreal Paris Makeup in Warsaw, Poland. Her research focuses on the credibility of beauty influencers. She has a BA in Public Relations from Bournemouth University.

Benjamin G. Voyer, Ph.D., is Professor in the Department of Entrepreneurship at ESCP Business School. His research investigates how self-perception and interpersonal relations affect cognition and behaviors in various contexts (consumption, organizational, cross-cultural...). His research has appeared in psychology journals (*Behavioural and Brain Sciences, Review of General Psychology, Frontiers in Psychology, Journal of Economic Psychology, Journal of Advanced Nursing*...) and management journals (*Journal of Business Research, AMS Review*...).

Weronika Waśkiw, Account Executive, Travel PR. She has worked across multiple travel brands in both in-house and agency-side roles. She also continues to work on digital communications activities within the industry, including influencer relations and social media management.

Introduction

Sevil Yesiloglu and Joyce Costello

It wasn't long ago, when waiting in line at a grocery store, that one of the authors overheard a young boy tell his mom that he wanted to grow up and become an influencer. The mother asked him if he would rather be an astronaut or a fireman. But the boy was resolute that he wanted to have a job on YouTube talking about his favorite stuff. Indeed, even at our universities, we started to notice a few years ago that many of the dissertations were focusing on influencers and if they would be different than celebrities. Agencies started emerging and promised aspiring influencers an exciting career and brands a way to improve how they could reach new audiences. Together, each of these events and our own research into motivations and behavior led us to develop this book.

We wanted a book that addresses the key elements behind influence and what it means to be influential. Ever since the internet revolution's with social media, how marketers and advertisers operated has changed. Brands have traditionally focused on creating direct communication paths with their audiences on social media. However, this book shows that third-party endorsers (a.k.a. influencers) have a huge impact on people, their online community, and their decisions. Individuals tend to seek others like themselves to share their opinions or are knowledgeable and reliable to reduce the risk they might face as a result of their buying decision. Therefore, marketers consider incorporating these influencers as part of their campaigns because the audience trusts them and listens to them when making some purchase decisions.

Social media influencers have been emerging as a new source of content creators and opinion leaders. We assert that influencers have been enhancing the knowledge of how these technologies can be used to market or advertise a product, service, or the brand itself. Influencers and influencer marketing are promising ways for brands to reach their potential and actual consumers. Hence, the book looks at different aspects of influencer marketing focusing on four different areas including Part 1 Exploring influencers and influencer marketing; Part 2 Influencers as a part of marketing communication campaigns; Part 3 The dark side of influencers; and Part 4 Legal and future aspects of influencer marketing.

Firstly, it is important to understand the meaning of influence and being influential as it is the key approach for both practitioners and scholars to understand the different type of influencers and their role in marketing. Part 1 addresses influencers and their roles in marketing and social media in different ways. It explores the difference between what is an influencer and what "being influential" means. By understanding the differences between traditional and digital influencers, brands can then focus on how to select the right influencers in the digital era. Finally, this section addresses the criteria to choose the right influencers for marketing campaigns. Consequently, Part 1 focuses on examining and identifying influencers and their role in digital and traditional media.

With this base understanding, Part 2 investigates influencers and their role in marketing communication campaign plans. Different frameworks are presented to help identify influencers for different marketing communication as well as explore the key motives behind influencers' brand-related engagement on Instagram. Although understanding the engagement between influencers and their audience is essential, brands also need to consider exploring this relationship between influencers and their audience further. Hence, in Part 2, this book explores the nature and types of parasocial relationships that can be developed as a result of the communication between influencers and their followers in order to strengthen the relationship in order to impact the audiences' decisions. Through looking at the role of influencers in marketing communication campaigns, we realize that understanding influencers and their role in the context of current global movement sustainability and sustainable consumption is essential for both practitioners and scholars. Therefore, we include two chapters that provide information on influencers who specialize in the specific area of sustainability and sustainable consumption.

Although using third-party endorsers "influencers" as a part of marketing communication campaigns is a positive strategic approach taken by organizations, we acknowledge that using influencers can bring specific considerations likely unintended damage for the relationship between brands created by influencers and their content. Therefore, Part 3 looks at the dark side of influencers in different ways: there is a comparison between sponsored and non-sponsored post and their impacts on credibility and trust; an exploration into different aspects of covert endorsement practices in influencer marketing; and the impact of fake followers of influencers on trust and credibility. Each chapter in Part 3 investigates a different aspect of influencers and their content, starting by exploring the differences between sponsored and unsponsored posts shared by influencers and their impact on trust and credibility.

Because of the unlimited access that social media offers to users, influencers and brands need to consider legal and ethical aspects of communication influencers create between themselves, brands, and consumers. Therefore, Part 4 sheds light on legal and ethical aspects of influencer marketing through investigating copyright issues related to influencers and their content on social media and the legal implication in influencer marketing communications. Similarly, with the evolving nature of

sevil yesiloglu and joyce costello

the technology and social media, marketers also need to consider the future of influencer marketing including virtual influencers as well as legal implications.

Finally, we include practical illustrations of key aspects of influencers marketing through case studies and examples to help the reader access their own beliefs and behaviors. We hope that those aspiring to be influencers, practitioners, and brands looking into influencer marketing enjoy the book and engage in building this new field.

Dr Sevil Yesiloglu and Dr Joyce Costello

part 1

Exploring influencers and influencer marketing

chapter 1

The rise of influencers and influencer marketing

Sevil Yesiloglu

Learning outcomes

- To define the terms influence, influencers and being influential.
- To understand the evolution of influencers.
- To understand key content strategies to identify key components of influencer marketing.

Being influential and influencers

To find what influences people and their decisions has always been enigmatic and a challenge for marketers, brands, and advertisers. To understand how to influence others, we need to firstly look at how influence has been identified historically by scholars and psychologists. In Cialdini's (2009) exploratory research, he investigated the power to influence using the six principles of compliance: consistency, reciprocation, social proof, authority, liking, and scarcity. He looked at how these determinants have an incredible force and influence on society to vote, purchase, donate, and so on. Cialdini characterized these six principles as "weapons of influence" (p. 1).

He explains reciprocation as a principle that is paying someone back if they do a favor for us. For example, influencers will often share each other's content as a means of reciprocating the favor of engagement. Consistency refers to a commitment that forces people to commit to a routine. It may be that an influencer consistently posts discounts for top products as a means of enticing followers to check their page routinely. Social proof implies things we commit to and find the right to do, if we see others doing it. For instance, if popular influencers are not clearly disclosing that their content is sponsored, it might inadvertently become the norm. Liking suggests it is a principle that makes us comply with requests from individuals we like. Many vloggers will ask their viewers to like their post and subscribe. Authority principle means that people tend to accept requests if they come from trustful and/or accepted sources. This becomes a deeply debated topic later in this book. Lastly, scarcity refers to when the availability is limited, opportunities become more attractive and valuable. While this last principle may seem contradictory to the explosion of influencers, if one applies it to the opportunities brands may present for sponsorship, then scarcity can drive influence. Together these six principles have proven to be extremely useful to help understand the process of influence and strengthen persuasion skills to influence the target audiences' purchase decision. However, Cialdini's (2009) principles have not revealed comprehensively the secret of how to be influential.

Increasingly though, scholars seek to identify the concept of how to be influential when it comes to other's decisions and behaviors. To add further clarity to this complex term, Hesketh (2010) looked at the ways of building relationships and investigated how we can master influence and persuasion. Hesketh (2010) discussed that if you are a newbie to any group (industry, work, media channel, etc.), first you need to understand the nature of the group you want to impress and influence through respecting them, their beliefs, and views. Rather than focus on the characteristics, strategic approach, he argued the importance of being accepted within a community first to have an influence on people.

While scholars and psychologists have debated the key traits of being influential, some researchers have begun to focus on certain "ordinary" people who gain tremendous influential power over people who follow them. First of all, to understand what classifies a non-celebrity (or an ordinary person) as an "influencer," scholars describe and name these groups of people in different ways including "instafamous" (Marwick 2015), micro-celebrity (Khamis et al. 2017), "market maven," or opinion leader (McQuail and Windahl 1993; Northouse 2016; Lin et al. 2018). For example, Van den Bulte and Joshi (2007) looked at individuals and their characteristics rather than principles of influence, and they posited that people became influential based on having social status and specific personality traits. However, Northouse (2016) argued that we need to look beyond personal traits to understand the concept of "being influential." He emphasized "... people likely to follow leaders who seem to know what they are doing..." (p. 418). As Song et al. (2007) emphasized, individuals gain their power through being knowledgeable and disseminating new information to others.

When it comes to identifying who these influential people are, scholars focus on the group of influential people who are characterized as a powerful information source (Gladwell 2000) and named as influencers. It has also been discussed that social media has a significant role in these influential people becoming influencers or even celebrities (Chae 2018). However, with a constant change in social media applications, it can become difficult to define influencers and understand how they gain their influential power. Abidin and Ots (2015) proposed a broad definition of influencers as:

sevil yesiloglu

Every day, ordinary Internet users who accumulate a relatively large following on blogs and social media through textual and visual narration of their personal lives and lifestyles, engage with their following in digital and physical spaces, and monetize their following by integrating "advertorials" into their blog or social media posts. (p. 1)

Although Abidin and Ots (2015) clearly emphasized the importance of the activities influencers focus on to influence their followers, as Enke and Borchers (2019) pointed out, Abidin and Ots had ignored the importance of a strategic approach behind their activities on online platforms.

By considering this significant point and taking into consideration the various definitions of influencer (Table 1.1), I define an influencer as a person who has a strategic approach and ability to influence individuals and their (buying) decisions within digital communication platforms. An influencer's space can include any communication platform, although they mainly have a niche audience that would already believe their power, authority, and expertise in a subject, product, industry, or brand. These key elements (power, authority, and expertise) can make the influencer marketing system work – having a niche and a target audience who believe what influencers say. This distinction about the relationship between influencing and purchase behavior is explored further in Chapter 2 (Leban and Voyer 2020).

Becoming an influencer on social media

Solis (2010) defines the characteristics of social media as "the democratization of information, transforming people from content readers into publishers… the shift from a broadcast mechanism, one-to-many to a many-to-one model, rooted in conversations between authors, people, and peers" (p. 37). With the innovative and democratic nature of social media platforms, the production, creation, and distribution of any content has become extremely easy. This is because it does not require people to know any technicality of these platforms to become content creators or eventually an influencer. As it is stated by Labrecque et al. (2011):

No longer does a person need to be familiar with complex coding languages or other technicalities to build Web sites, because virtually anyone can upload text, pictures and video instantly to a site from a personal computer or phone. With technological barriers crumbling and its increasing ubiquity, the Web has become the perfect platform for personal branding. (p. 38)

With the equal and innovative features that online platforms offer, Bolter and Grusin (1996) predicted that when these platforms emerged that it would become the new way for "construction and definitions of the self." This self in a digital world was taken further by Belk (2013), who argued that in the visual digital environment, particularly on social media, individuals are "disembodied and re-embodied as avatars, photos, and videos" (p. 481). In this way, we can argue that users are experiencing different ways of constructing their identity through sharing content that reflects their ideal

Table 1.1 Different types of definitions for influencers

Authors	Term/label	Definition
Senft (2008)	Micro-celebrity	"… involves people amping up their popularity over the Web using techniques like videos, blogs and social networking sites" (p. 25)
Freberg et al. (2011)	Social media influencers	"a new type of independent third-party endorser who shapes audiences' attitudes through blogs, tweets, and the use of other social media." (p. 90)
Marwick and Boyd (2011)	Micro-celebrity	"using social media to develop and maintain an audience." (p. 140)
Wong (2014)	Social Media Influencer	"a form of marketing that identifies and targets individuals who have influence over potential buyers"
Ge and Gretzel (2018)	Social Media Influencer	"individuals who are in a consumer's social graph and have a direct impact on the behavior of that consumer" (p. 1273)
Influencer Marketing Hub (2019)	Influencer	"…an individual who has the power to affect the purchase decisions of others because of his/her authority, knowledge, position or relationship with his/her audience"
Lou and Yuan (2019)	Social Media Influencer	"…is first and foremost a content generator: one who has the status of expertise in a specific area, who has cultivated a sizable number of captive followers – who are of marketing value to brands – by regularly producing valuable content via social media." (p. 59)

selves on social media. With these unlimited communications and content creation opportunities, individuals have begun practicing self-branding through producing text, content, images, and videos on online platforms, particularly on social media channels (Khamis et al. 2017). This has implications for influencers who can benefit monetarily by creating their best digital self.

By adding a strategic approach to self-branding with one's online activities, influencers can start creating distinctive stories and content which help them to create high visibility, engagement, and "online fame" (Khamis et al. 2017). Essentially, individuals began to gain fame through the visibility and engagement they received and built on online platforms to be considered famous through creating valuable and engaging content as part of building their ideal online presence. By practicing continuous self-presentation and branding activities on social media, they started to grow their number of followers and build an enormous online presence.

Social media creates an interactive environment for every user where they have equal opportunities to view or create any content in any form. However, users are not expected to be celebrities or famous brands. Yet, they can create their communities and become micro-celebrities with a high volume of engagement with their audiences in this virtual digital world. Khamis et al. (2017) proposed that social media frees individuals from the top-down dynamic which does require individuals to have "existing power" to be influential. But, for an individual to tap into the real impact on social media to grow any community, they must use strategic practices to gain influential power. As Marwick (2015) stated, "ordinary" people can become "famous" or a "micro-celebrity" by using social networking applications purposefully, including sharing eye-catching content including videos, selfies, images of their food, friends, and their daily routines.

Micro-celebrities (influencers) can range from high school students to fitness gurus, travelers, and beauty experts (e.g. Marwick 2015; Abidin and Ots 2015; Saul 2016). Scholars have challenged this vague term further to investigate potential key features that can validate individuals whether they can be classified as influencers or micro-celebrities. Some scholars believe that there are no specific criteria to measure how people perceive and accept an individual as an opinion leader or not (Xiong et al. 2018). Other scholars argue what is considered a high or low number of followers to consider if an individual should be classed as an influencer (De Veirman et al. 2017). Although quantifying can help brands to measure how many people these influencers can potentially reach, this should be evaluated as only a starting point to identify the right influencers and their social reach (e.g. Basille 2009; Straley 2010; Özçelik and Levi 2020).

Kusumasondjaja and Tjiptono (2019) highlight the need to look beyond quantitative data and focus on the engagement individuals receive in each post to identify influential people. Similarly, Freberg et al. (2011) argue that these groups of influential individuals can be identified through looking not only at the number of followers they have, but also engagement and interaction they build within their online space through likes, comments, tags, etc. Lin et al. (2018) stress that influencers gain specific online leadership authority based on their social reach (e.g. number of comments and likes). When influencers build their social reach, they also make sure they maintain their relationship with existing followers through increasing social capital by sharing new information (Marwick 2015). In this way, influencers benefit from having tremendous social reach both socially and commercially by having a "unique selling point, or a public identity that is singularly charismatic and responsive to the needs and interest of target audiences" (Khamis et al. 2017, p. 1).

Hearn and Schoenhoff (2016) stated: "the social media influencers work to generate a form of 'celebrity' capital by cultivating as much attention as possible and crafting an authentic 'personal brand' via social networks, which can be subsequently used by companies, and advertisers for consumer outreach" (p. 194). Not surprisingly, practitioners now pay closer attention to opinion leaders who have high social reach and the most authentic relationships with their followers (Yesiloglu and Gill 2020). Equally, as a part of social media marketing strategies, partnering with influencers has become one of the most emerging strategies for brands and marketers (Brown and Hayes 2008; Kafka and Molla 2017).

Influencers and content creation

Influencers typically build their content strategies around structuring aspirational photos of brand or product through using hashtags, filters, and photoshops which help them to become self-made micro-celebrities (Dewey 2014). In a meta-analysis of 167 studies about influencers and content, Chen and Chua (2020) found that influencers try to ensure they create content that represents them consistently. Some researchers suggest that influencers and their content tend to be highly influential when they mix exposure of both online and offline, self-branding, and strategic self-presentation (Hearn and Schoenhoff 2016). As a part of self-branding and presentation that was noted earlier, Uzunoglu and Kip (2014) found that physical attractiveness can lead to admiration and become a reason for individuals to follow an influencer on Instagram. Quintana Ramos and Cowie (2020) discovered that the causes influencers support and the supporting content related to drives increased engagement.

Additionally, we begin to see influencers start glorifying their selfies and posts they share to get noticed on Instagram. Saul (2016) maintains that successful influencers who attract a high volume of engagement, usually have some common characteristics including a sense of humor and original perspective. This approach helps influencers to be considered as more "relatable" trendsetters, as opposed to traditional celebrities and brands itself (Mediakix 2018), which fuel the buzz effect among the followers. People share information published more by someone (influencer) they feel close or relate to than individuals or brands they do not feel connected to.

Although all social networking platforms enable online and social interaction, they do not all offer influencers the exact same services, nor do they have the same functions (Hughes et al. 2019). This can impact the content of the influencer's posts. Initially, Instagram was photo-based but with IGTV and video capabilities and more recently live stories, content can be more dynamic than its original photo-sharing capabilities. To date, Instagram is the most popular social media platform for influencers to create an appealing online presence and large networks, with more than 1 billion active users monthly (Statista 2019). This has been supported by some scholars who argue that the influencer and their persuasion power substantially result from Instagram's characteristic features which allow any content creators to design their content in a creative and innovative way.

Idea fairy: Influencer content

Influencers are probably one of the most popular groups of people that media and marketers talk about. Think about influencers you follow on Instagram and list the things you like about their content. What does it say about the influencers you follow? What kind of influencer content consistently grabs your attention? Has the content ever led you to purchase something?

Influencer marketing: What makes it work?

From a practitioner and academic perspective, there are two types of terms defining influencers and their role in the marketing and advertising industry: influencer marketing and influencer relations. Influencer marketing refers to influencers' marketing activities related to short-term and paid activities. Influencer relations refer to activities in which influencers use unpaid, earned, and share media content which aims for a long-term relationship with their audience (Schach and Lommatzsch 2018). When we look into the term "influencer marketing" further, because of the wide range use of influencers by marketers and advertisers, it implies a comprehensive range of marketing activities fueled by brands and advertisers through investing in influencers and their relevant posts and content to brands' target audiences and products (Yodel 2017).

Although brands enhance their interaction with their desired audiences more on social media, they are still perceived by consumers as an organization trying to sell their products. Since influencers and their branded message (e.g. eWOM) are often perceived more authentic and credible than any brand-generated content created by marketers or advertisers (Talavera 2015), brands started seeking third-party endorsers who can deliver engaging branded content and enhance the communication with the brand's intended target audience and consumers on social media sites (Uzunoglu and Kip 2014). Therefore, brands started seeking strategic ways of working with digital influencers who already have a powerful impact on their established community and their followers' purchase decision. This way, brands have an opportunity to build closer relationships with their audiences through influencers' electronic word of mouth (eWOM) power and influencers' strong connections with their followers.

The power of electronic word of mouth

As noted earlier, social media offers unlimited tools for consumers who freely create and disseminate brand and product-related information through using their social connections (e.g. Boyd and Ellison 2007; Jansen et al. 2009; Knoll 2016). In recent years, marketers have become increasingly interested in directly managing these brand-related communications between consumers (e.g. word of mouth (WOM)) as well as consumers' communication with brands. This is because consumers have become active co-producers of value and meaning regarding brands, products, and services (e.g. Brown et al. 2009; Kozinets et al. 2010) through engaging brand-related posts on social networking sites. Initially, the idea of searching and understanding consumer opinion on social media websites attracts a greater interest from organizations, since any positive product-related post was also viewed as having value as great promotional vehicles for marketers and organizations for the length of the lifecycle of the post (Duan et al. 2008).

The reason eWOM becomes a powerful way to promote any brands, products, or services is because people are more likely to trust more their peers' opinions than advertisers (De Veirman et al. 2017). Villanueva et al. (2008) contend that people who buy any products recommended by others, have a tendency to add twice as much long-term value to the organization than the ones who did not buy the product as a result of their social connections' recommendations. Similarly, Swant's (2016) study evidenced that consumers trust social media influencers and their endorsements just as they would trust their friends. As consumers trust any product or service endorsement by influencers and purchase those products accordingly, eight out of 10 consumers have purchased something after seeing it on an influencer's social media post (Rakuten Marketing 2019).

Consequently, brands have begun partnering with influencers who are interpreted as credible electronic word of mouth sources rather than traditional advertising methods to reach a wide range of audiences as a part of their branding and marketing activities (e.g. Fransen et al. 2015; Abidin and Ots 2015; De Veirman et al. 2017). For brands, the whole point of using influencers is to create a reliable and trustworthy eWOM effect. Brown and Hayes (2008) describe this powerful eWOM effect as "like being on a trial" where you need a witness to support your case that whatever you say is credible and trustworthy (p. 23). Therefore, in order to target large audiences with a powerful eWOM strategy, brands seek influencers (witnesses) who have a high impact on their followers and fans on social media networks, as their followers tend to perceive their endorsement as word-of-mouth communication (Liu et al. 2015). In this way, brands and organizations can influence consumers' purchase decisions in an indirect way through using powerful eWOM method influencers as well as a viral effect which helps to disseminate influencer generated branded content among the followers (De Veirman et al. 2017). While we cannot deny that the use of eWOM strategy helps influencers' marketing become an important form of marketing and advertising, it is also true that the eWOM effect is increased by using creative and engaging content strategy.

Influencers, branded content, and purchase decisions

In general, social media influencers focus on three main objectives to achieve through their content when interacting with brands. First, influencers try to increase the number of followers they have. Even though scholars recommend focusing on quantifying numbers (Kusumasondjaja and Tjiptono 2019), there remains monetary advantages for influencers to have more followers to convince brands they can deliver an appropriate amount of reach. Secondly, influencers tend to try to increase

sevil yesiloglu

product knowledge among their followers through their content creation. For influencer marketing campaigns that are focusing on increasing brand awareness, this is especially pertinent. Finally, influencers make it an objective to influence their fans' purchase intention and/or decision. While increasing brand awareness is important, many brands will want that awareness leading to an action such as purchases. To achieve these objectives, several strategies have been applied by influencers and brands, particularly in content creation, to disseminate their ideas (Thomas 2004).

Content that is produced by influencers largely relies on the effectiveness of user-generated content (UGC) and is considered one of the major factors influencing consumer behavior (Hoffman and Fodor 2010). This may be due to users believing user-generated content contains more trustworthy, reliable, and up-to-date information than other branded sources (Gretzel and Yoo 2008). Similarly, Cwynar-Horta (2016) argued that if branded content is created by influencers in a user-generated content nature, it creates stronger relationships between influencers and their followers, which has an indirect impact on brand–consumer relationships. In line with this argument, Zhu and Chen (2015) argued that Instagram is a content-based site and its users primarily engage with posts because they like the content more than they like the person behind the profile. The subject of each content is mainly constructed around the exhibition of their exotic lives, purchases, daily routines that their followers do not have but wish to have (Abidin and Ots 2015; Saul 2016).

To clarify the value of influencer generated branded content further, some scholars investigated the type of content and its impact on the interaction and engagement between influencers and their followers (Yesiloglu 2018). Firstly, as social media was specifically founded as a platform for individuals to satisfy their needs related to information, the value of informative content on social media engagement has been discussed by several scholars (e.g. Park et al. 2009; Muntinga et al. 2011). Lou and Yuan (2019) suggested that influencers' informative branded content has a positive impact on followers' brand awareness and purchase decisions. Whereas other scholars discuss that product knowledge itself is what has a significant impact on people's purchase decisions (Kay et al. 2020). This may be because the internet and social media influencers have become a trusted source for updated product information (Mallipeddi et al. 2018). Therefore, the tactic that has been implemented by influencers to show they have a solid product knowledge is to emphasize key features of a product (Lou and Yang 2019) in different "how to" posts, including "how to make healthy food," "how to match blazers with different trousers," "the best places to go in London," etc.

As we begin to see influencers' strategic approach to content creation on social media enhance the interaction with their followers, practitioners and scholars began to seek further tactics that can be implemented by influencers to impact consumers' purchase decisions. Particularly on social media channels such as Instagram, showcasing content including photos and videos on sellers' Instagram posts, has been considered as one of the most important tactics to encourage users to make impulsive purchases (Lo et al. 2016).

Although brands acknowledge the fact that influencer-generated videos, images, and content can have a positive impact on users' purchase decision, they need to look for further integration of social media characteristic features to increase the effectiveness of influencer-generated branded content on purchase decisions. For example, in 2016, Instagram added a call-to-action button to help online businesses to share their product and brand-related content (Instagram 2016). This form of direct purchase also helps branded content become more attractive and engaging in terms of triggering potential consumers to make impulsive purchases (Handayani et al. 2018). Likewise, influencers integrate "buying tags" features on Instagram, which provide the greatest usefulness for users to buy products directly from brands' e-commerce sites. To explore influencers and their marketing activities on social media, we need to explore the partnership relationship between influencers and brands further.

Work relationship between influencers and brands

Since influencers started becoming an important part of marketing and advertising strategies in different industries, they have been called "a new type of independent third-party endorser who shape audience attitudes through blogs, tweet and the use of other social media" (Freberg et al. 2011, p. 90). To explain their role in marketing further, scholars focus on Katz and Lazarsfeld's (1955) concept of "two-step flow" theory of communication with the audience; which helps to explain the role potential opinion leaders play as a third-party endorser to pass brand-related information to them. Based on the "two-step flow" theory of communication framework in influencer marketing and influencer relations, brands engage with key opinion leaders (influencers) to endorse their products and services within the community they establish on digital platforms.

Thomas (2004) maintains that finding these key opinion leaders is crucial for brands to engage with larger audiences and spread brands' messages to their followers more effectively. So, brands started seeking outright influencers who either had the same type of audiences these brands target or can help them tap into a market where the brand does not have influence yet. Therefore, for brands to achieve any digital marketing goals which involve influencers, they need to have strategies in place.

It has been discussed by several researchers that people's decisions are mostly influenced by information they receive from others and this interaction has been found the most influential way to receive information for consumers (Keller 2007). As a part of eWOM and viral marketing strategies, brands recognize the power of referral marketing for acquiring new customers (Van den Bulte et al. 2018). For example, the Freberg et al. (2011) statement about third-party endorsers has drawn attention to the importance of influencers and their activities as a part of referral marketing strategy as influencers also have been employed not only for endorsing a brand or an organization (Liu et al. 2015), but also influencing a brand's reputation (Freberg et al. 2011).

One of the major challenges for organizations to achieve successful referral marketing is to identify and select the right influencers who can have a powerful impact on their followers and influence these followers to buy a new product, or help them to diffuse them in their social networks through their content (Momtaz et al. 2011; Pophal 2016). Hence, several scholars investigated influencers and how their strategic approach to marketing works in general (Rosenthal and Arcuri 2020).

Researchers looked at influencers and their marketing strategy from different angles, including how an organization needs to approach influencers (Uzunoglu and Kip 2014), how social media influencers impact stakeholders (Djafarova and Rushworth 2017), and how to integrate organizational activities external resources influencers bring to the relationship between organizations and influencers (Enke and Borchers 2019), and social media influencers' working routine (Pang et al. 2016).

Another important aspect of influencer marketing that requires further discussion is how the relationship between influencer and organization needs to be identified and managed in different ways. Organizations use influencers as a part of their marketing, public relations, and advertising strategies, but not necessarily in the same way. For example, a brand may use influencers in a public relations campaign to help gain awareness or educate them about the products' benefits or uses and employ influencers in marketing campaigns to generate sales. Each discipline lends itself to different tactics and outputs and so should the strategic use of influencers.

As influencers are not just limited to blogs anymore, companies need to look at this collaboration with influencers in more comprehensive ways (Enke and Borchers 2019) through a more complex strategic approach. Enke and Borchers (2019) defined this strategic social media influencer communication as "the purposeful use of communication by organizations or social media influencers in which social media influencers are addressed or perform activities with strategic significance to organizational goals" (p. 261). To explain different aspects of strategic communication between influencers and brands, they proposed a comprehensive framework to shed light on the management process. Enke and Borchers (2019) propose strategic communication in three different ways, including "managed strategic social media influencer communication, unmanaged strategic social media communication, and strategically insignificant social media influencer communication" (p. 271).

Managed strategic social media influencer communication is characterized as the influencer's activities aligned with the organization's objectives. Unmanaged strategic social media influencer communication refers to the influencers' activities that are only managed by influencers themselves without organization involvement. Lastly, strategically insignificant social media influencer communication describes the influencer's activities which are purposely insubstantial to the organization and their objectives. These activities can include the influencer's daily eating routine, exercises, or self-care routine, etc. They discuss that organizations need to employ both substantial and insubstantial approaches for influencers' communication.

As a part of referral marketing, which is mainly managed by brands, brands can work with influencers in different marketing forms including sponsored content, product placement, documenting daily life, affiliate links, partnerships, and gifted posts. To take the relationship with influencers further, brands start seeking more efficient and direct ways to reach their audience to increase engagement which can grow sales. As a result, brands decide to work with influencers directly involving launching a product range together. For example, *In the Style* shows a great partnership example with influencers (Geoghegan 2019). In 2019 clothing retailer *In the Style* announced a new product range collaborated with social media influencer Lorna Luxe. As a result, they revealed that they have the fastest-selling collection and the highest conversion in Europe, the US, and Australia since 2014 when the brand was launched. Please explore evidence of credibility between sponsored and non-sponsored content in Chapter 10 (Costello and Urbanska 2020).

As noted earlier, eWOM is an effective strategy in influencing purchase decisions; brands therefore begin to seek out influencers that genuinely endorse products or services of a brand that have a positive impact on purchase decisions. Therefore, as a part of the referral marketing strategy, influencers begin to focus on managed strategic social media influencer communication through affiliate links which are integrated on their posts and stories on Instagram to sell their product directly on social media (Affiliate Marketing 2019).

However, since brands encourage influencers to create eWOM effect as it seems that their paid or unpaid recommendations are perceived genuine, influencers began to face legal regulations for disclosing the commercial content they share on social media (e.g. Evans et al. 2017; Den Jans et al. 2019). For example, the UK Advertising Standards Authority (ASA) took a crucial step to clarify potential issues paid advertising can bring. As consumers cannot always differentiate between paid or unpaid posts influencers share on their social media profile, certain rules such as including the word #ad or #sponsored must now be included. The UK Code of Non-broadcast Advertising and Direct & Promotional Marketing (the CAP Code) requires that: "*Marketing communications must not falsely claim or imply that the marketer is acting as a consumer or for purposes outside its trade, business, craft or profession; marketing communications must make clear their commercial intent, if that is not obvious from the context.*" Furthermore, The CAP Code requires that users need to know whether the post they see is paid by brands or not, for example paid or organic content. Please see Chapter 13 for further information (Bosher 2020).

Idea fairy: Who can be an influencer

Think about can anyone be an influencer? What makes them an influencer?

Please make a list of activities (e.g. content creation, engagement with brands, use key traits of personality, etc.) an ordinary person needs to do to become an influencer.

Summary

- There is a difference between influence and being influential.
- Converging various applications of social media channels, together with influencers' content strategies and their relationship with the brands, make influencer marketing the potentially most significant type of marketing in the future.
- Marketers and advertisers need to focus on how they can enhance their engagement with influencers who have a significant power in their followers' purchase decisions.

Case study: The rise of an influencer – Joe Wicks as a healthy living guru

In a digital world, it cannot be denied that influencers and their strategies have become one of the key impacts on consumers' decisions and their lifestyle in general. One recent example is Joe Wicks, known as "The Body Coach" on social media and television. Joe is a British fitness coach and TV presenter. He has been recognized by several major publications including *Harper's Bazaar*, *Elle UK*, and *Forbes* for his effort and success in the fitness industry. His career started in television and traditional media and continues growing on different social media channels, specifically on Instagram and Facebook. After he became popular on social media, he launched his fitness and nutrition plan website, www.bodycoach.com.

His digital content includes High-Intensity Interval Training (HIIT) workouts, healthy food recipes, and snapshots of his daily family life. Through the self-branding method, his personal brand has become one of the most followed accounts on Instagram and YouTube. His content mainly consists of healthy recipes and tailored workouts.

With a book deal, upcoming TV show, and numerous product endorsements, Wicks's business is now earning £1 million a month. It is growing so fast that he's hired a large team, led by his brother and best friend, to run it.

His content strategy on social media: What makes him an influencer?

Although he has started earning his fame through his appearance on several TV shows, a well-planned content strategy behind his social media posts provides him further success in society, particularly in digital platforms. He started posting content on Instagram in 2014, including images of simple healthy food recipes, short intensive workout videos, and his daily life routine. He began posting fitness content to his YouTube channel, named "The Body Coach TV," in 2014. His first video garnered over 6 million views. The channel has amassed over 2.2 million subscribers and more than 128 million views.

Wicks has reached 3.6 million followers on Instagram and 2.3 million subscribers on YouTube. He provides content that meets people's needs to learn about healthy living styles, recipes, and workouts as a part of his self-branding activities. His content strategy has been built on providing informative content that is integrated with entertaining and fun content. Research suggested that the integration of informative and entertaining content in digital posts increases engagement (Hollebeek and Macky 2019). He also avoids disturbing branded content, relying, therefore, more on subtle product suggestions placed within healthy food recipes he shares across different social media channels. When he shares his content on social media channels, he is also aware of the power of positive and inspirational words on people and their engagement as he stated in his interview: "It's the power of social media, the power of a good message" (Heritage 2016). By posting about his passion for social media, Joe Wicks has gained immense internet popularity, allowing him to shape and influence his audiences through his eye-catching videos, recipes, and funny images. While his engagement mostly relies on his characteristics and both informative and entertaining content he shares, he also designed his content strategy linked to altruistic content during global pandemic COVID-19. During the COVID-19 pandemic lockdown in the UK, he started "P.E with Joe" on YouTube to help children and families stay active. This series of videos had a wide impact and was viewed more than a million times by followers. The result of his content strategy was astonishing, and he was awarded a Guinness World Record for "most viewers for a fitness workout live stream on YouTube," after achieving almost a million viewers on March 24, 2020 for his live stream.

Questions to consider:

1. What type of content strategy does Joe Wicks follow? What factors do you think make Joe Wicks such a successful influencer?
2. Do think influencers need the support of traditional media as well as social media channels to be more influential?
3. Do you have any other ideas on how influencers can get more engagement? Are there any content strategies you can suggest?

References

Abidin, C., and Ots, M., 2015, August. The influencer's dilemma: the shaping of new brand professions between credibility and commerce. In *AEJMC 2015, annual conference*.

Affiliate Marketing, 2019. How to Combine Affiliate Marketing and Influencer Marketing. Available from: www.postaffiliatepro.com/blog/how-to-combine-affiliate-marketing-and-influencer-marketing/

Asch, S.E., 1951. Effects of group pressure upon the modification and distortion of judgments. In H. Guetzkow (Ed.), *Groups, Leadership, and Men* (177–190). Pittsburgh, PA: Carnegie Press.

Barnhart, B., 2019. Everything you need to know about social media algorithms. *Sprout Social*. Available from: https://sproutsocial.com/insights/social-media-algorithms/

Basille, D., 2009. Social media influencers are not traditional influencers. Available from: www.briansolis.com/2009/11/social-media- influencers-are-not-traditional-influencers/

Belk, R.W., 2013. Extended self in a digital world. *Journal of Consumer Research*, 40(3), 477–500.

Bolter, J.D., and Grusin, R.A., 1996. Remediation. *Configurations*, 4(3), 311–358.

Boyd, D.M., and Ellison, N.B., 2007. Social network sites: Definition, history, and scholarship. *Journal of Computer-mediated Communication*, 13(1), 210–230.

Bosher, H., 2020. Influencer Marketing and the Law in Ch. 13 in *Influencer Marketing: Building Brand Communities and Engagement* Ed. Yesiloglu, S., and Costello, J. Routledge: London.

Brown, D., and Hayes, N., 2008. *Influencer Marketing*. Routledge.

Brown, E., Dury, S., and Holdsworth, M., 2009. Motivations of consumers that use local, organic fruit and vegetable box schemes in Central England and Southern France. *Appetite*, 53(2), 183–188.

Chae, J., 2018. Explaining females' envy toward social media influencers. *Media Psychology*, 21(2), 246–262.

Chen, X., and Chua, A., 2020. "Reviewing the Landscape of Research on Influencer-generated Content," 6th International Conference on Information Management (ICIM), London, United Kingdom, 2020, 244–248, DOI: 10.1109/ICIM49319.2020.244706

Cialdini, R.B., 2009. *Influencer: The Power of Persuasion*. New York. William Morrow.

Costello, J., and Urbanska, K., 2020. "Hope this is not sponsored" – Is an Influencers' credibility impacted when using sponsored versus non-sponsored content? Ch. 10 in *Influencer Marketing: Building Brand Communities and Engagement* Ed. Yesiloglu, S., and Costello, J. Routledge: London.

Cwynar-Horta, J., 2016. The commodification of the body positive movement on Instagram. *Stream: Culture/Politics/Technology*, 8(2), 36–56.

De Jans, S., Van de Sompel, D., Hudders, L., and Cauberghe, V., 2019. Advertising targeting young children: an overview of 10 years of research (2006–2016). *International Journal of Advertising*, 38(2), 173–206

De Veirman, M., Cauberghe, V., and Hudders, L., 2017. Marketing through Instagram Influencers: the impact of the number of followers and product divergence on brand attitude. *International Journal of Advertising*, 36(5), 798–828.

Dewey, C., 2014. Inside the world of the "Instafamous." *Washington Post*. Available from: www.washingtonpost.com/news/arts-and-entertainment/wp/2014/02/19/inside-the-world-of-the-instafamous/

Djafarova, E., and Rushworth, C., 2017. Exploring the credibility of online celebrities' Instagram profiles in influencing the purchase decisions of young female users. *Computers in Human Behavior*, 68, 1–7.

Duan, W., Gu, B., and Whinston, A.B., 2008. Do online reviews matter?—An empirical investigation of panel data. *Decision Support Systems*, 45(4), 1007–1016.

Enke, N., and Borchers, N.S., 2019. Social media influencers in strategic communication: A conceptual framework for strategic social media influencer communication. *International Journal of Strategic Communication*, 13(4), 261–277.

Evans, N.J., Phua, J., Lim, J., and Jun, H., 2017. Disclosing Instagram influencer advertising: The effects of disclosure language on advertising recognition, attitudes, and behavioral intent. *Journal of Interactive Advertising*, 17(2), 138–149.

Fransen, M.L., Verlegh, P.W., Kirmani, A., and Smit, E.G., 2015. A typology of consumer strategies for resisting advertising, and a review of mechanisms for countering them. *International Journal of Advertising*, 34(1), 6–16.

Freberg, K., Graham, K., McGaughey, K., and Freberg, L.A., 2011. Who are the social media influencers? A study of public perceptions of personality. *Public Relations Review*, 37(1), 90–92.

Galeotti, A., and Goyal, S., 2009. Influencing the influencers: a theory of strategic diffusion. *The RAND Journal of Economics*, 40(3), 509–553.

Gardner, S., 2005. *Buzz Marketing with Blogs for Dummies*. John Wiley & Sons.

Ge, J. and Gretzel, U., 2018. Emoji rhetoric: a social media influencer perspective. *Journal of Marketing Management*, 34(15–16), 1272–1295.

Geoghegan, J., 2019. Record-breaking influencer collaboration for In The Style. Available from: www.drapersonline.com/news/record-breaking-influencer-collaboration-for-in-the-style/7035925.article.

Gladwell, M. 2000 *The Tipping Point: How Little Things Can Make a Big Difference*. London: Abacus Books.

Gretzel, U., and Yoo, K.H., 2008. Use and impact of online travel reviews. *Information and Communication Technologies in Tourism 2008*, 35–46.

Handayani, W., Anshori, M., Usman, I., and Mudjanarko, S., 2018. Why are you happy with impulse buying? Evidence from Indonesia. *Management Science Letters*, 8(5), 283–292.

the rise of influencer marketing

Hearn, A., and Schoenhoff, S., 2016. From celebrity to influencer. In *A Companion to Celebrity*. London: Wiley, 194–212.

Heritage, S. 2016. Meet the Body Coach, the man with the million-dollar muscles. Accessed: www.theguardian.com/lifeandstyle/2016/jun/18/joe-wicks-meet-body-coach-million-dollar-muscles.

Hesketh, P., 2010. *How to Persuade and Influence People: Powerful Techniques to Get Your Own Way More Often*. John Wiley & Sons.

Hoffman, D.L., and Fodor, M., 2010. Can you measure the ROI of your social media marketing? *MIT Sloan Management Review*, 52(1), 41.

Hollebeek, L.D., and Macky, K., 2019. Digital content marketing's role in fostering consumer engagement, trust, and value: framework, fundamental propositions, and implications. *Journal of Interactive Marketing*, 45, 27–41.

Hudson, S., Huang, L., Roth, M.S., and Madden, T.J., 2016. The influence of social media interactions on consumer-brand relationships: a three-country study of brand perceptions and marketing behaviors. *International Journal of Research in Marketing*, 33, pp. 27–41.

Hughes, C., Swaminathan, V., and Brooks, G., 2019. Driving brand engagement through online social influencers: An empirical investigation of sponsored blogging campaigns. *Journal of Marketing*, 83(5),78–96.

Influencer Marketing Hub, 2018. Instagram Testing Creator Accounts [online], *InfluencerMarketingHub.com*. Available from: https://influencermarketinghub.com/instagram-creator-accounts/

Instagram, 2016. Enhancing the Way Instagrammers Interact with Ads. *Instagram Business Team*. Available from: https://business.instagram.com/blog/call-to-action-update

Jaakonmäki, R., Müller, O., and vom Brocke, J., 2017. "The impact of content, context, and creator on user engagement in social media marketing." In *Proceedings of the 50th Hawaii international conference on system sciences*.

Jansen, B.J., Zhang, M., Sobel, K., and Chowdury, A., 2009. Twitter power: Tweets as electronic word of mouth. *Journal of the American Society for Information science and technology*, 60(11), 2169–2188.

Kafka, P., and Molla, R., 2017. 2017 was the year digital ad spending finally beat TV. Available online: www.vox.com/2017/12/4/16733460/2017-digital-ad-spend-advertising-beat-tv

Katz, E., and Lazarsfeld, P., 1955. Personal Influence. In *The Part Played by People in the Flow of Mass Communication*. New York.

Kay, S., Mulcahy, R., and Parkinson, J., 2020. When less is more: the impact of macro and micro social media influencers' disclosure. *Journal of Marketing Management*, 36(3–4), 248–278.

Keller, E., 2007. Unleashing the power of word of mouth: Creating brand advocacy to drive growth. *Journal of Advertising Research*, 47(4), 448–452.

Khamis, S., Ang, L., and Welling, R., 2017. Self-branding, "micro-celebrity", and the rise of Social Media Influencers. *Celebrity Studies*, 8(2), 191–208.

Klostermann, J., Plumeyer, A., Böger, D., and Decker, R., 2018. Extracting brand information from social networks: Integrating image, text, and social tagging data. *International Journal of Research in Marketing*, 35(4), 538–556.

Knoll, J., 2016. Advertising in social media: a review of empirical evidence. *International Journal of Advertising*, 35(2), 266–300.

Kozinets, R.V., De Valck, K., Wojnicki, A.C., and Wilner, S.J., 2010. Networked narratives: Understanding word-of-mouth marketing in online communities. *Journal of Marketing*, 74(2), 71–89.

Kusumasondjaja, S., and Tjiptono, F., 2019. Endorsement and visual complexity in food advertising on Instagram. *Internet Research*, available at: https://doi.org/10.1108/IntR-11-2017-0459.

Labrecque, L.I., Markos, E., and Milne, G.R., 2011. Online personal branding: Processes, challenges, and implications. *Journal of Interactive Marketing*, 25(1), 37–50.

Leban, M., and Voyer, B., 2020, Social Media Influencers versus Traditional Influencers: Roles and consequences for traditional marketing campaigns. Ch. 2 in *Influencer Marketing: Building Brand Communities and Engagement*. Ed. Yesiloglu, S., and Costello, J. Routledge: London.

Lin, H.C., Bruning, P.F., and Swarna, H., 2018. Using online opinion leaders to promote the hedonic and utilitarian value of products and services. *Business Horizons*, 61(3), 431–442.

Liu, S., Jiang, C., Lin, Z., Ding, Y., Duan, R., and Xu, Z., 2015. Identifying effective influencers based on trust for electronic word-of-mouth marketing: A domain-aware approach. *Information Sciences*, 306, 34–52.

Lo, L.Y.S., Lin, S.W., and Hsu, L.Y., 2016. Motivation for online impulse buying: A two-factor theory perspective. *International Journal of Information Management*, 36(5),759–772.

Lou, C., and Yuan, S., 2019. Influencer marketing: how message value and credibility affect consumer trust of branded content on social media. *Journal of Interactive Advertising*, 19(1), 58–73.

Mallipeddi, R., Kumar, S., Sriskandarajah, C., and Zhu, Y., 2018. A Framework for Analyzing Influencer Marketing in Social Networks: Selection and Scheduling of Influencers. *Fox School of Business Research Paper*, (18–042).

Marwick, A., and Boyd, D., 2011. To see and be seen: Celebrity practice on Twitter. *Convergence*, 17(2), 139–158.

Marwick, A.E., 2015. Instafame: Luxury selfies in the attention economy. *Public Culture*, 27(75), 137–160.

McQuail, D., and Windahl, S., 2015. *Communication Models for the Study of Mass Communications*. Routledge.

Mediakix, 2018. The 2018 Influencer Marketing Industry Ad Spend, available at: http://mediakix.com/2018/03/influencer-marketing-industry-ad-spend-chart/#gs.vpRbqRs

Momtaz, N.J., Aghaie, A., and Alizadeh, S., 2011. Identifying opinion leaders for marketing by analyzing online social networks. *International Journal of Virtual Communities and Social Networking*, 3(3), 19–34.

Muntinga, D.G., Moorman, M., and Smit, E.G., 2011. Introducing COBRAs: Exploring motivations for brand-related social media use. *International Journal of Advertising*, 30(1), 13–46.

Northouse, P., 2016. *Leadership: Theory and Practice*. 7ed. Sage: London.

Özçelik, A., and Levi, E., 2020. Choosing the right influencer for your brand: a guide to the field. Ch. 5 in *Influencer Marketing: Building Brand Communities and Engagement* Ed. Yesiloglu, S., and Costello, J. Routledge: London.

Pang, A., Yingzhi Tan, E., Song-Qi Lim, R., Yue-Ming Kwan, T., and Bhardwaj Lakhanpal, P., 2016. Building effective relations with social media influencers in Singapore. *Media Asia*, 43(1), 56–68.

Park, N., Kee, K.F., and Valenzuela, S., 2009. Being immersed in a social networking environment: Facebook groups, uses and gratifications, and social outcomes. *CyberPsychology & Behavior*, 12(6), 729–733.

Pophal, L., 2016. Influencer marketing: turning tastemakers into your best salespeople. *EContent*, 39(7), 18–22.

Quintana Ramos, I., and Cownie, F., 2020. Female Environmental Influencers on Instagram. Ch. 9 in *Influencer Marketing and Relations: Changing the Ways Companies Communicate* Ed. Yesiloglu, S., and Costello, J. Routledge: London.

Rakuten Marketing, 2019, Influencer marketing global survey consumers. Rakuten Marketing. Available at: www.iab.com/wp-content/uploads/2019/03/Rakuten-2019-Influencer-Marketing-Report-Rakuten-Marketing.pdf

Riboldazzi, S., and Capriello, A., 2020. Identifying and selecting the right influencers in the digital era Ch. 3 in *Influencer Marketing: Building Brand Communities and Engagement* Ed. Yesiloglu, S., and Costello, J. Routledge: London.

Rosenthal, B., and Arcuri, A., 2020. How to map and select digital influencers for Marketing Campaigns. Ch. 4 in *Influencer Marketing: Building Brand Communities and Engagement* Ed. Yesiloglu, S., and Costello, J. Routledge: London.

Saul, H., 2016. Instafamous: Meet the social media influencers redefining celebrity. *The Independent*. Retrieved from www.independent.co.uk/news/people/instagram- model-natasha-oakley-iskra-lawrence-kayla-itsines-kendall-jenner-jordyn-woods- a6907551.html

Schach, A., and Lommatzsch, T., 2018. *Influencer Relations*. Springer Fachmedien Wiesbaden.

Scott, D.M., 2015. *The new rules of marketing and PR: How to use social media, online video, mobile applications, blogs, news releases, and viral marketing to reach buyers directly*. John Wiley & Sons.

Senft, T.M., 2008. Camgirls: Celebrity and community in the age of social networks (Vol. 4). Peter Lang.

Solis, B., 2010. *Engage: The complete guide for brands and businesses to build, cultivate, and measure success in the new web*. John Wiley & Sons.

Song, X., Chi, Y., Hino, K., and Tseng, B., 2007, November. Identifying opinion leaders in the blogosphere. In *Proceedings of the sixteenth ACM conference on Conference on information and knowledge management*, 971–974.

Statista, 2019. Social Media Advertising. *Statista*. Available from: www.statista.com/outlook/220/100/social-media-advertising/worldwide

Straley, B., 2010. How to: Target social media influencers to boost traffic and sales. *Mashable*. Available at: https://mashable.com/2010/04/15/social-media-influencers/?europe=true.

Swant, M., 2016. Twitter says users now trust influencers nearly as much as their friends. *Retrieved February*, 19, p. 2018.Available at: www.adweek.com/digital/twitter-says-users-now-trust-influencers-nearly-much-their-friends-171367/.

Talavera, M., 2015. "10 Reasons Why Influencer Marketing Is the Next Big Thing," *Adweek*, July 14, www.adweek.com/digital/10-reasons-why-influencer-marketing-is-the-next-big-thing/

Thomas Jr, G.M., 2004. Building the buzz in the hive mind. *Journal of Consumer Behaviour: An International Research Review*, 4(1), 64–72.

Uzunoglu, E., and Kip, S., 2014. Brand Communication through digital Influencers: Leveraging blogger engagement. *International Journal of Information Management*, 34, 592–602.

Van den Bulte, C., and Joshi, Y.V., 2007. New product diffusion with influentials and imitators. *Marketing Science*, 26(3), 400–421.

Van den Bulte, C., Bayer, E., Skiera, B., and Schmitt, P., 2018. How customer referral programs turn social capital into economic capital. *Journal of Marketing Research*, 55(1), 132–146.

Villanueva, J., Yoo, S., and Hanssens, D.M., 2008. The impact of marketing-induced versus word-of-mouth customer acquisition on customer equity growth. *Journal of Marketing Research*, 45(1), 48–59.

Wong, K. 2014. The Explosive Growth of Influencer Marketing and What it Means For You. Forbes. 10 September 2014. Accessed on 17 November 2015. Retrieved from www.forbes.com/sites/kylewong/2014/09/10/the-explosive-growth-ofinfluencer-marketing-and-what-it-means-for-you/.

Xiong, Y., Cheng, Z., Liang, E., and Wu, Y., 2018. Accumulation mechanism of opinion leaders' social interaction ties in virtual communities: Empirical evidence from China. *Computers in Human Behavior*, 82, 81–93.

Yesiloglu, S., 2018. *To post or not to post: examining motivations of brand/product-related engagement types on social networking sites* (Doctoral dissertation, Bournemouth University).

Yesiloglu, S., and Gill, S., 2020, An exploration into the motivations behind post-millennials' engagement with influencers' brand-related content on Instagram. Ch. 6 in *Influencer Marketing: Building Brand Communities and Engagement* Ed. Yesiloglu, S., and Costello, J. Routledge: London.

Yodel, G., 2017. What Is Influencer Marketing?. *Huffington Post, July 6*. Available from: www.huffpost.com/entry/what-is-influcner-marketing_b_10778128?guccounter=1&guce_referrer=aHRocHM6Ly93d3cuZ29vZ2xlLmNvbS8&guce_referrer_sig=AQAAAJeI_JJojDB6qAdjLN4QmESpT_IbYsnDQH8jz-lXfFDAqGroFgEK2POlhj1QNEnoMfoqSUN2X5p_zdPdj9kxLoPLYppq6Skv5Cw3BF3RIe4UUqgG2W1HfHWBPNFJeobRGFj9ybphHoHme M6GFw_o d9t8l1rl1s2IDTuZRuNtgAqV

Zhang, M., Guo, L., Hu, M., and Liu, W., 2017. Influence of customer engagement with company social networks on stickiness: Mediating effect of customer value creation. *International Journal of Information Management*, 37(3), 229–240.

Zhu, Y.Q., and Chen, H.G., 2015. Social media and human need satisfaction: Implications for social media marketing. *Business Horizons*, 58(3), 335–345.

chapter 2

Social media influencers versus traditional influencers

Roles and consequences for traditional marketing campaigns

Marina Leban and Benjamin G. Voyer

Learning outcomes

On completing this chapter, you should be able to:

- understand the difference between celebrity endorsement marketing strategies and social-media influencer marketing strategies;
- know the main models of celebrity endorsement;
- recognize the difference between traditional celebrities, and micro-celebrities and social media influencers; and
- understand the success criteria that contribute to influence from social media celebrities.

The rise of social media in the last decade has enabled "ordinary users" – as opposed to already established celebrities – to create and develop an online personal brand, leading to the emergence of micro-celebrities. Although not as prominent as traditional "Hollywood-type" celebrities on social media platforms such as Instagram, consumers are becoming increasingly interested in micro-celebrities over more established ones. This has led to the rise of social media influencers, who are seen as more relatable and more familiar to their fans. Marketers have first observed this emerging phenomena, and have started – albeit reluctantly – to move away from more traditional forms of celebrity endorsement marketing campaigns. Social media influencers appear to be the gateway to reaching out to more consumers and building better, stronger, and longer-lasting brand relationships.

Furthermore, in recent decades, the field of marketing has seen major changes with the rise of the internet – and disruptive e-commerce platforms and social media platforms – paving the way for new forms of communication and inter-action. In particular, traditional marketing communication, which traditionally relied on advertising through media channels such as television, radio, and print press, has started to incorporate, and at times shift to using, social media as an inherent part of their marketing communication mix (Lee and Hong 2016). The rise of social media has also led to changes in the way marketers work with influencers. Traditional influencers – also known as celebrities, or "stars" – were extensively used as brand endorsers. However, with the rise of social media platforms, ordinary individuals can gain notoriety through developing an audience of followers, thus creating a new type of influencers: social media influencers.

Over the last decade, social media platforms such as Facebook, Instagram, Twitter, and YouTube have been growing in the number of monthly active users, from 97 million in 2010 to a projected 3.08 billion in 2020 (Statista 2019). Of special interest is Instagram, a visual social media platform, in which users engage in the cre-ation of self-presentation content (Eagar and Dann 2016), which has been the fastest growing social media platform, with 1 billion monthly active users to date (Statista 2018). A new generation of influencers have been using this platform to build a personal brand and to acquire popularity through amassing followers (Marwick 2015). Marketers have quickly realized the potential of social media influencers and started to develop new influencer marketing strategies – also known as influencer marketing 2.0. As such, influencers have been shown to influence consumer behavior and decision making (Godey et al. 2016). Two main reasons explain the use of social media influencers and the positive contribution influencers make to marketing. First, social media influencers are able to reach out directly to more consumers, compared to companies. Second, influencers post information that consumers are genuinely interested in seeing (Casaló et al. 2018; Lin et al. 2018).

Traditional forms and types of influencers

A brief history of "celebrification"

In the early twentieth century, the development of the cinema industry in Hollywood led to the rise of celebrities the way we know them today. These celebrities were rap-idly seen as idols, unique individuals that portrayed the idealized American dream (Marshall 2014). The fact that the number of celebrities in the early twentieth century was limited by the scarce production of movies, further reinforced their audience's admiration (Kaikati 1987). Companies quickly seized the opportunity to capitalize

Table 2.1 Typology of past and current influencers

Emergence	Type of celebrity	Examples	Content	Media/Channels	Compensation	Communication strategy
Early 1900s –	Traditional celebrities/influencers	Actors, artists, politicians	Brand endorsement, advertisements	Traditional media (TV, radio, magazines)	Occasional monetary compensation for endorsement	Parasocial relationship Unidirectional One-to-many
2000s –	Reality TV celebrity	Talk shows and reality TV ordinary personalities	Entertainment and commercial	Traditional media (TV, radio, magazines)	Occasional monetary compensation for media appearances	Parasocial relationship Unidirectional One-to-many
1950s –	Corporate influencer network	Procter and Gamble, Vogue influencers	Market-specific product through network	Traditional media (TV, radio, magazines) and new media channels	Receive product samples Not necessarily compensated	Parasocial relationship Unidirectional One-to-many
2010 –	Micro-celebrities	Miranda Singsl,	Entertainment, niche content	New media unichannel social media platform	No compensation	Strong perceived interconnectedness one-to-many, one-to-one

marina leban and benjamin g. voyer

2013 –	Independent influencers	Beauty, lifestyle, health gurus	Entertainment and commercial Commercial only (specific products such as beauty products)	New media multi-channel social media platforms	Monetary compensation through collaboration with companies Gifted products	Strong perceived interconnectedness one-to-many, one-to-one
2018 –	Virtual influencers	Lil Miquela, …	Entertainment and commercial Created by a company	New media Instagram	Collaboration with brands	Parasocial relationship Unidirectional One-to-many (for now)

Sources: Adapted from Abidin (2015, 2018) and Piskorski and Brooks (2017).

on the audience's nascent admiration of celebrities, by collaborating with them on product endorsement. From the 1970s onwards, the number of films produced started to proliferate, and the number of celebrities rose accordingly. This, in turn, allowed companies to more easily find celebrities willing to become brand endorsers (Thompson 1978), and to improve targeting, by better matching which celebrity would fit a brand's image (Erdogan 1999). Although the very notion of celebrities has often been solely associated with Hollywood-type movie stars, scholars have considered other types of celebrities. These have traditionally been defined in a broad sense to incorporate, in addition to actors, artists, musicians, politicians, or sportsmen (e.g. Erdogan 1999; Piskorski and Brooks 2017). Table 2.1 depicts a historical continuum of influencers.

Marketing strategies and traditional influencers: the case of celebrity endorsement

Companies first started to identify possible brand endorsers in the form of traditional celebrities (Erdogan 1999). The marketing objective of such a strategy is to identify a celebrity that has matching personality traits to the brand personality and image. In the marketing literature, a celebrity endorser is "any individual who enjoys public recognition and who uses this recognition on behalf of a consumer good by appearing with it in an advertisement" (McCracken 1989, p. 310). For marketers, celebrity endorsement has become a powerful way to advertise a brand, influence consumers, and increase purchase intention (e.g. Amos et al. 2008; Erdogan 1999; Ohanian 1991).

The literature identifies three main marketing strategies using celebrity endorsement: Source Credibility Model, Source Attractiveness Model, and Meaning Transfer Model.

Starting with the *Source Credibility Model* (Ohanian 1990), marketing scholars have investigated how consumers perceive the source of a message, more specifically in terms of how much information can be gained about a target product or service. This model explores three main aspects: trustworthiness, attractiveness, and expertise of the celebrity endorser. Results suggest that if a consumer has a negative perception of all of these three aspects, then this will create a negative halo effect in terms of the celebrity endorser and brand perception. Thus, according to marketers, this model is important in order to choose the right celebrity to collaborate with. Studies relating to the source credibility model are discussed extensively in Chapter 7 (Närvänen et al. 2020) and are later tested empirically in Chapter 12 (Costello and Biondi 2020).

Other marketing scholars have deemed that attractiveness may be the most important aspect of a potential endorser. In the *Source Attractiveness Model* Singer (1983) argues that physical attractiveness, in addition to intellectual and personality aspects, does matter for a celebrity endorsement to work. The premise is that the higher the celebrity's attractiveness, the more power the celebrity has on consumer influence. In the field of social psychology, attractive individuals are usually considered to be smarter and more trustworthy (e.g. Eagly et al. 1991; Langlois and

marina leban and benjamin g. voyer

Roggman 1990). This concept of attractiveness is covered extensively in Chapter 4 (Rosenthal and Arcuri 2020).

In contrast, the *Meaning Transfer Model* (McCracken 1989) offers a less rigid approach to identifying suitable celebrity endorsers. The core argument is that, in a culturally constituted world, celebrities carry a cultural meaning, which is then transferred to a brand or product via the celebrity endorsement. This cultural meaning is further transferred into a brand or product through advertising, and then once again transferred from the product or service to the consumer. Altogether, the model suggests that consumers pick and choose specific products and brands in order to construct their identity. The careful creation of a celebrity image, as well as the way she or he is portrayed in an advertisement, is therefore crucial in determining how and if consumers will end up consuming a product or service.

As marketing techniques became more sophisticated in the 1980s onwards, companies have been looking at ways to better understand celebrity endorsement effects through the quantification of celebrity performance, and the use of these models (Hearn and Schoenhoff 2016). In recent years, however, changes in the nature of influencers have led companies to rethink previous top-down, rigid models, and the adoption of celebrity endorsement as part of their marketing strategies. For instance, marketing researchers have assumed that celebrities serve well only as brand ambassadors but have overlooked them as being individual human brands (Wohlfeil et al. 2019). These changes have called for marketing strategies to be adapted to each type of influencer, and saw companies having less control over influencers.

The emergence of a new category of influencers

Rise of micro-celebrities: from unknowns to celebrities

The rise of social media platforms in the 2010s has allowed traditional celebrities to keep – and extend – their large-scale fandom. But it has also allowed for the emergence of a new form of celebrities to emerge – referred to as "micro-celebrities." The notion of micro-celebrities was first introduced by Senft (2008), who observed that people online were able to gain popularity through blogs and social networking sites. In order to maintain their newly acquired popularity, micro-celebrities need to maintain a steady relationship with the viewers, by constantly communicating and actively interacting with their audience. The popularity of micro-celebrities is typically measured through their number of followers, likes, or comments (Marwick and Boyd 2011). Unlike traditional celebrities, micro-celebrity is considered "a state of being famous to a niche group of people" (Marwick 2013, p. 114). Micro-celebrity status is achieved through personal branding strategies in developing a human brand and followership.

To refer to this phenomenon, some scholars have coined the term "megaphone effect" (McQuarrie et al. 2012). According to McQuarrie et al. (2012), ordinary consumers are able to "take the megaphone" using social media, even though they may lack any professional experience in terms of communication. Thus, by definition, and contrary to the case of celebrities, micro-celebrities, at least initially, do not have any ties with brands. Their primary motive is therefore to gain attention and raise their popularity. This phenomenon is particularly prevalent on visual social media platforms such as Instagram, which has also been referred to as "Instafame," in which micro-celebrities are therefore able to easily reach thousands of followers. Micro-celebrities and Hollywood-type celebrities are comparable in the sense that they both publicly display their lives in order to create aspirational consumption (Marwick 2015).

Following Kozinets and Cerone (2014), although micro-celebrities are rapidly expanding on Instagram, there is a "celebrity threshold," in which being a micro-celebrity on Instagram does not automatically give you a stable popularity anymore. In fact, in order to maintain a high level of popularity, micro-celebrities have to develop new and increasingly sophisticated tactics to attract followers. Some of these strategies include drifting their brand image into dreamlike or utopian content, rather than aspirational content. However, such strategies may backfire, as followers cannot always identify themselves anymore with some of these micro-celebrities.

With the rise of micro-celebrities, there is still a gap in terms of understanding how micro-celebrities influence consumers. Some scholars have argued that micro-celebrities have almost as much influence on consumers as celebrities or well-established bloggers (McQuarrie et al. 2012). Moreover, contrary to previous assumptions, researchers have shown that consumers will not necessarily purchase celebrity-endorsed products, regardless of how much they like the celebrity (Banister and Cocker 2014). In fact, celebrities who have not been created or manipulated by companies have been proven to be more long-lasting, commercially profitable, and successful all together (Kendall 2008). Ultimately, understanding personal branding strategies of micro-celebrities may be a step forward in linking marketing managerial benefits and micro-celebrity collaborations.

Social media influencers as micro-celebrities

Among micro-celebrities, social media influencers – also known as "influencers" – are content creators or opinion leaders. They constitute a sub-category of micro-celebrities. Micro-celebrities typically become influencers once they have reached a wider popularity and audience on multiple media platforms (e.g. digitally but also in print) (Abidin 2015). The personal brand they created can then be directly associated with the brands they collaborate with, as a way for brands to influence consumers' purchase directly, by nurturing a consumer audience on social media (Abidin 2016a; Hearn and Schoenhoff 2016). A key distinction between micro-celebrities and social media influencers is that, while the former are usually considered "hobbyists," the latter are considered to be professionals. In fact, many of them will be monetizing their endorsement by creating specific content on social media platforms, including sponsored posts. This can, however, backfire, as their audience might be wary of such "sponsored" content.

Among all social media platforms, social media influencers' preferred platforms tend to be visual social media platforms. Whereas text-based social media platforms

marina leban and benjamin g. voyer

serve as a political, or conversational platform, visual social media serves as a self-presentation platform, in which images are favored over text (Marwick 2015). Instagram is currently favored as there seems to be a higher level of consumer engagement on this platform (Casaló et al. 2018; Marwick 2015). On visual social media platforms, social media influencers can end up fostering online communities in which they allow their followers to contribute to content creation, through direct message interaction, re-sharing content, or giving feedback. Thus, followers can also be co-producers of a social media influencer's online personal brand (Vargo and Lusch 2008, 2014). Moreover, followers consider social media influencers to be knowledgeable and experts about the products and other types of content they display on their accounts (Bao and Chang 2014).

Companies have mostly looked at social media influencers as a potential positive business opportunity to reach out to more consumers. As consumers are increasingly relying on online advertising and social media platforms to make purchase decisions, the weight of social media influencers in the decision-making process becomes more important. Another reason behind the fact that consumers seem to be attracted by social media influencers rather than more traditional celebrities, is that consumers tend to see social media influencers as more authentic and relatable than traditional celebrities (Hearn and Schoenhoff 2016). Marketing and consumer research has recently uncovered specific criteria inherent to social media influencers, which make them more successful than traditional influencers. These criteria are discussed in detail in the following section.

> ### Idea fairy: Micro celebrities influencers
>
> When considering social media influencers such as the Kardashians, how have they morphed into celebrities? Which other micro celebrities who started off as social media influencers can you identify? As a consumer, do you interact with celebrities and influencers differently? Why or why not?

Success criteria of social media influencers compared to traditional influencers

Interestingly, scholars are yet to reach a consensus or establish a model on what makes social media influencers more successful online than traditional celebrity influencers. In the literature, three main criteria are discussed as possible reasons for the stronger influence: being relatable, being reachable, being perceived as trustworthy or credible.

Relatability

Social media influencers tend to be more relatable than traditional celebrities. Whereas traditional, Hollywood-type celebrities tend to use social media platforms to showcase an extravagant and luxurious lifestyle, social media influencers appear to be more down-to-earth, and therefore more relatable. However, as noted by McQuarrie et al. (2012), appearing relatable may be more related to the performance techniques used by influencers, rather than reflecting an actual reality. McQuarrie et al. (2012) identify several practices used by social media influencers to emphasize and generate relatability. A first strategy is referred to as *"feigning similarity."* In this strategy, bloggers combine extravagant and privileged lifestyle posts with posts displaying the practice of more mundane activities. Doing so, they are able to signal to their audience that they are "just like them." Social media influencers can vlog about their daily routines, for instance stating a need to do their laundry, hang it out in their bedrooms, or washing the dishes (Piskorski and Brooks 2017). A second strategy is that of *"self-deprecation."* In this strategy, bloggers attempt to depreciate their achievements. For instance, social media influencers may tell their audience they would never have gotten the status they have without the help of a certain person, or without their loyal followers (McQuarrie et al. 2012). Finally, another way the social media influencer appears more likable and relatable is through the use of friendly language (e.g. "you guys") and directly addressing their viewers (Piskorski and Brooks 2017).

Reachability

In addition to appearing relatable – by showcasing their daily intimate lives – social media influencers also try to appear as reachable to their audience. They do so by actively and promptly interacting with their followers and responding to their comments or engaging in other live activities (Khamis et al. 2017). As Marwick (2016) suggests, this tactic is a way for social media influencers to maintain their popularity, as well as distancing themselves from traditional celebrities that are not, typically, engaging with their fans to the same extent. This, in turn, contributes to reinforcing the relationship between influencers and their audiences (Piskorski and Brooks 2017), as well as creating an illusion of closeness – also called *"perceived interconnectedness"* – with the social media influencers as followers deem the content to be exclusive and inaccessible in real life (Abidin 2015), giving followers a backstage access to the influencers' private life (Wohlfeil et al. 2019). Research has largely explored the concept of parasocial relationships between celebrities and fans (e.g. Rubin and McHugh 1987; Hwang and Zhang 2018; Wohlfeil et al. 2019). However, such reachability is often pictured as an illusion of fans feeling close to their idols. As Abidin (2015) points out, traditional celebrities use different communications strategies. More specifically, traditional celebrities foster parasocial relationships by using one-to-many communication strategies. Social media influencers, on the other hand, use both one-to-many and one-to-one communications strategies.

Trustworthiness

With a growing number of social media influencers and traditional celebrities actively using social media platforms, consumers have become more wary in terms of whom to trust. Since social media influencers appear more trustworthy than traditional

marina leban and benjamin g. voyer

celebrities, they also seem to carry a bigger weight on influencing the buying behavior of their followers (Djafarova and Rushworth 2017). Trustworthiness, in an influencer context, has been defined as "the honesty, integrity and believability of an endorser" (Erdogan 1999, p. 297). Thus, appearing authentic is an important aspect of trust-worthiness, something that social media influencers need to focus on when building their online personal brand (Khamis 2017). If social media influencers appear more trustworthy, they may, in turn, generate stronger electronic word-of-mouth (Djafarova and Rushworth, 2017), which may strengthen the weight of this in the buying decision-making process (Dost et al. 2019). Finally, Djafarova and Rushworth (2017) also note that consumers are more likely to follow new or unknown social media influencers, providing that they appear as genuine.

Idea fairy: Success criteria

Considering your own favorite influencers, how do they differ in terms of reliability, reachability, or trustworthiness? Does this impact how you engage with them online? How would you define success for an influencer?

Future research: Establishing an agenda to deepen our understanding of influencer marketing

With Instagram, a favorite platform among influencers, not even being a decade-old, research on social media influencers is understandably still in its infancy. In this chapter, we have discussed the ever-changing nature of influencers, from traditional celebrities to social media influencers, and to perhaps, in the coming years, virtual/artificial influencers (Marwick 2018). In addition, social media platforms are also constantly changing, adding new features or new applications within applications. Among social media platforms, visual social media platforms have appeared as being widely used by new and upcoming consumer segments such as generation Y and Z (Pew Research Center 2019). However, research on the type of content that social media influencers create on social media platforms has mostly been looked at on text-based platforms such as blogs and Twitter. More research is therefore needed to explore the type of practices that social media influencers display on visual social media platforms such as Instagram (Casaló et al. 2018).

Another area for future research would be to better understand the very nature of social media influencers, ultimately developing a typology of social media influencers. Scholars have either been looking at specific social media influencers such as bloggers (Erz and Christensen 2018; McQuarrie et al. 2012), fashion influencers (Abidin 2016a; Casaló et al. 2018), or have been using the term of social media influencers to describe any kind of social media influencer (e.g. Arora et al. 2019; Erz et al. 2018). Following other notable work on consumer cultures and communities (Schouten and McAlexander 1995), it is probable that social media influencers do not constitute a homogenous group, but that different types and levels and subcultures exist within the world of social media influencers. We thus encourage marketing scholars to deepen their understanding of the nature and types of influencers, as different influencers are likely to have different types of personal branding strategies and audiences. It is therefore crucial for marketing scholars and practitioners alike to understand the differences and similarities between each type of influencer, in order to devise better and more efficient marketing strategies.

A related area for future research lies in the importance of quantifying audience engagement, likes, comments, and other forms of engagement, to better understand and measure influencers' performance (e.g. Arora et al. 2019; Moro et al. 2016). As previously discussed, there may be other factors that carry an equal weight in terms of how social media influencers are able to influence consumer behavior. This is in line with a bigger issue in influencer marketing. Indeed, marketing practitioners and scholars have been dehumanizing celebrities, by considering them as only potential endorsers but not as brands themselves (Wohlfeil et al. 2019). Thus, as Fournier and Eckhardt (2019) put it, we urge researchers to "put the person back in person-brands," or in other words to rehumanize celebrities (Wohlfeil et al. 2019).

Most of the literature reviewed in this chapter reflects a Western, individualist, point of view on social media influencers. Research in cross-cultural psychology however suggests that individuals from different cultures perceive, process, and behave in strikingly different ways (Kastanakis and Voyer 2014). In addition, given the role that text plays in the social media culture, the very language that social media influencers speak (e.g. English vs. Korean) may affect the way they interact with their followers (Rhode et al. 2016). Cultural differences could thus play a role and affect the way social media influencers behave, especially in terms of how they may relate to their audiences. In addition, the motivations of followers, and the weight given to social media influencers' endorsement in the buying behavior process may differ across cultures. Finally, social media platforms differ around the world, with some platforms being predominantly used in one country or one region of the world. As platforms differ in terms of their functionalities, investigating cross-cultural differences in both social media influencers' behaviors and followers' perceptions and engagement with influencers may lead to fruitful results. Moreover, to the best of our knowledge, efforts have been made in exploring these cultural differences, especially for Asian influencer culture (Abidin 2016b; Abidin and Brown 2018; Abidin and Gwynne 2017) in media and communication studies. However, marketing literature remains underdeveloped in this area.

Finally, as the number of influencers on social media is fast increasing, staying unique is, in turn, increasingly difficult (Casaló et al. 2018). An interesting and emerging phenomenon has been the rise of virtual influencers. Virtual influencers have rapidly gained notoriety, amassing millions of viewers, and collaborating with luxury brands (Marwick 2018). Virtual influencers can be defined as being digitally and artificially fabricated human-like influencers, created by Artificial Intelligence agencies. To the best of our knowledge, no research has been conducted to explore the motivations behind following virtual influencers, how they are perceived, and the effect they carry on buying behaviors.

marina leban and benjamin g. voyer

Summary

- Celebrities play an essential role in marketing strategy as they influence consumer behavior, decision making, and have shown to effectively spread eWOM.
- Celebrity endorsement marketing strategies entail a top-down process in which marketers design and dictate how celebrities should market their brand. Social media influencer marketing strategies are freer to incorporate brands in the content they display, making them appear more authentic and genuine.
- The three main models of celebrity endorsement are: the Source Credibility Model (Ohanian 1990), the Source Attractiveness Model (Singer 1983), and the Meaning Transfer Model (McCracken 1989).
- Traditional celebrities have existed since the beginning of the twentieth century, and are usually well-established actors or artists.
- Micro-celebrities are ordinary consumers who became famous exclusively online, by posting niche content. They are often characterized as being "hobbyists." Social media influencers are professional micro-influencers who have become more established online as well as offline.
- Social media influencers are often successful due to them being relatable, being reachable and being perceived as trustworthy or credible

Case studies on social media influencers

Kylie Jenner: From socialite to influencer, turned product maker

Kylie Jenner, a social media influencer who rose to fame as part of a TV series (Keeping Up with the Kardashians) first broadcast in 2007, is a prime example of the power of social media when it comes to brand building. Seven years after the TV show started, she founded her own company, Kylie Lip Kits, offering initially a single product: lipsticks. Her company later expanded to other products and was renamed Kylie Cosmetics. Within 18 months of existence, Jenner's company had generated $420 million in revenue – when it took some traditional cosmetics companies such as Lancôme, decades to achieve similar turnovers. Kylie Jenner's brand success was such that she was named by Forbes, in June 2019, the youngest self-made billionaire ever, and the youngest billionaire in the world.

What can be learned from Kylie Jenner's brand-building success is twofold. First, social media and the effect of celebrity endorsement may work not only in the context of endorsing another brand, as research reviewed in this chapter suggests, but also in terms of developing a brand and product line from scratch. In doing so, SMIs may in fact bypass the traditional wariness that some consumers may have over celebrity and SMI-endorsed well-known brands. SMIs creating their own brand may be perceived as more trustworthy than those endorsing established brands. This may be further accentuated by the fact that, in the case of Kylie Cosmetics, the brand only has a dozen employees, while Kylie's mother, Kris Jenner, is also involved in the business, giving the company a small, family company feel.

The second lesson that can be learned from the case of Kylie Cosmetics is that social media influencers, who have successfully developed a personal brand, can then use their success to bypass traditional brands and become product and service creators themselves. This second lesson carries important consequences for marketers, pointing out the possibility that, in the coming years, celebrities increasingly act as competitors to traditional brands. This could then reshape the marketing world and the role of influencers in general. In the case of Kylie Jenner, much use was made of adopting a novel marketing approach to rapidly penetrate the teen cosmetics market. For example, the codes adopted on the packaging and online advertising were noticeably different from those of the beauty industry, by adopting bold colors and sleek, plain designs. Story-telling was used, for instance referring to Jenner's childhood insecurities about the appearance of her lips.

The rise of Kylie Cosmetics also raises a series of questions about the durability and future of such brands. Given that brands, when harnessing the power of social media, are able to grow at a fast, steady pace, it raises questions about whether such growth is both sustainable and durable. The risk may be that social media and SMI give rise to "meteorite brands," which rise to fame and disappear in a short period of time. Another possible strategy would be for these brands to eventually cease to be a social media influencer brand and join a bigger cosmetic group, such as L'Oréal or Estée Lauder. In addition, the rapid change of social media platforms, constantly requiring new skills as a communication medium and technique change – from text to photos, videos, and in the coming years, augmented and virtual reality – may further reinforce the questions around the future of such brands.

Questions to address:

- How can you explain Kylie Cosmetics rapid growth compared to traditional beauty brands?
- What are the success criteria, which could be replicated by other social media celebrities looking at launching their own cosmetic brands?
- What would be the risks and benefits of Kylie Jenner collaborating with another major cosmetic brand such as L'Oréal or Estée Lauder?

Glossier: Defying current cosmetic giants by adopting influencer marketing strategies

Glossier is yet another example of how social media can have an impact on brand building and consumer engagement. Glossier is a cosmetic company that was originally created by Emily Weiss in 2010. Weiss started a beauty blog called IntotheGloss.com to discuss issues between the current beauty industry and the real beauty needs of women. Emily Weiss then later in 2014 launched the official website Glossier.com containing four main cosmetic products. In the space of four years, Glossier increased in popularity. This led to the company exceeding $100 million in annual revenue.

Glossier's marketing approach, targeting mainly millennials, allowed it to grow fast over a short period of time. It relied on a strong social media presence, not

marina leban and benjamin g. voyer

only with traditional platforms such as Facebook or Twitter, but more specifically paying particular attention to Instagram, as millennials spend more time on that specific platform than other generations. The company amassed followers by creating "Instagrammable content," through designing their own products to be simple, not overly polished or glamorous, using color-friendly pastel-like colors, and most specifically, Instagrammable.

One particular marketing strategy that really allowed Glossier to grow fast was the use of social media influencers. Unlike traditional and more established beauty companies, which use traditional celebrity endorsers to promote their brands, Glossier's strategy was based on a more down-to-earth approach, hiring more "common" social media influencers, such as bloggers or vloggers – and this, regardless of how many followers they had on social media. Glossier referred to their social media influencers as "Glossier girls" and promoted them as "ordinary women" who enjoy using their products.

Glossier's strategy of sponsoring social media influencers follows the clear success criteria of social media influencers discussed in this chapter. The hiring of social media influencers, considered to be different than traditional celebrities, increased the brand's relatability. In turn, consumers following these social media influencers were able to identify themselves with the brand. Moreover, the use of "Glossier girls" meant that Glossier had a better consumer reach, as these social media influencers actively interacted with their audience. Lastly, because "Glossier Girls" were not necessarily established social media influencers, with some "only" having over 8,000 followers per account – as opposed to hundreds of thousands or millions of followers for traditional celebrities or established SMIs – these were seen as trustworthy and genuine in the type of content and advice they created on Instagram.

Altogether, Glossier is a prime example of how new brands can win an edge when it comes to targeting younger generations of consumers who: i) feel a need to interact with brands directly, and ii) like to gather information on brands through social media platforms. This can also illustrate the fact that younger generations may now be seen as more wary of the use of traditional celebrities in marketing campaigns.

Questions to address:

- What are the key factors that can explain Glossier's success?
- Why did Glossier choose to work with micro-celebrities rather than only work with established social media celebrities?
- How can Glossier replicate this success on new social media platforms?

References

Abidin, C., 2015. Communicative intimacies: Influencers and perceived interconnectedness. *Ada*, 8, 1–16.

Abidin, C., 2016a. "Aren't these just young, rich women doing vain things online?": Influencer selfies as subversive frivolity. *Social Media+ Society*, 2(2), 2056305116641342.

Abidin, C., 2016b. Visibility labor: Engaging with Influencers' fashion brands and# OOTD advertorial campaigns on Instagram. *Media International Australia*, 161(1), 86–100.

Abidin, C., and Brown, M.L., 2018. *Microcelebrity Around the Globe*: Emerald Publishing Limited.

Abidin, C., and Gwynne, J., 2017. Entrepreneurial selves, feminine corporeality, and lifestyle blogging in Singapore. *Asian Journal of Social Science*, 45(4–5), 385–408.

Amos, C., Holmes, G., and Strutton, D., 2008. Exploring the relationship between celebrity endorser effects and advertising effectiveness: A quantitative synthesis of effect size. *International Journal of Advertising*, 27(2), 209–234.

Arora, A., Bansal, S., Kandpal, C., Aswani, R., and Dwivedi, Y, 2019. Measuring social media influencer index-insights from Facebook, Twitter, and Instagram. *Journal of Retailing and Consumer Services*, 49, 86–101.

Banister, E.N., and Cocker, H.L., 2014. A cultural exploration of consumers' interactions and relationships with celebrities. *Journal of Marketing Management*, 30(1–2), 1–29.

Bao, T., and Chang, T., 2014. Finding disseminators via electronic word of mouth message for effective marketing communications. *Decision Support Systems*, 67, 21–29.

Casaló, L. V., Flavián, C., and Ibáñez-Sánchez, S., 2018. Influencers on Instagram: Antecedents and consequences of opinion leadership. *Journal of Business Research*. https://doi.org/10.1016/j.jbusres.2020.02.014

Costello, J., and Biondi, L., 2020. The Art of Deception: Will fake followers decay trust and can authenticity preserve it? Ch. 12 in *Influencer Marketing: Building Brand Communities and Engagement*. Ed. Yesiloglu, S., and Costello, J. Routledge: London.

Djafarova, E., and Rushworth, C., 2017. Exploring the credibility of online celebrities' Instagram profiles in influencing the purchase decisions of young female users. *Computers in Human Behavior*, 68, 1–7.

Dost, F., Phieler, U., Haenlein, M., and Libai, B., 2019. Seeding as Part of the Marketing Mix: Word-of-Mouth Program Interactions for Fast-Moving Consumer Goods. *Journal of Marketing*, 83(2), 62–81.

Eagar, T., and Dann, S., 2016. Classifying the narrated# selfie: Genre typing human-branding activity. *European Journal of Marketing*, 50(9/10), 1835–1857.

Eagly, A.H., Ashmore, R.D., Makhijani, M.G., and Longo, L.C., 1991. What is beautiful is good, but...: A meta-analytic review of research on the physical attractiveness stereotype. *Psychological Bulletin*, 110(1), 109–128.

Erdogan, B.Z., 1999. Celebrity endorsement: A literature review. *Journal of Marketing Management*, 15(4), 291–314.

Erz, A., and Christensen, A., 2018. Transforming consumers into brands: tracing transformation processes of the practice of blogging. *Journal of Interactive Marketing*, 43, 69–82.

Erz, A., Marder, B., and Osadchaya, E., 2018. Hashtags: Motivational drivers, their use, and differences between influencers and followers. *Computers in Human Behavior*, 89, 48–60.

Fournier, S., and Eckhardt, G.M., 2019. Putting the Person Back in Person-Brands: Understanding and Managing the Two-Bodied Brand. *Journal of Marketing Research*, 56(4), 602–619.

Godey, B., Manthiou, A., Pederzoli, D., Rokka, J., Aiello, G., Donvito, R., and Singh, R., 2016. Social media marketing efforts of luxury brands: Influence on brand equity and consumer behavior. *Journal of Business Research*, 69(12), 5833–5841.

Hearn, A., and Schoenhoff, S., 2016. From celebrity to influencer: Tracing the diffusion of celebrity value across the data stream. *A Companion to Celebrity*, 194–212.

Hwang, K., and Zhang, Q., 2018. Influence of parasocial relationship between digital celebrities and their followers on followers' purchase and electronic word-of-mouth intentions, and persuasion knowledge. *Computers in Human Behavior*, 87, 155–173.

Kaikati, J.G., 1987. Celebrity advertising: a review and synthesis. *International Journal of Advertising*, 6(2), 93–105.

Kastanakis, M.N., and Voyer, B.G., 2014. The effect of culture on perception and cognition: A conceptual framework. *Journal of Business Research*, 67(4), 425–433.

Kendall, T.D., 2008. Durable good celebrities. *Journal of Economic Behavior and Organization*, 66(2), 312–321.

Khamis, S., Ang, L., and Welling, R., 2017. Self-branding, "micro-celebrity", and the rise of Social Media Influencers. *Celebrity Studies*, 8(2), 191–208.

Kozinets, R., and Cerone, S., 2014. Between the suit and the selfie: Executives' lessons on the social "micro-celebrity". *GfK Marketing Intelligence Review*, 6(2), 21.

Langlois, J.H., and Roggman, L.A., 1990. Attractive faces are only average. *Psychological Science*, 1(2), 115–121.

Lee, J., and Hong, I.B., 2016. Predicting positive user responses to social media advertising: The roles of emotional appeal, informativeness, and creativity. *International Journal of Information Management*, 36(3), 360–373.

Lin, H., Bruning, P.F., and Swarna, H., 2018. Using online opinion leaders to promote the hedonic and utilitarian value of products and services. *Business Horizons*, 61(3), 431–442.

Marshall, P.D., 2014. *Celebrity and Power: Fame in contemporary culture*. U of Minnesota Press.

Marwick, A., 2016. You may know me from YouTube. *A Companion to Celebrity* (pp. 333–350). Wiley Blackwell.

Marwick, A.E., 2013. *Status Update: Celebrity, publicity, and branding in the social media age*. Yale University Press.

Marwick, A.E., 2015. Instafame: Luxury Selfies in the Attention Economy. *Public Culture*, 27(175), 137–160.

Marwick, A.E., 2018. The Algorithmic Celebrity: The Future of Internet Fame and Microcelebrity Studies. *Microcelebrity Around the Globe* (pp. 161–169): Emerald Publishing Limited.

Marwick, A.E., and Boyd, D., 2011. I tweet honestly, I tweet passionately: Twitter users, context collapse, and the imagined audience. *New Media and Society*, 13(1), 114–133.

McCracken, G., 1989. Who is the celebrity endorser? Cultural foundations of the endorsement process. *Journal of Consumer Research*, 16(3), 310–321.

McQuarrie, E.F., Miller, J., and Phillips, B.J., 2012. The megaphone effect: Taste and audience in fashion blogging. *Journal of Consumer Research*, 40(1), 136–158.

Moro, S., Rita, P., and Vala, B., 2016. Predicting social media performance metrics and evaluation of the impact on brand building: A data mining approach. *Journal of Business Research*, 69(9), 3341–3351.

Närvänen, E., Kirvesmies, T., and Kahri, E., 2020 Parasocial relationships of Generation Z consumers with social media influencers Ch. 7 in *Influencer Marketing: Building Brand Communities and Engagement*. Ed. Yesiloglu, S., and Costello, J. Routledge: London.

Ohanian, R., 1990. Construction and validation of a scale to measure celebrity endorsers' perceived expertise, trustworthiness, and attractiveness. *Journal of Advertising*, 19(3), 39–52.

Ohanian, R. (1991). The impact of celebrity spokespersons' perceived image on consumers' intention to purchase. Journal of Advertising Research, 31(1), 46–54.

Pew Research Center, 2019. Share of U.S. adults using social media, including Facebook, is mostly unchanged since 2018. *Pew Research Center*. Retrieved from www.pewresearch.org/fact-tank/2019/04/10/share-of-u-s-adults-using-social-media-including-facebook-is-mostly-unchanged-since-2018/

Piskorski, M., and Brooks, G., 2017. Online Broadcasters: How Do They Maintain Influence, When Audiences Know They Are Paid to Influence. *American Marketing Association Winter Conference*, 28, D70-D80.

Rhode, A.K., Voyer, B.G., and Gleibs, I.H., 2016. Does language matter? Exploring Chinese–Korean differences in holistic perception. *Frontiers in Psychology*, 7, 1508. https://doi.org/10.3389/fpsyg.2016.01508

Rosenthal, B., and Arcuri, A., 2020. How to map and select digital influencers for Marketing Campaigns. Ch. 4 in *Influencer Marketing: Building Brand Communities and Engagement*. Ed. Yesiloglu, S., and Costello, J. Routledge: London.

Rubin, R.B., and McHugh, M.P., 1987. Development of parasocial interaction relationships, *Journal of Broadcasting and Electronic Media*, 31(3), 279–292.

Schouten, J.W., and McAlexander, J.H., 1995. Subcultures of consumption: An ethnography of the new bikers. *Journal of Consumer Research*, 22(1), 43–61.

Senft, T.M., 2008. *Camgirls: Celebrity and community in the age of social networks*: Peter Lang Publishing.

Singer, B.D., 1983. The case for using "real people" in advertising. *Business Quarterly*, 48(4), 32–37.

Statista, 2019. Number of social media users worldwide from 2010 to 2023 (in billions). Retrieved from www.statista.com/statistics/278414/number-of-worldwide-social-network-users/

Statista, 2018. Number of monthly active Instagram users from January 2013 to June 2018 (in millions). Retrieved from www.statista.com/statistics/253577/number-of-monthly-active-instagram-users/

Thompson, J.R., 1978. Celebrities strike it big as endorsers. *Industrial Marketing*, 63(1), 85.

Vargo, S.L., and Lusch, R.F., 2008. From goods to service (s): Divergences and convergences of logics. *Industrial Marketing Management*, 37(3), 254–259.

Vargo, S.L., and Lusch, R.F., 2014. Evolving to a new dominant logic for marketing. *The Service-Dominant Logic of Marketing* (pp. 21–46): Routledge.

Wohlfeil, M., Patterson, A., and Gould, S.J., 2019. The allure of celebrities: unpacking their polysemic consumer appeal. *European Journal of Marketing*, 53(10), 2025–2053.

chapter 3

Identifying and selecting the right influencers in the digital era

Sabina Riboldazzi and Antonella Capriello

Learning outcomes

On completing this chapter, you should be able to:

- understand the social media influencer categories and the consequences of covert marketing;
- appreciate how reach, relevance, and resonance can help you identify and select the right influencers; and
- understand the three steps in identifying and selecting influencers.

Influencer marketing aims to generate strategic word-of-mouth (WOM) that significantly affects brand visibility and brand awareness (Rezvani et al. 2012). Influencer marketing has increasingly turned to social media, so much so that we now refer to "social media influencers" (Gillin 2007). This marketing approach comprises a hybrid of new marketing tools, including celebrity endorsements, as part of content-driven marketing campaigns that aim to tell the brand story in such a way as to offer value to customers, build their trust and interact with the brand. Brand managers constantly evaluate influencer marketing as an element of their marketing strategy (Glucksman 2017), particularly as the traditional social media approach where a firm creates a fan page to share the success of specific events is increasingly less effective. Furthermore, consumers are moving away from advertising, losing interest and confidence in traditional media, and are instead evaluating figures or models to follow who are external to the company. The success or failure of a digital marketing strategy may thus depend on the ability to identify key influencers from among the increasing number of bloggers, celebrities, macro- and micro-influencers acting on digital platforms (Bailis 2019).

For Instagram, the average cost of a sponsored photo increased by 44 percent between 2018 and 2019; in 2015, the average cost was $381 and now stands at a hefty $1,643. For Twitter, the cost of sponsoring tweets grew from $34 in 2015 to $422 in 2019 (McCarthy 2019). In light of the rising cost of sponsored content on such social media platforms, a critical issue in the digital era is how to select the right influencers who create engaging content, post regularly, and appeal to the right audiences (Snyder 2019). Simply looking at the influencer's popularity is a limited perspective since the real goal is to elicit customer brand engagement.

In this chapter, we analyze the key role of influencers in the digital era and the related typologies. A conceptual framework for identifying and selecting influencers is presented which includes the core dimensions emerging from a case study comparison. We then propose three steps for identifying and selecting the right influencers. Finally, we present a case study integrating all the key variables for selecting influencers.

Influencers in the digital era

The growing complexity of the global market in which companies operate requires the development of dynamic relations with many heterogeneous individuals (Brondoni 2018). This in turn may affect the company's results depending on its objectives. In some markets, networking relations and information dissemination also involve the key role of influencers. According to Brown and Hayes (2008, p. 50), influencers may be defined as "a third-party who significantly shapes the customer's purchasing decision but may never be accountable for it." The authors identify multiple categories of influencers such as academics, authors, management thinkers, business, and trade journalists that they map into various influencer roles – for instance, idea planters, predictors, and trendsetters.

Lambin (2008) underlines the importance of influencer orientation in market-driven management. Influencer orientation implies the identification of key influencers to develop specific communications to motivate and obtain their support. Specifically, Lambin (2008) identifies three types of influencers who recommend products, services, or brands. The first type of influencers refers to prescribers or individuals/organizations that formally single out a product, service, brand, or company. The prescription phenomenon is found in several industries and professions, from doctors who prescribe medications, to educators who prescribe textbooks, to architects who prescribe equipment. The second type refers to certification agencies or independent organizations developing common international management standards. For instance, ISO is the International Organization for Standardization where ISO

sabina riboldazzi and antonella capriello

9000 refers to the standard for quality management. Finally, there are opinion leaders or individuals who condition and influence a purchasing decision in an informal way (Lambin 2008). This is associated with the idea of traditional social media influencers on Instagram or YouTube that may focus their discussions on a niche area such as beauty or fashion.

Integrating this perspective, and in accordance with Gladwell (2000), influencers can be classified into three categories: connectors or networkers communicating messages far and wide through word-of-mouth; salesmen that through their charisma and skills are able to build an instant relationship with people and gain their trust; mavens or knowledgeable people and information specialists with information on different products, prices, and places. Keller and Berry (2003) later identified five traits to help distinguish "influentials." Those termed "activists" have an activist approach to life, while "people with active minds" have a restless intellect continually taking input from what they read, hear, and see. "People who are connected" have ties to a significantly large number of groups but differ from "people with impact" who others look up to for advice. Finally, there are the "trendsetters" for the mainstream market. While Gladwell (2000) and Keller and Berry (2003) coined their terms prior to the explosion of social media platforms ripe for influencer marketing, they paved the way for how digital or e-influencers would later be termed.

Burson-Marsteller (2010) created the term *e-fluentials* to describe opinion leaders who exert an extraordinary impact on spreading information online. Indeed, a further category of influencers has emerged because of the growth of digital and social media as well as e-business. Social media influencers "have the potential to create engagement, drive conversation, and/or sell products/services with the intended target audience. These individuals can range from being celebrities to more micro-targeted professional or nonprofessional peers" (Interactive Advertising Bureau 2018, p. 5).

Yesiloglu (2020) in Chapter 1 attributes the emergence and subsequent power of electronic word of mouth (eWOM) as becoming the defining moment in the rise of influencers. eWOM can make social media influencers extraordinarily successful through their higher credibility, empathy, and relevance to customers (Gruen et al. 2006). Through web-based opinion platforms, customers share their opinions and experiences of goods and services with a multitude of other customers (Hennig-Thurau et al. 2004). It is in the interest of companies as well as influencers to hold positive online conversations and persuade other customers (Lee and Youn 2009).

In generating intentional WOM, celebrity endorsements are considered credible sources for positive eWOM regarding certain services and products (Djafarova and Rushworth 2017). The credibility of a celebrity endorser in turn positively affects the credibility of the endorsed brand (Spry et al. 2011). In analyzing the spread of positive WOM, Bughin et al. (2010, p. 5) introduce the concept of "word-of-mouth equity," representing "the average sales impact of a brand message multiplied by the number of word-of-mouth messages." The authors also underline that high WOM equity may be generated by an influential sender with few messages given a close/trusted network, the presence of a favorable buying factor, and the consumer's own positive experience.

Gorry and Westbrook (2009) highlight that web influencers might be viewed as hostile voices, since their posts may be reactive rather than proactive, thus potentially damaging the company's reputation. However, many other studies recognize the social media influencer phenomenon, underlining the opportunity to forge alliances with online influencers, and focusing on some specific aspects, such as the relationship with advertisers, metrics, nature, variables, effect, and audience perceptions of influencers (e.g. Subramani and Rajagopalan 2003; Booth and Matic 2011; Freberg at al. 2011; De Veirman et al. 2017; Childers et al. 2018; Quintana Ramos and Cownie 2020). According to Freberg et al. (2011), social media influencers are a new type of independent third-party endorsers who shape audience attitudes using social media channels. By tapping into the platforms such as Instagram, Facebook, YouTube, and Twitter, influencers can create content to communicate and promote certain products and brands with the goal of obtaining a following and brand recognition.

Social media influencer categories

Social media influencers are often classified according to their number of followers, such as mega, macro, micro, nano, and virtual influencers. However, there are other characteristics we discuss that differentiate mega and virtual influencers from those based solely on audience size.

Celebrities, or mega influencers, are actors, artists, or athletes with a high number of followers on social media channels, and their prevalence may condition customer decisions (Backaler 2018). Their celebrity status generally entails high costs for collaborating with companies. Indeed, the reach of celebrities is immense. Mega influencers can boost a product or brand even with a short campaign (Pedersen 2019). They are characterized by fame but also professionalism in that they are generally supported by a team specialized in paid endorsements. According to Malik and Qureshi (2017), gender, attractiveness, credibility, and multiple celebrity endorsements are some aspects that make the use of celebrities effective in influencing purchasing intentions. An example of a mega influencer is Kim Kardashian, a celebrity endorser (Lueck 2015) with around 12 million followers, and in 2018, the first recipient of the Council of Fashion Designers of America influencer award.

Macro influencers generally reach around 10K–1 million followers (SanMiguel et al. 2018) and may be experts, executives, journalists, researchers, or bloggers with an explicit field of mastery and ability to deliver a desired action from their audience. They are perceived as opinion leaders on a subject matter and are generally regarded as topic specialists. Macro influencers may also be professional social media personalities with a passion for a specific topic and experience in offer negotiation and content creation. They are not celebrities, but their following consists of a large, loyal fan base. Macro influencers allow marketers to reach a large portion of their target audience with high-quality content (Influencity 2018).

In contrast, micro-influencers have a community with a more limited size. They reach around 1K–10K followers (SanMiguel et al. 2018) and address smaller audiences that they strategically maintain through consistent communications (Gretzel 2018). They may be real people with a strong relationship with their audience, generally

sabina riboldazzi and antonella capriello

focusing on a specific niche or area. They post sponsored content less often than celebrities, providing a set of advantages exclusively to a specific audience such as friends and family members, and may garner greater trust thanks to their relatable nature, accessibility, and content quality (Backaler 2018). Chen (2016) underlines the credibility of their eWOM, since micro-influencers have the potential to generate more organic engagement per post to include likes, comments, retweets, sharing, and reactions. This orientation is consistent with the idea of generating high WOM equity, as discussed in the previous section (Bughin et al. 2010).

Nano influencers have a lower number of followers, but a similarly high level of commitment: they reach as few as 1,000 followers (Maheshwari 2018) and act as persuaders in their social groups with particular opinions of a product/company. Many companies use micro and nano influencers with a relatively small follower base. For example, Sephora in February 2019 put out a casting call to select a group of beauty influencers to create content for the powerhouse beauty retailer. The 24 influencers selected through the program represent a wide range of nationalities, ethnicities, gender, etc. The down-to-earth nature of the selected influencers makes it easy for viewers to relate to them. The company states, "We value unique, unfiltered, sorry-not-sorry storytellers, no matter the number of followers they have" (www. sephorasquad.com).

An emerging category is virtual influencers or "non-human influencers" who may have millions of followers and may be chosen or created by companies with characteristics they specifically define. An advantage associated with virtual influencers is the ability to control the behavior and content of the communications conveyed by these virtual subjects. Among the most famous virtual influencers on a global level is Lil Miquela, the fashion icon created in 2016 whose Instagram profile counts more than 1 million followers. Lil Miquela, a computer-generated model who virtually lives in Los Angeles, has been hired by the most important luxury brands, often endorsed by some of her virtual friends (Yurieff 2018). With over 200,000 Instagram followers, another is Noonoouri, the ambassador of a sustainable lifestyle who has worked for fashion brands such as Marc Jacobs, Dior, and Versace (Iglhaut 2019). Noonoouri is not just a model but is interested in beauty, fashion, luxury, lifestyle, travel, culture, art, and social issues, attracting many followers in relation to her activities. Shudu, employed by other prestigious brands (such as Ellesse), has 177,000 Instagram followers and is widely considered the world's first digital supermodel (Kane 2019) thanks to her beauty, elegance, and ability to attract thousands who follow her updates daily. Guthrie (2020) elaborates in Chapter 15 about the key debates concerning how virtual influencers may disrupt how human influencers operate and indeed influencer marketing.

Idea fairy: Does size matter?

Considering the influencers which you follow, how would you classify them according to mega, macro, micro, nano, or virtual? Do you engage differently with the various categories? Do they engage with you? What are the pros and cons of the different sizes in your opinion and experience?

How to identify and select the right influencers in the digital era

The identification and selection of influencers are important phases in influencer marketing strategy development. Among the different categories of influencers operating in a specific market, it is important to identify and select those that have the ability to generate positive eWOM and are more influential in relation to the budget and objectives of a specific influencer marketing campaign.

Kumar and Mirchandani (2012) suggest a seven-step framework to identify and recruit influencers on social media channels: *monitor the conversation* on social media channels, either in relation to the company itself or competitors, which will enable the company to *identify influential individuals* who have the ability to spread messages from the company perspective. Next, companies should *ascertain the factors that influential individuals share* to create profiles of typical influencers. To find potential influencers for a particular campaign, it is not enough to identify users with influence, so a company should *locate potential influencers* who have interests relevant to the campaign in order to *recruit* those influencers to talk about the company's products and services. Once a company has recruited influential users, the next step should be to *incentivize influencers* to spread positive WOM and *reap the rewards* from increasingly effective social media campaigns.

Many companies use platforms and agencies (e.g. Traackr, Hypr, Klear) to identify and choose influencers. These agencies recognize that influencer marketing is becoming a more prevalent approach to advertising (Childers et al. 2018), and increasingly specialize in offering services to support influencer marketing campaigns. From a general perspective, the answers to the following questions can determine the choice of influencers: Who specifically do they influence and why? What decisions do they influence? At what point of the customer activity cycle do they become important? How powerful is their voice? (Lambin 2008).

An early attempt to answer these questions contemplates a four-dimension metric composed of market *reach, frequency of impact, quality of impact,* and *closeness to a decision* (Brown and Hayes 2008). Specifically, market reach and frequency of impact refer respectively to the number of people an influencer could connect with and the number of opportunities an influencer has to impact on customer decisions. Quality of impact can be explained as the esteem for the influencer's views, verdicts, and opinions held (Lambin 2008). Finally, closeness to decision refers to how close in timing the influencer's opinions are heard relative to the final customer decision, rather than how close in proximity the influencer is to the decision-maker (Brown and Hayes 2008).

To summarize the importance of the described variables, three main integrated dimensions (*reach, relevance,* and *resonance*) and related sub-dimensions should be evaluated when selecting influencers (see Figure 3.1). Considering the specific objectives of an influencer marketing campaign, these dimensions are key factors and practical tools to uncover the power of the selected influencers.

Reach

Reach refers to the number of people who can potentially see the influencer's content and considers all of the influencer's users. Indeed, a metric to estimate potential

sabina riboldazzi and antonella capriello

reach is the number of followers an influencer has (SanMiguel 2018), and after the campaign launch, some key reach metrics include followers' growth rate, number of impressions, website, and/or loading page traffic. *Target reach* concerns the potential size of an influencer's audience considering the target audience of a specific influencer marketing campaign. To identify and estimate the potential size of this target audience (Bailis 2019), an *audience demographics analysis* can be conducted referring to variables such as the country of origin and the language of the influencers' followers, as well as their education, age, income, interests, occupation. These variables allow estimating the number of influencer users in coherence with the selected audience of a defined marketing campaign.

Reach and target reach: the example of Pupa

Pupa (Micys Company S.p.A. Group) is an Italian company founded in 1976 representing "Made in Italy" cosmetics in the world. The company distributes its products in 65 countries, continually innovating its offer. Among Pupa's product innovations are the Sport Addicted line designed for women who wear make-up even during sporting activities (www.pupa.it). For this line, Pupa has chosen three ambassadors/influencers: Valentina Vignali, basketball player and model; Carlotta Ferlito, Olympic gymnast; and Elena D'Amario, first dancer of the Parsons Dance Company. The influencers have high reach and target reach potential, considering that their followers are respectively 1,500,000 (Instagram), 714,000 (IG), and 695,000 (IG) (www.launchmetrics.com). Moreover, many of the influencers' followers according to the "demographic variables" are consistent (by age, gender, occupation, etc.) with the target audience of the Sport Addicted campaign, foreshadowing the effective development potential of the influencer marketing campaign.

Relevance

Relevance refers to the level of alignment, similarity, and closeness of values and interests between the company and the influencer (Solis and Webber 2012). Relevance may also depend on the type of content/platform (audio, photos, recorded video, live streaming video, long and short text, curated content, etc.) that the influencers use to transmit their messages. According to Backaler (2018, p. 30), "from a brand's perspective, relevance also related to how closely an influencer's community matches up to the brand's target audience, as well as how closely the influencer's content aligns with key topics that the brand wants to be associated with."

Assessing relevance requires evaluating several influencer characteristics, including *authority*, that is, the influencer's ability to be recognized as an expert on a given topic or subject, level of *trust*, which directly depends on the honesty and truthfulness of the opinions the influencer expresses, and *affinity*, i.e., a natural linking or the empathy established by an influencer within a community (Solis and Webber 2012). *Authenticity* is also an important sub-dimension used to assess relevance and refers to the influencer's ability to be recognized as someone who transmits genuine passion through content without being viewed as a "sell-out" (Backaler 2018). Napoli et al. (2014) underline that sincerity is an important factor to evaluate authenticity. Audrezet et al. (2018) distinguish between passionate authenticity and transparent authenticity. Passionate authenticity emerges when influencers are driven by "their inner desires and passions more so than by commercial goals," transparent authenticity refers to the influencer's ability to provide "fact-based information about the product or service at the center of the brand partnership" (Audrezet et al. 2018, p. 9). For example, the influencers discussed in the case of Pupa could exhibit passionate authenticity when they are already wearing Pupa products, as opposed to transparent authenticity if they were only endorsing the products for commercial gain.

Ferchaud et al. (2018) specify that self-disclosure adds to the influencers' perceived authenticity. Self-disclosure remains a challenge despite policies emerging by advertising standards bodies around the world (Bosher 2020). According to Kowalczyk and Pounders (2016, p. 9), "a perception of authenticity fosters an emotional bond or relationship between the consumer and the celebrity." Relevance may be evaluated by reviewing the influencer's prior sponsorships and social media posts to ensure the content, values, passions, language, and expertise are consistent with the company and its brand values.

Relevance: Gucci uses works of art with expert commentary

Gucci, one of the most renowned fashion houses in the world and part of the Kering Group, recently inaugurated the Instagram account @guccibeauty. Through this account, the company traces, post-by-post, the evolution of styles, language, and theories on beauty with the help of some excellent influencers: great works of art. These have become a source of inspiration in terms of fashion and beauty. Each image is in fact accompanied by commentary from writers and art critics who contextualize the work and focus attention on the most "glamorous" details. The captions of this series of portraits are the work of a group of art writers, critics, journalists, and artists, with different backgrounds and origins. The group includes Tatiana Berg, Britt Julious, Larissa Pham, and Antwaun Sargent, with reviews edited by Kyle Chayka. Relevance derives from these experts' authority and the affinity and empathy generated through the alignment between Gucci's values and the artistic expressions of the works of art (www.gucci.com).

Resonance

Resonance relies on the influencer's ability to elicit actions, reflections, and emotions from the target audience. Resonance emerges when influencers make people understand that their community is not just a number but is interested and engaged in their content (Backaler 2018). Resonance is therefore linked to eWOM, and an evaluation of this dimension includes the *period of time* that the subject/content is discussed starting from its first appearance, the *frequency* with which the topic is included in the conversations, and *amplitude* that refers to the extent a topic is shared by the community or more simply, the level of engagement within a network (Solis and Webber 2012). With reference to this aspect, influencers can also amplify the effects of traditional communications, spreading their content through social media, and increasing the level of engagement.

sabina riboldazzi and antonella capriello

Coca-Cola Italia: an example of integrating traditional and influencer communications

For Christmas 2017, Coca-Cola Italia developed a television commercial whose basic values were family, friendship, and sharing. The commercial ended with the phrase "Thanks to those who make a gesture for others" to highlight Coca-Cola's support of the "Banco Alimentare" activity of collecting 3 million meals, for a total of 1,500 tons of food, for the needy. Coca-Cola chose to amplify its message through influencers, well-known faces in the Italian scene with the aim of achieving a high target reach and amplifying the effects of the TV spot. To achieve higher resonance, the influencers Michele Bravi, Lisa Casali, Camihawke, The Show, Guglielmo Scilla, and The Pozzolis Family were the protagonists of a video with over 600,000 views on Facebook and Twitter. Each influencer re-shared the video to increase reach, engagement, and strengthen the effects of the communication. To note is that Coca-Cola frequently uses influencers in its communication strategy. Consequently, the company has developed a policy for the clear and precise identification of influencers who use their social networks to promote sponsored content concerning the company. For example, Coca-Cola asks influencers to openly declare their connection with the company through the addition of the #AD + #CocaCola hashtags in communications on social networks every time an influencer is compensated (www.coca-colaitalia.it).

Engagement is typically used to measure how influencers demonstrate resonance. *Engagement* refers to the influencer's ability to involve users, activating them in the topics discussed, and incentivizing referrals, conversations about products/brands, and customer feedback (Hughes et al. 2019). According to Ray et al. (2014), engagement concerns a proactive behavior rather than treating all interactions as simple exchange propositions. Di Gangi and Wasko (2016, p. 4) specify the concept of user engagement as a "user's state of mind that warrants heightened involvement and results in a personally meaningful benefit." These authors underline that user engagement is divided into two psychological components: individual involvement, or the intensity with which a user perceives her/his role within a platform; and personal meaning, or the degree to which a user perceives the fulfillment of his/her interests and needs.

The evaluation of influencer engagement may include (Kumar and Mirchandani, 2012): the number of times the message is forwarded by receivers, with or without modifications; the number of connections that the messages jumped (for example, a message has jumped two connections if the message from one individual was received by a second individual and then forwarded to a third individual); and the number of replies and comments to each message. Furthermore, engagement may be assessed considering metrics such as the number of likes/dislikes, comments, shares, reactions, emotions, and retweets related to influencer content. Finally, an evaluation of *connection to other influencers* may better qualify influencer resonance.

The three steps in identifying and selecting influencers

In developing and implementing a marketing communication strategy in the digital era, the following steps are key to identifying and selecting influencers. First, listening to and analyzing social media conversations. Next, identifying influencers in accordance with the company values. Finally, in selecting the right influencers considering three dimensions: reach, relevance, and resonance, and their corresponding sub-dimensions as depicted in Figure 3.1.

This chapter has focused on the factors that impact the identification and selection of influencers in implementing digital marketing strategies. In analyzing the digital marketplace, influencers could generate positive WOM, even if their potential depends on the objectives and budget available for a specific influencer marketing campaign.

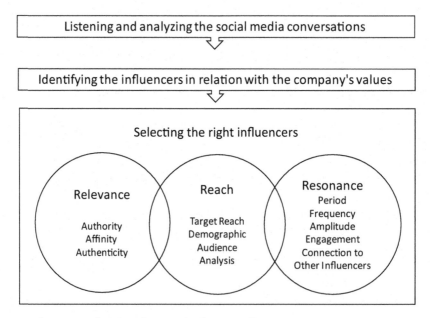

Figure 3.1 Three steps for identifying and selecting influencers.

sabina riboldazzi and antonella capriello

In choosing the influencers, we have identified three integrated dimensions (*reach, relevance, resonance*) and related sub-dimensions. These connected dimensions should be assessed in selecting influencers in view of the specific objectives of a digital marketing campaign.

Reach and *target reach* are the first determinant to identify and choose influencers in relation to the activities generated on online platforms. More specifically, in the case of Pupa, influencers are selected in accordance with their potential in terms of high target reach. The second dimension, *relevance*, refers to authority, affinity, and authenticity, as emerged in the Gucci case. More specifically, writers and art critics interact by contextualizing masterpieces and focusing attention on the most "glamorous" details in the captions of the series of portraits. Resonance is linked to eWOM in relation to *period, frequency*, and *amplitude*. In the Barilla case, the involvement of cultural icons amplified the campaign effects, generating high levels of engagement, whilst the Coca-Cola case shows the inference of combining traditional communications with the key role of influencers.

Summary

- In developing an effective marketing communications strategy, we have identified three steps to identify and select influencers.
- To test the validity of the proposed steps, future studies should analyze other companies to evaluate the implications on digital marketing policies, and extend the research to other dimensions in relation to selecting influencers.
- To evaluate the effectiveness of the influencer identification and selection processes, companies should adopt social media marketing metrics, as in the following illustrative case studies.

Case study: The Coop Lombardia choice of influencers

Coop Lombardia, a cooperative of Coop Italia, a leading Italian large-scale grocery retailer with 1,167 points of sale and a turnover of around 12,000 million euros, collaborates with "the boys of Casa Surace." Casa Surace is a factory founded in 2015 focused on the production of ironic videos with two million fans on the web, counting over 400 million viewers on Facebook and YouTube, collaborating as an influencer with important national and international brands, including Disney, Nutella, Samsung, Universal, Campari, and Western Union.

> STEP 1 – *Listening and analyzing social media conversations.* Coop's process of identifying and selecting influencers started with understanding and monitoring the local social media market and conversations considering numerous individuals across various social network sites in search of those coherent with the company's communication objectives and values.
>
> STEP 2 – *Identifying influencers in accordance with the company values.* Coop Lombardia identified "the boys of Casa Surace" through their social media activity, their number of connections, and their ability to generate engagement

thanks to similarities and common interests with their network friends. In particular, the company analyzed the initiatives previously developed by Casa Surace specifically with reference to the number of followers, content, and value transmitted, language used, comments, and reactions to the campaigns. Coop wanted to work with Casa Surace with the goal of transmitting cooperative values.

STEP 3 – *Selecting the right influencers considering three dimensions (reach, relevance, resonance) and the related sub-dimensions.* The *reach* dimension was evaluated considering the high potential reach of Casa Surace, which through a *demographic audience analysis* was identified as on target with the Coop Lombardia campaigns. Moreover, Coop Lombardia assessed the *relevance* and *resonance* of Casa Surace in the development of communications on social issues to spread the consumer cooperation values. The "boys of Casa Surace" had a high potential level of *resonance* and *relevance* in that through their ironic sketches and videos they communicated the values of Southern Italy, the lifestyle in small towns, cooking, family, etc., and were followed by a community that shared their values (*affinity*), recognized their *authenticity*, and got involved and *engaged* in their initiatives.

In implementing the communications strategy, Coop Lombardia decided to develop several initiatives/videos with Casa Surace including "#pigliatinacosatour," "Casa Surace against Waste," "Casa Surace for November 25," and "Casa Surace for Feeding Love."

For example, "Pigliatinacosatour" materialized as an itinerant journey (10 cities in 17 days) undertaken by Casa Surace to deliver packages containing Coop Libera Terra products (organic private label products grown on land free from the mafia) and meet their community in person. The initiative was narrated on the Casa Surace social pages and many people contributed using the hashtag #pigliatinacosatour on Facebook, Instagram, and Twitter. The challenge to win packages with Coop products was simple: Casa Surace published an announcement on Facebook inviting its fans to state, through different channels, the reasons why they wanted to receive the prize. The most exciting and amusing stories were rewarded with a delivery of the package to the place where the winners lived where events were held that many people participated in.

In monitoring the effectiveness of the communications strategy, the metrics affirmed the results of the campaign. For example, the video posted on YouTube launching the tour achieved 28,747 views and 386 likes, while the two selfie videos taken on the boys' arrival in Milan and posted on the Facebook page reached 29,818 views and 84,954 people. Furthermore, the influencers' ability to engage their followers generated a high level of resonance measured by the high number of conversations, sharing, and positive comments during the tour and the related events organized to support the tour. As regards the other initiatives ("Casa Surace against Waste," "Casa Surace for November 25," and "Casa Surace for Feeding Love"), Casa Surace transmits in an amusing and emphatic way, using simple language, the topics that are part of the Coop value system, which are respectively the reduction of food waste, the elimination of violence against women, and love for animals. The metrics endorsed Coop's choice: as regards "Casa Surace against Waste," the video shared on the Casa Surace Facebook page and in cross-postings on the Coop Lombardia page totaled 2.9 million views. "Casa Surace for November 25" achieved 130 positive interactions (reactions, comments, and shares), reaching 14,362 people and 3,975 views. The "Casa Surace for Feeding Love" video obtained 8.1 million views, 798,520 interactions, and reached 5,613,953 people (throughout Italy, aged 18 to 65, and with interests related to pets).

Questions:

1. How could Coop confirm it identified their most ideal influencers in the social media market?
2. How could Coop endure that the influencers they choose were in accordance with the company objectives and values?
3. How could Coop monitor the effectiveness of the influencer communication campaign other than the way that is provided in the case study?
4. What changes would you suggest based on evaluating the effectiveness of the influencer marketing campaign?

References

Audrezet, A., Derviler, G., and Moulard, J., 2018. Authenticity under threat: When social media influencers need to go beyond self-presentation. *Journal of Business Research*, in press. https://doi.org/10.1016/j.jbusres.2018.07.008.

Backaler, J., 2018. *Digital Influence. Unleash the power of influencer marketing to accelerate your global business*. Glendale, CA, USA: Palgrave Macmillan.

Bailis, R., 2019. The State of Influencer Marketing: 10 Influencer Marketing Statistics to Inform Where You Invest. *Big Commerce*. Retrieved from www.bigcommerce.com/blog/influencer-marketing-statistics/#what-is-influencer-marketing

Booth, N., and Matic, J., 2011. Mapping and leveraging influencers in social media to shape corporate brand perceptions. *Corporate Communications: An International Journal*, 16(3), 184–191. https://doi.org/10.1108/13563281111156853.

Bosher, H., 2020. Influencer Marketing and the Law. Ch. 13 in *Influencer Marketing: Building Brand Communities and Engagement*, Ed. Yesiloglu, S., and Costello, J. Routledge: London.

Brondoni, S.M. (Ed.), 2018. *Competitive Business Management: A Global Perspective*. Oxon: Routledge (Routledge-Giappichelli Studies in Business and Management).

Brown, D., and Hayes, N., 2008. *Influencer Marketing. Who really influences your customers?* Oxford: Butterworth-Heinemann.

Bughin, J., Doogan, J., and Vetvik, O.J., 2010. A new way to measure word-of-mouth marketing. *McKinsey Quarterly*, 2, 113–116. Retrieved from www.mckinsey.com/business-functions/marketing-and-sales/our-insights/a-new-way-to-measure-word-of-mouth-marketing

Burson-Marsteller, E., 2010, June. The power of online influencers. Available from https://issuu.com/burson-marstteller-emea/docs/e-fluentials_brochure/4.

Chen, Y., 2016. The rise of "micro-influencers" on Instagram. *Digiday*. Retrieved from https://digiday.com/marketing/micro-influencers/.

Childers, C., Lemon, L., and Hoy, M., 2018. #Sponsored #Ad: Agency perspective on influencer marketing campaigns. *Journal of Current Issues & Research in Advertising*, 40(3), 258–274.

De Veirman, M., Cauberghe, V., and Hudders, L., 2017. Marketing through Instagram influencers: The impact of the number of followers and product divergence on brand attitude. *International Journal of Advertising*, 36(5), 798–828.

Di Gangi, P.M., and Wasko, M.M., 2016. Social media engagement theory: Exploring the influence of user engagement on social media usage. *Journal of Organizational and End User Computing* (JOEUC), 28(2), 53–73.

Djafarova, E., and Rushworth, C., 2017. Exploring the credibility of online celebrities' Instagram profiles in influencing the purchase decisions of young female users. *Computers in Human Behavior*, 68, 1–7.

Ferchaud, A., Grzeslo, J., Orme, S., and LaGroue, J., 2018. Parasocial attributes and YouTube personalities: Exploring content trends across the most subscribed YouTube channels. *Computers in Human Behavior*, 80, 88–96.

Freberg, K., Graham, K., McGaughey, K., and Freberg, L.A., 2011. Who are the social media influencers? A study of public perceptions of personality. *Public Relations Review*, 37(1), 90–92.

Gillin, P., 2007. *The New Influencers: A Marketer's Guide to the New Social Media*. Sanger, CA: Quill Driver Book.

Gladwell, M., 2000. *The Tipping Point: How little things can make a big difference*. Boston, MA: Little, Brown.

Glucksman, M., 2017. The Rise of Social Media Influencer Marketing on Lifestyle Branding: A Case Study of Lucie Fink. *Elon Journal of Undergraduate Research in Communications*, 8(2), 77–87.

Gorry, G.A., and Westbrook, R.A., 2009. Winning the internet confidence game. *Corporate Reputation Review*, 12(3), 195–203.

Gretzel, U., 2018. Influencer marketing in travel and tourism. Ch. 10 in *Advances in social media for travel, tourism, and hospitality: New perspectives, practice, and cases*. Ed. Sigala, M. and Gretzel, U. New York: Routledge.

Gruen, T.V., Osmonbekov, T., and Czaplewski, A.J., 2006. eWOM: The impact of customer-to-customer online know-how exchange on customer value and loyalty. *Journal of Business Research*, 59(4), 449–456.

Guthrie, S., 2020. Virtual Influencers: More Human Than Human. Ch. 15 in *Influencer Marketing: Building Brand Communities and Engagement*. Ed. Yesiloglu, S., and Costello, J. London: Routledge.

Hennig-Thurau, T., Gwinner, K.P., Walsh, G., and Gremler, D.D., 2004. Electronic word-of-mouth via consumer-opinion platforms: What motivates consumers to articulate themselves on the Internet? *Journal of Interactive Marketing*, 18(1), 38–52.

Hughes, C., Swaminathan, V., and Brooks, G., 2019. Driving Brand Engagement through Online Social Influencers: An Empirical Investigation of Sponsored Blogging Campaigns. *Journal of Marketing*, 83(5), 78–96.

Iglhaut, C., 2019. The influencers of tomorrow will be virtual. *Deutschland.de*. Retrieved from www.deutschland.de/en/topic/culture/who-is-noonoouri-fashion-avatar-conquers-the-fashion-world

Influencity, 2018. The Difference between Micro, Macro, and Mega Influencers. *Influencity*. Retrieved from www.influicity.com/wp-content/uploads/2018/03/MegaMacroMicro-Whitepaper-min.pdf

Interactive Advertising Bureau, 2018, January. Inside Influence. Why publishers are increasingly turning to influencer marketing – and what that means for marketers. *IAB*. Retrieved from www.iab.com/wp-content/uploads/2018/01/IAB_Influencer_Marketing_for_Publishers_2018-01-25.pdf

Kane, H., 2019, July. Meet Shudu: The world's first digital supermodel. *Phoenix Magazine*. Retrieved from: www.phoenixmag.co.uk/article/meet-shudu-the-worlds-first-digital-supermodel/

Keller, E.B., and Berry, J.L., 2003. *The Influentials*. New York: The Free Press.

Kowalczyk, C., and Pounders, K., 2016. Transforming celebrities through social media: The role of authenticity and emotional attachment. *Journal of Product and Brand Management*, 25(4), 345–356.

Kumar, V., and Mirchandani, R., 2012. Increasing the ROI of social media marketing. *MIT Sloan Management Review*, 54(1), 54–61.

Lambin, J.J., 2008. *Changing Market Relationship in the Internet Age*. Louven: UCL Presses Universitaires de Luoven.

Lee, M., and Youn, S., 2009. Electronic word of mouth (eWOM): How eWOM platforms influence consumer product judgment. *International Journal of Advertising*, 28(3), 473–499.

Lueck, J.A., 2015. Friend-zone with benefits: The parasocial advertising of Kim Kardashian. *Journal of Marketing Communications*, 21(2), 91–109.

Maheshwari, S., 2018. Are You Ready for the Nanoinfluencers? *NY Times*. Retrieved from www.nytimes.com/2018/11/11/business/media/nanoinfluencers-instagram-influencers.html

Malik, H.M., and Qureshi, M.M., 2017. The impact of celebrity endorsement on consumer buying behavior. *Advances in Social Sciences Research Journal*, 4(3), 159–170.

McCarthy, N., November, 2019. How influencer marketing costs explode. *Statista*. Retrieved from www.statista.com/chart/19976/average-cost-of-a-sponsored-post-by-platform/?fbclid=IwAR3_FjP7q_Qh7DF8yrn7VIfTjzBSYBvMYyMnv3U8-zUfOsDJTQCsl4F4XNs

Napoli, J., Dickinson, S.J., Beverland, M.B., and Farrelly, F., 2014. Measuring consumer-based brand authenticity. *Journal of Business Research*, 67(6), 1090–1098.

Pedersen, M., July, 2019. The Power of Influencers: Mega, Micro, and Nano. *Stellar Agency*. Retrieved from https://medium.com/@stellaragency/the-power-of-influencers-mega-micro-and-nano-88b0d801356

Quintana Ramos, I. and Cownie, F., 2020. Female Environmental Influencers on Instagram. Ch. 9 in *Influencer Marketing: Building Brand Communities and Engagement*. Ed. Yesiloglu, S., and Costello, J. London: Routledge.

Ray, S., Kim S.S., and Morrison, J.G., 2019. The central role of engagement in online communities. *Information Systems Research*, 25(3), 528–546.

Rezvani, M., Hosseini, K.H., and Samadzadeh, M., 2012. Investigating the Role of Word of Mouth on Consumer Based Brand Equity Creation in Iran's Cell Phone Market. *Journal of Knowledge Management, Economics and Information Technology*, 2(8), 1–15.

SanMiguel, P., Guercini, S., and Sádaba, T., 2018. The Impact of Attitudes towards Influencers amongst Millennial Fashion Buyers. *Studies in Communication Sciences*, 18(2), 439–460.

Snyder, M., 2019. How to Choose the Right Influencers for Your Campaign. Retrieved from https://blog.jconnelly.com/how-to-choose-the-right-influencers-for-your-campaign

Solis, B., and Webber, A., 2012. The Rise of Digital Influence. Retrieved from http://indianstrategicknowledgeonline.com/web/soci%20media%20the%20rise%20of%20digital%20influence.pdf

Spry, A., Pappu, R., and Cornwell, T.B., 2011. Celebrity endorsement, brand credibility, and brand equity. *European Journal of Marketing*, 45(6), 882–909.

Subramani, M.R., and Rajagopalan, B., 2003. Knowledge-sharing and influence in online social networks via viral marketing. *Communications of the ACM*, 46(1), 300–307.

Yesiloglu, S., 2020. Rise of Influencers and Influencer Marketing. Ch. 1 in *Influencer Marketing: Building Brand Communities and Engagement*. Ed. Yesiloglu, S., and Costello, J. London: Routledge.

Yurieff, K., 2018. Instagram star isn't what she seems. But brands are buying in. *CNN*. Retrieved from https://money.cnn.com/2018/06/25/technology/lil-miquela-social-media-influencer-cgi/index.html

chapter 4

How to map and select digital influencers for marketing campaigns

Benjamin Rosenthal and Adriana Arcuri

Learning outcomes

On completing this chapter, you should be able to:

- understand the ICA framework and how the three components interact;
- distinguish between persona prioritization, domain identification, and audience quantification;
- identify the different criteria that can be used in selecting the best influencer; and
- understand the provision of guidelines that can help marketing executives in the selection of individuals for influencer marketing campaigns.

How should marketing managers choose a set of digital influencers for an influencer marketing campaign? Should they choose based on the personality, style, domain, brand fit, and the number of followers of each digital influencer? Should they take into account the narrative style and credibility of the content of these individuals? Or should they also look at the audience of these influencers, searching for elements that could help to increase the efficacy of the campaign? In this chapter, we integrate the literature on the topic and develop a framework with the criteria that can be used to select digital influencers for marketing campaigns. We also conducted a qualitative study showing how practitioners are currently selecting digital influencers. We incorporate our findings into the framework to give nuance to the process of selecting digital influencers.

According to the practitioner-oriented magazine *Business Insider*, influencer marketing generated revenues of US$ 8 billion in 2019 and is expected to generate US$ 15 billion in 2022 (Schomer 2019). The emergence of the influencer marketing is symptomatic of an evolving context for brands (Erz and Christensen 2018). Consumers are flocking to online social networks in search of information to consume, in a multi-fragmented and niche-oriented media landscape in which interests are specific, and communities are formed (Casaló et al. 2018). However, content is provided by a myriad of specialized amateurs (McQuarrie et al. 2013). In this media landscape, the content being produced is huge and decentralized, constituting an environment that is not controllable by the old traditional content producers (Holt 2016). In this situation, brands are forming partnerships with digital influencers to produce content and/or communicate to audiences that, otherwise, would be hard-to-reach for brands.

While these brand–influencer collaborations are increasing, the identification of influencers is difficult (Jacobson et al. 2019). Mapping and selecting digital influencers are important steps in the influencer marketing given the many possibilities as companies moved from merely communicating through a few traditional celebrities to communicating through dozens of creators (influencers) with varied audience sizes, from hyper-influencers to micro-influencers (Djafarova and Rushworth 2017). Several authors have explored the challenge to select individuals for influencer marketing campaigns (e.g. Probst et al. 2013; Arora et al. 2019). Often authors focus on characteristics of the individuals (Song et al. 2017; Sokolova and Kefi 2019) such as personality factors or physical attractiveness, the content (Ge and Gretzel 2018; Deborah et al. 2019), and the audience (Casaló et al. 2018; Lutkenhaus et al. 2019). Occasionally authors use multiple characteristics of the aforementioned elements (e.g. Djafarova and Ruthworth 2017; Audrezet et al. 2018), but the academic literature from management fields is far from consolidated (Arora et al. 2019; Deborah et al. 2019). What is missing is an integrative perspective of all the criteria that can be used to select individuals for influencer marketing campaigns.

The objective of this chapter is to fulfill this gap and to suggest one way that those involved in influencer marketing as well as those technological platforms that give access to thousands of potential digital influencers can best select digital influencers. We begin with a review of what the academic literature discloses on the criteria that can be used to select digital influencers for marketing campaigns, integrating the criteria belonging to individuals, content, and audiences into our proposed framework – the ICA framework (Figure 4.1). We then explain the qualitative methodology used in our research where we conducted interviews with the main players of the influencer marketing industry in Brazil. Afterward, we present two communication logics that influence the way companies practice influencer marketing and the way they select digital influencers. We then integrate the findings of the qualitative interviews into the ICA framework, showing how practitioners are currently working to select digital influencers. This allows us to illustrate with one case how the ICA framework can be used to select digital influencers and how the communication logics operating in the

benjamin rosenthal and adriana arcuri

marketing department shape the choice of criteria for selecting digital influencers. Finally, we discuss two potential contributions of the ICA framework, the first being the integration of the literature, and the second being the provision of guidelines that can help marketing executives in the selection of individuals for influencer marketing campaigns.

An integrative perspective on selecting individuals for influencer marketing campaigns

the academic literature still lacks an integrative perspective of the criteria that can be used to map and select digital influencers for marketing campaigns (Probst et al. 2013; Arora et al. 2019). Extant research mostly discusses some of the criteria belonging to one or two of three categories: the individual, the content, and the audience, but with little discussion on how these three categories intertwine and, when adopted in combination, may maximize the selection of digital influencers.

Individual characteristics are the most common criteria adopted in the literature. Influencer marketing signifies a marketing practice based on the influencer, possibly an evolution of the marketing practice of working with traditional celebrities and choosing them to be an endorser based on celebrity's characteristics – trustworthiness, expertise, similarity to a consumer segment, familiarity, likability, and the celebrity–brand image fit (Erdogan et al. 2001). Although Erdogan et al.'s (2001) study belongs to a pre-online time when television was the main media for brand messages, it assumes the centrality of the distinguished individual in the meaning transfer process. The alleged centrality of the individual in the social influence[1] process has been present in the literature since Katz and Lazarsfeld's (1955, p. 3) original definition of influencers as "individuals who were likely to influence other persons in their immediate environment." The literature that explores the social influence on online platforms is coherent about the importance of individual traces such as identity (Cocker et al. 2015), authenticity (Fillis 2015; Cocker and Cronin 2017), charisma (Probst et al. 2013; Cocker and Cronin 2017), personality (McQuarrie et al. 2013; Song et al. 2017), taste (McQuarrie et al. 2013), credibility (Djafarova and Ruthworth 2017; Sokolova and Kefi 2019), narrative form (Silva and Campos 2019), expertise and knowledge (Katz and Lazarsfeld 1955) to foster social influence in social networks.

Some authors state individual trace is important in the structural position in online social networks (Watts and Dodds 2007; Liu-Thompkins and Rogerson 2012). This is based on the criteria of degree centrality – the number of direct connections to other nodes, closeness centrality – the degree of proximity to the other nodes, betweenness centrality – the proximity to other nodes not directly connected to it, and eigenvector centrality – proximity to other influencers who add more to his influence potential (Probst et al. 2013). This literature on social network analysis comes mostly from information systems. According to Probst et al. (2013), the use of sociometry to find the right influencers for marketing purposes is not trivial and is still in its infancy. Some examples of sociometric applications that try to solve the social influence "maximization problem" can be seen in Bakshy et al. (2012), Araujo et al. (2017), and Deborah et al. (2019).

The literature addresses the importance of several content qualities (Berger 2014) in fostering social influence but it does not properly indicate how to use the content as criteria for selecting digital influencers. Content is what an audience consumes and, therefore, an important source of trust between the influencer and the audience, with trust here referring to the belief that the influencer truly believes in his content (Childers et al. 2018). Content fosters relationships, perceived authenticity (Fillis 2015; Cocker and Cronin 2017), and credibility (Djafarova and Ruthworth 2017). Several content qualities have been enumerated by Berger (2014) as important to foster social influence – entertaining, useful, sense-making, dissonance-reducing, risk- and uncertainty-reducing, own-bias confirming, emotion-arousing, polarizing, and self-concept-relevant content. The importance of the influencer's rhetoric to foster social influence was examined by Ge and Gretzel (2018) in their study of the use of emojis in digital influencers' narratives. Domain expertise has also been shown to build trust (Liu et al. 2015). Recently, content frequency has been used as criteria for developing a "hub index," which could measure how active a certain user is in communicating with other central users in a network (Deborah et al. 2019), which may help to set the conversations around a topic.

Only recently some authors began to combine characteristics of the audience with attributes from individuals and content to provide a broader perspective of how social influence can be fostered. For instance, Lou and Yuan (2019) highlighted the importance of content's informative value, together with the individual's trustworthiness and attractiveness. They also mentioned the importance of profile similarity between an audience and the digital influencer. Casaló et al. (2018) showed the importance of content quality together with the individual's authenticity and fit with the audience. Lutkenhaus et al. (2019) provide perhaps the most interesting use of the audience in the process of selecting digital influencers. These authors, researching in the health field, started the selection of individuals by first looking at the audiences interested in the health topic (specifically, vaccination issues). Only after conducting text mining and qualitative content analysis in health-related communities and understanding the audience's beliefs and social norms related to the topic, they selected individuals who could influence these audiences, given some individual attributes – their position in the network as opinion leaders and gatekeepers, their authenticity, and their position towards vaccination.

We integrated the criteria present in the literature into the ICA framework, which discloses the criteria available and the studies that support them (Figure 4.1). While the integration of the literature provides an extensive conceptual map, how the available criteria are currently being adopted by practitioners is an under-researched area. One exception is Stoldt et al.'s (2019) study on the role of intermediaries in influencer marketing. From their study, we can see that the tourism industry selects digital influencers based on brand fit, content quality, influence power, and the capacity to cultivate relationships with the audience. This single case informs us that the industry is indeed using the elements present on the ICA framework, albeit in a simplified manner (Figure 4.1).

Gräve (2019) also shows how marketers are currently selecting digital influencers for influencer marketing campaigns. The author conducted a survey with marketing, advertising, and public relations executives in Germany. Gräve (2019) found that although managers declare evaluating influencer marketing campaigns based on reach and interaction

benjamin rosenthal and adriana arcuri

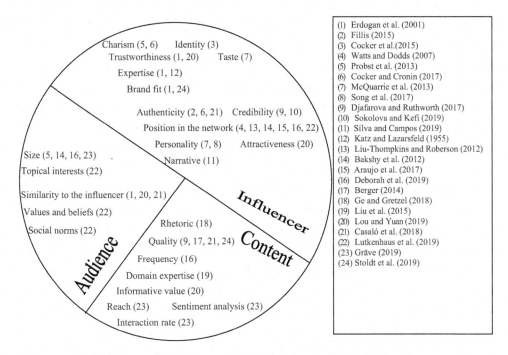

Figure 4.1 The ICA Framework: The available criteria to select digital influencers.

rate, they trust more on sentiment analysis to evaluate the performance of the campaign (content). This finding reveals the presence of trade-offs in the decision of which key performance indicators to use in order to evaluate an influencer marketing campaign (and, consequently, how to select influencers). However, the survey conducted had limitations in the number of options to answer, so many other variables, such as those present in the ICA framework, were not tested. As the present chapter sustains, based on our qualitative interviews with practitioners, managers use a varied number of criteria to select individuals, and this selection of criteria is conditional to the communication logic operating in the marketing department and to the objectives of the campaign.

We now want to explore the ways the industry is using isolated or combined criterium present on the framework in their influencer marketing campaigns. Before we do that, we intend to state here that we are not affirming that all these studies have neglected the combined importance of individual, content, and audience as criteria to select individuals for influencer marketing campaigns. What we suggest is that their specific research objective produced a vast literature that has not yet, to the best of our knowledge, produced an integrative perspective of all the criteria that can be applied to select digital influencers for marketing purposes.

Methodology

Our research is informed by the tradition of abductive analysis, an inferential process that builds theory in contrast to the literature. According to Timmermans and Tavory

(2012), this tradition seeks for "anomalous and surprising empirical findings against a background of multiple existing sociological theories..." (p. 169).

Data collection

To investigate how practitioners are currently selecting individuals for influencer marketing campaigns we adopted two procedures. First, the first author conducted semi-structured interviews (Kvale 2008) with 21 practitioners within the influencer marketing ecosystem in Brazil – nine marketing executives, two talent managers working with digital influencers, two advertising executives, three public relations executives, two technological platform and online marketplace executives, and three advisors on the industry were interviewed between May 2017 and January 2019, usually at their place of work or places of their convenience (e.g., coffee shops). These marketing executives were chosen through purposive sampling since they are responsible for influencer marketing campaigns at companies that represent key parts of this market in Brazil (Table 4.1), and individuals in certain positions in certain types of organizations were needed (Arsel 2017). The 21 informants provided thematic saturation for the authors' qualitative work (Guest et al. 2006). Social media penetration in Brazil was 62 percent in January 2018, a figure close to that in countries such as France (58 percent) and Mexico (64 percent) and well above the world average of 42 percent (Statista 2018), thus constituting a relevant context for studying the topic. The marketing executives interviewed work for companies in several segments of the market, such as food, beauty, alcoholic beverages, airline company, finance, health, cleaning, and personal care. The choice to interview executives from varied parts of the market allowed the triangulation of positions and viewpoints, increasing the depth and richness of the data (Saldaña 2011).

The interview protocol covered several aspects of the influencer marketing practice, such as its objectives, the process for developing campaigns, content creation, KPIs, the advantages and tensions of the practice, cases of success and failures, and their overall perception of the practice in the market. We specifically asked how they select

Table 4.1 Informants' profile

Interviewee codename	Position	Company sector
I-o	Marketing Manager	Food Industry (varied products)
I-b	Marketing Manager	Beauty/Personal Care
I-s	Marketing Manager	Alcoholic Beverages (spirits)
I-m	Brand Manager	Food Industry (varied products)
I-a	Marketing Manager	Airline Company
I-B	Marketing Manager	Financial Company
I-p	Marketing Manager	Health/Cleaning/Personal Care
I-d	Marketing Manager	Food Industry (dairy)
I-E	Marketing Manager	Alcoholic Beverages (beer)

benjamin rosenthal and adriana arcuri

digital influencers for marketing campaigns, and what criteria they use. The interviews lasted between 38 and 188 minutes and were recorded (with the interviewees' permission), and transcribed, totaling 690 pages of data.

Furthermore, the first author attended two events, one promoted by a technological platform in 2018, and another promoted by a consulting company in the field in 2019. In these events the first author spent two days listening to influencers, agents, marketing and advertising executives' comments on the practice, extensively taking notes on presentations and informal conversations to support the analysis.

Data analysis

The data analysis followed the logic of abductive theorization (Timmermans and Tavory 2012), while inductive thematic analysis (Braun and Clarke 2006) was conducted to generate the codes and categories emerging from the data, specifically the criteria being used to select digital influencers, constantly contrasting them to the literature. During the data analysis, the authors exchanged opinions, in an iterative process between data, theory, and theorization. As per Braun and Clark (2006) guidelines, our codes were generated at the semantic level, reflecting what is explicit in the data – e.g., the criteria used to select digital influencers and the practices involved in the selection process. Additionally, axial coding was performed to understand the relationship between codes and categories (Miles and Huberman 1994), specifically the relationship between the practices for selecting digital influencers and the logic behind these practices, as it will be presented in the results session.

Additionally, we profited from the second author's three years of experience as a marketing executive in a Brazilian battery company that has conducted many influencer marketing campaigns. This company worked in a way that, as we explain in the next session, operates in a media logic and a public relations logic. So, we illustrate our analysis with this battery company case, highlighting how and why the company has practiced influencer marketing (and selecting influencers) based on a media logic and a public relations logic.

Two logics behind the influencer marketing practice

Behind our informants' influencer marketing practice, we could apprehend the existence of two logics operating in their marketing departments – the media logic and the public relations logic – which affect the way companies practice influencer marketing and the criteria they use to select digital influencers. All the marketing executives interviewed practiced influencer marketing based on a media logic and three of them also adopted ways of thinking belonging to a public relations logic. The findings suggest that organizations can build more value if they work on both logics.

Influencer marketing based on a media logic

All of the marketing executives interviewed described ways of working with digital influencers that fall under a "media logic." In this chapter, media logic is defined as an organizational way of thinking and doing influencer marketing that resembles traditional media communication in its objectives and procedures. They perceive influencers as a media vehicle through which brand messages can be transmitted. The media logic affects the marketing objectives they pursue, the choice of criteria used to map and select digital influencers, and the creation of content, subsequently.

Marketing objectives in the media logic are similar to the ones used on television campaigns. Brand awareness, reach (e.g., imprints and visibility), attribute reinforcement, brand image, and conversion were common elements describing the objectives behind influencer marketing campaigns. As the brand manager of a beverage company selling spirits stated:

> We had our goal... it was to achieve one million impacts (impressions) so we went to the agency and they brought some options of digital influencers... (I-s).

Furthermore, some of the interviewees reported that the company has joined the practice of influencer marketing due to fear of missing out (FOMO), as the brand manager of a food company explained:

> Everyone else is doing it so there is pressure to do the same (I-m).

At the same time, she recognizes that executives, especially in top management positions, still do not understand what influencer marketing is and how it works. So, they tend to adopt the same reasoning that they have always worked with, with the same marketing objectives, with consequences for the criteria they use to map and select influencers.

Brands working in the media logic carefully design the campaign briefing to the digital influencers with the expectation that the desired brand elements will be transmitted and that the brand media goals will be achieved. Usually, the briefings were very detailed, recalling the cautious steps towards the production of a TV commercial, as can be seen in the words of the marketing manager of a food company:

> We make clear in the briefing the brand context, the brand benefits, the hashtags they must use, what kind of media, photos, stories, videos, how many, to guarantee that the brand message is communicated, but we leave him or her to speak to their public in their way, after all, no one works with influencers to make them speak like the brand... we also state whether he can use or not a hat, accessories, or the kind of ambiance we want for the picture if we want the product to appear or not, if open or sealed, the mood – like "feeling tired after workout" – how many times they must speak the brand name, the words they must use, like "yummy" or "healthy", if they need to insert some link in the video, that kind of thing... (I-d)

One can see from this excerpt that marketing executives working with a media logic think and practice influencer marketing aiming to control the content produced and the message communicated. Furthermore, brands working in the media logic were unaware of the possibilities of also working with a public relations logic. Now, we explain how some of the brands went beyond the media logic and engaged with influencer marketing from a public relations logic interjected in the marketing department.

Influencer marketing based on a public relations logic

Three of the nine marketing executives interviewed described influencer marketing ways of working that suit on a public relations logic. In this chapter, public relations logic is defined as an organizational way of thinking and doing influencer marketing that resembles public relations communication in its objectives and procedures. This logic is distinct because it takes the audience (the fans) and the influencer ongoing content production and conversation with the audience as the locus of brand content exposure. This logic emphasizes the co-constitutive roles of the influencer and the audience as value creators. It also emphasizes brand content as a co-creational act between brands, agencies, and digital influencers, which is crucial to engage the audience and deliver the campaign results.

A public relations logic involves understanding the dynamics of the conversation between the influencer and the audience and planning for brand content that enters into the timeline of the digital influencer without friction, without sounding overly commercial, with adequacy to the narrative style and life context of the influencer. A public relations logic also involves a concern for developing a relationship with influencers, which consequently facilitates branded content co-creation.

Unsurprisingly, the three marketeers working on a public relations logic knew the value of lasting partnerships with influencers, a practice of influencer marketing increasingly more common for brands (Pathak 2018). This was illustrated in the following excerpt from a marketing executive in a financial institution:

> I don't just want to use it and throw it away... we are together with all of them. If I did something today with one of them, I'm sure to do it tomorrow, in the next month, in the next year. We build this relationship to be truly perennial. (I-B).

A public relations logic also involves considering the digital influencer as a co-creator of branded content and not merely as a media vehicle that sends branded messages. As we show in the next excerpt, from a marketing executive who openly embraces content co-creation as a mantra, brand managers working on a public relations strategy emphasize the importance of co-creation to engage the audience and, at the same time, amplify the voice of the brand, a marketing objective also present in companies working only on a media logic:

> So, the co-creation work with creators began at this point, when we realized that it makes sense to use the gift that creators have, the tools they know how to use, to get us to amplify the brand voice. (I-B)

Working on a public relations logic demands a high level of involvement of brand executives with the mapping and selecting phase of influencer marketing campaigns and the development of curatorship of influencers for the brand. Brands that worked with a public relations logic tended to either internalize the mapping and selecting work, with the collaboration of advertising and PR agencies, or to work very close to the agencies when outsourcing the responsibility for producing a list of possible influencers. Some of these brands have a dedicated structure to influencer marketing campaigns, with professionals focused on getting to know the influencers and their relationship with the audiences.

Companies working on a public relations logic can either separate or integrate media-oriented and PR-oriented campaigns. Media-oriented projects aim at reach, frequency and brand awareness; PR-oriented projects aim at the quality of conversations between the brand, the influencer, and the audience, at seeding the conversations (Dost et al. 2019) between the influencer and the audience, with the brand appearing as an enabler, a sponsor, or even as content within these conversations. As previously said, brands that aim at PR-oriented objectives are not abandoning the traditional marketing objectives, such as brand awareness, reach, frequency, or brand image, but mostly changing the way these objectives are pursued.

Finally, working with a public relations or a media logic affects why and how marketing executives select influencers, as we further develop in the next session.

Current practices for selecting digital influencers

Based on the interviews conducted with practitioners, we apprehend three business practices currently being performed in the selection of individuals for influencer marketing campaigns: *persona prioritization*, *domain identification*, and *audience quantification*. Next, we describe these three business practices and how companies are adopting the criteria present in the literature in their influencer marketing practice.

We plotted all the criteria mentioned by the nine marketing executives we interviewed, and the criteria used in the battery company case as shown in Figure 4.2. We then triangulated our understanding of how decisions regarding the selection of influencers are currently taken through interviews with other agents in this market (e.g., with advertising and PR agency executives). The individual is the element that executives most refer to when asked how they select digital influencers. Criteria such as identity, personality, credibility, trustworthiness, brand-fit, and narrative style were mentioned as important to select them, a practice that we named *persona prioritization*, given the predominance of the public persona of individuals in the selection process. However, most of our informants use the individual's criteria in a simplified way. They usually navigate on the influencer's page for a while, forming a holistic perception of who one is based on elements of identity, personality, and narrative, and also how credible, trustworthy, and suitable for the brand and the campaign. As one executive says:

> the selection of an individual is a qualitative work... the perception of a certain "truth", something that makes you think that she is going to be able to tell the brand story in a compelling way. (I-p)

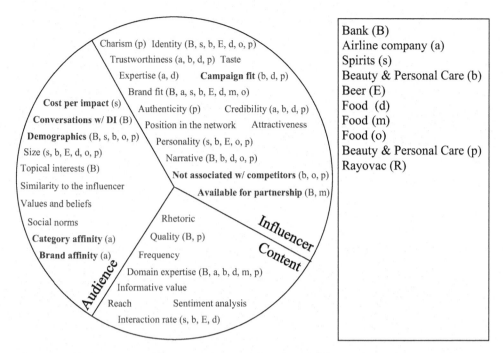

Figure 4.2 The criteria used by companies to select digital influencers.

Simplifying the set of variables connected to the individual may be a strategy adopted by marketing executives in the absence of simple ways of measuring other individual's factors, such as the position of the individual in a network, a criteria often cited in the literature (e.g. Liu-Thompkins and Roberson 2012; Bakshy et al. 2012; Araujo et al. 2017; Deborah et al. 2019; Lutkenhaus et al. 2019). In short, for *persona prioritization*, after selecting some individuals on the platform or receiving a list from an advertising or PR agency, marketing executives spend some time navigating in the timelines of digital influencers, form perceptions, and select individuals but also based on two other elements: the content and the audience.

To map possible influencers for a campaign, marketing executives engage in what we call the *domain identification* practice. This means they increasingly rely on technological platforms, such as Airfluencers and Celebryts, to map the influencers who concentrate their content in a certain domain. Through the use of keywords connected to certain types of content (e.g., beauty or health), they narrow down to a list of potential candidates. This is the reason why influencers usually focus on one specific topical area to build a network interested in that topic and also to achieve higher levels of engagement and perform according to the rules of the algorithms, thus becoming attractive for brands. After having a list of potential influencers for a certain domain, marketing executives navigate in their timelines, apprehending the specific topics they post and the level of expertise they demonstrate. This is an important criterion as one marketing executive from the food sector explains:

> *We were looking for individuals who were discussing topics of health... like (Flavia) Pavanelli... we were also concerned with finding people who cover several regions of Brazil because we are a national brand. (I-d)*

We believe that the domain identification practice is crucial for selecting digital influencers as the domain of expertise of the influencer is a form of approaching an audience that might have an interest in what the brand has to say regarding that topic.

Finally, the third practice we identified is based on the goal of marketing executives to communicate to a certain target. So, they concomitantly engage in the *audience quantification* practice. This is defined here as deciding on the selection of influencers for marketing campaigns based on the quantification of the audience's size and demographics (for instance, gender, age, location, and the perception of social class). Gender split, age range, and geographical location are all information disclosed by the technological platforms to their clients. The readiness of this information, together with the marketing objectives that are part of the media logic, lead marketing executives to a simplification and quantification of the audience, as illustrated in the following excerpt, from a marketing manager of a spirits company:

> *the target is the man, from 21 to 29 y.o., from the upper-level socioeconomic classes, so I asked the agency and they brought me the description of the profile (of a group of influencers)... 60/40, 60% are man, around 700.000 individuals in total, that's reasonable... (I-s)*

Furthermore, we noticed that audience quantification is a practice even more frequent for the selection of influencers with smaller audience sizes, in line with Carter (2016) in that "While the identification of celebrities often relies on intuition or implicit indicators of attention, the identification of smaller influencers relies heavily on data made available through APIs" (p. 8).

Now, we illustrate how the ICA framework can be used to select digital influencers and how the communication logics operating in the marketing department shape the choice of criteria for selecting digital influencers with the case of a traditional battery company with operations in Brazil.

Selecting digital influencers – the battery company case

The battery company is an American battery company with operations in Brazil since 1950. The brand is widely known in Brazil, but it does not have the top of mind position that it used to have in the 80s and 90s when the communication strategy counted with heavy TV advertising investments and the endorsement of the Brazilian soccer celebrity Pelé. In the past 20 years, after some mergers and acquisitions, the company diminished considerably its media investment, losing reputation and recognition in the battery segment. Moreover, competitors such as Duracell and Panasonic increased their media investments and gained market share in the same period (Nielsen and Media Monitor 2019).

benjamin rosenthal and adriana arcuri

In this scenario, the marketing objectives for the brand in 2018 and 2019 included increasing brand awareness and relevance through content on social media. These objectives were challenging since batteries are not a topic that easily grabs attention in social media. So, the goal was to communicate with battery users on Facebook and Instagram, finding a way to be relevant to the target while rescuing the reputation the brand once had.

In 2018, the brand engaged in a partnership with Paramount Pictures for the launch of the retro-oriented and pop culture movie Bumblebee, from the Transformers' franchise. The marketing strategy involved social media communication, and an influencer marketing campaign, targeting retro-culture lovers (millennials) and heavy users of batteries (parents with kids between 3 and 13 years old who are heavy users of batteries for toys), geeks and gamers between 15 and 30 years old (who play video games daily). The social media campaign was nostalgic, linking the battery to the character. Bumblebee movie had two key elements that helped to connect the character to the battery brand – it was placed in the 1980s and the yellow color of Bumblebee, equal to the brand's key color.

For the influencer marketing campaign, the company needed to select influencers who could reach the targets. In consonance to the media logic, influencers were seen as a media vehicle who could increase brand awareness and communicate the brand message associated with the movie. The criteria used for the selection of influencers was the size of the audience and the influence power, measured by the level of engagement of the audience with the content. Also, influencers should be campaign-fit, meaning that their identity should be connected with the movie message (e.g., they should be pop culture lovers, gamers, or connected to the nostalgia theme). Hence, considering the ICA framework, the criteria was an integration of elements from the individual and the audience.

Fri.to was the digital agency in charge of the Bumblebee campaign. Fri.to used the platform Airfluencers and their knowledge and experience to recommend an initial list with 50 influencers that should be contacted to attend the premiere of the movie. This list was narrowed down to 30 influencers. Since the influencers were not paid to attend, the criterion was mainly their availability to go to the premier. The influencer marketing campaign had two key moments: the invitation to the movie premiere and the streaming lives of the influencers on Instagram to generate brand visibility. Three influencers were selected for a paid action. They were female pop culture and game influencers, with a solid base of followers that had fit with the campaign. In December 2018, just before the release of the movie, three lives were aired on Instagram by @dianazambrozuski, @lullylucky, and @emanuellebarros. They received a specific briefing with a small room for co-creation. They needed to show the themed package in their hand while the live show on Instagram was happening. They also should enter the battery company website and play and stream the Bumblebee game, to increase brand awareness.

For the movie premiere in Sao Paulo, on December 15, 2018, 30 influencers were invited and 15 attended the event, resulting in 35 stories and 2 posts on Instagram mentioning the brand and marking the brand hashtag. In total, 1,493,574 people were impacted by the lives on Instagram, stories, and posts, with 148,413 interactions, and an average engagement level of 9.9 percent.[2]

The second campaign with digital influencers targeted the consumer of another product segment in the company – hearing aid batteries (HAB), the source of energy for hearing aid devices (HAD), a crucial item for those who want to overcome hearing loss and deafness. The typical consumer is deeply engaged with the HAB, using it every day, for many hours, attached to the body. In the case of cochlear implants, the device is inserted in the cochlea of the user (inside the head) after surgery, enabling a deaf person to hear again and allowing speech development.

The objective of the second influencer marketing campaign was to increase the knowledge and reputation of the brand in the deaf target by connecting with the base of a well-known and admired personality in this field. In this context, the criteria to select the influencers followed the public relations logic, focusing on the identity (the influencer should be a user of HADs or cochlear implants), personality (which should match with the brand positioning), and the capacity to produce engaging content for the target audience (individuals who use regularly HABs, have hearing loss or are deaf). Also, ideally, the influencer should be a real user of the brand HABs.

Paula Pfeifer, a user of cochlear implant and the brand HABs who had previously contacted the company to ask for sponsoring, was selected as the influencer at the beginning of 2018. Paula was well known (she has 28,5k followers on Instagram) and admired among the community of individuals with hearing loss and cochlear implants. The hashtag #surdosqueouvem (#hearingdeaf) that is her identification and the name of her project with Facebook, has 16.7k publications. In 2019 she won a Facebook Prize as "Community Resident," the only one to receive this recognition in Latin America. Since she was not a HAD user (she has a cochlear implant instead) and could not test the batteries herself, she recommended running a product test for one month with 20 followers and members of her Facebook closed group. She wanted to be sure of the quality before starting the campaign, to have the support of her followers. The followers that accepted to participate in the test received the appropriated batteries and committed to using only the partner brand during one month, giving daily feedback about their experience, helping Paula to understand more about the partner company through the perception of her followers so that she could co-create content with the company executives. This initial step showed Paula's commitment to her audience and critical position towards brand content and the products she promotes.

During this test, Paula and the company learned that batteries finish in the worst moments, and not necessarily in working hours. It was hard for individuals to find batteries on weekends or in 24-hour drugstores and retailers. When the battery finishes, the device stops working and the individual stops hearing – momentarily facing deafness. After learning that, the company team worked on a channel strategy to increase the availability of the product and communicated it to Paula's audience on Facebook, Instagram, and Paula's blog Chronicles of Deafness.

This is an example of how to find a relevant topic for the audience and use it in the communication, co-created between the influencer and the brand, connecting the brand content with the audience's needs and interests. Additionally, the project brought results beyond message reach and brand awareness: in one year, 3,000 new stores were selling the company HAB versus 300 stores at the beginning of the

benjamin rosenthal and adriana arcuri

project. For each new supermarket and drugstore chain that listed the batteries, there were stories and posts on Instagram informing the audience about the availability in the new places.

The campaign had three additional moments: the second one was a contest inviting followers to go to the stores and post when they find brand Battery, fostering audience engagement with the brand's interest. The third moment was the sponsorship of the Ear Parade, with Paula being one of its ambassadors. It was the first Ear Parade in Sao Paulo, with big ear sculptures in the city informing people about hearing loss and prevention. The company sponsored three ear sculptures, in another example of content that addresses the audience's interests. The fourth moment was the launch of the partner brand cochlear implant batteries, at the time not available in Brazil. Paula used to buy these batteries abroad and her followers started to ask the company to bring them to Brazil. The overall result of the four campaign moments were: 34,409 interactions, with an engagement rate of 284 per cent with 26 stories and 2 posts on both Instagram and Facebook. The level of engagement was very high because the community formed around Paula was committed to the topics that she posted. Furthermore, the brand invested money to increase the visibility of the campaign amongst a select audience.

The partnership with Paula Pfeifer brought the company more than just a communication campaign with a digital influencer. During this period, besides her role as a brand content co-creator, she also became a consultant for the brand (e.g., by conducting a full-day workshop with the advertising agency in August 2019), and a partner (e.g., by giving a speech in sales conventions).

Companies that work through the public relations logic may bring the influencer closer to the brand's interest in the same way that the brand should aim to get closer to the influencer's interest, fostering win–win relationships, as the case illustrates. The intention with this case is not to provide an extensive list of possibilities of partnership formats, as they are contextually connected to the brand's and the influencer's interests. The intention with this case, instead, is to provide examples of how this relationship can be built.

Discussion: how to improve the selection of digital influencers

The central contributions of this chapter are to integrate the literature on the criteria that can be used to select individuals for influencer marketing campaigns – the ICA framework – and to present three practices which show how marketing executives are taking into consideration criteria from the individual, the content, and the audience in this selection. Now, we discuss how marketing executives can improve the practices of persona prioritization, domain identification, and audience quantification to select individuals for influencer marketing campaigns.

First, marketing executives can improve the persona prioritization practice by often contextualizing the choice of the individual. What we mean by "contextualizing" is that the choice of digital influencers should be based on an alignment between the topic of the campaign and the persona of the influencer. For instance, in the case, Paula was a perfect fit for a campaign focused on batteries for individuals with hearing loss or deafness, a criterion named "campaign fit" (Figure 4.2). There is no objective way to decide who is "campaign fit" or not. This is a decision based on a judgment taken by marketing managers after getting to know potential influencers. This criterion should be used together with other personas' criteria such as identity, brand fit, trustworthiness, credibility, and narrative style.

Second, marketing executives can improve the domain identification practice by looking beyond the domain expertise of the individual. We believe that as important as the area of specialization is the quality of the content, as well as the interactions that it fosters. Some of our interviewees are already doing that (Figure 4.2). Just as for "campaign fit" there is no direct measure of content quality, although recent research (Arora et al. 2019; Gräve 2019) has attempted to use sentiment analysis in the comments of posts to access the quality level of the content. This is a judgment that marketing executives should make, based also on the objectives of the brand for the campaign, and on the kind of content that the brand wants to be associated with. Regarding the interactions fostered by the content, this is a criterion that is simple to measure, for instance through the number of comments on a series of posts. Together, domain expertise, content quality, and interaction rate can provide a simple yet efficient combination of criteria for the selection of digital influencers.

Third, marketing executives can improve the audience quantification practice by not only using the audience size and profile similarity to the influencer but also the demographics of the audience, the affinity, values, and beliefs with the related topic or product category (Lutkenhaus et al. 2019). As the case illustrates, when the audience of a digital influencer is involved with a topic and approves the products or services provided by a company, the efficacy of an influencer marketing campaign increases. This suggestion is in line with recent research showing that groups with a high level of homophile tend to share information that confirms their own beliefs (Yuan et al. 2019). Therefore, marketing executives should choose digital influencers based on the influencer audience's values and beliefs regarding the topic of interest, beyond its size and profile.

Notes

1 Often, the literature investigates the variables (e.g., individuals' or content' characteristics) that increase social influence, so in this chapter, we will often refer to the increase of social influence because these characteristics can be used as criteria to select digital influencers.
2 The engagement level is calculated by summing the number of interactions (likes, comments, and shares) and dividing this total by the number of followers (of the N digital influencers involved in the campaign).

References

Araujo, T., Neijens, P., and Vliegenthart, R., 2017. Getting the word out on Twitter: The role of influentials, information brokers and strong ties in building word-of-mouth for brands. *International Journal of Advertising*, 36(3), 496–513.

Arora, A., Bansal, S., Kandpal, C., Aswani, R., and Dwivedi, Y., 2019. Measuring social media influencer index-insights from Facebook, Twitter and Instagram. *Journal of Retailing and Consumer Services*, 49, 86–101.

benjamin rosenthal and adriana arcuri

Arsel, Z., 2017. Asking questions with reflexive focus: A tutorial on designing and conducting interviews. *Journal of Consumer Research*, 44(4), 939–948.

Arvidsson, A., Caliandro, A., Airoldi, M., and Barina, S., 2016. Crowds and value. Italian directioners on Twitter. *Information, Communication and Society*, 19(7), 921–939.

Audrezet, A., De Kerviler, G., and Moulard, J.G., 2018. Authenticity under threat: When social media influencers need to go beyond self-presentation. *Journal of Business Research*.

Bakshy, E., Rosenn, I., Marlow, C., and Adamic, L., 2012. The role of social networks in information diffusion. In Proceedings of the 21st international conference on World Wide Web, 519–528. ACM.

Berger, J., 2014. Word of mouth and interpersonal communication: A review and directions for future research. *Journal of Consumer Psychology*, 24(4), 586–607.

Braun, V., and Clarke, V., 2006. Using thematic analysis in psychology. *Qualitative Research in Psychology*, 3(2), 77–101.

Casaló, L. V., Flavián, C., and Ibáñez-Sánchez, S., 2018. Influencers on Instagram: Antecedents and consequences of opinion leadership. *Journal of Business Research*.

Childers, C.C., Lemon, L.L., and Hoy, M.G., 2018. # Sponsored# Ad: Agency Perspective on Influencer Marketing Campaigns. *Journal of Current Issues and Research in Advertising*, 1–17.

Cocker, H.L., and Cronin, J., 2017. Charismatic authority and the YouTuber: Unpacking the new cults of personality. *Marketing Theory*, 17(4), 455–472.

Cocker, H.L., Banister, E.N., and Piacentini, M.G., 2015. Producing and consuming celebrity identity myths: unpacking the classed identities of Cheryl Cole and Katie Price. *Journal of Marketing Management*, 31(5–6), 502–524.

Deborah, A., Michela, A., and Anna, C., 2019. How to quantify social media influencers: An empirical application at the Teatro alla Scala. *Heliyon*, 5(5), e01677.

Djafarova, E., and Rushworth, C., 2017. Exploring the credibility of online celebrities' Instagram profiles in influencing the purchase decisions of young female users. *Computers in Human Behavior*, 68, 1–7.

Dost, F., Phieler, U., Haenlein, M., and Libai, B., 2019. Seeding as Part of the Marketing Mix: Word-of-Mouth Program Interactions for Fast-Moving Consumer Goods. *Journal of Marketing*, 83(2), 62–81.

Erdogan, B. Z., Baker, M. J., and Tagg, S., 2001. Selecting celebrity endorsers: The practitioner's perspective. *Journal of Advertising Research*, 41(3), 39–48.

Erz, A., and Christensen, A.B.H., 2018. Transforming consumers into brands: tracing transformation processes of the practice of blogging. *Journal of Interactive Marketing*, 43, 69–82.

Fillis, I., 2015. The production and consumption activities relating to the celebrity artist. *Journal of Marketing Management*, 31(5–6), 646–664.

Ge, J., and Gretzel, U., 2018. Emoji rhetoric: a social media influencer perspective. *Journal of Marketing Management*, 34(15–16), 1272–1295.

Guest, G., Bunce, A., and Johnson, L., 2006. How many interviews are enough? An experiment with data saturation and variability. *Field Methods*, 18(1), 59–82.

Gräve, J.F., 2019. What KPIs are key? Evaluating performance metrics for social media influencers. *Social Media+ Society*, 5(3), 1–9.

Hackley, C., and Hackley, R.A., 2016. The iconicity of celebrity and the spiritual impulse. *Consumption Markets and Culture*, 19(3), 269–274.

Holt, D., 2016. Branding in the age of social media. *Harvard Business Review*, 94(3).

Jacobson, J., Gruzd, A., Kumar, P., and Mai, P., 2019. Networked Influence: An Introduction. *Social Media+ Society*, 5(3), 1–5.

Katz, E., and Lazarsfeld, P., 1955. *Personal Influence: The part played by people in the flow of mass communications*. New York, NY: The Free Press.

Kvale, S., 2008. *Doing Interviews*. Thousand Oaks, California: Sage.

Liu, S., Jiang, C., Lin, Z., Ding, Y., Duan, R., and Xu, Z., 2015. Identifying effective influencers based on trust for electronic word-of-mouth marketing: A domain-aware approach. *Information Sciences*, 306, 34–52.

Liu-Thompkins, Y., and Rogerson, M., 2012. Rising to stardom: An empirical investigation of the diffusion of user-generated content. *Journal of Interactive Marketing*, 26(2), 71–82.

Lou, C., and Yuan, S., 2019. Influencer marketing: How message value and credibility affect consumer trust of branded content on social media. *Journal of Interactive Advertising*, 19(1), 58–73.

Lutkenhaus, R.O., Jansz, J., and Bouman, M.P., 2019. Tailoring in the digital era: Stimulating dialogues on health topics in collaboration with social media influencers. *Digital Health*, 5, 2055207618821521.

McQuarrie, E.F., Miller, J., and Phillips, B.J., 2013. The megaphone effect: Taste and audience in fashion blogging. *Journal of Consumer Research*, 40(1), 136–158.

Miles, M.B., and Huberman, A.M., 1994. *Qualitative Data Analysis: An expanded sourcebook* (2nd ed.). Thousand Oaks, CA, US: Sage Publications, Inc.

Pathak, S., 2018. How Influence Marketing Has Changed in 5 Charts. Retrieved from https://digiday.com/marketing/influencer-marketing-changed-5-charts/

Probst, F., Grosswiele, L., and Pfleger, R., 2013. Who will lead and who will follow: Identifying Influential Users in Online Social Networks. *Business and Information Systems Engineering*, 5(3), 179–193.

Saldaña, J., 2011. *Fundamentals of Qualitative Research*. New York, NY: Oxford University Press.

Schomer, A., 2019. Influencer Marketing: State of the social media influencer market in 2020. *Business Insider*. Accessed January 13, 2020: www.businessinsider.com/influencer-marketing-report

Silva, N. D., and Campos, R.D., 2019. The 2.0 Critic: Blended Discourses in Blogging. *Latin American Business Review*, 20(2), 1–25.

Sokolova, K., and Kefi, H., 2019. Instagram and YouTube bloggers promote it, why should I buy? How credibility and parasocial interaction influence purchase intentions. *Journal of Retailing and Consumer Services*.

Song, S. Y., Cho, E., and Kim, Y. K., 2017. Personality factors and flow affecting opinion leadership in social media. *Personality and Individual Differences*, 114, 16–23.

Statista, 2018. Active social network penetration in selected countries as of January 2018. Retrieved from: www.statista.com/statistics/282846/regular-social-networking-usage-penetration-worldwide-by-country/

Stoldt, R., Wellman, M., Ekdale, B., and Tully, M., 2019. Professionalizing and Profiting: The Rise of Intermediaries in the Social Media Influencer Industry. *Social Media+ Society*, 5(1), 2056305119832587.

Timmermans, S., and Tavory, I., 2012. Theory construction in qualitative research: From grounded theory to abductive analysis. *Sociological Theory*, 30(3), 167–186.

Watts, D.J., and Dodds, P.S., 2007. Influentials, networks, and public opinion formation. *Journal of Consumer Research*, 34(4), 441–458.

Yuan, X., Schuchard, R.J., and Crooks, A.T., 2019. Examining Emergent Communities and Social Bots Within the Polarized Online Vaccination Debate in Twitter. *Social Media+ Society*, 5(3), 1–12.

part 2

Influencers as part of marketing communication campaigns

chapter 5

Choosing the right influencer for your brand

Ayse Bengi Ozcelik and Eser Levi

Learning outcomes

On completing this chapter, you should be able to:

- understand the right influencer concept and how brands may benefit;
- appreciate how consumer-based antecedents can impact choosing the best influencer;
- recognize how different influencer antecedents will attract brands; and
- understand the potential consequences of brands engaging with the right influencer.

Swipe up the screen and use the promotion code that I offer especially for my followers!

How many times a day do Instagram users see this message? And how many times do they really swipe up and make the purchase? People have always been influenced by other people's decisions or behaviors (Zietek 2016). Songs, fairy tales, oral histories, and even religious views are the evidence that word-of-mouth (WOM) marketing has existed for centuries (Weiss 2014).

Regarding new marketing paradigms, a common tendency for people today is to seek information through reviews and recommendations about the products on social media (Dinesh 2017). According to the findings of PwC Global Consumer Insights Survey (2018), social networks are found as the most influential channels for people who need inspiration about their purchases. The human-to-human contact, even if it is via the internet, is considered as more targeted and more effective than trad-itional marketing activities (Weiss 2014), providing a unilateral relationship between the brand and the consumer.

Consumers pursue genuine comments about the products or services they plan to purchase. They generally use their mobile phones to access information, and as a result, social media platforms have become one of the most functional tools regarding the purchase act. Hence, due to the increased time spent on these platforms, marketing professionals now need to adopt new practices in order to attract customers. Influencer marketing is one of these new methods providing the opportunity to build an authentic bond between brands and consumers (Woods 2016; Zietek 2016).

The influencer, acting as the opinion leader for the purchase advice (Casalo et al. 2018), has become the online endorser who is shaping consumers' attitudes and behaviors (Freberg et al. 2011). Influencers are creating content through Instagram posts, blogs, YouTube, videos, tweets, etc. to express their opinions and experiences using everyday life settings (Bladow 2018; Veirman et al. 2017). That is, an influ-encer can be defined as an online persona who periodically shares images, videos or texts about his/her views and comments on specific products or services, mostly embedded in their daily activities, with the intention of affecting consumers' choices. Defining the influencer should be the first step in utilizing influencer marketing. However, finding an influencer and making the deal is not enough to be able to reach the targeted customers and create a positive perception about the brand. The compel-ling part of this process is to find the right influencers who will serve as ambassadors of brands using their social media posts.

The purpose of this chapter is to provide a definition for the right influencer con-cept and a novel framework including its antecedents and consequences. Brands may then take this framework into consideration in order to utilize influencer marketing in a manner in which they can reach their targeted consumers with relevant content. Furthermore, the chapter aims to enhance the understanding and also present the key elements of this method in order to contribute to the field.

Who is the right influencer?

Finding the right influencer is a big challenge for brands today. The Global Insights Survey 2018 Report mentions that posts of friends or strangers alike have a great influence on buying decisions (PwC 2018). "Friends" and "strangers alike" being mentioned in the same sentence is worth considering. When consumers follow an influencer, they usually want to be a part of his/her life (Hearn and Schoenhoff 2016). Although they are strangers, they need to look alike in order to get connected. A good fit between the influencer and the consumer ensures the acceptance of and engage-ment with the influencer (Shalev and Morwitz 2011). Since they are seen as trusted trendsetters (Veirman et al. 2017), the content should be given in a coherent story to appeal to consumers (Pophal 2016) who are seeking for authenticity from their trusted so-called opinion leaders.

　　　　　　　　　　　　　　　　　　　　　ayse bengi ozcelik and eser levi

These online and social opinion leaders can be managed by marketers by means of their potential to affect people's choices in a way that brands can meet consumers' needs (Brown and Hayes 2016). Although the return on investment of influencer marketing is estimated to be 11 times more than traditional marketing annually (Woods 2016; Kirkpatrick 2016) with its less expensive and proper access to the targeted audience (Evans et al. 2017); marketers should use the technique carefully in order to yield expected results in such a growing sector. With increasing popularity of eWOM, hereafter influencer marketing, anyone can be an influencer on one's own (Weiss 2014). Stimulating the influencers to contribute to the marketing activities of giant brands, social media platforms have become full of influencers. On Instagram alone, over 200,000 posts are shared by influencers (Bladow 2018). It was reported that there was a huge increase in the influencer marketing-focused agencies in 2018 (Influencer Marketing Hub 2019).

This popularity motivates many social media users to become full-time influencers and do it as a job (Bladow 2018). The danger bell starts to ring here. The more exposure to influencers on social media, the more authenticity may be threatened. Accordingly, ethicality and trust decrease, and consumers do not believe in the endorsements and influencers do not generate positive attitudes and behaviors towards brands. Hence, there should be a regulation, but not a formal one, to use the influencer marketing technique. To help regulate the use of this practice, this chapter presents a framework for utilizing influencers including the antecedents and consequences (see Figure 5.1).

This framework suggests a positive relationship between the perception of consumers, influencers' manner and characteristics, and the attitudinal and behavioral outcomes for brands. If the antecedents exist for the influencer, then he/she is

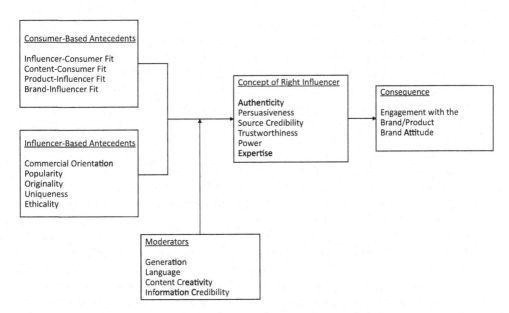

Figure 5.1 The framework of the right influencer: Antecedents and consequences.

perceived as more authentic, persuasive, credible, trustworthy, powerful, and expert. Previous studies show that there is a positive relationship between the perceived fit of the account with the consumer's personality and the effect of the influencer (e.g. Casalo et al. 2018; Lagner et al. 2013). Thereby, consumers engage with the brand or the product more, form a positive brand attitude and they become more likely to have buying intentions.

The concept of the right influencer is not a certain one since influencer marketing is a novel method. Today's social media influencers are acting like online opinion leaders who are defined as "the individuals who were likely to influence other people in their immediate environment" (Katz and Lazarsfeld 1955, p. 3). These new-age opinion leaders have the power to influence the attitudes, decisions, or behaviors of their followers through their social media postings (e.g. Veirman et al. 2017; Watts and Dodds 2007; Lyons and Henderson 2005). Although the number of followers may show a level of influential strength, there are a lot more than the numbers to evaluate influencers.

Social recommendations have an effect on 26 percent of online purchase decisions across all product categories (Pophal 2016). Hence, marketers invest in the potential of those persuasive communicators in order to disseminate the information by using their social network with a certain message about a product or a service (Veirman et al. 2017; Zietek 2016; Keller and Berry 2003). However, the use of that potential is critical for the brands in terms of using the proper influence in a proper context. Hence, conceptualizing the right influencer is crucial in terms of ensuring a return on investment.

The major challenge is to specify the ones who have the potential of influence on the targeted consumers with his/her social media behavior (e.g. Veirman et al. 2017; Araujo et al. 2017; Pophal 2016; Momtaz et al. 2011). Since influencers are accepted as having larger groups to influence compared to the average (Keller and Berry 2003), some different key points from traditional advertising techniques should be considered in order to use their influencing power correctly. Figure 5.2 suggests a recipe for defining the right influencer. A brand should use such a persona who is authentic in their words used in posts, persuasive and trustworthy enough to make the customer take action, credible in their social network, powerful to be able to affect the followers and an expert about what they are talking about. Each topic is explained in the following section. Although those concepts are interrelated, this chapter introduces them separately in order to emphasize the importance of each.

Authenticity

Authenticity can be considered as the most critical dimension for the right influencer, since it is the main underlying reason why the market needs a new technique. The traditional advertising methods are not enough to persuade consumers due to their aggressive and exaggerated nature. When marketers seek for less commercial and more intimate solutions to catch consumers (Dinesh 2017), authenticity becomes an important requirement for brands. For instance, the cooperation between Duygu Özaslan, a lifestyle blogger, and Bobby Brown, a make-up brand is a critical example of authenticity. The

Figure 5.2 The concept of the right influencer.

influencer is one of the pioneers of the sector, however she made too many agreements with irrelevant brands and lost her authenticity as a result. The reactions to these collaborations show that followers are aware of the monetary issues between the brand and the influencer which in turn harms both the influencer and the brand.

A message directly coming from the advertiser is perceived as less authentic and credible than a message coming from an ordinary consumer (Veirman et al. 2017). Likewise, it is important for social media users whether the influencer has a commercial motivation or not (Audrezet et al. 2018). They prefer to see a genuine person instead of a celebrity (Hearn and Schoenhoff 2016). Thus, influencers are not expected to be the direct endorsers; indeed, they are supposed to tell personal stories involving a particular product or brand (Casalo et al. 2018).

Persuasiveness

The main aim of advertising is to persuade consumers to purchase products or services. This persuasion approach is changing due to the transformation of consumers' needs. However, this need might not always be about a product or a service. It may also be about the persuasion process. According to the Persuasion Knowledge Model, individuals learn about persuasiveness in the life span and it shapes how they respond to persuasion tactics (Friestad and Wright 1994). In parallel with this, it is not a surprise that consumers nowadays are suspicious about advertisements (Veirman et al. 2017). They have the power to judge the credibility of the source and the message; and if it is irritating for them, they can skip the advertising (Xiao et al. 2018; Veirman et al. 2017).

Thus, marketers should use persuasive influencers which are perceived as trustworthy (Wathen and Burkell 2002), authentic (Abidin 2015), experts in that specific area (Xiao et al. 2018; Gass and Seiter 2011) and have fit with the product (Veirman et al. 2017). Although persuasiveness of an advertising technique is critically important, the advertising content should be relevance-oriented rather than persuasion-oriented (Kozinets et al. 2010) in order to keep the authenticity level high.

Idea fairy: Persuasiveness going wrong

One example related to the persuasiveness issue is the sponsorship of a diaper brand with insta-moms. The brand sent the same text to three different insta-moms and they all shared the content as the caption of their posts in an exact way as if it was their personal opinions. Some of the followers noticed the situation and declared it in a comment under the post. This not only backfired in terms of persuasiveness but also eroded the trustworthiness of the brand and harmed the authenticity of those insta-moms. That was an interesting case since it made people question the way the agencies and influencers work.

When have you seen examples of influencers trying to persuade you or others to do something that has gone horribly wrong? Should influencers always try to persuade? Why or why not?

Source credibility

Source credibility is defined as the judgment and the value that the message-receiver gives to the speaker (Gass and Seiter 2011). Credibility affects the perception of believability (O'Keefe 1990), persuades the message-receivers (Metzger et al. 2003), and is driven by trustworthiness and perceived expertise of the message-giver (Xiao et al. 2018; Veirman et al. 2017). Hence, it can be said that source credibility has two dimensions: *trustworthiness* and *expertise*.

After YouTube influencer videos have become popular, their rise is nourished by the perceived credibility of the content (e.g. Xiao et al. 2018; Alvarez 2017; Fidelman 2017). Especially social media celebrities such as YouTube vloggers, bloggers, or "instafamous" profiles have become more and more powerful than traditional celebrities due to the credibility levels (Djafarova and Rushworth 2017).

The source credibility is in a positive relationship with persuasiveness of the message (Wathen and Burkell 2002), information credibility (e.g. Xiao et al. 2018; Luo et al. 2013; Cheung et al. 2009), and trustworthiness (Veirman et al. 2017). Those relationships are mainly affected by the reduced perceived risk before giving a purchase decision (Djafarova and Rushworth 2017). When social media users evaluate the influencers' suggestions of products or services, they try to reduce the risk of being deceived. Hence, credible influencers may be more likely to influence the followers. In this sense, 49 percent of consumers trust influencer recommendations, and 40 percent of them make purchase decisions after seeing the product on social media (Digital Marketing Institute 2019). Source credibility is empirically tested in Chapter 10 by Costello and Urbanska (2020).

ayse bengi ozcelik and eser levi

Trustworthiness

The most critical difference of influencers from traditional celebrities is the intimacy and trustworthiness involved as they share their personal lives on social media (Veirman et al. 2017; Abidin 2016). Trustworthiness is the perceived reliability which is different from source credibility in that source credibility is about an individual's perception. Indeed, trustworthiness is a main dimension of source credibility (Xiao et al. 2018). For an influencer, being trustworthy is critical as it provides an attitudinal and behavioral influence on consumers and the persuasive power of the message content (Uzunoglu and Kip 2014). Consumers do not buy a product offered by someone that they do not trust. Although celebrities are regarded as more attractive (Grave 2017), influencers have more of an advantage than traditional celebrities in terms of trust, because if the influencer's message is perceived as noncommercial, it is perceived more trustworthy than an advertorial (Audrezet et al. 2018; Mudambi and Schuff 2010). Additionally, purchasing intention related to influencer marketing, namely eWOM, is mainly based on the feeling of trust because of reducing the risk when consumers trust their social media idols (Djafarova and Rushworth 2017).

Expertise

Along with the aforementioned characteristics of the right influencer, expertise stands as a supportive dimension. It is defined as the level of knowledge of a communicator in a certain area (Xiao et al. 2018). The perceived expertise level of the spokesperson, namely the influencer, may affect all of the dimensions of persuasiveness, source credibility, and trustworthiness. Additionally, previous research shows that it has a positive effect on the attitudes and behaviors of the consumers through the ad (e.g. Xiao et al. 2018; Braunsberger 1996; Ohanian 1991).

Idea fairy: Identifying expertise

Turkish YouTube influencer Refika Birgül is regarded as a credible source with regard to her area of expertise. She is a cook in real life and she executes her profession on YouTube. One of her most memorable brand partnerships was with a dried nuts brand called Peyman. She was suggesting Peyman nuts to be added as an ingredient in Asure, a traditional dessert in Turkey. The followers matched the suggestion with her expertise and trusted her, so the campaign resulted in success.

What influencers do you know that you consider experts? What makes them an expert to you? How would you identify experts?

Power

The credibility, trustworthiness, persuasiveness, and authenticity of an influencer's social media account is based on its power in consumers' perception. Besides, the power of an Instagram or YouTube account is measured by the number of followers. Consumers may judge the influencer on such peripheral cues (Veirman et al. 2017);

however, the number of followers of the followers is becoming a second-order characteristic when evaluating an account. Authenticity is more critical for an influencer to be powerful. That's why micro-influencers who are supposed to have high authenticity and expertise are on the stage (Zietek 2016). They seem to have non-commercial motivations to advertise a product or service. Hence, such a profile with 2,000 followers is considered more powerful than a profile with millions of followers. All of those dimensions provide that an influencer's personal narrative messages may be perceived as unbiased opinions and helps the influencer to be perceived as persuasively powerful (Abidin 2015). The ability to communicate the message as a tool to warn the followers among social, political, and consumption issues is the main power of the influencer (Uzunoglu and Kip 2014; Nisbet and Kotcher 2009).

Influencers who were celebrities before they became influencers may be regarded as more powerful when compared to the ones who gained their fame after being influencers. People generally evaluate public figures with respect to their personal lives and celebrities have a relatively long history in people's minds. Thus, it is possible to say that the celebrities who succeeded in gaining and sustaining a positive image in the eyes of audiences are more likely to be perceived as powerful figures. The number of followers is thought to make a positive contribution to the perceived power; nevertheless, it is not necessarily one of the most important determinants. Riboldazzi and Capriello (2020) explored this previously in Chapter 3.

How can we find the right influencer?

There are numerous antecedents of choosing the right influencer. Customer-based antecedents include the perceived fit between endorsers and the product or brand being endorsed, as well as the perceived fit between the consumer and the influencer and also the content the influencer delivers. Just as in the traditional celebrity endorsement approach, marketers need to provide consonance among all the actors in this practice. Conversely, influencer-based antecedents cover influencers' characteristics and the way they influence, such as commercial orientation, self-presentation, popularity, originality, uniqueness, and ethicality. Brands may easily determine the right influencers if these requirements are met.

Consumer-based antecedents

Influencer–consumer fit

The fit between the influencer and the consumer is one of the critical consumer-based antecedents of choosing the right influencer. Individuals are inclined to associate with their peers. The notion of homophily is used to explain this tendency of message receivers to bond with similar information sources (McCroskey et al. 1975). Correspondingly, consumers are likely to pay attention to the recommendations of

ayse bengi ozcelik and eser levi

the opinion leaders they identify themselves with, engage with, accept influence from, and get persuaded by a source that renders a good fit with how they perceive themselves (Shalev and Morwitz 2011). For this reason, brands must contemplate deeply on choosing the suitable influencer that would address their target (Djafarova and Rushworth 2017). The target audience of the brand that is recommended by the influencer should correspond to the follower profile of that influencer in order for the practice to be meaningful (Casalo et al. 2018; Uzunoglu and Kip 2014).

Content–consumer fit

The fit between the message content and the consumer is another consumer-based antecedent. The content of an influencer's account is a critical determinant while choosing the right influencer (Uzunoglu and Kip 2014). The brand that is recommended by the influencer may be compatible with the influencer's interests but may still be incongruent with the content of the account (Zhang et al. 2017). Therefore, influencers should be attentive about designing their content accordingly with their followers' interests. It is important for influencers to construct a coherent identity not because it would appeal to relevant consumers but because it would reinforce their identity as well (Childers et al. 2018).

Product–influencer fit

The fit between the influencer and the product that is being communicated by the influencer is also another consumer-based antecedent. An influencer who promotes an apparel that does not provide a good match with his/her public persona would be perceived as fake, since followers would anticipate a compatibility between the persona and the product being presented (Audrezet et al. 2018). Similarly, the relevance between the influencer and the product is a critical necessity for gaining success in social media advertising (Djafarova and Rushworth 2017). This is a common approach adopted by marketing professionals; celebrity endorsements are mostly configured in regard to the celebrities' congruence with the product.

Brand–influencer fit

The fit between the influencer and the brand being advertised is also another important consumer-based antecedent. It is highly crucial for brands to choose influencers that would be representative of their identity (Childers et al. 2018). Influencers should avoid making collaborations with brands that do not provide a good match with their interests (Audrezet et al. 2018). The consistency between the brand and the influencer may play a significant role in the effectiveness of this practice (Veirman et al. 2017). Evans et al. (2018) claims that a mutually beneficial relationship between the two sides may be established if brands choose influencers whose interests are compatible with their attributes.

Influencer-based antecedents

Commercial orientation

Consumers' perception regarding whether the influencer has a commercial orientation or not is a critical issue in influencer marketing practice. Pophal (2016) claims that brands may be negatively affected if consumers feel that the influencer made a financial agreement in return for endorsing the brand. This happened in the case of a comedian influencer, male and 30 years old, who promoted a cleaning supply and received harsh criticism as a result of the post in question. It is not only brands that may have trouble but also the influencers themselves may face unfavorable repercussions if the consumers understand that the brand is endorsed in exchange for a payment (Casalo et al. 2018). In a similar vein, consumers appreciate non-commercial orientation and they may lose their interest in influencers if they give the impression that they have overly commercial orientation (Audrezet et al. 2018).

Self-presentation

Goffman's (1959) theory of self-presentation refers to individuals' systematic efforts for building and managing a complete persona in the eyes of the public. Influencers also design their identities on social media to be able to address their audiences (Dinesh 2017). They create their online images to attract the attention of their target audience (Chae 2018). It is important for influencers to manage an extensive process on building an online persona since they should portray themselves as a consistent being, including their identity, personality, the content they convey, the language they use, etc. (Childers et al. 2018). Hearn and Schoenhoff (2016) point out an important matter regarding this issue; they state that social media influencers may not have full control over their public personas compared to traditional celebrities.

Popularity

Popularity on social media is generally measured by quantities, namely the number of followers, likes, or comments. An influencer who has many followers may be considered very reliable and therefore the products he/she promotes are perceived in a positive way. Consumers' perception of influencer's popularity is an important factor; however, popularity cannot be limited to the number of followers the influencer has. An influencer's perceived opinion leadership is not directly dependent on the quantity of the influencer's followers (Veirman et al. 2017). Besides, consumers are now highly conscious about how influencers can buy followers, therefore it is possible to say that numbers alone cannot indicate popularity. For instance, it is not the best idea to collaborate with influencers who have great numbers of followers if the aim is to endorse unique products or brands (Veirman et al. 2017). This is because such collaboration bears discrepancy since the endorsed product and the influencer do not fit each other. Consequently, popularity should not be measured by numbers; brands should seek influencers who are well-accepted among their targeted audience.

ayse bengi ozcelik and eser levi

Originality

Since there are countless influencers on social media, originality is an important determinant in order to stand out amongst others. Casalo et al. (2018) characterize originality by referring to a number of qualities such as newness, distinctness, unusualness, innovativeness, and sophistication. An insta-mom who gives advice about parenting in a humorous and self-mocking way may attract more attention when compared to a common insta-mom. Instead of endorsing a brand in a mechanical way, influencers should convey an original and sincere story that they integrate with the brand.

Uniqueness

Online marketing tactics often get copied by others. Uniqueness, therefore, is a must in order to gain and sustain a competitive advantage in the jungle of online platforms. It is vital in order for an influencer to be respected (Casalo et al. 2018). It would be beneficial to remember that influencers who have a large number of followers may not be perceived as unique by audiences although the likeability is higher (Veirman et al. 2017). For instance, if an influencer with 1 million followers is seen as a hardly accessible Instagram pop-star, an influencer with 50,000 followers may be perceived as an alternative singer whose followers feel that they are the selected people who discovered that singer. In fact, followers may feel that they are unique if the influencer they are following is unique. Hence, being perceived as exclusive leads to positive attitudes towards brands (Veirman et al. 2017).

Ethical

One of the most widespread criticisms that influencer marketing attracts is about the deceptive nature of this method. Similar to embedded advertising, it is believed that consumers mostly are not aware of the paid structure of the content they are exposed to. By law, influencers must disclose their financial engagement with the brand as well as remain ethically correct (Evans et al. 2017). With the spread of influencer marketing, consumers became aware of the materialistic relationship between influencer and brand. Hence, their perceptions can be easily changed according to the brand–influencer sponsorship. For example, if followers feel that the content is posted only for commercial motivations, they may question the ethicality of the influencer and it may affect all the aforementioned characteristics of the influencers.

Additional determinant factors

Given the reviewed literature; generation, language, content creativity, and information credibility are proposed as potential other factors which are shown as moderators in Figure 5.1. Whether the age groups of the influencer and consumer are similar or not; whether the influencer discloses the financial deal one has made with the brand or not; whether the content the influencer offers is creative or not; and lastly, whether the information delivered by the influencer is perceived as credible or not seem to be the major issues that affect the relationship this chapter deals with.

Generation

Ways of thinking and acting of specific age groups may play a role in how influencer marketing works. Woods (2016) found that almost half of millennials have made purchases based on the recommendation of an influencer. In a report by e-Marketer, it was stated that nearly 20 percent of Gen Z and Millennial members are affected by influencers before making a decision. This ratio is approximately 10 percent when it comes to Gen Xers and Baby Boomers (Droesch 2019).

Besides, the equivalence between the influencer and the consumer regarding the generation they belong to is also effective in this relationship. Influencers may impress consumers in a more effective way if the two actors of this communicative act are demographically similar (Langner, 2013).

Language

On their posts, some of the influencers disclose the deal he or she made with the brand, while some of them may not be very clear about their financial motivation and hide behind semantics. Influencers who adopt a transparent authenticity completely disclose information about the partnership they got into with brands with clear, understandable language such as #ad, #advert, #sponsored. Passionate influencers, on the other hand, focus only on being the emotional layer of the communication, leaving the financial language clarification aside (Audrezet et al. 2018). It is also recommended that influencers avoid partnerships when brands demand non-disclosure as that will convolute the legal language which must act as necessary disclosure (Audrezet et al. 2018).

Content creativity

Influencers must design creative content that would truly attract the attention of their target audiences (Uzunoglu and Kip 2014). Instead of recommending the product or the brand in a straightforward way, influencers should integrate the product or the brand product into their personal stories (Casalo et al. 2018). In addition, images also should be attractive and high quality in order for the influencers to be worth following (Djafarova and Rushworth 2017). Besides, the quality and variety of the writing is also as important as stories and images (Uzunoglu and Kip 2014).

Information credibility

Consumers generally feel distrust against the information provided on social media. In order for the information to be evaluated as credible, the first step is to ensure the credibility of the source. The information credibility is directly linked to source credibility since people tend to rely more on the information which comes from a credible

ayse bengi ozcelik and eser levi

source (Xiao et al. 2018). In addition to source credibility, the source's expertise, trustworthiness, and homophily are other dimensions that affect information credibility. Besides, as mentioned above, information is perceived as more credible if it is delivered by a peer, not a source authorized by companies (Veirman et al. 2017).

What if we find the right influencer?

The world of the audiences has been converted into one in which people are looking for some influencer suggestions on purpose, from a world of zapping the advertisements on TV or ad blocking on websites. Thus, marketers expect influencers to build brand reach and attract attention through their followers (Chae 2018; Childers et al. 2018). Other effective consequences of finding the right influencer include increased interaction, loyalty, and sharing online which can be classified as: engagement, attitude, purchase intention.

Engagement with the brand/product

Engagement is commonly defined as the consumer behavior beyond purchase (e.g. Bowden et al. 2015; Vivek et al. 2012; van Doorn et al. 2010). Customer brand engagement is "the level of a customer's motivational, brand-related, and context-dependent state of mind characterized by specific levels of cognitive, emotional, and behavioral activity in brand interactions" (Hollebeek 2011, p. 6). Having a state-of-mind, an engaged customer may not purchase or even plan to purchase (Vivek et al. 2012). Hence, the main aim of firms is to create a voluntary bond between the customer and the brand by using some authentic tools such as influencers.

When evaluating influencer marketing, a sector representative indicates that it is based on a unique content which can touch the brain and heart of the consumer and create a relationship with the influencer (Mert 2018). In this sense, social media influencers help brands to build a direct and organic connection with the consumers (Glucksman 2017).

This connection may manifest in different ways, such as interaction. Influencer marketing is mainly based on having a community including people with similar tastes. Hence, when people see the brand on a powerful influencer, they interact with the account and recommend it to friends. For instance, if an influencer mother uses a new bottle for her baby, follower mothers share it with other mothers and build a trusted relationship with the brand of that bottle. Various thoughts could occur in the consumer's mind: "The influencer uses it; therefore, I can trust and use this brand." Or: "Even the influencer recommends it, this is the best and I should suggest it to my friends." This is not only interaction but also a recommendation of the brand. Although the influencer marketing itself is a form of eWOM activity, WOM of that eWOM may be made by the followers. Resharing the post of the account is the main recommendation method. While resharing the content, the engaged consumer does not expect a financial or social outcome. So, it is an expected result of influencer marketing.

Brand attitude

After the advent of ad-blocking technology, consumers are able to skip ads online making it harder for brands to reach customers (Veirman et al. 2017). Since consumers' attitudes toward the brand and the product is often shaped by the advertisements (Jahnson-Boyd 2010), influencers' messages on social media have become the main content which is expected to be effective for brand attitude. The brands aim to create brand recognition by producing social media content and promoting the brands via social media influencers (Glucksman 2017). Engagement on social platforms ensures stronger relationships with the advertising brands are built (Vinarean 2017; Hudson et al. 2015).

Brand attitude is a critical criterion because it directly affects the purchase intention of consumers (Hausman and Siekpe 2009). People who are exposed to content by an influencer create an attitude toward that brand. If the influencer is perceived as authentic, persuasive, credible, trustworthy, powerful, and expert in their area, the consumer forms a positive brand attitude and this attitude may lead to a future buying intention.

Buying intention

Influencer marketing, as an eWOM technique, is strongly related to buying intention through trust (Djafarova and Rushworth 2017). The potential buyers can go into action after they see the influencer's message about the brand, since the influencers are the targets of consumers to look at and listen to (Woods 2016). Endorsement of the products by someone who is not a celebrity creates a more believable situation because of celebrities' bad reputation for abusing their fame for commercial motivations (Djafarova and Rushworth 2017). Studies show that lower-scale celebrities are perceived as more influential as the products or services they use in their messages are perceived as more affordable (Djafarova and Rushworth 2017). Influencers, in this sense, may be more effective on the purchase decisions of consumers than celebrities. Accordingly, effective influencers are expected to pursue their credibility, trustworthiness, and persuasiveness in their network and to have the ability to use their power to influence their followers with recommendations, brand and purchase decisions (Liu 2015). A right influencer choice can trigger the consumers' buying intention.

Summary

- Influencer marketing can be a priceless technique that utilizes the virtues of social media and is perfectly suited for brands to create sincere connections with consumers.
- Influencers have the power to make the information they convey more valuable and matchups between customers and influencer can be made along with the influencer marketing practices that are beneficial to brands.
- Marketing professionals need to be more attentive when choosing influencers to represent brands

ayse bengi ozcelik and eser levi

- Influencers should convey their messages in an enthusiastic way as it is necessary for them to act as real supporters of the brands they endorse.
- The content needs to be original and unique in order to make the influencer stand out from the crowd.
- Influencers should offer distinctive content in order to gain a competitive advantage in terms of both themselves as brands and the brands they endorse.

Case study: What if there is a self-created influencer? #hihieved

In Turkey, new moms on Instagram, so-called insta-moms, have an increasing popularity with their mom- and child-related content. They mainly share their daughters and sons in order to attract followers to their story and give information about some products. The process of influencer–brand partnership works as follows: brands reach the influencer agency, the agency gets into contact with the influencers in the portfolio, gives the text and content to them, and the influencer shares the post. Sometimes brands may directly reach the influencer. Since the content is prespecified and shared by plenty of influencers, the believability and authenticity are questioned by the followers.

In such a growing popularity of influencer marketing, some accounts are dissociated from others. "@hihieved[1]" is one of them. Hande Birsay, a former media specialist worked for corporations, and started to share her own pregnancy experiences on Instagram as @hiheved with a motivation and need to not feel alone:

> During and after my pregnancy, I experienced a lot of strange things that no one had ever told me before. I thought that I cannot be alone getting through all of those. I had to share them with other people. Then I started to use Instagram and realized that I am not alone.

Her authentic and socially sensitive posts are discovered from the followers organically. After her first post where she ironically mentions paying attention to her beauty during pregnancy with a photo of herself eating dessert recklessly, the account gets attention. Her style of mocking herself arises from a feeling of intimacy.

Her key point is not to share any products or brands that she does not use. Indeed, most posts are about the books she read, mainly about child-care. Those book posts get the followers' attention so much that the sales of certain books show an increasing performance after she has posted about them online. Publishers became aware of this and they started to send her some books. Hande read the books and if she believed in the book, she shared details online. Hence, a natural influencer–brand relationship was built between hihieved and publisher brands.

In the last three years, @hihieved formed just three sponsored partnerships with brands, which were medical products which she already used for her son. This included social responsibility partnerships such as donating toys to children suffering from cancer. She does not work with an agency because she thinks that would not be sincere. Her aim is to share unique content about a brand because she does not want to lose her credibility. She has created her own influencer world and if a brand reaches her with a perfect fit with the product/brand or the target consumer, she is in the game.

Hihieved is now a self-created well-read influencer thanks to her non-commercial oriented, unique, creative, and original content. What publishers do wisely is to find her and use her as an influencer for their marketing activities. Similar matches between brands and influencers can be made. Foremost, brands should find the perfect fit between their products, their brand identities, target audiences with the influencer who is authentic, trustworthy, and credible with authentic, original, unique, and creative posts. It is obvious that agency-based influencers are going to lose their power in the near future unless they do not recreate themselves again.

Questions

1. Is it possible to create a new influencer from an off-topic field?
2. What are the critical factors for determining the right influencer?
3. How can brands manage the relationship with agencies and influencers wisely?
4. How should brands plan future marketing activities in terms of influencer marketing?

Note

1 "Hihi eved" addresses an ironic usage of "uh-huh yes."

References

Abidin, C., 2015. Communicative intimacies: Influencers and perceived interconnectedness. Retrieved from: http://adanewmedia.org/2015/11/issue8-abidin/

Abidin, C., 2016. Visibility labour: Engaging with influencers' fashion brands and #OOTD advertorial campaigns on Instagram. *Media International Australia*, 161(1), 86–100.

Alvarez, E., 2017. YouTube stars are blurring the lines between content and ads. *Engadget*. Retrieved from www.engadget.com/2017/07/25/youtube-influencers-sponsored-videos/

Araujo, T., Neijens, P., and Vliegenthart, R., 2017. Getting the word out on Twitter: The role of influentials, information brokers and strong ties in building word-of-mouth for brands. *International Journal of Advertising*, 36(3), 496–503.

Audrezet, A., de Kerviler, G., and Moulard, J.G., 2017. Authenticity under threat: When social media influencers need to go beyond self-presentation. *Journal of Business Research*. Retrieved from: *https://doi.org/10.1016/j.jbusres.2018.07.008*

Bladow, L.E., 2018. Worth the click: why greater ftc enforcement is needed to curtail deceptive practices in influencer marketing. *William & Mary Law Review*, 59(3), 1124–1163.

Bowden, J.L.H., Gabbott, M., and Naumann, K., 2015. Service relationships and the customer disengagement–engagement conundrum. *Journal of Marketing Management*, 31(7–8), 774–806.

Braunsberger, K., 1996. The effects of source and product characteristics on persuasion (Doctoral dissertation). University of Texas at Arlington. Retrieved from http://dspace.nelson.usf.edu:8080/xmlui/handle/10806/6778

ayse bengi ozcelik and eser levi

Brown, D. and Hayes, N., 2016. *Influencer Marketing: Who really influences your customers?* London: Routledge, Taylor & Francis Group.

Casalo, L.V., Flavian, C., and Ibanez-Sanchez, S., 2018. Influencers on Instagram: Antecedents and consequences of opinion leadership. *Journal of Business Research.* Retrieved from *https://doi.org/10.1016/j.jbusres.2018.07.005*

Chae, J., 2018. Explaining Females' Envy Toward Social Media Influencers. *Media Psychology*, 21(2), 246–262.

Cheung, C.M., Sia, C., and Kuan, K.K.Y., 2012. Is this review believable? A study of factors affecting the credibility of online consumer reviews from an ELM perspective. *Journal of the Association for Information Systems*, 13(8), 618–635.

Childers, C.C., Lemon, L.L., and Hoy, M.G., 2018. #Sponsored #Ad: Agency Perspective on Influencer Marketing Campaigns. *Journal of Current Issues & Research in Advertising*, 40(3), 258–274.

Costello, J. and Urbanska, K. (2020) "Hope this is not sponsored" – Is an Influencers credibility impacted when using sponsored versus non-sponsored content? Ch. 10 in *Influencer Marketing and Relations: Building Brand Communities and Engagement.* Ed. Yesiloglu, S. and Costello, J. London: Routledge.

Digital Marketing Institute, 2019. 20 Influencer Marketing Strategies that will Surprise You. Retrieved from: https://digitalmarketinginstitute.com/blog/20-influencer-marketing-statistics-that-will-surprise-you

Dinesh, D., 2017. Why micro-influencers are a social media marketing imperative for 2017. *Industry Insights*, 3, 14–15.

Djafarova, E. and Rushworth, C., 2017. Exploring the credibility of online celebrities' Instagram profiles in influencing the purchase decisions of young female users. *Computers in Human Behavior*, 68, 1–7.

Droesch, B., 2019. Influencers More Likely to Inspire Gen Zer and Millennial Purchases. *eMarketer.* Retrieved from: www.emarketer.com/content/influencers-more-likely-to-inspire-gen-zer-and-millennial-purchases?ecid=NL1014

Evans, N.J., Phua, J., Lim, J., and Jun, H., 2017. Disclosing Instagram Influencer Advertising: The Effects of Disclosure Language on Advertising Recognition, Attitudes, and Behavioral Intent. *Journal of Interactive Advertising*, 17(2), 138–149.

Festinger, L., 1954. A Theory of Social Comparison Processes. *Human Relations*, 7(2), 117–140.

Fidelman, M., 2017. Here's how to crush it with YouTube influencers. *Entrepreneur.* Retrieved from www.entrepreneur.com/article/293257

Freberg, K., Graham, K., McGaughey, K., and Freberg, L.A., 2011. Who are the social media influencers? A study of public perceptions of personality. *Public Relations Review*, 3, 90–92.

Friestad, M. and Wright, P., 1994. The Persuasion Knowledge Model: How People Cope with Persuasion Attempts. *Journal of Consumer Research*, 21(1), 1–31.

Gass, R.H. and Seiter, J.S., 2011. Credibility. In K. Bowers, J. Zalesky, and M. Lentz (Eds.), *Persuasion: Social influence and compliance gaining* (4th ed., pp. 72–90). New York, NY: Pearson.

Glucksman, M., 2017. The Rise of Social Media Influencer Marketing on Lifestyle Branding: A Case Study of Lucie Fink. *Elon Journal of Undergraduate Research in Communications*, 8(2), 77–87.

Goffman, E. 1959 *The Presentation of Self in Everyday Life*. Garden City, N.Y.: Doubleday.

Grave, J.F., 2017. A New Type of Endorser? Investigating the Differences in Perception Between Social Media Influencers and Traditional Celebrities. AMA Summer Proceedings.

Hausman, A.V., and Siekpe, J.S., 2009. The effect of web interface features on consumer online purchase intentions. *Journal of Business Research*, 62(1), 5–13.

Hearn, A. and Schoenhoff, S., 2016. From Celebrity to Influencer: Tracing the Diffusion of Celebrity Value across the Data Stream. In P.D. Marshall and S. Redmond (Eds.), *A Companion to Celebrity* (pp. 194–211). UK: John Wiley & Sons, Inc.

Hollebeek, L.D., 2011. Demystifying customer brand engagement: Exploring the loyalty nexus. *Journal of Marketing Management*, 27(7–8), 785–807.

Hudson, S., Huang, L., Roth, M.S., and Madden, T.J., 2016. The influence of social media interactions on consumer–brand relationships: a three-country study of brand perceptions and marketing behaviors. *International Journal of Research in Marketing*, 33, 27–41.

Influencer Marketing Hub, 2019. The State of Influencer Marketing 2019: Benchmark Report, Retrieved from: https://influencermarketinghub.com/influencer-marketing-2019-benchmark-report/

Jannson-Boyd, C.V., 2010. *Consumer Psychology*. Glasgow: McGraw Hill.

Katz, E. and Lazarsfeld, P.F., 1955. *Personal Influence: The part played by people in the flow of mass communications*. New York, NY, US: Free Press.

Keller, E. and Berry. J., 2003. *The Influentials: One American in ten tells the other nine how to vote, where to eat, and what to buy*. New York, NY: The Free Press.

Kirkpatrick, D., 2016. Influencer Marketing Spurs 11 times the ROI over Traditional Tactics: Study. Marketing Dive. *Industry Dive*, Retrieved from: www.marketingdive.com/news/influencer-marketing-spurs-11-times-the-roi-overtraditional-tactics-study/416911/

Kozinets, R., de Valck, K., Wojnicki, A.C., and Wilner, S.J.S., 2010. Networked Narratives: Understanding Word-of-Mouth Marketing in Online Communities. *Journal of Marketing*, 74(2), 71–89.

Langner, S., Hennings, N., and Wiedmann, K.P., 2013. Social persuasion: targeting social identities through social influencers. *Journal of Consumer Marketing*, 30(1), 31–49.

Liu, S., Jiang, C., Lin, Z., Ding, Y., Duan, R., and Xu, Z., 2015. Identifying effective influencers based on trust for electronic word-of-mouth marketing: A domain-aware approach. *Information Sciences*, 306, 34–52.

Luo, X.R., Zhang, W., Burd, S., and Seazzu, A., 2013. Investigating phishing victimization with the heuristic–systematic model: A theoretical framework and an exploration. *Computers & Security*, 38, 28–38.

Lyons, B., and Henderson, K., 2005. Opinion leadership in a computer-mediated environment. *Journal of Consumer Behaviour*, 4(5), 319–329.

McCroskey, J.C., Richmond, V.P., and Daly, J.A., 1975. The development of a measure of perceived homophily in interpersonal communication. *Human Communication Research*, 1(4), 323–332.

Mert, Y.L., 2018. Influencer marketing application in the scope of digital marketing. *Gumushane University e-Journal of Faculty of Communication*, 6(2), 1299–1328.

Momtaz, N.J., Aghaie, A., and Alizadeh, S., 2011. Identifying opinion leaders for marketing by analyzing online social networks. *International Journal of Virtual Communities and Social Networking*, 3(1), 43–59.

Mudambi, S.M. and Schuff, D. (2010). What makes a helpful review? A study of customer reviews on Amazon.com. *MIS Quarterly*, 34(1), 185–200.

Nisbet, M.C. and Kotcher, J.E., 2009. A two-step flow of influence?: Opinion-leader campaigns on climate change. *Science Communication*, 30(3), 328–354.

Ohanian, R., 1991. The impact of celebrity spokespersons' perceived image on consumers' intention to purchase. *Journal of Advertising Research*, 31(1), 46–54.

O'Keefe, D.J., 1990. *Persuasion: Theory and practice*. Newbury Park, CA: Sage.

Pophal, L., 2016. Influencer Marketing: Turning taste makers into your best salespeople. *Econtent*, September/October, 19–22.

ayse bengi ozcelik and eser levi

PwC (2018). Global Consumer Insights Survey. Available from: www.pwc.com/gx/en/consumer-markets/consumer-insights-survey/2019/report.pdf

Riboldazzi, S. and Capriello, A., 2020. Identifying and selecting the right influencers in the digital era. Ch. 3 in *Influencer Marketing and Relations: Building Brand Communities and Engagement*. Ed. Yesiloglu, S. and Costello, J. Routledge: London.

Shalev, E. and Morwitz, V.G., 2012. Influence via Comparison-Driven Self- Evaluation and Restoration: The Case of the Low-Status Influencer. *Journal of Consumer Research*, 38(5), 964–980.

Uzunoglu, E. and Kip S.M., 2014. Brand communication through digital influencers: Leveraging blogger engagement. *International Journal of Information Management*, 34, 592–602.

van Doorn, J., Lemon, K.N., Mittal, V., Nass, S., Pick, D., Pirner, P., and Verhoef, P.C., 2010. Customer Engagement Behavior: Theoretical Foundations and Research Directions. *Journal of Service Research*, 13(3), 253–266.

Veirman, M.D., Cauberghe, V., and Hudders, L., 2017. Marketing through Instagram influencers: the impact of number of followers and product divergence on brand attitude. *International Journal of Advertising*, 36(5), 798–828.

Vinarean, S., 2017. Importance of Strategic Social Media Marketing. *Expert Journal of Marketing*, 5(1), 28–35.

Vivek, S.D., Beatty, S.E., and Morgan, R.M., 2012. Customer Engagement: Exploring Customer Relationships Beyond Purchase. *Journal of Marketing Theory and Practice*, 20(2), 127–145.

Wathen, C.D. and Burkell, J., 2002. Believe it or not: Factors influencing credibility on the Web. *Journal of the American Society for Information Science and Technology*, 53(2), 134–144.

Watts, D.J. and Dodds, P.S., 2007. Influentials, networks, and public opinion formation. *Journal of Consumer Research*, 34(4), 441–458.

Weiss, R., 2014. Influencer Marketing How word-of-mouth marketing can strengthen your organization's brand. *Marketing Health Services*. 34(1), 16–17.

Woods, S., 2016. #Sponsored: The Emergence of Influencer Marketing. University of Tennessee Honors Thesis Projects. https://trace.tennessee.edu/utk_chanhonoproj/1976

Xiao, M. Wang, R., and Chan-Olmsted, S., 2018. Factors affecting YouTube influencer marketing credibility: a heuristic-systematic model. *Journal of Media Business Studies*, 15(3), 188–213.

Zhang, Y., Moe, W.M., and Schweidel, D.A., 2017. Modeling the role of message content and influencers in social media rebroadcasting. *International Journal of Research in Marketing*, 34, 100–119.

Zietek, N., 2016. The characteristics and components of fashion influencer marketing. The Swedish School of Textiles. Available from: www.semanticscholar.org/paper/Influencer-Marketing-%3A-the-characteristics-and-of-Zietek/c863c3aee3c3edc50d92358444da8f8c478dd9ee

Post-millennials and their motivation to engage with influencers' brand-related content on Instagram

Sevil Yesiloglu and Simrit Gill

Learning outcomes

On completing this chapter, you should be able to:

- critically discuss influencer marketing on Instagram;
- discuss different type of engagement;
- understand the motivational framework within the influencer marketing field; and
- discuss how motivations can shape different type of engagement with influencers and their brand-related activities on Instagram.

The emergence of influencer marketing

With the rise of social media, the phenomenon of word-of-mouth (WOM) appeared; society was able to share opinions and reviews mapping down WOM as a key marketing tactic, and influencer marketing revolutionized (Brown and Hayes 2008).

The aim of influencer marketing is to transform influencers into brand advocates who then share their brand or product-related views to build loyal customers through relationships (Messiaen 2017; Sudha and Sheena 2017). For brands and marketers, the shift has steered from celebrity endorsements, as influencers are seen to be more credible and trustworthy than celebrities, particularly as consumers are able to relate to these influencers through their personality (Talaverna 2015; De Veirman et al. 2017; Leban and Voyer 2020). The exposure of the staged advertisements has moved consumers to want an authentic and personal way to engage (Gilmore and Pine 2007), thus causing a power shift away from organizations and to consumers (O'Brien 2011).

Yesiloglu (2020) emphasizes the difference between paid and unpaid marketing activities of influencers further and divides influencer marketing into earned influencer marketing – influencers producing user-generated content – and paid influencer marketing, where influencers produce firm-generated content. Whilst firm-generated content refers to being sent products or receiving a commission of sales, or the brand may host an event that is documented, user-generated content relates to when the influencer purchases or is sent free samples or products and does not receive any remuneration (Messiaen 2017). The distinction between the two has become a legal area of contention. As a result, the Advertising Standards Association (ASA) has recently regulated influencer marketing content which needs to be identifiable by consumers for being paid or not (Bosher 2020). The use of "#ad" or "#sponsored" is used to highlight paid content to consumers, allowing them to have the choice of whether to engage with the post (Advertising Practice 2017).

Influencers' brand-related content on Instagram follows both firm and user-generated content practices and therefore we investigate both post types to maintain a rounded understanding of the motivations for engaging. By encompassing both types of posts, a comparison could be made between the ways in which consumers engage depending on its type on Instagram.

The rise of Instagram

Instagram was launched in 2010, won the iPhone app of the year in 2011, and now hosts 500 million daily active users (Instagram 2020). A survey by influencer platform Zine (2017) found that in a worldwide sample of social influencers, nearly 80 percent of respondents considered Instagram to be their primary platform to collaborate with brands, due to the simultaneous feedback when seeking reviews through comments and likes. Consumers can view influencers' brand-related posts through pictures, videos, and life stories and engage with them through liking, commenting, or sharing posts (Sheldon and Bryant 2016). Instagram is undisputedly one of the most important social media channels currently around (Hughes 2017). Out of 2,500 micro-influencers, 60 percent thought Instagram was the best overall platform for engagement, with Facebook only gaining 18 percent (Brenner 2017).

With social media sites becoming a honey pot for consumers to gain information about brands whilst simultaneously sharing their own reviews and experiences (Dahl 2018), this phenomenon has led to the rise of the modern-day "social media influencer" – third-party endorsers that can help shape consumers' purchase decisions through blogs, tweets, pictures, and other social media uses (Freberg et al. 2011). The success of these influencers can be determined by the intimate relationships they have established between themselves and their followers (Abidin and Thompson 2012), as well as their creative ways of using the features on social media channels.

To appreciate how social media changes the way we communicate, influencers can now reach a mass audience and their impact should not be underestimated. Zoella – dubbed the "Queen of the Web" – can now reach out to her 9.5 million followers at just the touch of a button (Instagram 2020). From a brand's perspective, influencers have already built their business, creating their own content often aligning with the vision of the brands they partner with and an established audience (Alcántara 2018). As discussed by Yesiloglu (2020), influencers truly serve as a crucial connection between a brand and consumers through using eWOM strategy. The ideal situation allows for brands to be able to collaborate with an established creator, whilst influencers are being paid for doing what they love and present the idea of living their "best life" (Alcántara 2018; Rosenthal and Arcuri 2020). Studies have shown that the brand-related content in an influencers' post is found to be 12.85 times greater in value than traditional media tools (Dilenschneider 2013), with 74 percent of consumers advising that they use social media sites before they decide whether to purchase a product or service (Barker 2018).

Influencer marketing and engagement on social media

Influencers aim to drive a brand message to a niche, targeted segment by publishing content on the latest promotions and products (Markethub 2016). The content they produce can be formed in various ways, including reviews, competitions, giveaways, casual information, or an insight into invitations to key events. In contrast to celebrity endorsements, where the celebrity does not partake in the creation of content, influencers can be guided by the brand but ultimately create the media themselves, enforcing the idea that influencers are transmitting their own message and not the brand's (Geppert 2016; Leban and Voyer), which helps them to engage with consumers and build a strong relationship in social media.

To build strong relationships with their followers, influencers recognize motivating followers to engage is more powerful than raising simple awareness (Yesiloglu 2017). Vargo and Lusch (2008) outlined the importance of engagement that creates relationships and the behavior of consumers as an outcome of interactive or co-creative experiences. Vivek et al. (2012) discovered motivational drivers can lead to engagement beyond transactions, resulting in loyalty, affective commitment, and WOM. This supports Keller and Berry's (2003) debate about how influencers have a dual role within the market, acting as both a consumer and marketer for their audiences. Considering the fundamental role of engagement in influencer marketing, it is important to understand different engagement types of individuals with influencers' brand-related content on social media.

Usage typologies can provide guidance to gain an understanding of engagement on social media platforms (Shao 2009), especially if brands investigate consumer to consumer brand-related content (Muntinga et al. 2011). For example, Shao et al. (2009) proposed a continuum, starting with consuming (for information or entertainment), participation (social interactions or community development), and finally produ-cing (for self-expression or self-actualization) to understand user-generated content online. Muntinga et al. (2011) advanced these concepts further by creating three usage typologies: consuming; contributing (to), and creating brand-related content on specific social media platforms.

To understand the passive engagement of consumers in online communities (e.g. Hagel and Armstrong 1996; Dholakia et al. 2004) and brand-related interaction on social media (Muntinga et al. 2011), scholars focused on this engagement type through looking at different activities as viewing, watching, and reading content. Consuming brand-related content represents the minimum level of activeness on social media (Muntinga et al. 2011) and consumers' passive participation without contributing any content on social media. Although studies by McQuail (2010) are based on user gratification theory, it shows that consumption of brand-related con-tent is for information seeking and enjoyment is similar to findings by Muntinga et al. (2011). This dimension represents the brand-related engagement between individuals and individuals to content (Shao 2009).

Furthermore, the "contributing" dimension which refers to interacting with posts about brands by making contributions through user to user and user to content interactions has been increasingly explored by practitioners and academics in order to investigate online consumer reviews (Ho-Dac et al. 2013); eWOM (Dellarocas et al. 2007), liking brand pages on Facebook (Phua and Ahn 2016) and sharing brand-related content on social media (Brettel et al. 2015; Craig et al. 2015). De Vries et al. (2012) pointed out that consumers' contribution activities including comments or likes can increase or decrease the attractiveness of brand posts if found to be negative.

Idea fairy: Usage typologies

Considering your own behavior on social media, do you spend more time consuming or con-tributing? Do you tend to favor one platform over another? Or are you motivated to different action due to the platform?

Self-determination theory: understanding motivations

Self-determination theory (SDT) (Deci and Ryan 1985) has often been observed in relation to understanding the intentions (e.g. Dholakia 2004; Zhang et al. 2010; Hoffman and Novak 2012) and human motivational behavior and dynamics (Lin and Huang 2013). SDT divides motivation types into extrinsic and intrinsic motiv-ations (Deci and Ryan 2000). Whilst intrinsic motivations are driven by enjoyment or helping others, extrinsic motivations are driven by either external pressure or reward (Razmerita et al. 2016). Consumers who are intrinsically motivated are more likely to engage with the influencer's brand-related posts on Instagram, to improve their skill set as well as their appearance, lifestyle inspiration they received by the engage-ment of the influencer's posts. On the other hand, extrinsic motivations pertain to the performance driven by outcomes, including reward or avoidance from pressure or punishment (Deci and Ryan 2006). Extrinsic motivation mainly focuses on goal-driven activities where consumers expect rewards (e.g. loyalty program, coupon, discount, etc.). Previous studies postulate that extrinsically driven consumers are likely to have a detrimental impact on social media marketing (Sook Kwon et al. 2014). Similarly, Kim and Drumwright (2016) illustrate empirically that a consumer who is extrinsically driven tends to be the primary target audience for social-relational marketing programs and community building on social media.

Thus it can be concluded that those who are extrinsically motivated relate to external reward and pressure and seek praise from others, whereas those that are intrinsically motivated can relate to positive effects and internal motivations such as enjoyment (Yesiloglu 2017). To understand consumers' engagement with influencers' brand-related posts, it is therefore useful to examine motivations which trigger two types of engagement: consuming and contributing.

Idea fairy: Motivations

Considering your own behavior on social media, which motivation factor gives you intrinsic pleasure? Do any of the motivations provide extrinsic motivation for you? Where can you see your motivations coming into conflict?

Empirical study

Whilst scholars have focused on identifying right influencers (Özçelik and Levi 2020), the authenticity of influencers' popularity (De Veirman et al. 2017), behavioral engagement with influencers (Yesiloglu and Waśkiw 2020), still little is known about what motivates consumers to engage with influencers which help influencers to understand how they can grow their community in the new digital world.

To see how self-determination theory can be applied to understand the motivations behind these specific engagement types, we carried out a qualitative study using semi-structured interviews with 14 participants from the age of 21–23. This strategy was implemented as the study required exploration of feelings in human behavior (David and Sutton 2009) and a story from participants (Arksey and Knight 1999).

The interview guide was formed using key topic areas such as motivations behind the consumption of influencers' brand-related content on Instagram including open-ended questions on the review of influencers' brand-related posts on Instagram as well as frequency and reasoning behind this. The interview guide then continued the motivations to contribute to influencers' brand-related content on Instagram in the form of likes, comments and shares, and the possible motivations behind this. The questions were designed to be open-ended to allow for flexibility within the conversation and allow new areas to be explored and possible additions to theory to be made (Creswell and Clark 2017). The interviews were transcribed verbatim and coded corresponding to motivations for engagement identified in literature, e.g. enjoyment or information seeking. If a statement did not fit within pre-existing motivations, this was classed as a new motivation and explored further.

sevil yesiloglu and simrit gill

Motivations of consuming influencers' brand-related content

In this study, we first identify the motivations of consumers when they consume (e.g. reading, viewing, watching) influencers' brand-related posts on Instagram. The data suggested post-millennials consume influencers' brand-related posts due to information seeking. Furthermore, it was found that the fear of missing out and using social media as a stimulation to relieve boredom was present, differentiating from findings of previous studies exploring the motivations behind engaging with brand-related content (Muntinga et al. 2011; Yesiloglu 2017).

Fear of Missing Out (FOMO)

FOMO is defined as "a pervasive apprehension that others might be having rewarding experiences from which one is absent and a desire to stay continually connected with what others are doing" (Przybylski et al. 2013, p. 1841). FOMO is not an entirely new concept and its application to social media increases (Abel et al. 2016). FOMO studies have shown it can be a mediator linking psychological needs to social media engagement and indicators of wellbeing (Oberst et al. 2017). Fear of Missing Out is found as a factor extending the amount of time people spend using social media (Hunt et al. 2018), and several individual factors including levels of need satisfaction and general mood (Przybylski et al. 2013). In line with self-determination theory (Deci and Ryan 2000), the deficit in psychological needs may increase the need to keep up to date and use social media as an effective self-regulation tool to satisfy psychological needs (Przybylski et al. 2013; Beyens et al. 2016). Hence, it can be expected that FOMO can be linked to consumers' engagement with influencers' brand-related posts on social media.

The need to keep up to date and the use of social media can act as self-regulation to satisfy psychological needs (Beyens et al. 2016). As one of the participants outlined that when not following influencer Kylie Jenner:

> *I hadn't seen it... went straight onto Instagram and followed her and it was the fear of missing out, and you get FOMO when there is stuff going on and you aren't aware of it... I don't think it is why I consume but it definitely takes a part in it ... you know what is going on, you're in the loop, and when you're out of the loop you're missing out on everything, I unfollowed Chris Brown because he posted so much... and now I am scared because I feel like I'm missing out.*

FOMO describes the motive for the need to stay continually connected with others to hinder the emotional feeling of being left out (Przyblyski et al. 2013). Participant 10 also identified with FOMO by revealing that if she unfollowed these influencers, she would feel "*a little bit left out... I would be falling behind.*" Although the motivation of FOMO has not been overtly explored within the realms of engagement with brand-related content, this research has shown it to be one of the leading motives to engage, which also increases the individuals' wellbeing through having a discussion with their peers (Oberst et al. 2017).

Information seeking

This motivation has been explored in the literature in four categories: pre-purchase, surveillance (Courtois et al. 2009), knowledge, and inspiration (Muntinga et al. 2011). Knowledge is the process of consumers viewing influencers' brand-related posts to receive information, mainly relevant to their pre-purchase decisions (Muntinga et al. 2011). The act of being inspired comes from consuming influencers' brand-related posts due to the need to feel inspired and gain new ideas (Muntinga et al. 2011).

Information seeking has been identified through a scope of research as being a key motivator in engagement with online activities (Muntinga et al. 2011; Whiting and Williams 2013; Yesiloglu 2017). Inspiration and surveillance were identified as the core motivations within information seeking (Muntinga et al. 2011) through post-millennials viewing influencers as role models, whilst keeping up with their latest trends and news. As there was a lack of enjoyment, content must have a purpose to increase engagement.

Inspiration

Information seeking is a core motivation for people to consume brand-related content, and this was found with all participants (Muntinga et al. 2011). One participant referred to inspiration:

> you want reviews and tutorials, recommendations and very much gain information... influencers tend to spark an interest.

Another participant stated:

> Instagram is all about living your best life and the influencer culture aligns with this.

Yet, another participant suggested that her sole reason to consume influencers' brand-related posts was:

> for inspiration and for me to keep on top of all the latest trends... it is for information and inspiration.

Surveillance

Information seeking is often found to be a key motivation for social media usage (Whiting and Williams 2013) as stemmed from Papacharissi and Rubin (2000), who contend that staying up to date on one's social environment through surveillance is imperative. In this study, we identified that users follow and consume influencers' brand-related content as they wish to observe and stay up to date on influencers and their content. As one of the participants outlined:

> Instagram is a good way to find out new products, it reveals new things, I don't have to go into a shop every day. The main reason is to get information, I think it's very convenient.

sevil yesiloglu and simrit gill

We found that this aspect of information seeking motivation is also a way to eliminate any opportunity of the fear that one could be missing out by their outdated knowledge in their social circle (Przyblyski et al. 2013).

Pre-purchase

Studies propose pre-purchase as being a key motivator for consumption (Muntinga et al. 2011; Yesiloglu 2017). However, one Participant outlined that influencers' brand-related posts make him *"more inclined to research but I would go on the site itself,"* whilst another Participant supported this, stating *"I do search for reviews but Instagram isn't where I would go for that."*

This shows individuals are online to seek information (Hennig-Thurau et al. 2004) but that Instagram would not be the participants' platform of choice. However, views were not unanimous. One participant outlined a motive for seeking information from these posts is because *"the information you pick up is credible"* and was supported by another Participant who said *"smaller influencers are more likely to do it for free so it is more honest and genuine."*

Enjoyment

Identification moves towards the idea of self-determination due to the acceptance of regulation on one's own accord (Deci and Ryan 2000). Intrinsically motivating activities should be enjoyable because of the psychological needs it fills of being competent and autonomous. Gretzel and Yoo (2008) outline that in the context of social media, enjoyment refers to the entertainment users' experience when engaging with brand-related content. Gretzel and Yoo (2008) found that enjoyment was one of the motivations that led to consumers engaging with electronic word of mouth, a proposed outcome of engagement (Vivek et al. 2012), leading a brand community sharing knowledge and experiences (Hung and Li 2007).

Enjoyment has also been investigated to investigate the perceived hedonic value of a post created by influencers on social media (Hughes et al. 2019). Research shows the hedonic value of a post captures attention as well as impacts attitudes and WOM (Berger and Schwartz 2011). Relatedly, Hughes et al. (2019) extended the findings of Berger and Milkman's (2012) study and pointed that a hedonic value of a post which influences the enjoyment, emotions, and an entertainment consumer experience, have a significant impact on the consumer to consume (e.g. read) blogs on Facebook.

Similarly, we investigate whether the motivation for enjoyment is the entertainment (Muntinga et al. 2011) that individuals gain from consuming influencers' brand-related content on Instagram. Consequently, we identified the motivation for enjoyment is a significant impact on consuming influencers' brand-related posts on Instagram. As one participant commented, the enjoyment comes:

> from the delivery and how it is presented, if they incorporate their personality into the brand.

Another participant mentioned: *"if it is aesthetically pleasing, I try to emulate it for my Instagram,"* also showing elements of inspiration.

Motives for contributing to influencers' brand-related content on Instagram

Remuneration and socialization are identified as key motivations to contributing to posts; however, established motivations such as personal identity and warning others were less apparent. The motivation to support the influencer was identified due to the established relationship that individuals encompass with those that they follow, yet opinions of peers did not pose important.

Remuneration

Extrinsic rewards can occur when a consumer needs remuneration or compensation for their actions (Hars and Ou 2001). In the consumer behavior research field, it has been discussed that consumers could therefore wish to contribute to brand-related content for want of external reward through prizes (Wang and Fesenmaier 2003). Extrinsic motivation could be the purpose for many consumers' engagement with brand-related content (Muntinga et al. 2011), having both a positive and negative impact on information sharing (Lin and Huang 2013; Bock et al. 2005), and can lead to perceived opportunistic behavior having a negative impact on the trustworthiness of the content producer or influencer (Morgan and Hunt 1994).

In this study, we found that consumers' motive for contributing is remuneration, where their online engagement with influencers' brand-related content activities is related to receiving rewards (Wang and Fesenmaier 2003; Muntinga et al. 2011) as five participants outlined that the remuneration is the sole motive to contributing (commenting or sharing) to influencers' brand-related posts. Another participant outlined:

> *commenting...will be more for personal gain... like these competitions.*

One of the participants agreed, stating that the engagement type would simply be commenting and not sharing a post:

> *but I think I only had to tag like friends in their posts, I didn't have to share any-thing, I feel a bit stupid when I get involved in competitions because I'm never going to win... I guess if it is a competition and I genuinely might have a chance... then I potentially would.*

Previous research has shown the external rewards are apparent in motivations behind consumers' online activities (Hennig-Thurau et al. 2004; Muntinga et al. 2011; Yesiloglu 2017), concurring with this research. Nevertheless, post-millennials are becoming increasingly aware of the low probability of winning, and influencers

sevil yesiloglu and simrit gill

should take care in the production of this content and communicate winners of prizes to avoid confusion with hoax posts.

Remuneration, or winning competitions, appeared to be the sole reason for contributing to influencers' brand-related content for most of the participants in this research. Similarly, the motive of commenting or sharing a post was with the hope of receiving money or other rewards; despite the belief of winning being low (Wang and Fesenmaier 2003; Muntinga et al. 2011). Without remuneration, motives to contribute were low as there was nothing to gain or exchange.

Socializing

The motivation to socialize or communicate with others has been explored due to the increase in the use of social media when the opportunity to socialize exists (Wise et al. 2010). Henning-Thurau et al. (2004) argued that consumers tend to be motivated to contribute to eWOM if they see others doing the same and this helps them to make appropriate purchasing decisions. It has been discussed further by Wolny and Mueller (2013) that through contributing to brand-related posts, consumers create a conversation about a product and service which helps them to communicate and socialize with others.

Socializing also appears as a motive to create a sense of belonging where it is suggested that an individual will contribute more to brand-related content if socializing is a key motivation (Shao 2008). If users have an intimate relationship with others, users can meet the need for relatedness (Deci and Ryan 2000). Therefore, to engage with influencers and followers on social media by contributing to influencers' brand-related posts, followers have an opportunity to satisfy their need for socializing as well as relatedness.

Wolny and Mueller (2013) outline the need to talk about a product or service to create conversation, which was apparent with post-millennials' engagement on Instagram. The motivation appeared to at first surround the desire to share information (Muntinga et al. 2011); however the key component of this was to initiate conversations between friends. We also acknowledge that socializing motive and FOMO are closely aligned to maintain a social belonging and the need to stay current amongst social circles when post-millennials engage with influencers' brand-related content. As one of the participants pointed out:

So... if I'm gonna put myself in someone's shoes... I'll tag you, you look at this new color it looks great, this color may look good on you.

This example of helping others was also touched upon with a fellow participant, who mentioned:

I live in a house with 3 other guys that are really big on their streetwear brands ... I'm not massively on the scene myself but if I see something that they would like, I'll 100% tag them.

Positive recognition from the influencer

Personal identity refers to the need for self-assurance and approval from others (Muntinga et al. 2011), however for further clarity not suggested in previous literature, positive recognition from the influencer has been separated into a further motivation, yet still encompasses the need for self-enhancement (Hennig-Thurau et al. 2004). Berger and Schwatz (2011) discussed that individuals engage with self-presentation activities on social media to get positive recognition from others. Therefore, the motives for engaging in need of approval from peers, can differ from the need of approval from the influencer creating the brand-related content; therefore the two motives are being separated for this research and for further clarification in future research.

Included in the motive of self-enhancement (Hennig-Thurau et al. 2004), we found that the need for positive recognition from the influencer is of the key motives for contribution. As one of the participants stated:

> I commented once on something Proudlock posted and he actually came back and replied to me which was quite a good feeling because he was actually taking time to go through it.

In this research, personal identity was omitted from the framework, as post-millennials did not desire approval from others (Muntinga et al. 2011). Instead, positive recognition from influencers appeared more prevalent when engaging with influencers' posts on Instagram.

Helping the influencer

In the existing literature, altruistic motivation has been explored in different terms. For example, Yap et al. (2013) explored this motivation through sharing experiences to support or help the company. When we look at the communication between brands and consumers on online platforms further, Jeong and Jang (2011) also discovered that the need to help the company can be a key motivation in creating brand-related content, where individuals are seeking ways to equalize the exchange between a brand and themselves (Gretzel and Yoo 2008). As current literature has pointed out that altruistic motivation impacts on consumers' brand communication on social media, in the context of this research we found that helping influencers is one of the motives that can have a significant impact on post-millennials to contribute to influencers' content on Instagram. As a participant outlined:

> I think I'm like supporting them in a way by liking what they are sharing... so the point is they are engaging... so yeah it's like supporting them in a way... if I am engaging by tagging other people it is benefiting the person I've tagged but also the influencer that is promoting something.

There is little literature surrounding the importance of the motivation around the helping of the influencer or the brand online; however, this motivation held more prominence than the wide research of helping others. Influencer marketing prides itself on the ability to establish and retain relationships (De Veirman et al. 2017), albeit individuals recognize communication may be one way, the motive to help the influencer through "likes" in particular is imperative in allowing the consumer to feel like they are giving back to the influencer. It therefore becomes a key motivation of post-millennials' engagement with brand-related posts on Instagram, allowing the consumer to contribute to the relationships that influential marketing thrives to establish (De Veirman et al. 2017).

Insights and applicability

The aim of this chapter was to understand the motivations behind post-millennials' engagement with influencers' brand-related content on Instagram. To summarize, the key motivations for engagement can relate to FOMO, socializing, and remuneration. However, there is scope for further research as outlined in this chapter alongside theoretical conclusions and managerial implications. Disparate to previous research asserting prominence of the motive of enjoyment; qualitative research found that post-millennials are consuming influencers' brand-related content as a form of stimulation to relieve the discomfort of boredom and gain a social belonging.

Influencers' brand-related posts should resonate with the consumer, provoking cognitive engagement (Grolnick and Ryan 1989). Posts encompassing information have higher levels of consumption, as post-millennials aim to maintain current knowledge and use Instagram as a source of inspiration, concurring with Muntinga et al. (2011). Dissimilar to previous literature it emerged that post-millennials consume influencers' brand-related content as a form of stimulation to relieve discomfort and boredom (Fishwick 2004), and the long-term taint of this has diminished feelings of pleasure that may once have been gained from consuming these posts (Fishwick 2004).

Using influencers' brand-related content as stimulation can also be because of the need to gain a membership with society (Scitovsky 1992), closely associated with the motive to consume these posts to eradicate any feelings of missing out (Przyblyski et al. 2013). Post-millennials use social media as a self-regulation tool, satisfying their psychological needs by maintaining current knowledge of trends and can socialize with their friends (Beyens et al. 2016). It can be concluded as a primary motive to consume influencers' brand-related content. In order to surpass the motives for consumption as a stimulus or to avoid FOMO, influencers should continue to establish the relationship they have with consumers and emulate a relationship that their audience regains pleasure in consuming and therefore could increase levels of engagement.

Remuneration has been identified as a significant motivation in past research (Wang and Fesenmaier 2003; Muntinga et al. 2011) and coincides with the findings of this chapter. Post-millennials are likely to contribute to an influencers' brand-related post if there is the opportunity to win a prize or reward. "Tagging" friends, or socializing, so they are able to see the post and share relevant information with them is a common motive to contributing to influencers' brand-related posts, correlating to the need to create conversation as an elimination tool for FOMO.

It was also interesting to observe the lack of a need for approval from peers and how the participant's engagement with influencers' brand-related posts was more focused on the positive recognition from influencers. The motive to help the influencer through liking posts or commenting was more prevalent than the need to warn others (Hennig-Thurau 2004; Muntinga et al. 2011; Jeong and Jang 2011). There was limited research surrounding the effect of positive recognition from the influencer, however research showed that it should be considered to increase contribution to posts. Post-millennials were found to not expect communication from the influencer but show feelings of happiness when influencers did respond to comments or return likes. It can be deduced that if engagement appears to be a two-way communication, it strengthens the relationship that influencers create with their consumers and therefore could lead to an increase in engagement on brand-related posts.

The conceptual framework was adapted from various literature surrounding consumer engagement (e.g. Hennig-Thauru 2004; Muntinga et al. 2011; Whiting and Williams 2013; Yesiloglu 2017). Consumption of influencers' brand-related posts derived from the motive of seeking information, as influencers present themselves in a certain light, portraying an "influencer" lifestyle of "living your best life" and acting as a source of inspiration to many. Remuneration (Wang and Fesenmaier 2003; Muntinga et al. 2011) was also a significant motive in contributing to posts due to the want or need to gain rewards; for many participants it was the sole reason for contributing to influencers' brand-related posts. However, it also provides new contributions to this area of research including the motive to reduce FOMO (Przyblyski et al. 2013; Beyens et al. 2016), the act of engaging with influencers' brand-related posts to relieve boredom (Scitovsky 1992; Fishwick 2004), and the desire to help the influencer (Jeong and Jang 2011).

Common motives identified in literature, such as entertainment (Papacharissi and Rubin 2000; Muntinga et al. 2011; Whiting and Williams 2013), were omitted from the framework as it was identified that these posts were consumed due to their use of a stimulus and the pleasure of consuming these products was diminishing, harmonizing the idea of the "Joyless Economy" (Scitovsky 1992) in a social media context. The motive of warning others (Hennig-Thurau 2004; Muntinga et al. 2011) was replaced with the motivation of gaining positive recognition from the influencer; as post-millennials were more inclined to contribute to influencers' brand-related posts as a means of helping them and if recognition was given by the influencer.

Summary

- Post-millennials use social media as a self-regulation tool, satisfying their psychological needs by maintaining current knowledge of trends and have the ability to socialize with their friends and engage with influencers' content in different ways based on the motivations they have.

sevil yesiloglu and simrit gill

- To understand different types of engagement further, we need to look at motivations individuals have behind the engagement. For example, while FOMO, information motives are primary motives for post-millennials to consume influencers' brand-related posts, remuneration, socializing, and helping the influencers are the key motives for consumers when they participate in influencers' brand-related posts on Instagram through liking, tagging, and commenting.
- Social media has offered a tremendous amount of engagement opportunities for both brands and influencers. For example, when brands and influencers look for a higher level of loyalty and engagement, they need to focus on motivations that trigger people to contribute to influencers' branded content. On the other hand, when they aim to raise brand awareness, they need to focus on what motivates consumers to read influencers' brand-related posts on Instagram.

Case study: GOODFOODS's recipe for influencer marketing success

Weronika Waśkiw, Travel PR

Influencer marketing aims at transforming influencers into brand advocates (Messiaen 2017), establishing long-lasting relationships with consumers (De Veirman et al. 2017). In order to refrain from posts being used as stimulation, where consumers are not gaining enjoyment from posts, social media managers and influencers should strive to work on content relevant to the influencers' target audience, complete with information that consumers are able to share with friends, and encourage socialization. Influencers should aim to encourage two-way communication with consumers by liking posts or comments to ensure audience support is valued. Furthermore, if the aim of the brand-related content is to drive contribution through reward, competition winners should clearly be announced to ensure it is not received as a hoax post. Managers should also aim to create a strong brand community, through exclusive pages or posts surrounding the influencer due to the motive of FOMO and there may be an increase of engagement if post-millennials feel they have a social belonging and are part of a larger society.

GOODFOODS is a US-based company that has worked with influencers since 2017; it is an environmentally friendly food brand known for its all-natural guacamole, snack dips, and juices. The niche company needed to find a way to build its online presence, brand awareness, and drive sales of its not-so-well-known products. In 2017, the niche company jumped on the influencer marketing bandwagon and successfully used the power of influencers to boost brand awareness and lift sales. With the help from Linqia, an influencer marketing agency, and a media company FRWD, GOODFOODS picked a total of 60 digital creators in niches ranging from food, lifestyle, home, and parenting to produce original content and recipes using GOODFOODS products.

The campaign was divided into three stages, all themed around key events in the American calendar – baseball game days, Thanksgiving, and Christmas and

Hanukkah. Ahead of the games, influencers were asked to share their own recipes for finger foods. For Thanksgiving, they needed to incorporate the GOODFOODS products into their traditional meals, whereas during the Christmas and Hanukkah time, influencers were supposed to show how guacamole and dips have become part of their festive celebrations. As a result, more than 2,000 pieces of original content were created, including photo and video pieces, blog stories, social media posts, and of course recipes – all featuring GOODFOODS products. The campaign generated 42.2 million impressions and drove over 21,750 people to the GOODFOODS website, where one-quarter of them used the company's store locator to find where they could buy GOODFOODS products. The high-quality influencer-generated content resulted in nearly 50,000 social media engagements, such as likes, comments, shares, and retweets – 294 percent above the initial goal that was set up by the brand.

Many of the assets created by the influencers were then favored over professionally produced content to be repurposed through native advertising and paid social ads to bring additional results. The engagement rate for paid Instagram ads using influencer content was 22.8 percent – more than twice the original brand-created content. The campaign primarily relied on blog-style recipes and in fact blog content is often viewed as more genuine and authentic. People were actively engaging with the influencer-created posts as they considered them a useful and practical source of cooking inspiration and other brand-related information. Since people often turn to online communities not just to connect but also to cultivate and explore their own hobbies, the campaign's content provided them with another value in addition to entertainment and social interaction. Since 2017, GOODFOODS has been employing influencers as a part of its marketing strategy.

The three stages of the influencer program were ideally planned around key events in the American calendar, which also helped the campaign and boosted engagement by creating an emotional connection between influencer-created content and the audience. Those moments, like baseball games or a Thanksgiving feast, are relevant to many American households and by linking them to GOODFOODS products, the campaign's content spoke to people personally.

The emotional connection was also strengthened by the choice of relevant influencers that the audience could easily identify with. The influencers had a highly relevant audience and as a result, their recipes and posts came across engaging and authentic in a natural way.

Questions to consider:

1. Consider GOODFOODS and think about the key advantages this company has in the market.
2. What are the key aspects of influencer marketing GOODFOODS employ?
3. What role does influencer-generated content play on consumers' engagement? Consider how it is relevant to individuals' motivations?
4. Can you suggest any content and campaign strategies influencers can consider to motivate their followers to engage with their branded content further?

sevil yesiloglu and simrit gill

References

Abel, J., Buff, C., and Burr, S., 2016. Social Media and the Fear of Missing Out: Scale Development and Assessment. *Journal of Business & Economics Research*, 14(1), 33.

Abidin, C. and Thompson, E., 2012. Buymylife.com: Cyber-femininities and commercial intimacy in blogshops. *Women's Studies International Forum*, 35(6), 467–477.

Advertising Practice, 2017. Affiliate Marketing: New Advertising Guidance for social influencers [online]. *Asa.org.uk*. Available from: www.asa.org.uk/news/Insight-affiliate-marketing-new-advertising- guidance-for-social-influencers.html

Alcántara, A., 2018. How Can Brands Effectively Use Influencers? This Marketing Company Explains Its Strategy [online]. *Adweek.com*. Available from: www.adweek.com/digital/how-can-brands-effectively-use-influencers-this- marketing-company-explains-its-strategy/

Arksey, H. and Knight, P., 1999. *Interviewing for Social Scientists*. London: Sage Publications.

Barker, S., 2018. How Social Media is Influencing purchase decisions [online]. *Social Media Week*. Available from: https://socialmediaweek.org/blog/2017/05/social-media-influencing-purchase-decisions

Berger, J. and Milkman, K.L., 2012. What makes online content viral? *Journal of Marketing Research*, 49(2), 192–205.

Berger, J. and Schwartz, E., 2011. What Drives Immediate and Ongoing Word of Mouth? *Journal of Marketing Research*, 48(5), 869–880.

Beyens, I., Frison, E., and Eggermont, S., 2016. "I don't want to miss a thing": Adolescents' fear of missing out and its relationship to adolescents' social needs, Facebook use, and Facebook related stress. *Computers in Human Behavior*, 64, 1–8.

Bosher, H., 2020. Influencer Marketing and the Law in Ch. 13 in *Influencer Marketing: Building Brand Communities and Engagement* Ed. Yesiloglu, S., and Costello, J. Routledge: London.

Brenner, M., 2017. Social Media Engagement – 2017's Surprising Best and Worst Performers [online]. *Marketing Insider Group*. Available from: https://marketinginsidergroup.com/social-media/social-media- engagement-2017s-surprising-best-worst-performers/

Brettel, M., Reich, J.C., Gavilanes, J.M., and Flatten, T.C., 2015. What drives advertising success on Facebook? An advertising-effectiveness model: Measuring the effects on sales of "Likes" and other social-network stimuli. *Journal of Advertising Research*, 55(2), 162–175.

Brown, D. and Hayes, N., 2008. *Influencer Marketing*. Amsterdam: Elsevier/Butterworth-Heinemann.

Courtois, C., Mechant, P., De Marez, L., and Verleye G., 2009. Gratifications and Seeding Behavior of Online Adolescents. *Journal of Computer-Mediated Communication*, 15(1), 109–137.

Craig, C.S., Greene, W.H., and Versaci, A., 2015. E-word of mouth: Early predictor of audience engagement: How pre-release "e-WOM" drives box-office outcomes of movies. *Journal of Advertising Research*, 55(1), 62–72.

Creswell, J.W. and Clark, V.L.P., 2017. 3rd Edition. *Designing and Conducting Mixed Methods Research*. California: Sage Publications.

Dahl, S., 2018. *Social Media Marketing: Theories and Applications*. London: Sage Publications.

David, M. and Sutton, C., 2009. *Social Research*. London: Sage Publications.

De Veirman, M., Cauberghe, V., and Hudders, L., 2017. Marketing through Instagram influencers: the impact of the number of followers and product divergence on brand attitude. *International Journal of Advertising*, 36(5), 798–828.

de Vries, L., Gensler, S., and Leeflang, P., 2012. Popularity of Brand Posts on Brand Fan Pages: An Investigation of the Effects of Social Media Marketing. *Journal of Interactive Marketing*, 26(2), 83–91.

Deci, E. and Ryan, R., 1985. The general causality orientations scale: Self- determination in personality. *Journal of Research in Personality*, 19(2), 109–134.

Deci, E. and Ryan. R., 2000. Self-determination theory and the facilitation of intrinsic motivation, social development, and well-being. *American Psychologist*, 55(1), 68–78.

Deci, E., and Ryan. R., 2006. Self-Regulation and the Problem of Human Autonomy: Does Psychology Need Choice, Self-Determination, and Will? *Journal of Personality*, 74(6), 1557–1586.

Dellarocas, C., Zhang, X.M., and Awad, N.F., 2007. Exploring the value of online product reviews in forecasting sales: The case of motion pictures. *Journal of Interactive Marketing*, 21(4), 23–45.

Dholakia, U.M., Bagozzi, R.P., and Pearo, L.K., 2004. A social influence model of consumer participation in network-and small-group-based virtual communities. *International Journal of Research in Marketing*, 21(3), 241–263.

Dilenschneider, C., 2013. 5 Key Reasons Why Social Media Strategies Are Different Than Traditional Marketing Strategies – *Colleen Dilenschneider* [online]. Available from: www.colleendilen.com/2013/06/18/5-key-reasons-why-social- media-strategies-are-different-than-traditional-marketing-strategies/

Fishwick, M., 2004. Emotional design: why we love (or hate) everyday things. *Choice Reviews Online*, 41(11).

Freberg, K., Graham, K., McGaughey, K., and Freberg, L., 2011. Who are the social media influencers? A study of public perceptions of personality. *Public Relations Review*, 37(1), 90–92.

Geppert, G., 2016. How Influence Marketing Differs from Celebrity Endorsement. [online] *Convince and Convert: Social Media Consulting and Content Marketing Consulting*. Available at: www.convinceandconvert.com/digital-marketing/influence-marketing-differs-from-celebrity-endorsement/

Gilmore, J.H. and Pine, B.J., 2007. *Authenticity: What consumers really want*. Boston. Harvard Business School Press.

Gretzel, U. and Yoo, K.H., 2008. Use and impact of online travel reviews. *Information and Communication Technologies in Tourism 2008*, 35–46.

Grolnick, W. and Ryan, R., 1989. Parent styles associated with children's self- regulation and competence in school. *Journal of Educational Psychology*, 81(2), 143–154.

Hagel, J. and Armstrong, A.G., 1996. The real value of on-line communities. *Harvard Business Review*, 74(3), 134–141.

Hars, A. and Ou, S., 2001. Working for free? Motivations of participating in open source projects. *Proceedings of the 34th Annual Hawaii International Conference on System Sciences*.

Hennig-Thurau, T., Gwinner, K.P., Walsh, G., and Gremler, D.D., 2004. Electronic word-of-mouth via consumer-opinion platforms: what motivates consumers to articulate themselves on the internet? *Journal of Interactive Marketing*, 18(1), 38–52.

Ho-Dac, N.N., Carson, S.J., and Moore, W.L., 2013. The effects of positive and negative online customer reviews: do brand strength and category maturity matter? *Journal of Marketing*, 77(6), 37–53.

Hoffman, D. and Novak, T., 2012. Why Do People Use Social Media? Empirical Findings and a New Theoretical Framework for Social Media Goal Pursuit. *SSRN Electronic Journal*. Available from: http://dx.doi.org/10.2139/ssrn.1989586

Hughes, C., 2017. 6 Reasons Why Instagram Marketing is Important for Your Brand [online]. *Iconosquare Blog*. Available from: https://blog.iconosquare.com/why-instagram-marketing-is-important/

Hughes, C., Swaminathan, V., and Brooks, G. (2019) Driving Brand Engagement Through Online Social Influencers: An Empirical Investigation of Sponsored Blogging Campaigns. *Journal of Marketing*, 83(5), 78–96.

Hung, K.H. and Li, S.Y., 2007. The influence of eWOM on virtual consumer communities: Social capital, consumer learning, and behavioral outcomes. *Journal of Advertising Research*, 47(4), 485–495.

Hunt, M.G., Marx, R., Lipson, C., and Young, J., 2018. No more FOMO: Limiting social media decreases loneliness and depression. *Journal of Social and Clinical Psychology*, 37(10), 751–768.

Instagram (2020), We bring you closer to the people and things you love. *Instagram*. Accessed from: https://about.instagram.com/about-us

Jeong, E. and Jang, S., 2011. Restaurant experiences triggering positive electronic word-of-mouth (eWOM) motivations. *International Journal of Hospitality Management*, 30(2), 356–366.

Keller, E and Berry, J., 2003. *The Influentials*. New York: Free Press.

Kim, E. and Drumwright, M., 2016, Engaging consumers and building relationships in social media. *Computers in Human Behavior*, 63, 970–979. https://dl.acm.org/doi/10.1016/j.chb.2016.06.025

Leban, M. and Voyer, B., 2020, Social Media Influencers versus Traditional Influencers: Roles and consequences for traditional marketing campaigns. Ch. 2 in *Influencer Marketing: Building Brand Communities and Engagement*. Ed. Yesiloglu, S., and Costello, J. Routledge: London.

Lin, F. and Huang, H., 2013. Why people share knowledge in virtual communities? *Internet Research*, 23(2), 133–159.

MarketHub, 2016. Influencer Marketing Vs Word-of-Mouth Marketing [online]. *MarketHub*. Available from: https://markethub.io/influencer-marketing-vs-word-of-mouth-marketing/

McQuail, D., 2010. *McQuail's Mass Communication Theory*. Sage publications.

Messiaen, J., 2017. Influencer Marketing: How the popularity threshold of Instagram influencers impacts consumer behavior: the moderating role of purchase involvement. *University of Ghent: Master of Science in Business Economics*.

Muntinga, D., Moorman, M., and Smit, E., 2011. Introducing COBRAs: Exploring motivations for brand-related social media use. *International Journal of Advertising*, 30(1), 13–46.

O'Brien, C., 2011. The emergence of social media empowered consumers. *Irish Marketing Review*, 21(1) 32–40.

Özçelik, A. and Levi, E., 2020. Choosing the right influencer for your brand: a guide to the field. Ch. 5 in *Influencer Marketing: Building Brand Communities and Engagement*. Ed. Yesiloglu, S. and Costello, J. Routledge: London.

Oberst, U., Wegmann, E., Stodt, B., Brand, M., and Chamarro, A., 2017. Negative consequences from heavy social networking in adolescents: The mediating role of fear of missing out. *Journal of Adolescence*, 55, 51–60.

Papacharissi, Z. and Rubin, A.M., 2000, Predictors of internet use, *Journal of Broadcasting and Electronic Media*, 44(2), 175–196.

Phua, J. and Ahn, S.J., 2016. Explicating the "like" on Facebook brand pages: The effect of intensity of Facebook use, number of overall "likes", and number of friends' "likes" on consumers' brand outcomes. *Journal of Marketing Communications*, 22(5), 544–559.

Przybylski, A., Murayama, K., DeHaan, C., and Gladwell, V., 2013. Motivational, emotional, and behavioral correlates of fear of missing out. *Computers in Human Behavior*, 29(4), 1841–1848.

Razmerita, L., Kirchner, K., and Nielsen, P., 2016. What factors influence knowledge sharing in organizations? A social dilemma perspective of social media communication. *Journal of Knowledge Management*, 20(6), 1225–1246.

Rosenthal, B. and Arcuri, A., 2020. How to map and select digital influencers for Marketing Campaigns. Ch. 4 in *Influencer Marketing: Building Brand Communities and Engagement*. Ed. Yesiloglu, S. and Costello, J. London: Routledge.

Scitovsky, T., 1992. *The Joyless Economy*. New York: Oxford University Press.

Shao, G., 2009. Understanding the appeal of user-generated media: a uses and gratifications perspective. *Internet Research*, 19(1), 7–25.

Sheldon, P. and Bryant, K., 2016. Instagram: Motives for its use and relationship to narcissism and contextual age. *Computers in Human Behavior*, 58, 89–97.

Sook Kwon, E., Kim, E., Sung, Y., and Yun Yoo, C., 2014. Brand followers: Consumer motivation and attitude towards brand communications on Twitter. *International Journal of Advertising*, 33(4), 657–680.

Sudha, M., and Sheena, K., 2017. Impact of Influencers in Consumer Decision Process: The Fashion Industry. *SCMS Journal of Indian Management*, 14–30.

Talaverna, M., 2015. 10 Reasons Why Influencer Marketing is the Next Big Thing [online]. *Adweek*. Available from: www.adweek.com/digital/10-reasons-why-influencer marketingis-the-next-big-thing/

Vargo, S. and Lusch, R., 2008. Service-dominant logic: continuing the evolution. *Journal of the Academy of Marketing Science*, 36(1), 1–10.

Vivek, S.D., Beatty, S.E., and Morgan, R.M., 2012. Customer Engagement: Exploring Customer Relationships Beyond Purchase. *Journal of Marketing Theory and Practice*, 20(2), 127–145.

Wang, Y. and Fesenmaier, D.R., 2003. Assessing motivation of contribution in online communities: an empirical investigation of an online travel community. *Electronic Markets*, 13(1), 33–45.

Whiting, A. and Williams, D., 2013. Why people use social media: a uses and gratifications approach. *Qualitative Market Research: An International Journal*, 16(4), 362–369.

Wise, K., Alhabash, S., and Park, H., 2010. Emotional Responses During Social Information Seeking on Facebook. *CyberPsychology: Behavior & Social Networking*, 13(5), 555–562.

Wolny, J. and Mueller, C., 2013. Analysis of fashion consumers' motives to engage in electronic word-of-mouth communication through social media platforms. *Journal of Marketing Management*, 29, 562–583.

Yap, K.B., Soetarto, B., and Sweeney, J.C., 2013. The relationship between electronic word-of-mouth motivations and message characteristics: The sender's perspective. *Australasian Marketing Journal*, 21(1), 66–74.

Yesiloglu, S., 2017. To post or not to post: examining motivations of brand/product- related engagement types on social networking sites. Ph.D. Thesis. Bournemouth University, Faculty of Management.

Yesiloglu, S., 2020, The Rise of Influencers and Influencer Marketing. Ch. 1 in *Influencer Marketing: Building Brand Communities and Engagement*. Ed. Yesiloglu, S. and Costello, J. Routledge: London.

Yesiloglu, S. and Waśkiw, W., 2020, An Exploratory study into consumer-influencer engagement on Instagram in the context of sustainability. Ch. 8 in *Influencer Marketing: Building Brand Communities and Engagement*. Ed. Yesiloglu, S., and Costello, J. Routledge: London.

Zhang, J.Q., Craciun, G., and Shin, D., 2010. When does electronic word-of-mouth matter? A study of consumer product reviews. *Journal of Business Research*, 63(12), 1336–1341.

Zine, 2017. ZINE – Influencer Marketing Technology [online]. *ZINE*. Available from: https://zine.co/

Parasocial relationships of Generation Z consumers with social media influencers

Elina Närvänen, Tytti Kirvesmies, and Elina Kahri

Learning outcomes

On completing this chapter, you should be able to:

- understand that influencer marketing operates at a more personal level when consumers form parasocial relationships with social media influencers;
- realize that parasocial relationships may end because of several different reasons related to the consumer or to the influencer; and
- recognize social media influencers and influencer marketing professionals need to be aware of the nature of parasocial relationships the followers may have with the influencer.

The influencer marketing phenomenon

Social media has revolutionized the interaction between consumers and companies. According to some statistics, people spent 135 minutes per day in 2017 on social media

elina närvänen et al.

(Global Web Index, n.d.); hence companies have become increasingly interested in reaching customers through the new, interactive Web 2.0 technologies. However, according to a recent Edelman Trust Barometer, three in four consumers avoid advertising, using one or more avoidance strategies (Edelman 2019). Consumers may not even pay attention to ads on social media or might consider them to be negative and intrusive (Bang and Lee 2016). Furthermore, many consumers use ad-blocking technologies to avoid online advertising.

Some consumers perceive social media influencers as more credible than companies in their decision-making (e.g. Carr and Hayes 2014; Djafarova and Rushworth 2017). The Edelman Trust Barometer from 2019 found that 63 percent of respondents trusted what influencers say about a brand much more than what the brand says about itself in its advertising (Edelman 2019). A social media influencer is defined as an opinion leader or tastemaker in one or more areas of consumption who has a considerable following on social media (De Veirman et al. 2017). Influencer marketing refers to companies using social media influencers to spread the word about a brand to the influencer's followers (De Veirman et al. 2017). As a format of marketing communications, influencer marketing spend has grown steadily over recent years, with an estimated market value of 5 to 10 billion dollars by 2020 (Mediakix 2018). Its benefits for marketers include that consumers may perceive it as word-of-mouth rather than as paid advertising. The industry has quickly become institutionalized and many influencers today make their living out of brand collaborations.

From admiring celebrities to forming personal connections

Influencer marketing relates to celebrity endorsement (Bergkvist and Zhou 2016), which has been a commonly used form of marketing communications, but which has changed its form online. In celebrity endorsement, the celebrity's degree of popularity is considered as important. A recent study suggested that the higher popularity of an influencer does not always lead to more effective influence in social media (Chung and Cho 2017). This may be because influencers with large amounts of followers may lack uniqueness and perceived authenticity (Audrezet et al. 2018). Instead, a personal connection felt by the consumer with the influencer is more important. Recent studies have suggested that this personal connection may also help influencer marketing to overcome its key challenge: disclosing paid advertising collaborations (e.g. De Jans et al. 2018; Evans et al. 2017). As soon as the influencer discloses paid advertising collaboration such as by using hashtags like #gifted or #affiliate, this activates the consumers' persuasion knowledge, and may influence their purchase intentions as well as their attitude toward the influencer negatively. This occurs as consumers may perceive that the influencer is no longer unbiased nor offering their honest opinion (De Jans et al. 2018). However, full disclosure is increasingly a requirement set by, for instance, the international chamber of commerce (ICC) and government agencies regarding marketing communication ethics. (This is later discussed in depth by Bosher (2020) in Chapter 13.) Yet, according to one recent industry study, only a fragment of influencer posts currently comply with these requirements (Influencer Marketing Hub 2019). In the same industry survey by the Influencer Marketing Hub, marketers state that the biggest challenge in influencer marketing is finding and selecting appropriate influencers for cooperation (36 percent) and that the audience relationship is the most important factor when running influencer campaigns (48 percent). To do this successfully, marketers must understand why consumers choose to follow particular influencers, and how such an audience relationship is created or severed. This study focuses on the consumer perspective and investigates the parasocial relationships as an explanatory factor behind why consumers may choose to follow or unfollow certain influencers.

Relationships with influencers

Consumers, particularly adolescents, typically admire social media influencers and consider them like their friends (De Jans et al. 2018). The theory that provides answers for why consumers trust and follow the advice of certain influencers and not others is the theory of parasocial interaction, which originates in psychology and media studies (Horton and Wohl 1956). Similar to the characters of our favorite television series (ibid.), consumers have been argued to form parasocial relationships with the influencers they follow on social media (e.g. Chung and Cho 2017; De Jans et al. 2018; Lueck 2015). Lee and Watkins (2016) have established that forming this kind of relationship with a YouTube vlogger led to more positive brand perceptions. These relationships are characterized by their one-sided relationship rather than the direct nature of the interaction. The consumer has been following the life of the influencer for a long time and feels like they know the person, even though they have never met. On the other hand, the influencer does not know almost anything about the follower, making the relationship one-sided. Hence, there is an illusion of intimacy (Lueck 2015). Studies within marketing and consumer research have begun to apply the above introduced parasocial relationship theory to influencer marketing phenomena (e.g. Chung and Cho 2017; Lueck 2015). However, so far these studies have focused more on the company perspective. The consumer perspective, i.e. how consumers themselves perceive and experience these parasocial relationships, has not been studied. However, to fully understand the relevance and value of the phenomenon in marketing, the consumer perspective is important.

Idea fairy: Relationships with influencers

Considering your own beliefs, how often do you feel your relationship with influencers is one-sided? Have you ever felt the urge to "break up" with an influencer because you felt they were not being true to themselves? Do you think that different generations will have different parasocial relationships with influencers? Why?

Theoretical background
Opinion leadership on social media

In its most basic sense, influencer marketing can be explained by the two-step flow theory of communication developed already by Katz and Lazarsfeld (1955). This theory

elina närvänen et al.

explains how messages move from senders to receivers in a marketing environment. Rather than perceiving a direct path between the sender (marketer) and receiver (consumer), the theory identifies the role of opinion leaders as mediators between the message sender (marketer) and the consumer. Hence there are two steps in the message flow – step one is mediators, and step two is the final consumer. The theory has been utilized in marketing to conceptualize celebrity endorsement (Bergkvist and Zhou 2016). It has also been applied to study brand communication through digital influencers, especially bloggers (Uzunoğlu and Kip 2014). Indeed, today's social media influencers engage in reciprocal and frequent conversations with consumers through different channels (Chung and Cho 2017). Furthermore, the notion of celebrity has changed as the social media influencers may be popular merely because of the content they produce online rather than as athletes or artists, for instance (Freberg et al. 2011). Hence, ordinary consumers can become tastemakers and gain influencer status through publicly demonstrating their amount of cultural capital in a specific field of consumption (McQuarrie et al. 2013).

Social media influencers are often admired for their lifestyle as a whole, and hence the influencer disclosing a lot of details about their daily lives, values, interests, and activities increases their perceived credibility (Djafarova and Rushworth 2017) and in turn, results in greater benefits for marketers (Chung and Cho 2017). Credibility is required to form trust because trust is needed for high quality, strong relationships with the influencer to form (De Jans et al. 2018). Conversely, when a celebrity does not disclose personal information about him or herself, they can be perceived as inauthentic and their value as an influencer may decrease (Chung and Cho 2017). According to previous research, the ability of the consumer to self-identify as similar to the influencer also plays a great role in choosing which influencer to follow (e.g. Chung and Cho 2017; Li and Chignell 2010).

Parasocial relationship theory

Parasocial relationship theory is one perspective explaining the effectiveness of influencer marketing in social media. Researchers in marketing and consumer behavior have utilized parasocial relationship theory to explore themes including consumer–brand relationships in social media (Labrecque 2014), parasocial advertising (Lueck 2015), the strength of parasocial relationships in social media (Bond 2016), as well as which social media channels (Colliander and Dahlén 2011) and what kind of influencer characteristics (Chung and Cho 2017; Giles 2002) are most likely to generate strong parasocial relationships. From the consumer perspective, a few studies have examined consumer motivations to form parasocial relationships (e.g. Escalas and Bettman 2017; Yuan et al. 2016), and several have studied the effects of such relationships on consumers' online and purchasing behavior (e.g. Chung and Cho 2017; Lee and Watkins 2016; Yuksel and Labreque 2016).

Even though consumers have formed parasocial relationships through traditional media such as television, social media offers even better opportunities for this due to its interactive and open nature (Labrecque 2014). With reference to interactive nature, Lueck (2015) argued that through interactive questions, social media influencers invite consumers to interact, creating an illusion of friendship even though their participation in the discussion is minimal. Bond (2016) found that two-sided social media interactions (e.g. the influencer responding to a comment made by a follower rather than just posting new things) strengthen the parasocial relationship. Colliander and Dahlén (2011) viewed blogs as a typical example of a media that generates parasocial relationships, as they focus on personal stories and photos of the bloggers' daily lives, as well as audience interaction. The drivers for parasocial relationships include features of the influencer themselves, such as coherent representation and perceived authenticity (e.g. Costello and Biondi 2020; Giles 2002), as well as credibility, trustworthiness, and attractiveness (e.g. Chung and Cho 2017; Costello and Urbanska 2020; McCracken 1988).

The consumer perspective has not yet been prominent in studies of parasocial relationships. However, a study by Yuan et al. (2016) has examined consumers' motivations to form parasocial relationships and argue that especially entertainment, relationship-building, and information-seeking motivations are central. Further, Escalas and Bettman (2017) examined parasocial relationships of adolescents and found that teens who have a high need for social connections form parasocial relationships with celebrities to transfer their images onto themselves. Parasocial relationships influence consumers' opinions and interests, their emotions and moods, as well as direct their activities both offline and online (Yuksel and Labreque 2016), through increasing intentions to buy (Chung and Cho 2017; Lee and Watkins 2016) and positive effects on customer equity and loyalty (Labreque 2014; Yuan et al. 2016). Even though the parasocial theory has increasingly been utilized to study influencer marketing and its effects on consumers, the ways in which consumers themselves experience their parasocial relationships is as yet largely unknown.

Methods and data

This study is positioned within the social constructionist paradigm (Eriksson and Kovalainen 2008) which views reality as subjective and knowledge as gained through interaction and interpretation. The interest is on how consumers have experienced their parasocial relationships with social media influencers. In recruiting the study participants, they needed to have personal experience of the study phenomenon. Generation Z (born between 1995 and 2000) young women who were active users of social media were chosen as the informants of the study. Generation Z are accustomed to endless messages and multiple information sources around them (Chaney et al. 2017). This generation values the authenticity and realness of social media (Djafarova and Rushworth 2016) and are more likely to form parasocial relationships with celebrities (e.g. Escalas and Bettman 2017; Theran et al. 2010).

Two qualitative methods were utilized to generate the data. In the first phase, four focus group interviews were organized. Focus groups offer a way to generate natural discussion data from participants' interaction with each other. This method is useful in social constructionist research because it captures the different subjective views through interaction between group members (Tadajewski 2016). The focus group interviewees were recruited via Instagram with the criteria that they belonged to

elina närvänen et al.

Table 7.1 Description of the data

Method/format of data	Participants	Amount of data
Focus group interview 1	4 young women, age 17–19	93 minutes
Focus group interview 2	6 young women, age 18–19	93 minutes
Focus group interview 3	7 young women, age 18–19	84 minutes
Focus group interview 4	6 young women, age 17–19	77 minutes
Interviewee 1	young woman, age 19	37 minutes
Interviewee 2	young woman, age 22	24 minutes
Interviewee 3	young woman, age 16	32 minutes
Interviewee 4	young woman, age 22	60 minutes
Interviewee 5	young woman, age 19	50 minutes
Interviewee 6	young woman, age 20	35 minutes
Total	**29 interviewees**	**585 minutes**

Generation Z and were active social media users (they had 400+ followers). Personal messages were sent to potential participants, and they were encouraged to bring a friend with them to facilitate joining the study. The focus group interviews were moderated by one of the authors, asking the participants questions about their social media usage, which influencers they follow and why, their purchasing behavior, and especially their experiences and views on brand collaborations. The interviews' duration varied from 77 to 93 minutes and the number of participants per group ranged from four to seven, amounting to 24 persons in total. Details of the data are portrayed in Table 7.1.

A first qualitative analysis that identified common themes across the groups' experiences was conducted based on the focus group data. Here, it was noted that the participants discussed not only their current parasocial relationships with influencers but also their relationships that had ended. Therefore, the authors decided to generate more data to explore this and other themes further. In the second phase, six in-depth interviews with a different set of individuals with the same demographic profile were conducted. These interviewees were recruited from the researchers' personal networks through snowball sampling. Similar questions were asked as in the focus group interviews but special focus was put on terminated parasocial relationships – the interviewees were asked before the interview whether they had any experience of stopping the following of an influencer. The duration of these interviews was 30–60 minutes. All the data were recorded and transcribed for analysis. The second round of analysis was conducted on all the data utilizing inductive content analysis techniques (Eriksson and Kovalainen 2008). First, the data were reduced into meaningful segments (keywords, concepts, ideas), then clustered into similar themes and finally abstracted into more theoretical categories. This process was cyclical in nature, in line with the hermeneutic approach where the researcher moves between parts and the whole, theory, and empirical material (Gummesson 2003).

Findings

Next, we present the key findings of the study. They have been divided into two main sections: four requirements of parasocial relationships that operate as a precondition for an illusion of intimacy to form, and three types of parasocial relationships.

Four requirements of parasocial relationships

The first requirement was that the influencer 1) *portrayed something real and relatable about their everyday lives* using different social media channels:

> Many celebrities are really active on social media and they post a lot of updates about their everyday lives too. Through Snapchat, you see their normal life and, like, that even they eat candy and stuff.
>
> (Focus group 2 interviewee)

Hence, for the interviewees, it was important that the influencers they followed posted mundane, ordinary things about their daily lives rather than only posting polished pictures and stories about extraordinary events. Endorsers eating candy, experiencing sad days or chaos at home, and talking about personal topics gave the followers a feeling that the influencers were just like their friends. This finding is in line with those of Ilicic and Webster (2016), who argued in the celebrity endorsement context that experiencing endorsers failing and living life like normal people helps consumers to relate to them. Some interviewees carefully chose to follow particular influencers only through specific channels, such as YouTube or Snapchat rather than Instagram, as described by one of the interviewees:

> I only follow [the influencer] on YouTube, because I get the most truthful picture of them there. And this other influencer I only follow on Snapchat. [Interviewer: Why do you do that? Why not Instagram, then?] Because I don't like them boasting about their bodies and appearance [on Instagram] and lack of truthfulness and the amount of commercial content they have there.
>
> (Interviewee 1)

The interviewees also reported how they appreciated that the influencer replied to the followers' comments and questions and thereby engaged in two-way parasocial interaction. This also made them feel closer to the influencer. This is in line with previous studies emphasizing social media's unique abilities for two-sided parasocial interactions (Bond 2016; Lueck 2015).

In addition to disliking overly commercial content, participants also appreciated those influencers who 2) *reported their company-sponsored posts* in a transparent manner. This is related to the notion of covert marketing. A study has found that covert marketing – marketing where the brand is hidden to appear more authentic – results in lower brand commitment and brand trust, especially when the consumer

elina närvänen et al.

has an emotional relationship with the brand (Ashley and Leonard 2009). This is the second identified requirement of parasocial relationships and was described in the data as follows:

> I really appreciate them [the influencer] adding a sponsorship hashtag there, or somehow indicating that it's an ad. I feel fooled when they don't.
>
> (Focus group 4 interviewee)

Hence, the findings are in line with recent studies on the effects of advertising disclosure – as long as the influencer's aims and purposes are clear, disclosure may be interpreted by consumers as fair and there may be positive effects on the brand and influencer perceptions (DeJans et al. 2018).

One aspect related to reporting collaborations honestly that was discussed in the interview data was the nature of the collaboration. If the brand fit the content of the influencer's post well, then it was more likely to be accepted by the follower. As one participant noted:

> I'm really annoyed at the type of posts like "use this discount code to buy this watch" [...] Instead I really like challenges, like building a gingerbread house, which was sponsored by this brand of candy that was used to decorate it – so then the content is fun and nice to watch. So it gives me the feeling that I'd like to buy the candy myself and decorate similarly.
>
> (Interviewee 1)

Hence, the fit between the brand or ad content and the content posted by the influencer is important. The lack of fit may also be perceived by the follower as an aesthetic and visual matter rather than related to the content itself, as described by one of the focus group participants:

> I'm annoyed by most of the ads on Instagram as they are often ugly and visually not fitting with those accounts I have decided to follow. In general, I hate it when ads are forced on me.
>
> (Focus group 2 interviewee)

Thus, like in the context of celebrity endorsement, also in influencer marketing the concept of fit or match is important as meanings may travel from brand to endorser and vice versa (McCormick 2016). However, followers can consider the fit between various aspects of the influencer marketing campaign including brand, the ad, the posted content, and the influencer's personality and style. All these aspects are filtered through the frame of the parasocial relationship.

The third identified requirement of a parasocial relationship is that consumers expected the influencer to 3) *be true to themselves* in different channels. It was described by one of the focus group participants as follows:

I immediately thought about her when I saw this picture. I've gotten to know her and she isn't only doing easy promotions, but always has beautiful photos like this one. (Focus group 4 interviewee)

As stated by this interviewee, they experienced a parasocial relationship over time and hence expected the influencer to remain truthful to their style that the follower had learned to appreciate. Coherent representation has been found in parasocial relationship theory to mediate the formation of such relationships (Giles 2002) and the findings of the current study support this notion. Also, the followers expected the influencer to not only boost brands and provide recommendations but also sometimes have negative things to say, to prove their credibility. Any doubts about the truthfulness or integrity of the influencer resulted in a threat to the parasocial relationship. One participant expressed her concerns in the following way:

I don't understand why anyone collaborates with that brand. I can't help thinking that she just wants money from the collaboration.

(Focus group 2 interviewee)

The fourth requirement identified from the data is that consumers preferred to engage in parasocial relationships with influencers who 4) *carefully chose which brands they support and personalized their endorsements* rather than only transmitted uniform marketing messages. One of the focus group participants described this as follows:

You really easily hear it from YouTubers if they've been told what they have to say. I mean, there's a huge difference between giving a speech someone planned for you beforehand and then just talking about it on Snapchat while you talk about other stuff too. I trust it more when it's just natural, I mean it's horrible when, for example, the endorsed products in a YouTube video are lined up nicely behind them. That's, that's like an ad.

(Focus group 1 interviewee)

Hence, brand collaborations that seemed to be more natural rather than prescribed by the brand were perceived as better by the interviewees. As also argued by Yuksel and Labreque (2016), the influencers receiving overly restrictive instructions from the brand may be detrimental to their perceived authenticity.

As proof of the credibility of the brands being used by the influencer, interviewees wanted to see the products in an authentic context such as running with the sponsored running shoes on or taking a shower with the sponsored shampoo brand actually seen there with the influencer:

I feel that it's good when they say some negative things too. That makes the messages more reliable. I mean, if someone is only praising every product, that's not reliable anymore. Or, they should share their real experiences using the products. (Focus group 1 interviewee)

elina närvänen et al.

These requirements can be related to perceived uniqueness and originality, which have been argued to characterize opinion leadership formation on Instagram (Casaló et al. 2018). However, even though authenticity was important to the interviewees, they still often expected a kind of "professional touch" to the way the influencer produced their content, as described by one of the interviewees:

> If I notice that the production is not good quality, I may stop following them. For instance, if they don't post videos when they're supposed to, or if the quality is really low, or you see that they have not made any effort, or the voice is bad. Or suddenly the camera is hazy or it's badly edited or they just use [a simple freeware program for video editing]. It shows that they're not really making an effort.
>
> (Interviewee 1)

The above quotation summarizes the way many interviewees felt that for them to form a long-term parasocial friendship with an influencer, many preconditions had to be fulfilled. Next, we will discuss the three types of parasocial relationships that were identified from the data, analyzing their dynamics in more detail.

The three types of parasocial relationships

Three types of parasocial relationships were identified from the data: close personal friendships, ex friendships, and casual friendships. The first type of parasocial relationship found in the analysis is that of a *close personal friendship*. In this type, the consumer identifies strongly with the influencer and feels the similarity in values and lifestyle choices. Also, the consumers feel that they have a lot of personal knowledge about the influencer generated over the long period they have followed them. This knowledge makes them trust the influencer more and makes them attached to the relationship, as described by one of the interviewees:

> Yea, I'm totally committed more to them [favorite influencer], if you've followed them for four years or so, you start to know them for real. I know that they don't show everything in there, but you start to know them and their routines. (Interviewer: What would it feel like if they suddenly stopped?) Interviewee: I would be totally upset (laughing), I would really be in shock, or I don't know... of course, I would get over it at some point, but if I think about my favorite influencer, for instance, if they take two weeks' break from posting, I'm totally panicked just waiting for the videos to appear. So, I would be really sad. 'Cause you just invest in some of them. (Interviewee 5)

The above quotation demonstrates the attachment and closeness felt by the interviewees with some of their favorite influencers who were seen as close friends.

Further, with close friends, consumers are more likely to have a stronger trust toward the influencer. One interviewee described having bought several things that the influencer had worn without acknowledging any paid collaborations. When asked whether she was sure that the influencer had not been paid by the fashion brands to wear the clothes, she reported:

> I know her, she's honest [...]. She wouldn't have done that for money, she would have told me if she had.
>
> (Focus group 1 interviewee)

Establishing the friendship was not a conscious decision, but one that occurred through days, months, and years of following the influencer. This personal knowledge helped consumers also appreciate and evaluate the brand recommendations better:

> Maybe you need some kind of knowledge of people so that you can evaluate what they say and write. I mean, if it's a collaboration blog text [...] then it helps if you know the background of the person and if you can trust her.
>
> (Focus group 1 interviewee)

These types of parasocial relationships also typically fulfilled all the requirements stated in the above analysis. On many occasions, the influencer was also perceived as a role model for the follower, who admired their style and way of posting content:

> I have followed this influencer for a long time... I've actually always followed her. She has a nice style and I really admire her. I would buy these things she recommends.
>
> (Focus group 4 interviewee)

The followers were also in these cases willing to forgive their favorite influencer for a few mistakes if they generally remained the way the followers had learned to know them. However, the influencer needs to be perceived as a friend rather than a stranger for the parasocial relationship to thrive.

The second type of parasocial relationship identified is that of an *ex-friendship*. This relationship type may result from a friendship somehow ending due to either the influencer's behavior or the consumer's changing life situation. In the first case, influencers may cause negative reactions due to their increasing fame. Hence, when the influencer loses their perceived authenticity and does not reveal enough about their daily life anymore or their content becomes too professional, it may be a reason for the consumer to end the relationship or distance themselves from it:

> Sometimes you notice when someone gets more followers that they start to more carefully think about what they post. For example, I have this one blogger I have followed since she started, and in the beginning, her posts were personal but now she isn't sharing much at all. I mean, maybe it's what you get used to, but sometimes I wish she would share something real about her life again, like how it's really going at the moment.
>
> (Focus group 1 interviewee)

elina närvänen et al.

Hence, this kind of behavior may decrease the perceived intimacy of the relationship and result in a parasocial breakup (Cohen, 2003).

Another reason for the parasocial breakup can be due to a perceived change in the values or lifestyle of the influencer:

> This influencer had similar values as I do for a long time. I could identify with her and she was such an inspiration to me. I wanted to be like her and then suddenly she started acting totally contradictory to my values.
>
> (Interviewee 1)

This quotation also shows how important it is for strong parasocial relationships that the influencer is perceived to have similar values and interests so that the follower can self-identify with them, as supported also by previous studies on influencer marketing (Chung and Cho 2017). Lack of interaction, especially in situations where the consumers felt that the influencer had promised them something or betrayed their trust, was another reason for ending the relationship:

> These [followers] are the people they [influencers] get paid for. You cannot just disappear. You have to have some respect.
>
> (Interviewee 5)

This quotation illustrates that the consumers expect the parasocial relationship to be honored by the influencers as well, in terms of respecting their followers and showing some reciprocity toward them. The interviewees also discussed that ex-friendships may actually have a negative impact on their consumption choices, as they may feel angry and disappointed at the influencer and turn against the brands they recommend:

> Now I've blocked the person from my life so that I would not buy the products that she recommends.
>
> (Interviewee 1)

Hence, the danger of severed close relationships with followers is a genuine risk for brands collaborating with these influencers.

The third identified relationship, *casual friendship*, is much less emotionally engaging for the consumer than either the close friendship or the ex-friendship. It concerns relationships that were described by the interviewees as ongoing at some level, but which were not seen to be very influential or important for them. These relationships could be with influencers that were only followed for entertainment purposes – for escaping the mundane everyday life. Rather than following people that the consumer can really identify with and relate to, they may follow influencers that are highly different in terms of lifestyle or life stage, for instance. A focus group participant describes this as follows:

> I'm looking for positive energy and motivation. I follow people who are quite different than I am who live differently than I do. I mean, it's cool to follow them.
> (Focus group 2 interviewee)

Consumers reported for instance that they kept following certain popular influencers in order not to miss anything important:

> Perhaps I like to keep the option open... if I stopped following them, then they would in a way disappear from my life, and then if something cool and crazy happened, I would miss it.

(Interviewee 5)

Hence, not all parasocial relationships are equally strong or influential, from the point of view of the consumers. The plurality of parasocial relationships also illustrates that consumers may follow influencers for various reasons.

Discussion

The findings illuminate the nature and types of relationships that young Generation Z women have with the influencers they follow on social media. These relationships are differently characterized by the influencer's perceived authenticity and credibility, the feeling of intimacy with the influencer as well as how consumers react to brand endorsements by the influencers. The study's findings provide further support for emerging studies on influencer marketing that specifically highlight the crucial role of authenticity and openness (e.g. Audrezet et al. 2018; Chung and Cho 2017; Djafarova and Rushworth 2017; Labrecque 2014).

All the identified requirements for parasocial relationships with social media influencers in this study are connected with this notion. First, the influencer needs to portray something real and relatable; second, they need to be transparent about their branded collaborations; third, they need to be true to themselves and finally, choose carefully which brands they collaborate with and personalize their endorsements. We argue that these requirements are all interlinked and filtered through the consumer's parasocial relationship. The parasocial relationship is temporal in nature, and the evaluation of whether the requirements are met by the influencer depends on past experiences of the consumer. Furthermore, we propose that the loss of authenticity in any of these requirements may lead to a lack of authenticity being transferred to the endorsed brand as well. Hence, our findings build a more nuanced, temporal perspective on how authenticity is evaluated by consumers in the context of influencer marketing.

The findings also add a contribution to the emerging literature that has focused on parasocial relationships in the social media context. These studies have utilized quantitative research designs and concentrated on the effects of parasocial relationships on variables such as customer equity (Yuan et al. 2016), brand attitude (De Veirman et al. 2017), and loyalty and purchase intentions (e.g. Labrecque 2014; Yuksel and Labreque 2016; Chung and Cho 2017). Using an interpretive perspective, the current study offers a more nuanced analysis of the temporal dynamics of these relationships. The findings of this study support previous studies that similarly highlight openness and interactivity as preconditions for parasocial relationships (Labrecque 2014), as

elina närvänen et al.

well as the need for followers to be able to self-identify and share similar values with the influencer (Chung and Cho 2017; Casaló et al. 2018). However, previous studies have not examined how parasocial relationships evolve and develop.

The three identified relationship types reveal that consumers have various parasocial relationships the strength of which varies, and they are dynamically changing over time. Some parasocial relationships may also be terminated and end up in a "break-up" that may be felt like a painful experience for the consumer. While the parasocial relationship theory has considered breakups in the context of media characters (e.g. Cohen 2003) and branding research has considered how consumer–brand relationships end (Fournier 1998; Hemetsberger et al. 2009), this study is the first to consider this aspect in the context of influencer marketing.

Managerial implications

The study has important managerial implications for brands considering influencer marketing as a marketing communications tool, as well as for influencer marketing agencies and influencers themselves. The findings reveal that not every influencer is able to affect their followers similarly, because the followers decide the nature of the parasocial relationship. This is a subjective issue, which is dependent on both the influencer's perceived behavior as well as the motivations of the follower. The study also illuminates the risks involved in terminated parasocial relationships, as they may result in consumers rejecting brands endorsed by their "ex."

The implications for influencers include that they need to be constantly monitoring their followers' opinions and feelings related to their content. This way, the influencer can detect when they are about to lose followers due to parasocial break-up and can change their content accordingly. Influencers could use the findings of this study as a checklist to ensure that their content is able to generate parasocial relationships. Influencers and their agencies could also use the findings to plan surveys for the followers in order to find out more about their experiences.

Implications for marketers include the need to build authentic, relevant, and interactive co-operation with influencers in order to avoid parasocial breakups and negative reactions. In order to do this, the brand really needs to know the influencer and their followers. They should also identify what kind of relationships the influencer has with their followers is crucial for brands investing in influencer marketing. If most of the followers are in a "close friendship" type of a parasocial relationship, there is the opportunity to do successful influencer marketing through establishing a long-term partnership with the influencer. This way, the brand is also able to develop and evolve its communications alongside the influencer's content. If some of the followers that belong in the brand's target group are rather in an "ex friendship" type, then collaborating with the influencer may result in a negative brand image and hence, should be avoided. Finally, with casual friendships, there is perhaps less risk as the consumers are not as emotionally committed to the relationship, but the effectiveness of the communications may be lower compared to true friendships.

Summary

- This study contributes to a more profound understanding of parasocial relationships on social media from the consumers' point of view.
- The current study provides a much-needed, deeper level perspective to consumers' experiences.
- Further research should be conducted on the consumer perspective to influencer marketing and parasocial relationships including the motivations of consumers to form a parasocial relationship, and especially on the notion of parasocial breakups with social media influencers.

Case study: Food bloggers promoting poultry resulted in mixed reactions

In 2016, a Finnish food producer brand Atria initiated an influencer marketing campaign with food bloggers and invited them to visit the farms where their poultry meat is being produced in order to create authentic content about it in their blogs. The brand wanted to try to change consumers' negative perceptions of the animals' living conditions and improve the brand image. As a result, many bloggers wrote very positively about their experiences at the farms, emphasizing their feelings of becoming convinced that the production is ethical and responsible. The blog posts written by these influencers were largely relatable to their followers, who were also interested in corporate responsibility and food production. Increasing the authenticity of their posts, some bloggers also included critical aspects in their texts, but all of them ultimately ended with a positive note about the brand. The influencers also praised the brand for its openness and willingness to engage in interaction with consumers. The company reported in its blog post that the campaign had been a success. However, the results of the campaign amongst the influencers' followers and the general public were mixed.

The comments the blog posts received from followers described how the followers themselves had had a negative perception of poultry production before, and how they had been concerned about its ethical aspects, clearly demonstrating the *relatability of the content*. Many followers thanked the bloggers for their courage in going to the farms and reporting their experiences. However, while some followers expressed a positive attitude toward the brand after reading about it, others criticized the bloggers for their lack of critical assessment and for being paid to promote the brand. They felt the campaign posts were not in line with the influencers' image or their other blog posts – thus, the influencers were not perceived as *being true to themselves*. Commentators in various discussions on both the blogs themselves and elsewhere on social media expressed feelings of sadness and disappointment at the influencers they had been following for a long time. Further, the participating bloggers were blamed in many comments for not *choosing more carefully which brands they collaborated with*, and indeed, the bloggers who had refused to cooperate were praised for their integrity. The resulting discussion amongst the followers of the influencers pointed out that they believed the bloggers were led to write mainly positive things. Some followers reported that they would stop

elina närvänen et al.

following these blogs and that the blogs' reputation would be tarnished forever by the collaboration. In addition, some consumers were concerned about the *transparency of the campaign* in terms of the bloggers failing to fully disclose that the company had paid them. In fact, the Finnish Council of Ethics in Advertising issued a statement that the campaign had broken the code of ethics in marketing communications because consumers were left unsure about the advertising intent of the campaign.

The practical lessons learned about this campaign are that brands need to carefully consider whether their collaboration with an influencer is likely to be perceived by their followers as authentic and genuine and whether it will strengthen or sever the parasocial relationship that the consumers have with the influencer. Especially popular influencers have a big audience which can be divided as a consequence of a branded collaboration. Some followers may become alienated and as a result, a great amount of negative publicity toward the influencer and also the brand. Being well aware of the values that are important for the followers, especially the ones that are in the brand's target market, is crucial, and the risks involved should be analyzed in advance, especially when touching issues that are controversial.

Questions:

1. What were the advantages and disadvantages of the aforementioned influencers' actions that could improve or degrade their parasocial relationships?
2. What examples of parasocial relationships can you identify with from your own experiences online?
3. Is it worth it for influencers to alienate those followers with whom they have had a positive parasocial relationship with for brand sponsorship?

References

Ashley, C., and Leonard, H.A., 2009. Betrayed by the buzz? Covert content and consumer-brand relationships. *Journal of Public Policy and Marketing*, 28(2), 212–220.

Audrezet, A., De Kerviler, G., and Moulard, J.G., 2018. Authenticity under threat: When social media influencers need to go beyond self-presentation. *Journal of Business Research*, in press. https://doi.org/10.1016/j.jbusres.2018.07.008

Bang, H.J., and Lee, W.N., 2016. Consumer response to ads in social network sites: an exploration into the role of ad location and path. *Journal of Current Issues and Research in Advertising*, 37(1), 1–14.

Bergkvist, L., and Zhou, K.Q., 2016. Celebrity endorsements: a literature review and research agenda. *International Journal of Advertising*, 35(4), 642–663.

Bosher, H., 2020. Influencer Marketing and the Law. Ch. 13 in *Influencer Marketing: Building Brand Communities and Engagement*. Ed. Yesiloglu, S., and Costello, J. London: Routledge.

Bond, B.J., 2016. Following your "friend": Social media and the strength of adolescents' parasocial relationships with media personae. *Cyberpsychology, Behavior And Social Networking*, 19(11), 656–660.

Carr, C. T., and Hayes, R.A., 2014. The effect of disclosure of third-party influence on an opinion leader's credibility and electronic word of mouth in two-step flow. *Journal of Interactive Advertising*, 14(1), 38–50.

Casaló, L. V., Flavián, C., and Ibáñez-Sánchez, S., 2018. Influencers on Instagram: Antecedents and consequences of opinion leadership. *Journal of Business Research*, in press. https://doi.org/10.1016/j.jbusres.2018.07.005

Chaney, D., Mourad, T., and Slimane, K.B., 2017. Marketing to the (new) generations: summary and perspectives. *Journal of Strategic Marketing*, 25(3), 179–189.

Chung, S., and Cho, H., 2017. Fostering parasocial relationships with celebrities on social media: implications for celebrity endorsement. *Psychology and Marketing*, 34(4), 481–495.

Cohen, J., 2003. Parasocial breakups: Measuring individual differences in responses to the dissolution of parasocial relationships. *Mass Communication and Society*, 6(2), 191–202.

Colliander, J., and Dahlén, M., 2011. Following the fashionable friend: The power of social media. *Journal of Advertising Research*, 51(1), 313–320.

Costello, J., and Biondi, L., 2020. The Art of Deception: Will fake followers decay trust and can authenticity preserve it? Ch. 12 in *Influencer Marketing: Building Brand Communities and Engagement*. Ed. Yesiloglu, S., and Costello, J. London: Routledge.

Costello, J., and Urbanska, K., 2020. "Hope this is not sponsored" – Is an Influencers' credibility impacted when using sponsored versus non-sponsored content? Ch. 10 in *Influencer Marketing: Building Brand Communities and Engagement*. Ed. Yesiloglu, S., and Costello, J. London: Routledge.

De Veirman, M., Cauberghe, V., and Hudders, L., 2017. Marketing through Instagram influencers: The impact of the number of followers and product divergence on brand attitude. *International Journal of Advertising*, 36(5), 798–828.

Djafarova, E., and Rushworth, C., 2017. Exploring the credibility of online celebrities' Instagram profiles in influencing the purchase decisions of young female users. *Computers in Human Behaviour*, 68, 1–7.

Edelman, 2019. 2019 Edelman Trust Barometer special report: In brands we trust? Edelman. Retrieved from www.edelman.com/research/trust-barometer-special-report-in-brands-we-trust

Eriksson, P., and Kovalainen, A., 2008. *Qualitative Methods in Business Research*. London: Sage.

Escalas, J.E., and Bettman, J.R., 2017. Connecting with celebrities: How consumers appropriate celebrity meanings for a sense of belonging. *Journal of Advertising*, 46(2), 297–308.

Evans, N. J., Phua, J., Lim, J., and Jun, H., 2017. Disclosing Instagram influencer advertising: The effects of disclosure language on advertising recognition, attitudes, and behavioral intent. *Journal of Interactive Advertising*, 17(2), 138–149.

Fournier, S., 1998. Consumers and their brands: Developing relationship theory in consumer research. *Journal of Consumer Research*, 24(4), 343–373.

Freberg, K., Graham, K., McGaughey, K., and Freberg, L.A., 2011. Who are the social media influencers? A study of public perceptions of personality. *Public Relations Review*, 37, 90–92.

Giles, D., 2002. Parasocial interaction: A review of the literature and a model for future research. *Media Psychology*, 4(3), 279–305.

Gummesson, E., 2003. All research is interpretive! *Journal of Business and Industrial Marketing*, 18(6/7), 482–492.

GlobalWebIndex. (n.d.). Daily time spent on social networking by internet users worldwide from 2012 to 2017 (in minutes). In Statista – The Statistics Portal. Retrieved from www.statista.com/statistics/433871/daily-social-media-usage-worldwide/

Hemetsberger, A., Kittinger-Rosanelli, C.M.T., and Friedmann, S., 2009. "Bye-bye love" – Why devoted consumers break up with their brands. *Advances in Consumer Research*, 36, 430–437.

Horton, D., and Wohl, R., 1956. Mass communication and para-social interaction: Observations on intimacy at a distance. *Psychiatry*, 19(3), 215–229.

Ilicic, J., and Webster, C.M., 2016. Being true to oneself: Investigating celebrity brand authenticity. *Psychology and Marketing*, 33(6), 410–420.

Influencer Marketing Hub, 2019. Influencer marketing benchmark report. Retrieved from: https://influencermarketinghub.com/influencer-marketing-2019-benchmark-report/

De Jans, S. Cauberghe, V., and Hudders, L., 2018. How an advertising disclosure alerts young adolescents to sponsored vlogs: The moderating role of a peer-based advertising literacy intervention through an informational vlog. *Journal of Advertising*, 47(4), 309–325.

Katz, E., and Lazarsfeld, P., 1955. *Personal influence: The part played by people in the flow of mass communications*. Glencoe: Free Press.

Labrecque, L.I., 2014. Fostering consumer-brand relationships in social media environments: The role of parasocial interaction. *Journal of Interactive Marketing*, 28(2), 134–148.

Lee, J.E., and Watkins, B., 2016. YouTube vloggers' influence on consumer luxury brand perceptions and intentions. *Journal of Business Research*, 69(12), 5753–5760.

Li, J., and Chignell, M., 2010. Birds of a feather: How personality influences blog writing and reading. *International Journal of Human-Computer Studies*, 68, 589–602.

Lueck, J.A., 2015. Friend-zone with benefits: The parasocial advertising of Kim Kardashian. *Journal of Marketing Communications*, 21(2), 91–109.

Mediakix, 2018. The 2018 Influencer Marketing Industry Ad Spend. Retrieved from: http://mediakix.com/2018/03/influencer-marketing-industry-ad-spendchart/

McCormick, K., 2016. Celebrity endorsements: Influence of a product-endorser match on Millennials attitudes and purchase intentions. *Journal of Retailing and Consumer Services*, 32, 39–45.

McCracken, G., 1989. Who is the celebrity endorser? Cultural foundations of the endorsement process. *Journal of Consumer Research*, 16(3), 310–321.

McQuarrie, E.F., Miller, J., and Phillips, B.J., 2012. The megaphone effect: Taste and audience in fashion blogging. *Journal of Consumer Research*, 40(1), 136–158.

Tadajewski, M., 2016. Focus groups: history, epistemology, and non-individualistic consumer research. *Consumption Markets and Culture*, 19(4), 319–345.

Theran, S.A., Newberg, E.M., and Gleason, T.R., 2010. Adolescent girls' parasocial interactions with media figures. *The Journal of Genetic Psychology*, 171(3), 270–277.

Uzunoğlu, E., and Kip, S.M., 2014. Brand communication through digital influencers: Leveraging blogger engagement. *International Journal of Information Management*, 34(5), 592–602.

Yuan, C.L., Kim, J., and Kim, S.J., 2016. Parasocial relationship effects on customer equity in the social media context. *Journal of Business Research*, 69(9), 3795–3803.

Yuksel, M., and Labrecque, L.I., 2016. "Digital buddies": Parasocial interactions in social media. *Journal of Research in Interactive Marketing*, 10(4), 305–320.

chapter 8

Can you make the world more sustainable with influencers?

Exploring consumers' motivations to engage with influencers' sustainable content on Instagram

Sevil Yesiloglu and Weronika Waśkiw

Learning outcomes

- To explore influencers and influencer marketing within sustainability subject area.
- To understand motivations behind users' engagement with sustainable influencers.
- To identify different content types that impact consumers' willingness to engage with influencers.

Influencer marketing and influencers

The ever-evolving internet and the increasing digital empowerment of consumers have transformed the traditional ways of conveying a message. This has made social media marketing essential for influencing the modern consumer (Opreana and Vinerean 2015). One of the reasons behind its effectiveness is that it is based on the well-established power of word-of-mouth (WOM), which over the years has evolved into electronic word-of-mouth (eWOM) (Kietzmann and Canhoto 2013). Furthermore, eWOM became a foundation of influencer marketing (De Veirman et al. 2017; Yesiloglu 2020) – a phenomenon proved to be highly effective by scholars (e.g. De Veirman et al. 2017; Hoffman and Fodor 2010) and the industry (Gallagher 2018).

Nonetheless, influencer marketing is relatively new and thus, further research of digital influencers is essential, especially in the case of Instagram. With Instagrammers[1] who in 2018 posted nearly 40 percent of branded content more than the year before (Klear 2019), the platform is fast becoming a key tool for influencer marketing (Hutchinson 2019). Instagram's platform developers recognized the value of their influencers and developed new features such as the Creator Account option to further facilitate their activities (Influencer Marketing Hub 2018). Considering the creative features of Instagram, the combination of both visual information and verbal messages are believed to be a highly effective marketing approach (Pavel 2014). This could be a reason why Instagram is characterized by the highest engagement rate amongst social media platforms (Buryan 2018). Indeed, Instagram influencers are generating engagement rates over twice as high as brands (Gallagher 2018). Most marketers (85 percent) consider engagement data the most important metric for influencer marketing (Influencer Intelligence 2018). Lorenz (2019) suggests that the content in the comment section can be equally insightful and has the potential to provide a further, deeper understanding of consumer–influencer engagement on this platform.

By understanding these metrics, it can help marketers implement successful influencer-led campaigns. However, well-implemented online campaigns and efficiently managed social media networking sites are also believed to be an effective instrument to serve ethical and educational purposes (Grocher et al. 2018), while having a real sustainable impact (Langley and Van den Broek 2010). Therefore, while the recognition of influencers is consistently increasing (Uzunoglu and Kip 2014), there is also a debate about promoting sustainable development and environment-friendly lifestyle, and the role that influencers can play in this process (Styles 2019). Although society has a largely positive attitude towards sustainability (Langley and Van den Broek 2010) and it seems to be a growing trend (Kane et al. 2012), human activity is continuing to have a seriously damaging impact on the environment. Therefore, current lifestyles and consumption behavior need an urgent *eco-cultural revolution* (Wang et al. 2011), which could be also encouraged by the marketing industry and particularly influencers.

The overall purpose of this chapter, therefore, is to examine user engagement with sustainable content posted by Instagram influencers to establish how environment-friendly products and services (e.g. eco-food or sustainable travel) could increase the popularity of influencers. We do this by first identifying the motivations of Instagram users to engage with sustainable content. We then explore how different content types and features affect the two-way communication between Instagram users and influencers. Finally, we identify the most effective approaches to popularize a sustainable lifestyle through Instagrammers.

Influencers and their followers on social media

Digital conversations between influencers and their audiences have started to reflect the two-way communication model where "every receiver is a potential sender" (Uzunoglu and Kip 2014, p. 598). The concept was proposed decades ago by Turnbull and Meenaghan (1980), who stated that the transmission of messages does not necessarily have to be initiated by the opinion leader. Similarly, Myers and Robertson (1972) added that "opinion leadership is two-way: people who influence others are themselves influenced by others" (p. 41). (Opinion leadership is discussed extensively by Yesiloglu (2020) in Chapter 1.)

Nevertheless, the two-way relationship could also result from the more recent societal change as many of today's consumers have been immersed in technology that facilitates two-way relationships. Consequently, consumers naturally expect to be able to embrace relationships with brands (in this case, influencers) instead of just being passive recipients of their messages (Williams and Chinn 2010). Moreover, social network systems effectively facilitate building those relationships as they are often characterized by their conversational nature (Weinberg and Pehlivan 2011). Indeed, they were developed to "[create] an environment that encourages a two-way conversation" (Papasolomou and Melanthiou 2012, p. 325) between influencers and their followers. However, the extent to which followers engage in the conversation varies and depends on factors such as an individual's interests, level of involvement, personality, and motivations (Uzunoglu and Kip 2014).

The power of Instagram influencers

De Veirman et al. (2017) emphasized the effectiveness of Instagram as a tool for eWOM because it allows users to generate content that contains both visual and textual messages. Similarly, Zhu and Chen (2015) classified Instagram as being a content-based site. This means Instagram's users engage with posts because they like the content probably more than they like the person behind the profile, and their conversations tend to be related to the subject of the post instead of its author. Furthermore, content that is produced by Instagrammers largely relies on the effectiveness of user-generated content, which has become one of the major factors influencing consumer behavior nowadays (Hoffman and Fodor's 2010). This user-generated content is generally believed to contain more trustworthy, reliable, and up-to-date information than other sources (Gretzel and Yoo 2008). Since it tends to be more relatable for influencers' followers, it can create stronger connections between the audience and the brand or concept that influencers advocate (Cwynar-Horta 2016).

Nonetheless, the notion of a content-based site does not diminish the social aspect of Instagram as user-generated visuals on the platform allow users to efficiently communicate with large groups of people (Bakhshi et al. 2014). With approximately 70 million daily photo updates (Lee et al. 2015), Instagram is one of the most important platforms for eWOM and influencer marketing (Jaakonmäki et al. 2017), especially when rising influencers are considered (Evans et al. 2017). Moreover, the sense of immediacy on the platform facilitates the creation of communities around influencers (Casaló et al. 2018), which is also supported by professional publications that often consider Instagrammers to be leaders in driving social engagement (RhythmOne 2017).

The concept of engagement

Engagement has received a fair amount of attention over the last few decades across various disciplines, including social psychology (Achterberg et al. 2003), politics (Mondak et al. 2010), and organizational behavior (Saks 2006). The concept is still relatively new to the marketing literature, but the number of relevant studies has increased significantly in recent years (e.g. Brodie et al. 2011; Hollebeek et al. 2014; Vivek et al. 2014). Consumer engagement in social media has also started gaining more attention from scholars due to it being "a promising concept expected to provide enhanced predictive and explanatory power of focal consumer behavior outcomes" (Hollebeek et al. 2014, p. 150). The broader definition of engagement as either positive or negative "[behavioral] manifestations that have a brand or firm focus ... resulting from motivational drivers" (Van Doorn et al. 2010, p. 254) could be used in this context but there is a need to apply additional perspectives that will allow this concept to be explored in relation to influencers in more detail.

Parasocial interaction approach

The relationship with social media personalities was previously discussed with the concept of parasocial interaction (Ngai et al. 2015). The theory was originally used to understand the effect of TV and film celebrities on consumers in the 1950s to explain the one-way relationship between these two (Stever and Lawson 2013). However, it was promptly adapted to more current marketing phenomena when some of the first online creators, bloggers, emerged (Colliander and Dahlén 2011).

Based on the conversational and informal nature of blogs and social networking sites (Uzunoglu and Kip 2014), readers and followers are expected to be characterized by a high level of parasocial interaction as the "conversational style" and "informal settings" are the main factors influencing parasocial interaction (Rubin et al. 1985). Parasocial interaction aims to explain the illusionary relationship between media personalities and media users (Lee and Watkins 2016) who "believe they are engaged in a direct two-way conversation" (Labrecque 2014, p. 135), as opposed to having a real two-way communication. However, engagement with media personalities is prompted by exactly the same motivations as real interpersonal interactions, i.e.

searching for advice, seeking friends, trying to be part of someone's life, or a desire to eventually meet the media personality in the real world (Rubin et al. 1985). Therefore, parallel dimensions can be expected to motivate consumer–influencer engagement. This concept was explored further in Chapter 7 (Närvänen et al. 2020).

Types of online engagement

Different scholars propose both unidimensional and multidimensional definitions of online consumer engagement, but the multidimensional view is largely preferred (e.g. Dessart 2015; Harrigan et al. 2017). This is because of its focus on cognitive, emotional, and behavioral dimensions (e.g. Brodie et al. 2011; Brodie et al. 2013; Hollebeek et al. 2014; So et al. 2014; Vivek et al. 2014). Even though Ilic (2008) developed two additional components, aspirational and social engagement, they were then rejected by Hollebeek (2011), who argued that these should be included as subcomponents of the emotional facet.

Dessart et al. (2016) argues that the above conceptualizations and proposed scales were created to find their applicability across different contexts and types of online platforms. Yet, previously Baldus et al. (2015) noticed that none of them focuses specifically on the explicit dimensions of engagement for online brand communities to "capture motivations tied to the channel, other consumers, and the brand simultaneously" (p. 979), making it also relevant for the exploration of consumer–influencer engagement. Moreover, Baldus et al.'s (2015) work largely reflects the motivations proposed in the Self-Determination Theory (SDT) (Deci and Ryan 1985). SDT is considered by several scholars to be a valuable framework in helping researchers to understand eWOM engagement (e.g. Wang et al. 2016; Yesiloglu and Gill 2020). Therefore, due to the lack of extensive research specifically on consumer–influencer engagement on Instagram, the scale proposed by Baldus et al. (2015) is considered for this chapter. Moreover, based on the notion that proposed conceptualizations do not necessarily need to refer to behavioral, cognitive, and affective components to encompass these dimensions (Harrigan et al. 2017), our study will extend their work and categorize the proposed 11 dimensions into the three facets. A full overview of the reviewed conceptualizations of engagement in the marketing literature is shown in Table 8.1.

Investigating influencers' sustainable behavior and their engagement with consumers

The phenomenon of social media has had a significant impact on the awareness of environmental issues among its users (Too and Bajracharya 2015). Social networking sites effectively "combine the effects of observing [role models] and the actions of other people" (Langley and Van den Broek 2010, p. 18). However, it has been argued that the above notion strongly indicates the potential of influencers (the "role models") to be used for this purpose. Following this discussion, Olsen (2014) refers

sevil yesiloglu and weronika waśkiw

Table 8.1 Overview of the reviewed engagement conceptualizations

	Behavioral	Emotional	Cognitive
Hollebeek et al. (2014, p. 154)	**Activation** "A consumer's level of energy, effort, and time spent on a brand in a particular consumer/brand interaction."	**Affection** "A consumer's degree of positive brand-related effect in a particular consumer/brand interaction."	**Cognitive Processing** "A consumer's level of brand-related thought processing and elaboration in a particular consumer/brand interaction."
So et al. (2014, p311)	**Interaction** "Various participation … that a customer has with a brand organization or other customers outside of purchase."	**Identification** "The degree of a consumer's perceived oneness with or belongingness to the brand." **Enthusiasm** "The degree of excitement and interest that a consumer has in the brand."	**Absorption** "A pleasant state which describes the customer as being fully concentrated, happy and deeply engrossed while playing the role as a consumer of the brand." **Attention** "The degree of attentiveness, focus, and connection that a consumer has with a brand."
Vivek et al. (2014, p.407)	**Enthused participation** "The zealous reactions and feelings of a person related to using or interacting with the focus of their engagement."	**Social connection** "Enhancement of the interaction based on the inclusion of others with the focus of engagement, indicating mutual or reciprocal action in the presence of others."	**Conscious attention** "The degree of interest the person has or wishes to have in interacting with the focus of their engagement."
Baldus et al. (2015, p. 981)	**Seeking assistance** "The degree to which a community member wants to receive help from fellow community members."	**Brand passion** "The ardent affection a community member has for the brand."	**Brand influence** "The degree to which a community member wants to influence the brand."

(continued)

Table 8.1 Cont.

Behavioral	Emotional	Cognitive
Self-expression	**Connecting**	**Rewards (hedonic)**
"The degree to which a community member feels that the community provides them with a forum where they can express their true interests and opinions."	"The extent to which a community member feels that being a member of the brand community connects them to some good thing bigger than themselves."	"The degree to which the community member wants to gain hedonic rewards … through their participation in the community."
Like-minded discussion "The extent to which a community member is interested in talking with people similar to themselves about the brand."	**Validation** "A community member's feeling of the extent to which other community members affirm the importance of their opinions, ideas, and interests."	**Rewards (utilitarian)** "The degree to which the community member wants to gain utilitarian rewards … through their participation in the community."
Helping "The degree to which a community member wants to help fellow community members by sharing knowledge, experience, or time."		**Up-to-date information** "The degree to which a community member feels that the brand community helps them to stay informed or keep up-to-date with brand and product-related information."

to Cialdini's (2007) principles of social influence, the principle of social proof that relies on the conformity of human nature. By doing so, Olsen (2014) confirms the suitability of social networking sites to motivate for lower energy consumption, especially when it prompts the competitiveness of social media users.

Furthermore, Kane et al.'s (2012) study emphasizes that Facebook is an effective tool to build the connection between consumers and their green attitudes. This results from the nature of the platform that encourages users further to share their experiences and recommendations. As Kane et al.'s (2012) study confirms, these two are the primary drivers when choosing sustainable products or services. Moreover, Zeng and Gerritsen (2014) point out that there is a particular link between social media and sustainable tourism due to the power of user-generated content as well as the capability of social media to "reflect and influence tourists' perceptions and attitudes towards *green* or *eco-activities*" (p. 30). This view could be extended with Langley and Van den Broek's (2010) observation that since social networking sites are currently available nearly everywhere at all times, they can also support sustainable choices of consumers during any other activities, e.g. shopping online. Given that Instagram is used for similar purposes as the aforementioned social networking sites, e.g. to share or follow recommendations (Casaló et al. 2018), it can be assumed that there is also a link between Instagram influencers and sustainable attitudes of their audience.

Idea fairy: Sustainability and influencers

Growing concern for the environment is probably one of the most important global movements shaping individuals' current activities on online platforms. When you consider these global trends, think about your own activities online and try to answer the following questions: what sources do you follow when you do want to receive more information about the environment and the issues raised by the society? Is social media playing an important role in your engagement (e.g. searching for news, posts, content etc.)? Are there any certain influencers that you follow sharing posts within sustainable context? What are the reasons you follow these types of influencers?

The study

To investigate the motivations and content of Instagram users to engage with sustainable content noted earlier, we collected the observatory data for this study from the publicly available Instagram accounts. The selection of influencers was based on the inclusion of the keyword "sustainability" or at least one of the relevant hashtags (e.g. #ecofriendly, #sustainableliving, #zerowaste) in their recent posts. The relevant hashtags were identified with a Keyhole tracker, a tool that provides a set of the trending hashtags used by Instagram users alongside the main keyword (i.e. "sustainability") at the time of searching.

To accurately address the current trend within the industry, only 20 of the most recent posts were collected from each of the five chosen influencers. Paid posts (e.g. posts, which included hashtags #sponsored or #ad, or were marked as *Paid partnership*) were not collected due to their questionable credibility (Evans et al. 2017). Moreover, the so-called giveaways were also omitted as their only aim is to offer incentives, and taking them into consideration could cause biased results.

All textual data that was collected (including hashtags) needed to be written in English to avoid incorrect or inaccurate translations. Despite the popularity of emojis on social media and a notion that they can become a new language (Gaffey 2015), they were not taken into account in this study to minimize the risk of misunderstanding their meaning due to the differences between linguistic and non-linguistic (e.g. visual) forms of communication (Dresner and Herring 2010).

Data analysis

In this research, we followed the three-stage process of inductive content analysis, including the stages of preparation, organizing, and reporting (Elo and Kyngäs 2008). In the first coding pass, we created several nodes to mark the types of Instagram posts that influencers create (e.g. image, video) or briefly report on the visual elements that an image contains (e.g. human face). Moreover, several comments were recorded in the form of numeric codes. The number of likes was not taken into consideration due to the recent updates from Instagram that began to hide likes to decrease the implied importance of this metric (Constine 2019).

Even though the first three initial nodes to code the sustainable themes (i.e. *sustainable fashion*, *zero waste*, and *climate change*) were also taken from the Keyhole tracker that was previously used to identify relevant hashtags, all textual content was then open-coded "to describe all [its] aspects" (Elo and Kyngäs 2008, p. 109) – a practice that allowed us to recognize all the other existing themes. To get further insights into the two-way communication between Instagram influencers and their audience, a specific type of content (e.g. emotional, informative) was also reported at this stage. Although some of the content types mentioned in the reviewed literature were used as a foundation, additional nodes were subsequently created during the process of coding.

In this study, we adopted the well-established engagement scale proposed by Baldus et al. (2015). However, a large portion of comments on the posts was open coded with the use of effective methods (Saldaña 2013) to identify additional motivations to engage with influencers. Figure 8.1 shows the list of all the initial tree nodes that allowed a hierarchical structure to form.

Motivations and content of Instagram users to engage with sustainable content

A hundred Instagram posts were collected from five sustainable influencers that resulted in 4,881 publicly available comments. During the first stage of analysis, we excluded some of the comments as they were published by authors-influencers (922 comments), did not include any textual message (333 comments), were written in languages other than English (48 comments) or were identified as spam and other unrelated messages (47 comments). The remaining 3,525 comments were suitable for the thematic analysis.

After two cycles of coding, we observed *like-minded discussion* to be the most prominent motivational dimension. However, this includes both user-influencer discussions as well as conversations between other commenters. Interestingly, *like-minded discussion* was significantly more prominent than any other proposed dimension, including the desire to connect (*Connecting*). This implies that even though Instagram users willingly engage in conversations with influencers who share the same views, they are not motivated enough to build a strong connection with the influencer or the influencer's community. The summary of the motivational dimensions identified through the analysis and their prominence is presented in Table 8.2.

sevil yesiloglu and weronika waśkiw

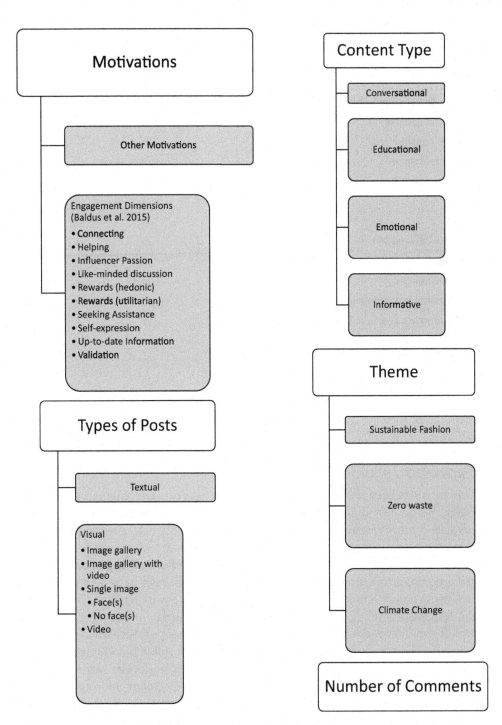

Figure 8.1 Tree nodes created for initial coding.

Table 8.2 Prominence of the engagement motivations identified through the analysis

Motivations	Number of comments
TOTAL	**3,525**
The proposed engagement dimensions	1,960
Like-minded discussion	897
Influencer passion	283
Seeking assistance	238
Self-expression	203
Helping	113
Validation	111
Up-to-date information	60
Connecting	38
Influencer influence	11
Other motivations to engage	1,571
Other comments & unidentified motivations	437
Non-contributive affection	372
Tags	361
Non-contributive like-mindedness	275
Inspiration	92
Content appreciation	34

Information seeking

Information has been found to be an important trigger for consumers to engage with content on social media (e.g. Muntinga et al. 2011; Yesiloglu 2018). Previous user-generated content research on traditional and new media has revealed information seeking for media consumption (Shao 2009). Consumers with an opinion-seeking behavior are likely to search for information and advice from other people when they make a purchase decision (Flynn et al. 1996). This can help in understanding why consumers consume brand-related content on social networking sites. On the other hand, Muntinga et al. (2011) explore this motivation further and categorize it under four different subheadings: surveillance, knowledge, pre-purchase information, and inspiration. Their study broadly focuses on consumers' online brand-related engagement. They found information seeking is one of the main motives why people read others' brand-related content on Facebook and Twitter. To explore information motive further, this study includes a sub-motivation of information seeking inspiration refers to reading content to get a new idea (Muntinga et al. 2011), *seeking advice* and *up-to-date information*.

When looking at Instagram users and their engagement behavior with sustainable influencers, we found that looking for inspiration is one of the main motives followers have. The emergence of an additional behavioral dimension, *inspiration*,

sevil yesiloglu and weronika waśkiw

and its dominance over some of the other items proposed by Baldus et al. (2015), such as seeking up-to-date information, is a particularly unexpected result, knowing that social media has been recognized as the primary source of online stories, with Instagram being one of the leading news providers (Reuters Institute 2018). When we consider the content type influencers published on their profile, our findings revealed that the most effective informative content type was primarily posts about the "zero waste" movement, which generated on average a relatively high number of comments per post and the majority of them were prompted by a desire to have a *like-minded discussion*. This indicates that the *zero-waste* theme is more likely to be an effective engagement driver but further investigation to understand the correlation between the specific post themes and motivations to engage is needed.

When we looked at followers' need to seek advice further, we found that Instagram users were more likely to seek help in case of posts about *sustainable beauty* and they only used comments to tag other users when an influencer shared generic information about *nature conservation*. Despite the purpose of *educational* posts to share practical solutions and educate Instagram users on how to implement sustainable solutions into their lives, *seeking* [further] *assistance* was a dominant motivation for users to engage with influencers' posts. This indicates that influencers who share sustainable tips and instructions not only provide their audience with valuable guidance, but they are also the most likely to popularize the idea of a sustainable lifestyle amongst those users who require additional clarity or information. Informative Instagram content where influencers share their practical solutions to the daily life of the followers, tend to increase the popularity of the content of influencers.

Like-minded conversation and socializing

Most of the motivations that were identified through this study reflected the dimensions proposed by Bladus et al. (2015), whose scale served as a foundation for this study. By finding this, we highlighted the multidimensionality of consumer–influencer engagement on Instagram. Furthermore, knowing that *like-minded discussion* was the primary motivation for Instagram users to engage with influencers, this study confirms the conversational nature of this platform alongside other social networking sites that encourage two-way discussions (Weinberg and Pehlivan 2011; Papasolomou and Melanthiou 2012). It also aligns with the self-determination theory (SDT), which emphasizes intrinsic motivation to be enhanced by social factors (Deci and Ryan 1985). Berger and Schwartz (2011) also find that consumers often rely on online engagement with others as an input for small talk and everyday conversations with others. Hence, followers tend to engage with influencers' posts on different levels to try to compensate for their thwarted intrinsic needs by gratifications that are derived from these engagement types, which may be driven by a communication with others (socializing) motive, which is related to the desire to interact with others.

To take this discussion further out of the engagement dimensions, this study shows that conversing with people who have similar interests (*like-minded discussion*) was identified as the key motivation to comment, which can create valuable conversation for followers to socialize. In addition to this, it is essential to mention that this motivation encompasses discussion both with influencers and other Instagram users. Interestingly, *like-minded discussion* was significantly more prominent than any other proposed dimension, including the desire to connect. This implies that even though Instagram users willingly engage in conversations with influencers who share the same views, they are not motivated enough to build a strong connection between them and the influencer or the influencer's community if they do not have a sense of like-minded discussion.

Self-expression

Alongside the prominence of *like-minded discussion*, the frequency of *self-expression* supports the multi-step flow theory (Weimann 1982) and emphasizes the importance of Instagram users and their comments in the conversation with influencers. It is questionable whether they should be considered as opinion leaders on the same level as influencers (as suggested by Myers and Robertson's (1972) view of two-way opinion leadership) but their willingness to contribute and a motivation to express their own opinions is vital in this two-way communication model and signifies their role as message senders, not just receivers (Uzunoglu and Kip 2014). Similarly, their contribution to eWOM was further highlighted by a significant number of comments where commenters only tagged other users. Despite not being included in the original scale and their low relevance to the subject of conversation, these results greatly support the notion that influencer marketing not only emerged from eWOM but in fact, maximizes its capabilities. This finding also supports the discussion of De Veirman et al. (2017) that pointed out the message of influencers can easily create viral effects among their audience. When we consider the viral effect of influencers' messages on users' engagement, we also need to consider the significant effect of the need for users to express themselves through engaging with influencers' posts.

Helping others

Altruistic behavior is commonly regarded as a substantial motivation to trigger people's engagement in online media. When scholars investigate this motive, they mainly look at the engagement consumers have with content not owned by brands such as eWOM, user-generated content, networking social media sites etc. This study, therefore, brings further attention to the altruistic dimension of engagement that has already been widely recognized in different contexts by other researchers (e.g. Sundaram et al. 1998; Hennig-Thurau et al. 2004).

Inspiration for these studies has come from finding the reasons for a genuine need individuals have to help others in virtual communities. To investigate this motive further, we found that followers are driven by altruistic motives (helping others) when they comment on sustainable influencers' posts. However, when we look at communication between influencers and their followers within a sustainable context in existing literature, there is an interesting dissonance between altruistic motivations to engage with sustainable content confirmed in this study and Olsen's (2014) findings that suggested appealing to the competitiveness of social media users in order to motivate them for sustainable behaviors (i.e. by offering utilitarian rewards). Although utilitarian reward has been investigated in literature as an external reward or benefit that motivates users in engaging crowdsourcing (Hirth et al. 2013) and online games (Chang et al. 2014), this term has not been comprehensively investigated to understand altruistic behavior and engagement in the interaction between influencers and followers. Therefore, our findings indicate the support for the well-researched attitude-behavior gap towards sustainability (Juvan and Dolnicar 2014; Terlau and Hirsch 2015).

Influencer passion

As discussed in Chapter 1 (Yesiloglu 2020), creative and eye-catching content clearly has a significant impact on consumers' engagement with influencers on social media. More specifically, on Instagram which is classified as a content-based site (Zhu and Chen 2015), using the creative features of Instagram significantly reflects influencers' passion and increases the level of engagement consumers show when they communicate with influencers. Similarly, Audrezet et al. (2018) evaluate influencers' passion in their content as a great opportunity for organizations to engage with their audience. They also argued, according to self-determination theory, authenticity involves an individual's engagement in intrinsically motivated behavior – which is centered by individuals' desire and passion (Deci and Ryan 2000). Audrezet et al. (2018) proposed that influencers' digital content has been found to be intrinsically motivated when influencers are passionately authentic. We can, therefore, argue that Instagram users are motivated to engage because the subject of the post involves influencers' passion and their genuine interest in sustainability rather than because of its author.

Types of content and their influence on engagement

While this chapter has hinted at the importance of motivations to understand the engagement between influencers and their followers, we also acknowledge the valuable impact of content types on engagement. The increasing importance of the comment sections on Instagram (Lorenz 2019) suggests that their content can be equally insightful and thus, they have the potential to provide a further understanding of consumer–influencer engagement on this platform. Given this, the average number of comments are depicted in Table 8.3.

Educational/informative content

As Lee et al. (2014, p. 5) pointed out, "informative content tends to drive engagement positively only when combined with [persuasive] content" (Lee et al. 2014, p. 5). Our finding revealed also that *conversational-informative* content is highly efficient in generating a high volume of comments on influencers' posts on Instagram. Despite the purpose of *educational* posts to share practical solutions and educate Instagram users on how to implement sustainable solutions into their lives, *seeking* [further] *assistance* was a primary motivation in case of the *informative-educational* content (19.64 percent) and a second most common dimension when posts were

Table 8.3 The average number of comments generated on specific content types.

Content Types	Average number of comments generated per post
Informative – conversational	78
Emotional	77
Informative – educational	66
Informative – emotional	66
Educational – conversational	64
Conversational	42
Emotional – conversational	38
Informative	35
Informative – educational – conversational	24
Educational	5

just *educational* (18.37 percent). This indicates that influencers who share sustainable tips and instructions not only provide their audience with valuable guidance, but they are also most likely to popularize the idea of a sustainable lifestyle as their audience intentionally seeks additional clarity or information. This is particularly important considering that *seeking assistance* was also one of the key motivations overall (as previously noted in Table 8.2). Moreover, users were also likely to express being inspired (*Inspiration*) when posts featured *informative-educational* (17.46 percent) or *educational* (10.2 percent) types of content, meaning that these two could have the largest real-life impact. Therefore, even though the educational approach is not necessarily the primary engagement driver on Instagram, when the number of comments is considered, this kind of content has the potential to have the most significant real-life impact by inspiring others and raising awareness of sustainable choices.

On the other hand, this study emphasizes the valuable contribution of education content which stimulates the engagement between influencers and their followers. Considering the identified motivations (*Inspiration* and *Seeking assistance*), they drive Instagram users to engage with *educational* posts implying their effectiveness in encouraging people to live sustainably as they particularly inspire people or prompt them to seek further help. Therefore, *educational* posts effectively increase the generic knowledge of sustainability and raise awareness of how accessible and effortless sustainable solutions are. This is particularly important knowing that "low awareness" has been found to be one of the primary barriers for eco-products and services (Kane et al. 2012).

Emotional content

An extensive body of research looked further at the positive impact of *emotional* messages on engagement in the context of textual posts on Facebook (Lee et al. 2014) or newspaper articles (Berger and Milkman 2012). For example, Berger and

sevil yesiloglu and weronika waśkiw

Milkman's (2012) looked at the textual content that contains emotional messages. Their study of the online *New York Times* articles shows that stories which evoke highly positive (awe) or negative (anger or anxiety) emotions were more likely to go viral in contrast with other emotions, e.g. sadness. Nonetheless, none of these studies explored content created by influencers and thus, little is known on whether these content types would affect consumer–influencer engagement on Instagram in the same way. To expand it further, we provide support for this notion in relation to influencers' content on Instagram.

Content and physical attractive (or attractive content?)

Particularly given the importance of physical attractiveness in influencer marketing discussed in Chapter 1, it has been brought to marketers' attention that the physical attractiveness of influencers has a positive impact on users and their engagement with influencers' posts. The results of this research align with Bakhshi et al.'s (2014) analysis and confirm that Instagram users favor the presence of at least one human face in a photo as this kind of content tends to generate more comments. This finding reflects the vast psychological research suggesting that human nature instinctively prioritizes looking at the human face as opposed to any other objects (Young et al. 1986), especially when the factor of physical attractiveness is being considered (Jaakonmäki et al. 2017). However, the presence of human faces could be also seen as a distraction as these posts attracted proportionally a high volume of brief and unrelated to sustainability comments, implying that Instagram users did not feel motivated enough to fully express their passion for the influencer or, more importantly, contribute to the meaningful discussion. Therefore, in the context of sustainable influencers whose aim is to spread eco-conscious messages (Salibian 2018), the seemingly higher engagement has the potential to act unfavorably and bring an undesired effect.

Future direction

The findings of this research aim to provide pro-environmental individuals, brands, or organizations with new insights into consumer–influencer engagement and guide them in creating engaging content that communicates more effectively with their audiences.

First and foremost, this study highlights the consumer need for information that is provided in a conversational, informal tone. While conversational content has been seen as one of the primary factors driving the success of influencer marketing (Scott 2017) and companies in many cases favor disseminating informative messages about their new products or promotions (Lee et al. 2014), the finding of this study emphasizes the need for a combination of these two content types to make sustainability more engaging. As shown above, information-carrying visuals have the potential to drive a relatively high number of comments that contribute to meaningful discussion. When communicating the right message is a priority, content creators should also take into consideration potential distractions, e.g. a face in the photo.

Furthermore, the analysis of motivations that drive Instagram users to engage with sustainable influencers implies a high level of altruistic motives. Therefore, influencers or marketers whose aim is to promote sustainable products or services through Instagrammers could use this finding to encourage consumers to engage by highlighting how others can benefit from their participation in the conversation or by emphasizing the mutual benefits of their engagement (Henning-Thurau et al. 2004).

Summary

- This chapter showed that Instagram users were highly motivated to have a like-minded discussion with influencers and the theme of the posts or the way they were written did not affect their motivations significantly. However, Instagram posts in the *emotional* or *conversational-informative* tone of voice generated the highest number of comments.
- Furthermore, the analysis revealed that Instagram users were more likely to engage with influencers to admit feeling inspired by them rather than to receive up-to-date information or any kind of incentives.
- The study also confirmed photos with a human face generate a higher number of comments. However, it also suggests that photos with objects, food, etc. could be more beneficial for the purpose of promoting sustainability as the presence of a human face significantly motivated Instagram users to share their non-contributive affection or thoughts, as opposed to posting relevant comments.
- Lastly, the findings of this study show support for educational posts that contain practical advice as they have a large potential to popularize the idea of a sustainable lifestyle amongst Instagram users despite generating a relatively lower number of comments.

Case study: An agency's adaptation to COVID-19

Raluca Rusoiu, Crowd – Global Creative Agency

When COVID-19 struck the UK, marketing, advertising, and public relations agencies all scrambled to adjust their services to help clients adjust to the new lockdown restrictions. Crowd started helping its clients by taking events online as well as bringing the client's services online. The agency even developed a virtual tour of its home county, Dorset.

Crowd was working with one brand, ExtraAF, that was wanting to do a new brand launch. ExtraAF is a sustainable fashion brand geared for all genders who want sustainable clothing without compromising on style. ExtraAF's goal is to change the status quo of the market and create demand for eco-friendly/sustainable fashion, trying to make it the new norm. However, with the COVID-19 restrictions, Crowd had to adjust its original campaign (an in-studio photo shoot and life-style photoshoot) to plan B. Crowd reacted quickly and formed an influencer-led content production plan to ensure that ExtraAF could still launch as planned. Influencers would be recruited to model and capture the new fashion line all from their own home.

Crowd had previously used influencers in an "Awesome in any language" campaign for Razor, a company that produced Hovertrax 2.0 which is a self-balancing electric scooter. Crowd worked with influencers to show the emotion and fun of using the product.

The new brand ExtraAF was planning on being an online brand only. But, with the lockdown and many individuals spending an inordinate amount of time on the internet – it was an opportunity, but also a challenge. For those fashion brands with an online presence, more potential customers had time to browse the internet. However, there is the potential that the individual is being bombarded with an increased amount of online communications.

Launching a new fashion line or sustainable brand is hard under normal circumstances. Influencers have helped on many fronts. By taking their photos at home and sharing online, we are also able to use their content on the brand's website. This gives the brands a deeper connection with the influencer and their audience. This may be because it is not a random model, but someone the audience may have already engaged with. Additionally, the influencers have done a great job of increasing awareness. This awareness boost informs the audience about the brand's sustainability efforts.

For ExtraAF's overall message to not get diluted, Crowd sent influencer packs with key messages. However, influencers were expected to ensure they produced content in their own tone of voice and style. Crowd says working with influencers that specialize in fashion, value sustainability, and fit with the overall brand personality is important for the success of the campaign. Crowd also tries to make sure their chosen influencers are as inclusive as possible.

Questions:

1. How hard do you think it is for brands to adapt their campaigns when hit with natural disasters or pandemics?
2. What are the advantages and disadvantages of working with influencers?
3. Why is it important that influencers produce content in their own tone of voice or style?

Note

1 For the purpose of clear and concise analysis, throughout the whole study the terms "Instagrammers" and "(Instagram) influencers" are being used interchangeably, whilst those who commented on their posts are referred to as *Instagram users*.

References

Achterberg, W., Pot, A.M., Kerkstra, A., Ooms, M., Muller, M., and Ribbe, M., 2003. The effect of depression on social engagement in newly admitted Dutch nursing home residents. *The Gerontologist*, 43(2), 213–218.

Audrezet, A., Caffier de Kerviler, G., and Guidry Moulard, J., 2018, Authenticity Under Threat: When social media influencers need to go beyond passion, *Journal of Business Research*, in press.

Bakhshi, S., Shamma, D.A., and Gilbert, E., 2014. Faces engage us: Photos with faces attract more likes and comments on Instagram. In: Proceedings of the SIGCHI Conference on Human Factors in Computing Systems. Toronto 26 April–1 May 2014. Toronto, ON: ACM, 965–974.

Baldus, B.J., Voorhees, C., and Calantone, R., 2015. Online brand community engagement: Scale development and validation. *Journal of Business Research*, 68(5), 978–985.

Berger, J., and Milkman, K.L., 2012. What makes online content viral?. *Journal of Marketing Research*, 49(2), 192–205.

Berger, J., and Schwartz, E.M., 2011. What drives immediate and ongoing word of mouth? *Journal of Marketing Research*, 48(5), 869–880.

Brodie, R.J., Hollebeek, L.D., Jurić, B., and Ilić, A., 2011. Customer engagement: Conceptual domain, fundamental propositions, and implications for research. *Journal of service research*, 14(3), 252–271.

Brodie, R.J., Ilic, A., Juric, B., and Hollebeek, L., 2013. Consumer engagement in a virtual brand community: An exploratory analysis. *Journal of Business Research*, 66(1), 105–114.

Buryan, M., 2018. Instagram Engagement: Everything You Need to Know [Exclusive Stats] [online], *Socialbakers.com*. Available from: www.socialbakers.com/blog/instagram-engagement

Casaló, L.V., Flavián, C., and Ibáñez-Sánchez, S., 2018. Influencers on Instagram: Antecedents and consequences of opinion leadership. *Journal of Business Research* [online], In Press. Available from: www.sciencedirect.com/science/article/pii/S0148296318303187

Chang, I.C., Liu, C.C., and Chen, K., 2014. The effects of hedonic/utilitarian expectations and social influence on continuance intention to play online games. *Internet Research*, 24(1), 21–45.

Cialdini, R.B, 2007. *Influence: The psychology of persuasion*. Revised Edition. New York: Collins.

Colliander, J., and Dahlén, M., 2011. Following the fashionable friend: The power of social media: Weighing publicity effectiveness of blogs versus online magazines. *Journal of Advertising Research*, 51(1), 313–320.

Constine, J., 2019. Instagram officially tests hiding Like counts [online], *TechCrunch.com*. Available from: https://techcrunch.com/2019/04/30/instagram-hidden-like- counter/?guccounter=1&guce_referrer_us=aHRocHM6Ly93d3cuZ29vZ2xlLmNvbS8&guce_referrer_cs=AdtybB_yYh_skdTEfJ1hpA

Cwynar-Horta, J., 2016. The commodification of the body positive movement on Instagram. *Stream: inspiring critical thought*, 8(2), 36–56.

De Veirman, M., Cauberghe, V., and Hudders, L., 2017. Marketing through Instagram influencers: the impact of the number of followers and product divergence on brand attitude. *International Journal of Advertising*, 36(5), 798–828.

Deci, E.L., and Ryan, R.M., 1985. The general causality orientations scale: Self-determination in personality. *Journal of Research in Personality*, 19(2), 109–134.

Deci, E.L., and Ryan, R.M., 2000. The "what" and "why" of goal pursuits: Human needs and the self-determination of behavior. *Psychological Inquiry*, 11(4), 227–268.

Dessart, L., 2015. *Consumer engagement in online brand communities*. Thesis (Ph.D.). University of Glasgow.

Dessart, L., Veloutsou, C., and Morgan-Thomas, A., 2016. Capturing consumer engagement: duality, dimensionality, and measurement. *Journal of Marketing Management*, 32(5–6), 399–426.

Dresner, E., and Herring, S. C., 2010. Functions of the nonverbal CMC: Emoticons and illocutionary force. *Communication Theory*, 20, 249–268.

Elo, S., and Kyngäs, H., 2008. The qualitative content analysis process. *Journal of Advanced Nursing*, 62(1), 107–115.

Evans, N.J., Phua, J., Lim, J., and Jun, H., 2017. Disclosing Instagram influencer advertising: The effects of disclosure language on advertising recognition, attitudes, and behavioral intent. *Journal of Interactive Advertising*, 17(2), 138–149.

Flynn, L.R., Goldsmith, R.E., and Eastman, J.K., 1996. Opinion leaders and opinion seekers: Two new measurement scales. *Journal of the Academy of Marketing Science*, 24(2), 137.

Gaffey, C., 2015. Are Emojis Becoming the New Universal "Language"? [online]. *Newsweek*, Available from: www.newsweek.com/emojiemojisemoji-meaningemoji-languageemoji-communicationemoji-unicodevyv-600005

Gallagher, K., 2018. The Influencer Marketing Report: Research, strategy & platforms for leveraging social media influencers [online]. *Business Insider*, Available from: www.businessinsider.com/the-influencer-marketing-report-2018-1?r=US&IR=T

Gretzel, U., and Yoo, K.H., 2008. Use and impact of online travel reviews. *Information and Communication Technologies in Tourism*, 35–46.

Grocher, K., Wolf, L., and Goldkind, L., 2018. Social Media in Agency Settings. In: Goldkind, L., Wolf, L., and Freddolino, P.P., eds. *Digital Social Work: Tools for Practice with Individuals, Organizations, and Communities*. Oxford: Oxford University Press, 168–184.

Harrigan, P., Evers, U., Miles, M., and Daly, T., 2017. Customer engagement with tourism social media brands. *Tourism Management*, 59, 597–609.

Hennig-Thurau, T., Gwinner, K.P., Walsh, G., and Gremler, D.D., 2004. Electronic word-of-mouth via consumer-opinion platforms: what motivates consumers to articulate themselves on the internet?. *Journal of Interactive Marketing*, 18(1), 38–52.

Hirth, M., Hoßfeld, T., and Tran-Gia, P., 2013. Analyzing costs and accuracy of validation mechanisms for crowdsourcing platforms. *Mathematical and Computer Modelling*, 57, 11–12, 2918–2932.

Hoffman, D.L., and Fodor, M. 2010. Can You Measure the ROI of Your Social Media Marketing? *MIT Sloan Management Review*, 52(1), 41–49.

Hollebeek, L.D., 2011. Demystifying customer brand engagement: Exploring the loyalty nexus. *Journal of Marketing Management*, 27(7–8), 785–807.

Hollebeek, L.D., Glynn, M.S., and Brodie, R.J., 2014. Consumer brand engagement in social media: Conceptualization, scale development and validation. *Journal of Interactive Marketing*, 28(2), 149–165.

Hutchinson, A., 2019. New Report Looks at the Growth of Influencer Marketing on Instagram [online]. *SocialMediaToday*, Available from: www.socialmediatoday.com/news/new-report-looks-at-the-growth-of-influencer-marketing-on-instagram/546245/

Ilic, A., 2008. Towards a conceptualization of consumer engagement in online communities: A netnographic study of vibration training online community. Unpublished master's thesis, University of Auckland (Department of Marketing), Auckland, New Zealand.

Influencer Intelligence, 2018. Influencer Marketing 2020 [online]. Available from: https://influencerintelligence.econsultancy.com/resource-article/HW/Influencer-Marketing-2020/

Influencer Marketing Hub, 2018. Instagram Testing Creator Accounts [online], *Influencer MarketingHub.com*. Available from: https://influencermarketinghub.com/instagram-creator-accounts/

Jaakonmäki, R., Müller, O., and Vom Brocke, J., 2017. "The impact of content, context, and creator on user engagement in social media marketing." In *Proceedings of the 50th Hawaii international conference on system sciences*.

Juvan, E., and Dolnicar, S., 2014. The attitude-behavior gap in sustainable tourism. *Annals of Tourism Research*, 48, 76–95.

Kane, K., Chiru, C., and Ciuchete, S.G., 2012. Exploring the eco-attitudes and buying behavior of Facebook users. *Amfiteatru Economic*, 31(1), 157–171.

Kietzmann, J., and Canhoto, A., 2013. Bittersweet! Understanding and managing electronic word of mouth. *Journal of Public Affairs*, 13(2), 146–159.

Klear, 2019. *The State of Influencer Marketing 2019* [online]. Available from: https://klear.com/instagram-influencers-report-2019

Labrecque, L.I., 2014. Fostering consumer-brand relationships in social media environments: The role of parasocial interaction. *Journal of Interactive Marketing*, 28(2), 134–148.

Langley, D., and van den Broek, T., 2010. Exploring social media as a driver of sustainable behavior: case analysis and policy implications. In: *Internet politics and policy conference*, 16–17 September 2011. Oxford: University of Oxford, 1–28.

Lee, D., Kartik, H., and Harikesh, N., 2014. *The Effect of Social Media Marketing Content on Consumer Engagement: Evidence from Facebook*, Working paper, The Wharton School, University of Pennsylvania, 1–51.

Lee, E., Lee, J.A., Moon, J.H., and Sung, Y., 2015. Pictures speak louder than words: Motivations for using Instagram. *Cyberpsychology, Behavior, and Social Networking*, 18(9), 552–556.

Lee, J.E., and Watkins, B., 2016. YouTube vloggers' influence on consumer luxury brand perceptions and intentions. *Journal of Business Research*, 69(12), 5753–5760.

Lorenz, T., 2019. How Comments Became the Best Part of Instagram [online], *The Atlantic*. Available from: www.theatlantic.com/technology/archive/2019/01/how-comments-became-best-part-instagram/579415/

Mondak, J.J., Hibbing, M.V., Canache, D., Seligson, M.A., and Anderson, M.R., 2010. Personality and civic engagement: An integrative framework for the study of trait effects on political behavior. *American Political Science Review*, 104(1), 85–110.

Muntinga, D.G., Moorman, M., and Smit, E.G., 2011. Introducing COBRAs: Exploring motivations for brand-related social media use. *International Journal of Advertising*, 30(1), 13–46.

Myers, J.H., and Robertson, T.S., 1972. Dimensions of opinion leadership. *Journal of Marketing Research*, 9(1), 41–46.

Närvänen, E., Kirvesmies, T., and Kahri, E. (2020) Parasocial relationships of Generation Z consumers with social media influencers. Ch. 4 in *Influencer Marketing: Building Brand Communities and Engagement*. Ed. Yesiloglu, S., and Costello, J. London: Routledge.

Ngai, E.W., Tao, S.S., and Moon, K.K., 2015. Social media research: Theories, constructs, and conceptual frameworks. *International Journal of Information Management*, 35(1), 33–44.

Olsen, C.S., 2014. Visualization of energy consumption: Motivating for a sustainable behavior through social media. In: 2014 International Conference on Collaboration Technologies and Systems (CTS). Minneapolis, MN: 19–23 May 2014, 641–646.

Opreana, A., and Vinerean, S., 2015. A new development in online marketing: Introducing digital inbound marketing. *Expert Journal of Marketing*, 3(1), 29–34.

Papasolomou, I., and Melanthiou, Y., 2012. Social media: Marketing public relations' new best friend. *Journal of Promotion Management*, 18(3), 319–328.

Pavel, C., 2014. Using visual content in your marketing. *Quaestus Multidisciplinary Research Journal*, 5(1), 164–168.

Reuters Institute, 2018. Reuters Institute: Digital News Report 2018 [online]. Available from: http://media.digitalnewsreport.org/wp-content/uploads/2018/06/digital-news-report-2018.pdf?x89475

RhythmOne, 2017. Influencer Marketing Benchmarks Report [online]. Available from: www. rhythmone.com/assets/insights/RhythmOne_FullYear2016InfluencerBenchmarks.pdf

Rubin, A.M., Perse, E.M., and Powell, R.A., 1985. Loneliness, parasocial interaction, and local television news viewing. *Human Communication Research*, 12(2), 155–180.

Saks, A.M., 2006. Antecedents and consequences of employee engagement. *Journal of Managerial Psychology*, 21(7), 600–619.

Saldaña, J., 2013. *The Coding Manual for Qualitative Researchers*. 2nd ed. Thousand Oaks, CA: Sage.

Salibian, S., 2018. Influence Peddler: The Sustainability Bunch [online], *WWD.com*. Available from: wwd.com/fashion-news/fashion-features/sustainable-influencers-1202934381/

Scott, S., 2017. How to use Instagram influencer tactics on your next photo series [online], *Medium.com*. Available from: https://medium.com/media-center-lab/how-to-use-instagram- influencer-tactics-on-your-next-photo-series-c50cf7bd4b7a

Shao, G., 2009. Understanding the appeal of user-generated media: a uses and gratification perspective. *Internet Research*, 19, 7–25.

So, K.K.F., King, C., and Sparks, B., 2014. Customer engagement with tourism brands: Scale development and validation. *Journal of Hospitality & Tourism Research*, 38(3), 304–329.

Stever, G.S., and Lawson, K., 2013. Twitter as a way for celebrities to communicate with fans: Implications for the study of para-social interaction. *North American Journal of Psychology*, 15(2), 339–354.

Styles, D., 2019. Influencer power vital for sustainable fashion? [online], *Ecotextile.com*. Available from: www.ecotextile.com/2019040224202/fashion-retail-news/influencer- power-vital-for-sustainable-fashion.html

Sundaram, D.S., Mitra, K., and Webster, C., 1998. Word-of-Mouth Communications: A Motivational Analysis. *Advances in Consumer Research*, 25, 527–531.

Terlau, W., and Hirsch, D., 2015. Sustainable consumption and the attitude-behavior-gap phenomenon-causes and measurements towards a sustainable development. *International Journal on Food System Dynamics*, 6(3), 159–174.

Too, L., and Bajracharya, B., 2015. Sustainable campus: engaging the community in sustainability. *International Journal of Sustainability in Higher Education*, 16(1), 57–71.

Turnbull, P.W., and Meenaghan, A., 1980. Diffusion of innovation and opinion leadership. *European Journal of Marketing*, 14(1), 3–33.

Uzunoglu, E., and Kip, S., 2014. Brand Communication through digital Influencers: Leveraging blogger engagement. *International Journal of Information Management*, 34, 592–602.

Van Doorn, J., Lemon, K.N., Mittal, V., Nass, S., Pick, D., Pirner, P. and Verhoef, P.C., 2010. Customer engagement behavior: Theoretical foundations and research directions. *Journal of Service Research*, 13(3), 253–266.

Vivek, S.D., Beatty, S.E., Dalela, V., and Morgan, R.M., 2014. A generalized multidimensional scale for measuring customer engagement. *Journal of Marketing Theory and Practice*, 22(4), 401–420.

Wang, R., Li, F., Hu, D., and Li, B.L., 2011. Understanding eco-complexity: social-economic-natural complex ecosystem approach. *Ecological Complexity*, 8(1), 15–29.

Wang, T., Yeh, R.K.J., Chen, C., and Tsydypov, Z., 2016. What drives electronic word-of-mouth on social networking sites? Perspectives of social capital and self-determination. *Telematics and Informatics*, 33(4), 1034–1047.

Weimann, G., 1982. On the importance of marginality: One more step into the two-step flow of communication. *American Sociological Review*, 764–773.

Weinberg, B.D., and Pehlivan, E., 2011. Social spending: Managing the social media mix. *Business Horizons*, 54(3), 275–282.

Williams, J., and Chinn, S.J., 2010. Meeting relationship-marketing goals through social media: A conceptual model for sport marketers. *International Journal of Sport Communication*, 3(4), 422–437.

Zeng, B., and Gerritsen, R., 2014. What do we know about social media in tourism? A review. *Tourism Management Perspectives*, 10(1), 27–36.

Zhu, Y.Q. and Chen, H.G., 2015. Social media and human need satisfaction: Implications for social media marketing. *Business Horizons*, 58(3), 335–345.

Yesiloglu, S., 2018. *To post or not to post: examining motivations of brand/product-related engagement types on social networking sites* (Doctoral dissertation, Bournemouth University).

Yesiloglu, S., 2020. The Rise of influencers and Influencer Marketing. Ch. 1 in *Influencer Marketing: Building Brand Communities and Engagement*. Ed. Yesiloglu, S., and Costello, J. Routledge: London.

Yesiloglu, S. and Gill, S., 2020, An exploration into the motivations behind post-millennials' engagement with influencers' brand-related content on Instagram. Ch. 6 in *Influencer Marketing: Building Brand Communities and Engagement*. Ed. Yesiloglu, S., and Costello, J. Routledge: London.

Young, A., Mcweeny, K., Hay, D., and Ellis, A., 1986. Matching familiar and unfamiliar faces on identity and expression. *Psychological Research*, 48(2), 63–68.

chapter 9

Female environmental influencers on Instagram

Irene Quintana Ramos and Fiona Cownie

Learning outcomes

On completing this chapter, you should be able to:

- acquire a systematically informed knowledge about how female environmental influencers are using Instagram to advance their activism;
- understand the opportunities an interpretative phenomenological analysis offers for researching into influencers' practice; and
- recommend approaches brands might take in working with influencers within the environmental sphere.

As the coverage of environmental challenges increases and scientists highlight the consequences of climate change, public concern grows. Traditional forms of activism, strikes, demonstrations, and petition-signing now sit alongside new forms of participation. Social media platforms provide an opportunity for people to express themselves, share opinions, and create communities based on common interests and causes. Environmental movements are among those causes uniting people within the online sphere. This chapter aims to understand how female influencers are promoting environmentalism on Instagram. Using interpretative phenomenological analysis, we examine Instagram posts, including their aesthetic presentation and textual content, as a reflection of the lived experience of female environmental influencers.

The chapter identifies female environmental influencers in the areas of veganism and zero waste living. We inductively examine Instagram posts from four influencers to understand the influencers' lived experience of online environmental activism. We also seek to understand these influencers' approaches to environmental activism through analysis of the content and style of their Instagram posts. The intent is to highlight key themes and theoretical insights that will inform our understanding of influencers and their practice.

Environmental activism

The rise of environmental activism finds its origins before the twentieth century prompted by an increasing concern about the use of chemicals in agriculture, or the development of nuclear energy (Rome 2003). During the 1960s a new "protest generation" emerged, more concerned about quality of life and social justice than previous generations (Sherkat and Blocker 1993). Later in the 1990s, the so-called "do-it-yourself" (DIY) culture emerged. Led by young people, the DIY culture was characterized by radical green activism through a range of activities including high-profile tree-sits and anti-road protests (Pickerill 2003).

Today, climate change is one of the most dangerous issues that humanity faces and one of the United Nations' Sustainable Development Goals (UN 2019). The focus on mitigating or adapting to climate change has many implications for society's approach to living and consumption. Internet platforms allow people to enhance their understanding of the causes of the climate crisis, alongside the possible solutions in which every individual can take part even with small actions. A rising number of documentaries speak to this context: *Cowspiracy* (Andersen and Kuhn 2014) presents the reality behind the mass production within the food industry; *Before the Flood* (Fisher and DiCaprio 2016), produced and presented by Leonardo DiCaprio, shows how the current production system is affecting climate change and how hidden interests confuse the public with disinformation campaigns; *Our Planet* (WWF 2019) sees David Attenborough present the biodiversity of the planet, warning of the dangers that every species of the planet faces due to human activities.

The public is now more aware of environmentalism than ever. The 2017 Special Euro-barometer report from the European Commission (2017) revealed that 94 percent of European citizens considered the protection of the environment as an important concern for them. 72 percent of Americans see global warming as a 'personally important' issue (Leiserowitz et al. 2018). The Euro-barometer report (European Commission 2017) shows that, despite television still being the first source of environmental information, there has been an important rise in the use of the internet and social media as a source of news about the environment over the past fifteen years. Social media networks not only serve as a news source for the public, but as platforms in which information flows in a multidirectional way. Instagram, the third most used social media network in the UK (YouGov 2018), is home to environmental activism found under hashtags including #zerowaste with almost four million posts, or #veganism – with more than six and a half million posts in April 2019. Important environmental organizations like the United Nations (@unenvironment), WWF International (@WWF), and Greenpeace International (@Greenpeace), make use of hashtags on Instagram to promote their campaigns. In parallel with this organizational content, we see the increasing power of influencers, such as the zero-waste movement founder @zerowastehome. These influencers help to create a sense of community among people who are part of the environmental movement, by posting images and text alongside environmentally focused hashtags.

The environmental movement can be seen as a social movement, defined as networks of individuals and organizations connecting thanks to a common identity, to fight against "conflictual issues" (Diani 1992, p. 17). Activism, characterized by such collective action, has traditionally been undertaken in the form of letters, demonstrations, or mass petitioning (Brunsting and Postmes 2002). However, technological development has opened the door to new forms of activism. Today social media networks reflect how society is changing and responding to important events in the world. Platforms such as Instagram are used to promote activist causes. We are seeing online environmental movements such as zero-waste, being led by women (Wicker 2019). Women are using social media to influence people's lifestyles to create a new wave of ethical and eco-friendly consumerism. To illustrate, the zero-waste movement was founded in 2008 by a Californian woman, Bea Johnson (@zerowastehome); one of its manifestations is a cohort of women around the world creating Instagram accounts focused on providing tips of how changes in people's lifestyle can positively impact the planet.

Drawing from previous research showing that women are more prone to show pro-environmental attitudes than men (e.g. Zelezny et al. 2000; Xiao and McCright 2015), this chapter seeks to understand the role of female influencers in the promotion of pro-environmental behaviors within Instagram.

Socialization theory and gender values

Women have always been an important part of the environmental movement. Women have worked to protect wildlife, stop pollution or save open zones, justifying their actions as "municipal housekeeping and civic mothering" (Rome 2003, p. 535). Scholars have studied gender differences in terms of environmentalism over the last two decades (e.g. Zelezny et al. 2000; Dietz et al. 2002; McCright 2010; Xiao and McCright 2015). Whilst McCright (2010) claims that there is little "theoretical depth" to work on public opinion about environmentalism, there is consensus that women show more pro-environmental behaviors and concerns than men.

Socialization theory establishes that individuals behave according to their gender and its consequent role within their cultural context (Zelezny et al. 2000). In an extensive review of previous literature, Davidson and Freudenburg (1996) concluded that safety concerns related to environmental risk were stronger among women. Corroborating this, McCright (2010) claims that women are more concerned than men about local environmental problems, especially if those problems threaten their health and safety, and that those differences are consistent when focusing on global environmental concerns. Gender differences in pro-environmental behaviors are rooted in values (Dietz et al. 2002), that is "points of reference in decision making" (Dietz et al. 2002, p. 354). In that sense, the socialization theory draws from assumptions that women tend to be more compassionate and caring than men. This explains women's tendency to be more concerned and protective toward nature (Blocker and Eckberg 1997). Moreover, while women tend to carry out actions within the private sphere, through their consumer behavior (Vicente-Molina et al. 2017), men are more prone to participate in the public sphere by joining environmental organizations, for instance. In contrast women's trust in institutions is lower than men's (Xiao and McCright 2015). Thus we see a series of scholarly arguments that support the notion that women have a greater tendency than men to have deep concerns about the environment and to play out these concerns in non-institutional contexts, for example through creating content on social media platforms. We note, however, that much of the extant material speaks to environmental concern prior to the declaration of a climate emergency in 2016; this prioritization of the environment may have stimulated increasing interest and action from both genders more equally.

Whilst we note the role of gender, environmental concern is ultimately dependent on the individual's perception of the relationship that humans have with the environment (Stern et al. 1993). The ecological value orientation embraces "concern for self, concern for other human beings, and concern for the biosphere" (Zelezny et al. 2000, p. 446). Thus, the fact that individuals show pro-environmental behaviors is not necessarily linked to love for nature, it could be related to more selfish reasons, such as fear of the devastating consequences of climate breakdown. Altruism is one of the values most clearly related to environmentalism. Dietz et al. (2002) found that women more than men not only considered altruism as a very important value, but also exhibited this value more than men. Therefore, women are socialized to take others' needs into account, demonstrating greater altruism and, therefore greater pro-environmental attitudes (Zelezny et al. 2000).

Women and online participation

Women's involvement in political activities and public participation within the online sphere has gained little attention (Keller 2012). Women use mediated communication such as social media more often than men do (Kimbrough et al. 2013). The use of online platforms allows women to express themselves, their lived experiences, as well as exposing themselves and their views publicly. While doing so, they contribute to participatory culture (Jenkins 2006), in which the traditional media consumers also become producers of media, hence transforming culture and social constructs. Further, they become opinion leaders, as others with similar values and beliefs look up to them as reliable sources of information and knowledge (Ertekin and Atik 2012). Thus women acting as opinion leaders and operating within the social media context have the characteristics of influencers and are the focus of our interest.

Female influencers are creators of their own agenda, communicating ideas and concerns through blogging, messages, comments, or sharing what others with similar views create online (Keller 2012). Moreover, Harris (2008, p. 483) suggests that "some young women are seeking alternative modes and spaces to engage in activism." We believe that women's engagement in politics through technology represents a new

irene quintana ramos and fiona cownie

form of activism in which female environmental influencers negotiate their role as consumers and actors of the collective participation in public matters.

Empirical study

We develop here a small-scale study that draws from these ideas of socialization and female online participation. Using interpretative phenomenological analysis, we examine the lived experience of four female influencers who offer content on Instagram related to the environment. We do this by exploring and interpreting how female influencers are experiencing and sharing content related to a significant phenomenon, the current environmental crisis. We seek to provide in-depth and detailed analysis, in order to avoid unremarkable and descriptive outcomes (Larkin et al. 2006). There is a real challenge in obtaining that depth of analysis from a social media platform like Instagram. However, autobiographical accounts (Sutherland et al. 2014) are also valid as they provide us with valuable descriptions developed by participants themselves (Smith 2004). Furthermore, our identity emerges from the way in which we tell stories about ourselves (Duero and Villegas 2018). Such stories are evident on Instagram where female influencers present themselves and their experiences in the form of images, written posts, and brief stories about phenomena such as veganism or zero waste.

The study focused on four influencers: cathkendall, soyvegana_jenny, trashisfortossers, and simply.living.well (Figure 9.1). We chose these influencers as their Instagram accounts reflected debate about environmentalism, and more specifically about veganism or zero waste. Veganism – a plant-based diet – is seen by some as one of the main solutions to the climate crisis alongside having fewer children and reducing travels by plane (Wynes and Nicholas 2017). Contrastingly, the zero-waste movement emerges from a growing concern about population increase and the rapidly growing consumption and disposal of resources. Influencer content was written in either English or Spanish, allowing us to faithfully understand and interpret the material. We examined these accounts from April to June 2019, a time period experiencing environmental momentum in the media following Greta Thunberg's speech at the European Parliament.

We selected data from the Instagram accounts by using hashtags such as #zerowaste, #veganism, #plasticfree, or #vegan. The four accounts are public and each influencer has at least 10,000 followers (see Table 9.1), the minimum number of followers which classify a micro-influencer (this was discussed extensively by Riboldazzi and Capriello (2020) in Chapter 3). We examined 69 posts including comments and responses from the influencers.

Table 9.1 Sample of female environmental influencers

Influencer	Followers	Posts (whole account)	Posts (April–June 2019)
cathkendall	21,800	3033	21
soyvegana_jenny	73,900	952	12
trashisfortossers	347,000	1653	23
simply.living.well	197,000	333	13

We recorded verbatim quotations, along with researchers' annotations, and used thematic analysis to search for patterns in the data (Sutherland et al. 2014, p. 414). After an initial analysis, themes and subthemes were coded to facilitate the extraction of commonalities and differences between the cases (Smith et al. 2009). Emerging themes were distinct for the two forms of activism. The vegan influencers' content comprised sub-themes of empathy, criticism of animal abuse, vegan consumption, veganism as a balanced diet. Sub-themes related to zero waste embraced Do-it-yourself, minimalist aesthetic, and making sustainable choices. The use of the interpretative phenomenological analysis is an innovative approach to be adopted with this form of data.

Activism

Influencers' pro-environmental behaviors and the promotion of public activism

Our chosen female influencers demonstrated different ways of promoting pro-environmental behaviors. Two of the accounts (cathkendall and soyvegana_jenny) were focused on veganism and the protection of animals and the planet, whereas trashisfortossers and simply.living.well promoted a zero-waste lifestyle addressing issues such as plastic waste, conservation of nature, and ethical consumption. Although messages were not always explicitly about environmentalism, the promotion of different lifestyles and nature-based content drove influencers' conversations towards a concern about the protection of the planet and the environment. Instagram profiles were used to present the accounts and anchored the tone and feed content. The two vegan participants present themselves as activists, while the zero waste participants as advocates for producing less waste.

Public activism

Just one influencer, cathkendall, showed explicit involvement in public activism using her Instagram account to encourage political action (Valenzuela 2013). She carries out her activism privately through her vegan lifestyle and also participates in public actions. This female influencer appears in several posts leading street demonstrations against animal exploitation, campaigning to spread awareness, or giving speeches.

irene quintana ramos and fiona cownie

She uses a metaphor to define for her the distinction between simply being vegan and being a vegan activist:

> *Being vegan is like seeing a dog being beaten up on the street and choosing not to join in on something you know is cruel, that's all lovely but who's going to stop it if not you? being an activist is walking over to that bastard and stopping that dog being beaten by any means possible.*

Thus, for this influencer a change of habits within the private sphere is not enough to have a real impact. She thinks it is necessary to become an active part of the collective movement to generate a bigger impact and instigate change. Clearly Instagram provides an opportunity to communicate this engagement with a collective movement. Indeed content generation on Instagram is part of the behaviors of this collective movement. However, we note that cathkendall's perspective challenges Szasz's (2007) argument that when people engage in a cause through private lifestyle changes, their contribution to other traditional and organizationally based forms of activism and political participation are diminished.

Similarly, soyvegana_jenny uses Instagram to promote her attempts to encourage followers to participate within the vegan movement. Author of two books, she invites people to buy her books with a contribution to animal sanctuaries, which financially benefit from sales. She demonstrates a shift from being a media consumer to a creator of media and culture and promotes this among her followers (Keller 2012).

The journey towards activism is the focus of the content of one of the zero waste influencers, trashisfortossers. She speaks about how her environmental activism started and how her perspective has changed over time. Like cathkendall, she was participating in public demonstrations to raise awareness of environmental challenges. However, she realized that her individual actions were inconsistent with the collective demands she was promoting. It appears that the essence of "conflictual issues" (Diani 1992 p. 17) surrounding waste reduction was present within this influencer's reflection upon her own choices. As she says, she *"was using plastic all the time, I was creating trash, and participating in fast fashion."* Her attitudes towards environmentalism are, therefore, rooted in her personal altruistic values (Dietz et al. 2002). Moreover, she realized that if individual actions don't align with personal values, collective actions will have little real impact. *"It made me feel frustrated, overwhelmed, and powerless,"* she says, reflecting on the fact that she was asking others to make a change whilst lacking the self-awareness that she wasn't doing it herself. She changed her behaviors, refocusing her activism on her home and the daily decisions which contribute to waste production and claims that this inspires her followers: *"living my values has not only changed my reality and lowered my impact on the environment but has also inspired so many others to do the same."* We can see that she is building her credibility as an influencer for the zero-waste movement, in turn becoming a role model for others to imitate (Ertekin and Atik 2012).

The influencers are part of public activism, sharing their commitment and beliefs through their social media platforms. The internet works as a "subaltern public sphere – a participatory forum" (Harlow and Sharp 2012, p. 199), in which different views and voices are shared and gain power. Therefore, while posting about their private lifestyle, influencers are also sharing their thoughts, inviting others to do the same, and creating a positive impact. To illustrate, trashisfortossers argues that, *"I have kept over 11.000 pounds of trash out of landfills and by living my values and talking about my lifestyle and as a result, many more have started reducing their waste too."*

Veganism

Two Instagrammers (cathkendall and soyvegana_jenny) were openly vegan and veganism was at the core of their lived experience within Instagram. For both influencers their vegan activism is essentially motivated by the defense of and love for animals. They consider themselves as animal rights activists, and the majority of their posts are animalism related. However, they bring different approaches to veganism: soyvegana_jenny promoting eating vegan food and consuming vegan products; cathkendall urging the cessation of animal agriculture and for her followers to stop eating animals. Within the overarching theme of veganism, four sub-themes emerged: empathy; criticism to human's abuse of animals; vegan consumption; and veganism as a balanced diet.

Empathy

Empathy is the ability to "put oneself" in others' situations, understanding and recognizing others' emotions and feelings (Singer 2015, p. 76). Cathkendall and soyvegana_jenny show immense empathy towards animals through their Instagram posts. Their journey within veganism is explicitly linked to their love for animals. We know that women are socialized to take into consideration other's needs (Zelezny et al. 2000); by choosing a vegan lifestyle, these influencers are opting to protect the interests of animals. Cathkendall, for instance, displays a repertoire of pictures in which she is hugging or kissing animals. She uses her content to encourage followers to understand that animals have the capacity to feel, and therefore they can love, feel pain, and suffer. She may be preaching to the converted. In one post, she explains that as she knows that chemicals are being tested on animals by the pharmaceutical industry, she does not use antibiotics when she is ill. In her words:

> *They cut monkeys[sic] and cats [sic] skulls off to expose their brains and perform brain experiments on them. For lots of people, pharma might be unavoidable right now, personally I have been able to refuse it up until now, I've been offered antibiotics 5x in my life and never once took them...*

Influencer soyvegana_jenny also shows her empathy towards animals, seeing veganism as a "sustainable and respectful" lifestyle. For her *"it doesn't make sense to harm them [animals] when there are other options."* She shares an image of her two dogs, demonstrating her empathy and love for animals. Soyvegana_jenny shows great care for the wellbeing of her dogs, and sadness when sharing with her followers the state in which abandoned dogs are found in shelters:

> She [her dog] lived there for 4 years, in which she suffered other dogs' attacks, insuffi-cient foo [sic] and lack of medical attention from a vet that didn't heal her physical or psychological wounds.

These two influencers try to spread awareness among followers about the suffering of animals and seek to evoke a sense of empathy in order to inspire followers to act. They use their content of them hugging animals to show how important it is to love and take care of the animals and to appreciate *"the gift"* that is *"to have the pos-sibility of cohabitating with them"* (soyvegana_jenny). The portrayal of these female influencers on Instagram relates to the idea of them acting in the role of compas-sionate and empathetic caregivers (Vicente-Molina et al. 2017).

Criticism of humans' abuse of animals

These two vegan influencers show signs of blaming humankind for the abuse of resources, especially the abuse and suffering of animals. Whilst soyvegana_jenny does so in a conservative way with gentle comments such as *"we [humans] have not known, and still don't know how to appreciate this gift [the animals],"* cathkendall shares her knowledge about the abuse that animals suffer every day for humans' benefit. She shows explicit pictures about animals in labs, pictures of her holding dead animals, as well as extensive descriptions of the exploitation of animals by different industries:

> The most horrific tests are carried out so we can enjoy these products, they spray per-fume into rabbits' eyes, they pour glue into their eyes, they cut the animals and put products into the cuts to see how they react. They force beagles to smoke ... they give rats cancer ...

Cathkendall's approach is to criticize a system that considers animals as mere objects in which to test products for human use. However, she is also appealing to what Maniates (2001, p. 34) called the "destructive consumer choice" of individuals, by which people have the power as consumers to achieve changes in the system by shifting their consumption patterns. In the post about tests on rabbits and beagles, a follower replies that some animals are bred to be killed for food. Cathkendall responds by blaming humans and humans' desire to own everything. She uses Instagram as an alternative source of information, in which she gives voice to animals and contradicts the mainstream media and its hegemonic messages (Harlow and Sharp 2012, p. 199).

Vegan consumption

Veganism is promoted differently by the two influencers. Whether the overlying cause is environmentalism or animalism, food consumption is a salient topic within their Instagram accounts. Both use their Instagram accounts to spread the idea of veganism as an ethical choice in which *"animals stop being seen as ingredients"* (soyvegana_jenny) and a counterculture that tries to break with ingrained cultural beliefs (Harlow and Sharp 2012): *"stop eating animals. It's weird"* (cathkendall). However, while cathkendall's mention or discussion about food is less present in her account than in soyvegana_jenny's, she promotes vegan consumption as the engine that moves the vegan movement forward. For instance, among several posts sharing purchases of vegan items from the supermarket or big food chains, she anchors her opinion about vegan consumption next to a picture of a new vegan burger in a famous fast-food chain:

> *Boycotting fast-food chains offering vegan options is doing animals an injustice. Supply and demand is the reason this movement has expanded so quickly.*

Although aware of these companies' exploitation of animals, she sees an opportunity for people as consumers to send a message by buying these vegan products. Cathkendall repeatedly reinforces the idea explored by Tripp (2018, p. 790) that by making "green lifestyle choices" she generates more awareness and calls for consumers as a collective body. Thus, the gradual shift of consumption patterns will – according to her views – eventually lead to end animal exploitation. We can see then that there is a place for influencers to address an issue, here vegan consumption, in distinctive ways through their online content.

Veganism as a balanced diet

For influencer soyvegana_jenny, whilst food is also at the core of her Instagram account, her approach to the promotion of the vegan diet is very different. She wants to help people understand that vegan food can be *"fun, easy and accessible."* Thus, the vast majority of the pictures of her Instagram account are food recipes also shared on her blog page. Soyvegana_jenny presents food recipes with great care for aesthetics by focusing on the photo's composition and lighting. Alongside images of food, she usually talks about the food or ingredients she particularly likes and provides informational content. For example, next to a picture of a bowl of oat and yogurt, she says:

> *I love having oat for breakfast. It is a cereal rich in fiber and very satiating, so it helps me to deal with those days when I know I will be out for hours.*

Therefore, she uses her Instagram feed to promote veganism as a healthy diet. However, she also tries to demonstrate that having a vegan diet does not require a strict organization of meals. As she says,

> *Sometimes I plan and sometimes I improvise. I just try to include veggies, fruits, legumes, cereals, nuts and seed regularly.*

Corroborating Keller's (2012) argument, the freedom of online platforms facilitates women setting their own agenda. The influencer soyvegana_jenny seeks to challenge myths about veganism being boring, strict, and expensive. She makes an effort to present a vegan diet as normal, in which it is good to be organized to avoid wasting food and to make the most of the ingredients you already have at home as would be the case for all diets. Thus, she seeks to enhance veganism, portraying an attractive lifestyle to which activists should commit (Garrett 2006).

Overall, for these female influencers, veganism is the obvious response to concern about animal suffering. Environmentalism might not seem to be the priority for these influencers as clearly as the welfare of animals. Though both influencers tell their followers that veganism is an essential step to tackle climate change. While, for instance cathkendall protests in a street demonstration that *"animal agriculture is the leading cause of climate destruction, GO VEGAN,"* for soyveganana_jenny the focus is the activism of individuals' daily decisions and personal choices making a difference to address climate change. For this influencer, our role as consumers is to send a message to those in power (companies, governments) about the kind of future people are willing to support and ways for this to be achieved.

Zero waste

We looked at two zero-waste influencers trashisfortossers and simply.living.well and it was evident that they took different approaches to their promotion of pro-environmental behaviors compared to our vegan influencers. Both zero-waste influencers showed great concern for the environmental impact of human consumption and waste. These two influencers foster sustainable consumption by refusing to use single-use items, reusing products and materials, and recycling. We identified three sub-themes within zero-waste: DIY, minimalist aesthetics, and making sustainable choices.

Do it yourself (DIY)

DIY is about "taking matters in your own hands" rather than leaving it for others to do it for you (Ratto and Boler 2014, p. 1). Thus DIY echoes notions of taking responsibility. The zero-waste influencers used their Instagram feed to advocate that their followers create their own products, rather than simply purchasing. The influencer simply.living.well spends a great deal of time in her garden cultivating plants that will later become the ingredients of home-made products. She crafts her posts to share recipes of home-made mouthwash, foot-soak, and a special tea to treat nerves. It is apparent from analyzing her feed that this influencer is educating her daughter into the same philosophy of harvesting, collection, and transformation of natural resources.

Both simply.living.well and trashfortossers use their knowledge and creativity to avoid contributing to the consumption of single-use plastics; this is the key focus of their Instagram content. Influencer simply.living.well encourages creativity to avoid plastic consumption, by reusing or recycling disposable packages, to becoming a self-sufficient producer of her own crafts, tools, or products; whereas trashisfortossers appears to be more concerned about the practicality of being your own producer of, for example, cleaning products. The opportunity for creativity to be part of the influencers' armory is clear. At the heart of the notion of being an influencer is creating a space for content to share. Thus creativity in terms of communicating new ideas, new ways of doing things as well as being a producer of creative artifacts is evident. The aesthetically attentive presentation of content by some influencers reinforces the creative aspect of being an influencer.

Minimalist aesthetics

One of the characteristic aspects of the influencers' promotion of the zero-waste life-style was their curation of the aesthetic of their content. We can clearly see that simply. living.well and trashisfortossers care about presenting the zero-waste lifestyle as well-organized, bright, and simple. By using a glass jar in which she has managed to keep her waste for seven years, trashisfortossers, sends a simple but clear message that sustainable consumption is feasible. She also advocates making life simple, having a *"minimalist home for the most part."* simply.living.well agrees and an underlying message from her content is keeping things simple. These two female influencers use Instagram as an artistic and practical strategy of activism (Harris 2008).

Curated photographs of tidy spaces occupied by plants, glass jars, and stainless-steel containers, are presenting these influencers' as aesthetically appealing living spaces. These women's lives are apparently constructed through the practices of restricting consumption and returning to the approaches we associate with the past (Lorenzen 2012) to minimize environmental impact. Values are clearly driving these influencers' practice both online and offline.

Making sustainable choices

The zero-waste movement represented by the influencers demonstrates the clear determination and concern of these women to protect nature (Vicente-Molina et al. 2017). The influencers intend to protect the oceans, reduce the waste they send to landfills, and preserve the quality of water – key environmental actions highlighted by Lorenzen (2012). These women choose to fight against climate change through their daily practices, including what they consume, how they consume, and how they dispose of products and materials. Trashisfortossers confesses that she is an *"insane list person,"* which helps her to be more organized when buying groceries, therefore reducing consumption and waste. Reflecting devotion and dedication to the environ-ment, simply.living.well seems to always make sure to prolong the products' life cycle, for example using a bamboo toothbrush for her teeth, to clean her house, and then finally composting the product.

For trashfortossers a recurrent topic is clothing. She only buys second-hand clothes. In one of her posts she explains why she stopped buying fast-fashion: *"Over 25 billion pounds of clothes go to waste every year in the U.S. alone."* Instead, she opts for a more sustainable and environmentally friendly option. In one post, she challenges clothes made from recycled plastics, explaining this is actually harmful for the environment:

> When plastic-based clothes are washed, they shed microfibers that break down into smaller and smaller plastics that are infinitely harder to filter and collect.

irene quintana ramos and fiona cownie

She appears knowledgeable, seeking to educate her followers to inform their decision-making. She addresses the ethical considerations of flying, highlighting its associated pollution and carbon emissions (Wynes and Nicholas 2017). However, she shares the tension of considering flying to spread her activism – again reflecting the "conflictual issues" (Diani 1992 p. 17) associated with this influencer space.

Reflecting on environmental influencers and Instagram

These female environmental influencers' Instagram accounts make clear the values that drive their distinctive forms of activism. Their astute use of Instagram allows them to use the platform as an alternative arena to enact political engagement (Harris 2008), and to showcase their own approaches to veganism and zero waste production in order to influence the transformation of their followers' behaviors (Muntinga et al. 2011). Clearly their followers may already exhibit similar behaviors; the influencers may be merely preaching to the converted. However, there is a sense that the influencers may play a role in stimulating new behaviors amongst their followers through the sharing of creative ideas and certainly in sustaining environmentally beneficial behaviors. Instagram emerges for these influencers as a platform, not only to express their concerns and spread their messages, but also as a means to generate debate and build a community of people with common interests (Boyd and Ellison 2007). We have seen how such common interests are more specific than a general interest in the protection of the environment. Our chosen topics for study, veganism and zero waste, may be complementary but they highlight quite distinct routes forward within the environmental movement and certainly may attract very different follower groupings.

We have seen that despite the chosen social media platform being defined and sustained by images, these influencers support their image-based content with extensive written posts in which they reflect on their own day-to-day life, relating their choices to the environmental cause. Indeed we can see that they treat Instagram as a micro-blogging site (Keller 2012).

Whilst concern about the environment and protection of natural resources is clearly at the core of the zero-waste focused content, the vegan influencers show a higher involvement in animalism and protecting animals from human exploitation and appear to give less direct focus to environmentalism. However, values such as altruism, empathy, and equality towards animals, are perceived through their discourses and promotion of behaviors forging a more ecological and fairer environment for every living being, not just humans.

We aimed to analyze our influencers' Instagram profiles as forms of lived experience through interpretative phenomenological analysis. We did this to examine influencers' meaning-making of the world (Sutherland et al. 2014) through a qualitative and interpretative analysis. We sought to understand the reasons behind the participants' involvement in environmentalism, by analyzing their content in Instagram as they presented it (Smith et al. 2009), rather than measuring it to obtain a representative result. The analysis allowed us to gather insights from our chosen influencers through images and text shared on Instagram. Whilst Instagram is essentially an image-based platform it was the written posts accompanying the images which facilitated our distinction of themes and provided a better understanding of the lived experiences of the participants.

We knew that this was an innovative approach to use on social media content alone. Indeed we concluded that interpretative phenomenological analysis using Instagram posts was limiting in the development of an in-depth and meaningful interpretation of the lived experiences of the four female environmental influencers. The time-frame for data collection inhibited our full understanding and exploration of the context and background of the participants (Larkin et al. 2006). Moreover, Instagram's newest feature – the story – in which content is uploaded for up to twenty-four hours – was excluded given its temporary nature. We knew that these stories would have added to the depth of our interpretations of influencer content. In that sense, an exploration of the whole profile, including stories and videos, within the platform would help to get a greater knowledge of influencers' social, cultural, and personal backgrounds. Whilst Instagram served as a means to gather data, we would recommend that future researchers support its interpretation with semi-structured interviews with influencers and followers depending on the focus of inquiry (Larkin et al. 2006; Smith et al. 2009).

This study aimed to understand how female influencers are promoting pro-environmental behaviors within Instagram. Drawing from the socialization theory that posits that women are more prone to show environmental attitudes than men (Zelezny et al. 2000; Xiao and McCright 2010), the research sought to analyze the promotion of environmentalism online from a gendered perspective. We explored the role of women in the promotion of pro-environmental behaviors on Instagram and reflected on the applicability of the interpretative phenomenological analysis as a research method for the lived experience within Instagram. The women behind the influencer accounts were the focus of our reflections, however it was the content obtained from the platform which was the basis of our interpretations of the lived experiences of the influencers.

Our small purposive sample of influencers clearly revealed the importance of values underpinning the environmental activism of these women on Instagram. While protection of the environment and nature was at the core of all four influencers' content, it seemed to be of particular importance to the zero-waste influencers; more so than for the vegan influencers. Indeed, it was striking how little overlap there was between the two types of influencers: the zero-wasters did not talk about veganism; the vegan influencers did not directly post about zero-waste. The clear focus for the vegan influencers was empathy for animals and their fight to defend animals from human exploitation. The zero-waste influencers were focused on the environmental impact of human consumption and waste.

This study reflects the ideas of Keller (2012); the women were developing and contributing to online communities of participation, in which they publicly spread their activism as citizens and consumers. Instagram provides these influencers with a form of expression of real-life experiences related to environmental activism. It is used by the influencers as a tool to promote not only political action (Valenzuela 2013), but also the protection of the environment through a shift in daily choices (Tripp 2018).

irene quintana ramos and fiona cownie

Implications

Environmental concern is a growing issue that surpasses the scope of mainstream media. Instagram, as many other online Social Networking Sites, is used as a tool, not only to participate in that debate, but also to promote certain behaviors among other users. These influencers demonstrate environmental behaviors that go beyond tackling the climate crisis. They promote pro-environmental behaviors by making environmental issues relatable to society's daily choices. Through their content, the influencers debunk misinformation and share their knowledge to spread awareness among followers and inspire followers to change their behaviors. They seek to act as role models. Moreover, the influencers are inviting people to think about the ethical implications of their decisions towards important issues, the use of animals for food production and testing, and the harm that human actions are causing to the planet. Whether they are successful in this invitation we do not know but we can see that these influencers are generating comments and debate from their followers. These female environmental influencers are an example of a growing group of people that are questioning pre-established cultural and social values, applying changes to their own lives, and spreading their message. They are part of a counterculture that is worried about the future and is seeking to do something about it.

Working with such environmental influencers demands authenticity from brands. It is clear that the influencers we examined have deep-seated feelings about their chosen form of activism. Whilst we cannot claim that this is generalizable to all environmental influencers we can see from this study that brands intending to develop their image or behaviors in line with environmental values must move from the generic and really connect with specific issues. We saw how this group of women serve as an example of the ethical deliberation that is taking place related to the purchase of products. Brands seeking to work with influencers must be prepared to transparently engage within the conflictual arguments which accompany environmental consumption. Greenwashing is not an option; brands must be clear that promotional activities at the margins of their sustainability are likely to create critique from their influencer partner or the influencer's followers.

As the prominence of the United Nations' Sustainable Development Goals increases and their centrality to many brands' thinking develops, working with environmental influencers in aligning activity to the goals may be fruitful. Whilst goal number 13 "Climate Action" has already been highlighted, it is goal number 12 "Responsible Production and Consumption" which most resonates with the work of our environmental influencers. The zero-waste influencers' activity aligns well with UN SDG number 12, in particular target 12.5: "By 2030, substantially reduce waste generation through prevention, reduction, recycling and reuse." The UN SDGs were not the focus of our influencers' discussions within the period of analysis. Therefore conversations about the goals aligned to collaborations with brands may be beneficial to influencers in potentially broadening the reach of influencers' content through hashtags such as #unsdgs (currently linked to 11.9k posts). Indeed the specific goals currently have relatively few hashtags relating to them; #unsdg12 has "100+ posts" at the time of writing. Therefore collaborations between influencers and brands, aligned to specific goals, will serve to advance the awareness and potency of the goals and will clearly map influencers and brands to the global sustainability project.

Brands seeking to work with influencers must be prepared to cede control and allow influencers to become translators rather than replicators of brand messages. The authenticity and creativity our influencers demonstrated will refract brand communications in a manner that makes messages more potent amongst followers and the Instagram community as a whole.

Summary

- The influencers within our study are powerful agents in the discussion about the environment and their presence complements the increasing evidence that brands and companies are more frequently considering the use of sustainable packaging, vegan food, or eco-friendly materials.
- Whilst small businesses are emerging to satisfy the growing demand for more ethical and sustainable products, big brands and corporations are looking to these influencers as role models for thousands of current and potential consumers who would support a shift towards more sustainable production and consumption.

References

Andersen, K., and Kuhn, K., (Directors), 2014. *Cowspiracy. The Sustainability Secret.* [Video File]. United States: A.U.M. Films & Media. Retrieved from: www.netflix.com/search?q=cowspiracy&jbv=80033772&jbp=0&jbr=0

Blocker, T.J., and Eckberg, D.L., 1997. Gender and environmentalism: results from the 1993 general social survey. *Soc. Sci. Q.* 78, 841–858.

Boyd, D.M., and Ellison, N.B., 2007. Social Networking Sites: Definition, History, and Scholarship. *Journal of Computer-Mediated Communication*, 12(1), 210–230.

Brunsting, S., and Postmes, T., 2002. Social Movement Participation in The Digital Age. Predicting Offline and Online Collective Action. *Small-Group Research*, 33(5), 525–554.

Davidson, D.J., and Freudenburg, W.R., 1996. Gender and environmental risk concerns: A review and analysis of available research. *Environment and Behavior*, 28(3), 302–339.

Diani, M., 1992. The concept of Social Movement. *The Sociological Review* [online]. 40(1), 1–25.

Dietz, T., Kalof, L., and Stern, P.C., 2002. Gender, Values, and Environmentalism. *Social Science Quarterly*, 83(1), 353–364.

Duero, D.G., and Villegas F.J.O., 2018. Phenomenological-narrative contributions to understanding the narrative strategies that shape the autobiographical account throughout different moments of the therapeutic process. *Research in Psychotherapy: Psychopathology, Process and Outcome*, 21, 98–115.

European Commission, 2017. *Special Eurobarometer 468 – October 2017. Attitudes of European Citizens towards the Environment. Summary.* European Union. 2017.6399

Ertekin, Z.Ö., and Atik, D., 2012. Word-of-mouth communication in marketing: An exploratory study of motivations behind opinion leadership and opinion seeking. *METU Studies in Development*, 39(3), 323–345.

Fisher, S. (Director and producer) and DiCaprio, L. (Producer), 2016. *Before the Flood*. [Video File]. United States: Appian Way Productions. Retrieved from: www.amazon.com/Before-Flood-Leonardo-DiCaprio/dp/B01M31RS3L/ref=tmm_aiv_title_0?_encoding=UTF8&qid=1492530172&sr=8-2

Garrett, R.K., 2006. Protest in an Information Society: a review of literature on social movements and new ICTs. *Information, Communication, and Society*, 9(2), 202–224.

Harlow, S., and Harp, D., 2012. Collective action on the web. *Information, Communication, and Society*, 15(2), 196–216.

Jenkins, H., 2006. *Convergence Culture. Where Old and New Media Collide*. New York and London: New York University Press

Keller, J.M., 2012. Virtual Feminisms. *Information, Communication, and Society*, 15(3), 429–447.

Kimbrough, A.M., Guadagno, R.E., Muscanell, N.L., and Dill, J., 2013. Gender differences in mediated communication: Women connect more than do men. *Computers in Human Behavior*, 29, 896–900.

Leiserowitz, A., Maibach, E., Rosenthal, S., Kotcher, J., Ballew, M., Goldberg, M., and Gustafson, A., 2018. *Climate Change in the American Mind: December 2018*. Yale University and George Mason University. New Haven, CT: Yale Program on Climate Change Communication.

Harris, A., 2008. Young women, late modern politics, and the participatory possibilities of online cultures. *Journal of Youth Studies*, 11(5), 481–495.

Larkin, M., Watts, S., and Clifton, E. 2006. Giving voice and making sense in interpretative phenomenological analysis. *Qualitative Research in Psychology*, (3), 102–120.

Lorenzen, J.A., 2012. Going Green: The Process of Lifestyle Change. *Sociological Forum*, 27(1).

Maniates, M.F., 2001. Individualization: Plant a Tree, Buy a Bike, Save the World? *Global Environmental Politics*, 1(3), 31–52.

McCright, A.M., 2010. The effects of gender on climate change knowledge and concern in the American public. *Population and Environment*, 32(1), 66–87.

Muntinga, D.G., Moorman, M., and Smit, E.G., 2011. Introducing COBRAs. Exploring motivations for Brand-related social media use. *International Journal of Advertising*, 30(1), 13–16.

Pickerill, J., 2003. *Cyber protest. Environmental activism online*. Manchester: Manchester University Press

Ratto, M., and Boler, M., 2014. *DIY Citizenship: Critical Making and social media*. Cambridge: The MIT Press.

Riboldazzi, S., and Capriello, A., 2020. Identifying and selecting the right influencers in the digital era. Ch. 3 in *Influencer Marketing: Building Brand Communities and Engagement*. Ed. Yesiloglu, S., and Costello, J. Routledge: London.

Rome, A., 2003. "Give Earth a Chance": The Environmental Movement and the Sixties. *The Journal of American History*, 90(2), 525–554.

Sherkat, D.S., and Blocker, T.J., 1993. Environmental activism in the protest generation: Differentiating 1960s activists. *Youth and Society*, 25(1), 140–161.

Singer, P., 2015. *The Most Good You Can Do*. New Haven and London: Yale University Press.

Smith, J.A., 2004. Reflecting on the development of interpretative phenomenological analysis and its contribution to qualitative research in psychology. *Qualitative Research in Psychology*, 1, 39–54.

Smith, J.A., and Osborn, M., 2007. Pain as an assault on the self: An interpretative phenomenological analysis of the psychological impact of chronic benign low back pain. *Psychology and Health*, 22(5), 517–534.

Smith, M., 2019. Concern for the environment at record highs. *YouGov*, 5 June 2019. Available from: https://yougov.co.uk/topics/politics/articles-reports/2019/06/05/concern-environment-record-highs

Stern, P.C., Dietz, T., and Kalof, L., 1993. Value Orientations, Gender, and Environmental Concern. *Environment and Behavior*, 27, 723–745.

Sutherland, O., Dawczyk, K.D.L, Cripps, J., and Lewis, S.P., 2014. Self-compassion in online accounts of nonsuicidal self-injury: An interpretative phenomenological analysis. *Counselling Psychology Quarterly*, 27(4), 409–433.

Szasz, A., 2007. *Shopping Our Way to Safety: How We Changed from Protecting the Environment to Protecting Ourselves*. Minneapolis: University of Minnesota Press.

Tripp, W.B., 2018. Being green: Patterns of participation in the environmental movement. *Current Sociology*, 66(5), 788–809.

United Nations, 2019. *Why does climate change matters?* Kenya: UN Environment. Available from: www.unenvironment.org/explore-topics/climate-change/why-does-climate-change-matter

Valenzuela, S., 2013. Unpacking the use of social media for protest behavior: The roles of information, opinion expression, and activism. *American Behavioral Scientist*, 57(7), 920–942.

Vicente-Molina, M.A., Fernandez-Sainz, A., and Izagirre-Olaizola, J., 2017. Does gender make a difference in pro-environmental behavior? The case of the Basque Country University students. *Journal of Cleaner Production*, 176 (2018), 98–98.

Wicker, A., 2019. The complicated gender politics of going zero waste. *Vox* [online]. 9 May 2019. Available from: www.vox.com/the-goods/2019/5/9/18535943/zero-waste-movement-gender-sustainability-women-instagram [accessed 29 May 2019].

WWF, Silverback & Netflix (Producers), 2019. *Our Planet*. [Limited Series]. United Kingdom: Silverback Films. Retrieved from: www.netflix.com/search?q=our%20plan&jbv=80049832&jbp=0&jbr=0

Wynes, S., and Nicholas, K.A., 2017. The climate mitigation gap: education and government recommendations miss the most effective individual actions. *Environmental Research Letters*, 12(7).

Xiao, C., and McCright, A.M., 2015. Gender Differences in Environmental Concern: Revisiting the Institutional Trust Hypothesis in the USA. *Environment and Behavior*, 47(1), 17–37.

YouGov, 2018. *YouGov Ratings. Digital and technology*. Available from: https://yougov.co.uk/ratings/technology/popularity

Zelezny, L.C., Chua, P.P., and Aldrich, C., 2000. Elaborating on Gender Differences in Environmentalism. *Journal of Social Issues*, 56(3), 443–457.

irene quintana ramos and fiona cownie

part 3

The dark side of influencers

"Hope this is not sponsored" – Is an influencer's credibility impacted when using sponsored versus non-sponsored content?

Joyce Costello and Klaudia Maria Urbanska

Learning outcomes

On completing this chapter, you should be able to:

*   understand how the source credibility model can be applied in influencer marketing;
*   appreciate sponsored and non-sponsored content leads to different sentiment; and
*   understand how the audience's perception of an influencer's attractiveness, trustworthiness, and expertise differ between sponsored and non-sponsored content.

Endorsements over original content

Each day, social media users are increasingly exposed to sponsored content in the form of advertising, native advertising and sponsored content from influencers. The problem arises when the user can no longer distinguish between sponsored and original content. In Chapter 7, Närvänen et al. (2020) explored the parasocial relationship between influencers and Generation Z. We build from their study to investigate whether influencer credibility would differ if the post were explicitly stating if they are sponsored or not.

Some scholars suggest that influencers are viewed as an objective and independent source of information and hence they can help influence opinions and shape attitudes and ultimately behaviors through their content (Freberg et al. 2011). Others argue that if an influencer's content becomes overwhelmingly sponsored, it could degrade the influencer's credibility and parasocial relationship with their audiences (De Vierman and Hudders 2020). By understanding if sponsored content impacts credibility, it can help influencers make a strategic decision prior to focusing on mainly producing sponsored content.

Bosher (2020) discusses in Chapter 13 how the US Federal Trade Commission and the UK Competition and Markets Authority have set out laws that force the influencers to disclose endorsed products. For instance, information about any content made in collaboration with a brand needs to be clearly displayed to a viewer (Bosher 2020). Nevertheless, some academics argue that there will always remain a lack of total clarity and transparency (Wu 2016). Influencers have not always disclosed that their content was sponsored (Bradbury 2017).

In the case of Scott Disick, this has resulted in massive backlash from fans. The reality TV personality posted an Instagram picture with a caption that included details of the agreement made with the brand. But there was no obvious information to say that this was an advertisement (Crossfield 2017). The Fyre Festival showed not only the power of influencers, but also questioned the influencers' credibility when they inadvertently endorsed what would eventually be known as a complete fiasco in the entertainment world (Keinmann 2019; White 2019). Because the influencers played a primary role in promoting the festival, some questioned if they should also be held accountable and the impact on influencer marketing (Stanwick and Stanwick 2019). Consequently, regulations are becoming more and more rigorous (Penny 2018).

The attraction to YouTube

The rise of YouTube influencers has contributed to the growth of influencer marketing (Lee and Watkins 2016; Pitz et al. 2018). Currently, Internet Marketing Hub's (2020) YouTube Earnings Estimator predicts that an Influencer with 20,000 video views a day could earn between $10K to $17K with AdSense alone. Add in sponsored content income from companies and suddenly making a career out of being a YouTube Influencer is very lucrative indeed. This is especially reinforced with research company Nielsen (2019) predicting that by 2022, Brands will spend up to $15 billion on influencer marketing.

Many YouTube influencers are considered to be "micro-celebrities" by some scholars as they are able to successfully promote almost anything that results in companies moving away from traditional advertising methods (Abidin and Ots 2016; Leban and Voyer 2020). With the drastic increase of advertisements and product

joyce costello and klaudia maria urbanska

placements in influencers' content, the debate is still centered around credibility and authenticity (Abidin and Ots 2016). Indeed, some scholars question whether influencers' content should be treated in a similar manner to advertisers' (MacRury 2020). Some aspiring influencers will even go to great lengths in faking sponsorship deals in order to be noticed by brands (Betches 2019). This has increasingly become a problem for brands that may find themselves inadvertently linked influencers under false pretenses as well as step up their online monitoring of the brand mentioned by influencers, aspiring or otherwise (Joffe 2018).

When examining top genres of influencers on YouTube, beauty influencers own some of the most subscribed channels (Leskin 2019). In the UK, some of the most recognizable ones are Jordan Lipscombe, Hannah Renee, and Sophdoesnails (Statista 2019). When looking at a list of *Highest Paid Beauty Influencers*, Eksouzian-Cavadas (2018) stated it is evident that what sets them apart from the rest is owning a YouTube channel. They have a significant reach, often more than a million followers, and are categorized as macro or mega influencers (Ruiz-Gomez 2018). (See Chapter 1 (Yesiloglu 2020) for more about the difference between macro or mega influencers.) Due to a strong online presence on multiple platforms, they are able to cross-promote products and create an influential product promotion (Ruiz-Gomez 2018). The paid-for-videos are often described as native advertising as they seamlessly incorporate promoted products (Wojdynski and Evans 2015). Nevertheless, viewers' reactions to watching sponsored and non-sponsored content could also differ because credibility is based on consumer perception (Rieh et al. 2014).

Idea fairy: Why the attraction to YouTube

Considering your own social media habits, why would you engage with an influencer on YouTube as opposed to other platforms such as Instagram or TikTok? Do you notice if the content has been sponsored or not? Does this impact whether you subscribed to the channel or engage with the influencer?

Source credibility model

This study draws upon Ohanian's (1991) source credibility model. She created the source credibility model to explain factors such as attractiveness, trustworthiness, and expertise impacting the levels of credibility of an individual (Ohanian 1991). While the model has been applied to a variety of scenarios (e.g. celebrity endorsement), it is also relevant to today's context of influencers because they are the new micro-celebrities (Abidin and Ots 2016).

The first dimension of credibility can be defined as the believability of the addresser and its perception in the listener's mind (Alder and Rodman 1999). This implies that credibility is determined by the individual within their own context. Therefore, influencers would need an overwhelming majority of their followers to believe that they (the influencer) have credibility. This becomes a problem if the influencer employed fake followers or bots, as discussed later in Chapter 12 (Costello and Biondi 2020).

Lowry et al. (2013) found that highly credible sources are not only more effective in marketing promotion but could produce a more positive attitude or opinion change. Nevertheless, the credibility of a person or a product can be very subjective and may be hard to estimate (Rieh et al. 2014). There remains a high level of discrepancy when it comes to measuring the spokesperson's credibility, with various scholars using different scales of measurement that look at various empirically derived dimensions (Eisend 2006). Accordingly, academics mainly focused on three dimensions that help to measure one's credibility: attractiveness, trustworthiness, and expertise (which are discussed in-depth in the following section) (Amos et al. 2008; Pitz et al. 2018).

In modern times, the initial classification has been applied to celebrity endorsements and its relation to brand attitude, brand credibility, as well as purchase intention (Seiler and Kucza 2017; Wang et al. 2017). More importantly it can be also applied to influencers on social media in the context of purchase intention (Ananda and Wandebori 2016) and influencer marketing credibility (Xiao et al. 2018). For scholars, one of the main areas of focus has been the application of the model in the field of celebrity endorsement. Attractiveness, expertise, and trustworthiness of the promoter also impacts attitudes towards the brand, as well as the advertisement and purchase intentions both in the case of celebrity endorsement (e.g. Goldsmith et al. 2000; La Ferle and Choi 2005; Amos et al. 2008) and YouTube influencers (Wang et al. 2017). Even though customers have a positive attitude towards a recommendation made by a popular person (O'Mahony and Meenaghan 1997), some studies found that the bigger the number of endorsements, the lower the credibility (Tripp et al. 1994). This suggests that overloading the amount of endorsements by an influencer might result in decreased trustworthiness and authenticity.

Yet, one of the key differences between celebrity endorsements and influencers is that the latter tend to have an interactive relationship with their audience (Brown and Fiorella 2013). Sanjay Nazeral, Carat's Global Chief Strategy Officer, emphasizes that even though influencer and celebrity marketing is different, "influencers were just as likely as celebrities to drive buying decisions" (Nazeral 2017, p. 3). This suggests that practitioners may expect the same outcomes when investing in marketing campaigns with influencers as they would have if they had used celebrities. Additionally, other studies identify influencers as micro-celebrities as they are popular amongst a niche group of people (Abidin and Ots 2016). While this could be advantageous to those wanting to reach a niche group, it also results in reaching a significantly smaller audience.

Many scholars focus primarily on the impact of YouTube and Instagram influencers' product reviews and found that the model's three dimensions had a significant impact on purchase intention (e.g. Ananda and Wandebori 2016; Djafarova and Rushworth 2017; Rebelo 2017; Lee 2018; Xiao et al. 2018). These studies suggest that trustworthiness, expertise, and quality of the review are the predominant factors in determining credibility. Furthermore, Fred (2015) states that YouTube influencers' expertise and trustworthiness were rated higher in non-sponsored videos. Nouri (2018) studied influencers in comparison to traditional

joyce costello and klaudia maria urbanska

celebrities and determined that influencers tend to be more believable. On the contrary, Lim et al. (2017) found that the source credibility has no impact on buying behaviors.

When the trust variable is introduced in the source credibility model, Lou and Yuan's (2019) findings suggest that influencers' credibility and content's informative value have an impact on followers' trust.

Credibility in sponsored and non-sponsored content

Sponsored content is prominent and can be effective in marketing (Lu et al. 2014), especially when concerning influencers. Lu et al. (2014) discovered that customers have a more positive attitude towards sponsored content if they know the brand, and the product is a commonly searched good. Moreover, even a paid-for-recommendation from a credible source was found to influence purchase intention. Colliander and Erlandsson (2015) tested this idea when they had two groups of people who were introduced to a blogger post; however, only one was told that this was in fact an advertisement. Even though the source's credibility suffered, the purchase intention and attitude towards the brand remained the same. On the contrary, Ballantine and Yeung (2015) found that sponsored online content does not influence perceived credibility, brand attitude, or purchase intention. According to their study, the source of the blog does not impact those qualities.

> ### Idea fairy: Noticing the difference
>
> Considering your own social media habits, when you are watching YouTube videos, how often do you open the description and see if it is sponsored or not? Does this change your viewpoint of the influencer once you know whether it is sponsored or not? How important is it to you that influencers are credible? What about brands?

Attractiveness in the eye of the beholder

The first dimension of the source credibility model is attractiveness, which is defined as the concept of one's perception of a perfect appearance (Hatfield and Rapson 2010). Nowadays, the perfect look is usually modeled on influencers, and includes characteristics such as full lips, perfect brows, great skin and body (Brucculieri 2018). However, as everyone's opinion on what is beautiful is very different, the definition of this factor can also be very subjective (Joseph 1982). But it is mostly understood on a physical level (appearance) (Bhatt et al. 2013).

Physical attractiveness is often found to have a significant impact on the source credibility and communication effectiveness when explored in the context of celebrity endorsement (La Ferle and Choi 2015; Seiler and Kucza 2017) and influencers (Wang et al. 2017). Additionally, attractive sources are often seen as more trustworthy and competent than unattractive ones (Hong et al. 2018). This could be due to the association between position and appearance as the current beauty standards require every well-known person to be attractive. According to Ohanian (1991), words associated with attractiveness include: classy, beautiful, elegant, and sexy. Indeed, the use of these words remain key indicators of attractiveness across time.

Attractiveness not only influences attitudes towards an advertisement but can increase sales (Seiler and Kucza 2017). Furthermore, physical appearance often has an overall influence on the persuasiveness of the communication or message (Pornpitakpan et al. 2017). Djafarowa and Rushworth's (2017) Instagram study found that attractiveness plays an especially important role amongst young females. Similarly, Rebelo (2017) found that the perceived attractiveness of an influencer highly affects credibility and purchase intention. Conversely, some scholars suggest that attractiveness has no impact. Ananda and Wandebori (2016) discovered that the appearance of a beauty YouTuber is the only element of the source credibility model that does not construct a change in customer behavior. Their results were later confirmed by Sokolova and Kefi (2019) on YouTube and Instagram. This might imply that the influencer might be able to influence attitudes towards a brand, but not sway behavior changes.

The role of attractiveness in the context of social media beauty influencers is especially important due to the nature of the industry. Even though recently many companies have started focusing on body positivity and diversity among men and women, many advertisements still only show perfect models as a representation of everyday women (Thiruchelvam 2017; Kemp 2018). According to Walker (2018), brands are now turning to influencers to use their authenticity and credibility to diversify their content and become more relevant. As such, beauty influencers' attractiveness should play a role in perceived credibility and can vary based on different types of content.

Trustworthiness

The second dimension of the source credibility model is trustworthiness. It focuses on the assumption of honesty, objectivity, and believability of the individual (Erdogan 1999). Ohanian (1991) stated the more trustworthy the source, the bigger the opinion change amongst the audience. Believable endorsers can "proxy the confidence consumers have in the reliability and integrity of a given source" (Amos et al. 2008, p. 224). This means that the endorser's qualities can influence the brand's ones. According to Erdogan (1999), likeability is the most significant determinant of trustworthiness. The term was also linked to words like dependability, honesty, reliability, and sincerity (Ohanian 1991). Similarly to attractiveness, this dimension has also been a subject of many studies, especially in the area of celebrity endorsement.

Expertise and trustworthiness were often associated with having the biggest impact on credibility (Amos et al. 2008); however, many studies found it was usually the latter which had the strongest effect when compared to other dimensions of the source credibility model (e.g. Amos et al. 2008; Seiler and Kucza 2017; Wang et al. 2017; Xiao et al. 2018). This was especially prominent in Xiao et al.'s (2018) study where even in the presence of non-source credibility model factors, trust was still of utmost importance. On the other hand, even though trustworthiness is a key component of the model, Rossiter and Smidts's (2012) research revealed that it does not have a positive influence on an endorsement as the public is aware that the promotion was paid for. Moreover, according to Ohanian (1991), trustworthiness is not related to the purchase intention of the endorsed brand.

In the context of social media influencers, trustworthiness is usually placed as an influential dimension. Researchers confirmed its high impact on the source's credibility (e.g. Ananda and Wandebori 2016; Rebelo 2017; Xiao et al. 2018). Ananda and Wandebori's (2016), as well as Rebelo's (2017) findings showed that this dimension has a high impact on purchase intention. Moreover, according to Xiao et al. (2018), trustworthiness is one of the dimensions with the most significant impact on an influencer's credibility.

The above research suggests that trustworthiness is not only a significant part of the source credibility model but also the most impactful one (Seiler and Kucza 2017). Therefore, to gain credibility and resonate with their audience, the influencer needs to be authentic. This is even more important nowadays with the rise of fake news on social media (Xiao et al. 2018). Therefore, if an influencer has multiple product endorsements or sponsored content it may impact their trustworthiness.

Expertise

The final dimension of the source credibility model is expertise, which is represented by the knowledge, skills, and experience acquired by the source (Ohanian 1991). In the case of beauty influencers that could include any professional qualifications from the industry. This component was also proven to have a direct effect on the credibility and persuasiveness of the communication (Rossiter and Smidts 2012; Seiler and Kucza 2017). According to Ohanian (1991), the words "experienced, knowledgeable, qualified or skilled" are ones that determine expertise. Similarly to other dimensions of the model, this one was also a concern of various academic studies including ones related to brand credibility, as well as celebrity endorsement.

Trustworthiness and expertise have generally been pointed out as dimensions with the most impact on credibility, however, the latter "appears to be the dominant dimension" (Homer and Kahle 1990, p. 30). Ohanian (1991) concluded that expertise is the only aspect of the model that is related to the purchase intention of the endorsed brand. This is because most celebrities are attractive, and they were paid to promote a product that is not trustworthy. According to Till and Busler (1998), expertise was also more effective compared only to attractiveness. Similarly, Rossiter and Smidts (2012) took both of these components into consideration and still determined expertise to be more important.

Other scholars found expertise effectiveness to be lesser, often placing it after trustworthiness (e.g. Amos et al. 2008, Seiler and Kucza 2017, Wang et al. 2017). Even though Amos et al.'s (2008) quantitative study was related to celebrity endorsement, trustworthiness was found to be the most predictive dimension of credibility. These findings were also later confirmed by several other studies that explored the relationship between credibility and purchase intention (Lim et al. 2017; Seiler and Kucza 2017; Wang et al. 2017). Lim et al. (2017) suggested that followers felt influencers sometimes lack expertise in the products they were trying to promote. This implies that companies with innovative products may need to ensure influencers understand fully all aspects of the product prior to producing content. Certainly, expertise was mostly proven to be significant to the endorser's credibility given the persuasiveness of the message. Additionally, specifically for celebrity endorsement, increased number of promoted products lessens the credibility, however expertise would be the least affected dimension of the model as it does not influence the endorser's knowledge in particular areas (Tripp et al. 1994).

In the studies related to influencers, expertise was mostly determined to have a significant impact (Ananda and Wandebori 2016, Xiao et al. 2018). It was found to be especially important amongst beauty YouTubers because they need to provide valid and accurate information (Ananda and Wanderbori 2016). According to Xiao et al. (2018) the prominence of expertise shows that the viewer perceives the influencer as an expert in a selected field. Nevertheless, there is a lack of influencer research when it comes to expertise as this dimension was often not taken into consideration. This could be because many influencers do not hold any industry-related professional qualifications or if they do, it is not explicitly stated in their profiles or in the description of their content.

Collectively, attractiveness, trustworthiness, and expertise should contribute to the overall credibility of the influencers. These dimensions, however, are decided based on the audience's perception. Brand sponsorship deals could signal the credibility of the influencer in the eyes of the brand, but it is the audience that engages – or not – with the influencer's content. Therefore, we seek to investigate if the relationship between attractiveness, trustworthiness, and expertise is significantly related to credibility given the conditions of sponsored versus non-sponsored posts.

The investigation

For this study, we first utilized netnography as this study focuses on the analysis of online data, in particular YouTube video comments (Kozinets 2015). This strategy has its beginnings in ethnography, which centers around studying people's behaviors and culture. This study focused on three top UK beauty influencers and compared three sponsored and three non-sponsored videos with a total of 2,591 comments (Table 10.1). For sponsored content, the influencer had to include the fact that the video is "sponsored by [company name]" or "made in partnership with [company name]." Subsequently, non-sponsored content included information "this video is not sponsored" or had no information about sponsorship at all.

Table 10.1 UK Beauty influencers and corresponding comments

Name	Hannah Renee	Jordan Lipscombe	Sophdoesnails
Sponsored comments	124	524	343
Non-sponsored Comments	168	599	833
Total of 2591 comments			

joyce costello and klaudia maria urbanska

Priori codes (parent nodes) were created on the basis of Ohanian's (1991) source credibility model such as attractiveness, trustworthiness, and expertise. Secondary codes were then developed by taking the key variables and running a word tree search off the data in NVivo; we were able to visualize the words most commonly associated with each term. For example, attractiveness was associated with positive terms such as attractive, classy, beautiful, elegant, and sexy. The variable trustworthiness was associated with dependability, reliable, honest, sincere, and trustworthy. Expertise was associated with expert experience, knowledgeable, qualified, and skilled.

Content that was not related to the source credibility model such as emojis or tagging someone were coded as neutral and not included in the final analysis. Additionally, the source's (influencer's) comments under their own videos were not coded. This is due to the fact that this study is trying to understand viewers' opinions on the source's credibility. This left us with 2,423 points of engagement.

It is important to note that the Nvivo analysis also identified comments specifically related to sponsored and non-sponsored content. Under the paid-for videos, users were found complaining about yet another advertisement. On the other hand, under normal videos, more than one viewer commented: "Hope this is not sponsored." Items such as this and those that were negative in terms of attractiveness, trustworthiness, and expertise were code also.

In order to explore the relationship between attractiveness, trustworthiness, and expertise in relation to sponsored and non-sponsored videos, we used binary logistic regression. In the literature review, we argue that the audience's perceived attractiveness should differ between sponsored and non-sponsored content and the results show that when the post was sponsored, the viewers who commented on it were one and a half times significantly more likely to find the source attractive (Exp(B)=1.573, p<.01) (model 1, Table 10.2), but if the post was non-sponsored, they were almost two-thirds less likely to find it attractive (Exp(B)=.636, p<.01) (model 1, Table 10.3). When exploring trustworthiness and sponsored content, the viewer was significantly less likely to find it trustworthy (Exp(B)=.028 p<.10) (model 2, Table 10.2), but if the post was non-sponsored, they were three and a half times more likely to find it trustworthy (Exp(B)=3.566, p<.05) (model 2, Table 10.3). In terms of expertise, there was no significant relation between expertise and sponsored content (Exp(B)=1.347, p=.337) (model 3, Table 10.2) or non-sponsored content (Exp(B)=.742, p=.337) (model 3, Table 10.3). Finally, when exploring collectively the source credibility dimensions to sponsored and non-sponsored content, the results were mirrored as if they were measured separately (model 4, Table 10.2; model 4, Table 10.3).

Attractiveness, trustworthiness, and expertise differ

This study aimed to discover whether viewers' perception of influencers' credibility is different in sponsored and non-sponsored content. We found that sponsored posts solicit significantly more evidence of attractiveness. This corresponds to social media influencer studies that show physical attractiveness was found to be important amongst young females (Djafarowa and Rushworth 2017). Yet, because the relationship was significantly more so when the post was sponsored, as opposed to the

Table 10.2 Binary logistic regression results – sponsored post

	Model 1		Model 2		Model 3		Model 4	
	DV: Sponsored post		DV: Sponsored post		DV: Sponsored post		DV: Sponsored post	
	Exp(β) Odds ratio	S.E.	Exp(β) Odds ratio	S.E.	Exp(β) Odds ratio	S.E.	Exp(β) Odds ratio	S.E.
Attractiveness	1.573**	0.154					1.630**	0.174
Trustworthiness			0.028†	0.769			.176*	0.815
Expertise					1.347	0.310	1.192	0.382
Constant (odds ratio)	.570***	0.044	.594***	0.042	.588***	0.042	.571***	0.044
Nagelkerke R^2	0.005		0.002		0.001		0.008	
Hosmer-Lemeshow	Chi-square .000, df 0,sig. = .00		Chi-square .000, df 0,sig. = .00		Chi-square .000, df 1,sig. = 1.00		Chi-square .003, df 1,sig. = .954	
Null predicted % correct	62.9		62.9		62.9		62.9	
Predictive capacity of model	62.9		62.9		62.9		62.9	
Observations	2,423		2,423		2,423		2,423	

Notes: *** p <.001, ** p <.01, * p<.05, † p<.10; Displayed coefficients are standardized coefficients.

opposite effect when it was not. This could be that the audience felt the influencer must be attractive because brands that they might like themselves had paid the influencer to promote their content. Given that we took an equal sample from each influencer of sponsored and non-sponsored content, it raises the question of whether attractiveness fluctuates because of, perhaps, a moderating effect of sponsorship. However, this relationship was not hypothesized so it was not tested.

Anada and Wandebori (2016) stated that attractiveness was the only dimension of the source credibility model that does not influence customer behavior. Their result could have been altered due to the lack of distinction between sponsored and non-sponsored content. Yet nowadays it is crucial to create high-quality sponsored content (Bradbury 2017). As such, the influencers may put more effort into looking attractive in a sponsored post, as they are being paid for promoting a product, brand, or event. Hong et al. (2018) found that attractive sources were also found to be more trustworthy and competent, thus inadvertently perpetuating the belief that an influencer does not need to be a believable expert in their field if they are perceived to be beautiful.

When we explored trustworthiness, the audience was significantly more likely to trust non-sponsored content. Trust is a key area prevalent in research related to social media influencers (Anada and Wandebori 2016; Rebelo 2017; Xiao et al. 2018) and

joyce costello and klaudia maria urbanska

Table 10.3 Binary logistic regression results – non-sponsored post

	Model 1		Model 2		Model 3		Model 4	
	DV: Non-Sponsored		DV: Non-Sponsored		DV: Non-Sponsored		DV: Non-Sponsored	
	Exp(β) Odds ratio	S.E.	Exp(β) Odds ratio	S.E.	Exp(β) Odds ratio	S.E.	Exp(β) Odds ratio	S.E.
Attractiveness	.636**	0.154					.613**	0.174
Trustworthiness			3.566*	0.765			5.684*	0.815
Expertise					0.742	0.310	0.839	0.382
Constant (odds ratio)	1.754***	0.044	1.683***	0.520	1.701***	0.042	.1.750***	0.044
Nagelkerke R²	0.005		0.002		0.001		0.008	
Hosmer-Lemeshow	Chi-square .000, df 0,sig. = .00		Chi-square .000, df 0,sig. = .00		Chi-square .000, df 1,sig. = 1.00		Chi-square .003, df 1,sig. = .954	
Null predicted % correct	62.9		62.9		62.9		62.9	
Predictive capacity of model	62.9		62.9		62.9		62.9	
Observations	2,423		2,423		2,423		2,423	

Notes: *** $p < .001$, ** $p < .01$, * $p < .05$; Displayed coefficients are standardized coefficients.

our findings are aligned with Fred's (2015) findings. So, the paradox arises that if a brand wants potential consumers to trust a brand, it may not be in the brand's interest to have a sponsorship deal with the influencers. According to Rossiter and Smidts (2012), this dimension does not have a positive impact on the endorsement as people are aware that payment was received for an advertisement. In a non-sponsored video, this prejudice is non-existent, therefore believability can be of high importance.

Nonetheless, some social media personalities are known for not always disclosing promoted brands and hiding behind the "I genuinely love it" slogan (Bradbury 2017). Through native advertising, influencers can easily promote products (Wojdynski and Evans 2015) and this can lead to confusion amongst viewers as to what content is paid for. Laws set out by the UK Competition and Markets Authority in relation to disclosing a promoted product rely mainly on the trustworthiness of the influencer (Bosher 2020). Videos chosen for the purpose of this research clearly stated that they were created in collaboration with a brand that explains the overwhelming difference in trusting non-sponsored over sponsored content. Trustworthiness was found to have a high impact on purchase intention (Ananda and Wandebori 2016; Rebelo 2017), therefore influencers may want to avoid too many sponsorships to avoid permanent damage to their credibility (Tripp et al. 1994).

sponsored versus non-sponsored content

Finally, expertise was found to have no significance with either video type. This means that beauty influencers' skills or qualifications may not be important when it comes to their credibility. The results of this research are inconsistent with previous academic findings such as Ananda and Wandebori (2016) who found this dimension to be important for beauty influencers. Other scholars also identified expertise to have a direct impact on credibility and persuasiveness (e.g. La Ferle and Choi 2005; Rossiter and Smidts 2012; Siler and Kucza 2017). According to Ohanian (1991), the creator of the source credibility model, expertise is the only dimension linked to the purchase intention of the endorsed brand. Nonetheless, the aforementioned studies focused on the typical understanding of the term "celebrity endorsement." Social media personalities can promote various products (Wojdynski and Evans 2015), which is easily noticeable on YouTube profiles of influencers chosen for the purpose of this research (Hannah Renee, Jordan Lipscombe, and Sophdoesnails). Even though their background is beauty, they also collaborate with fashion and even underwear brands. They may not hold any professional qualifications when it comes to what they are doing because they simply gained popularity online. As such, the results show that there is no more need for influencers to be experts in particular areas of interest.

The findings of this study suggest that factors leading to credibility vary based on a type of content created by an influencer. Whereas attractiveness and trustworthiness are highly significant, expertise is no longer important in the case of influencer marketing. When creating sponsored content, beauty influencers should focus on their attractiveness as it tends to have the highest impact on credibility. If they value their trustworthiness, they should avoid creating paid-for-videos. Ultimately, perception of the latter dimension was proven to be hard to change, with the new advertising standards and viewers being aware of advertisements and wary of dishonest opinions. Influencers can, however, alter their perceived attractiveness by delivering high-quality content at all times.

Furthermore, this study reveals several managerial implications and practical recommendations for public relations, marketing, and advertising practitioners focused on influencer marketing. Firstly, this study helps them to further understand the aspects that create influencer credibility. This is especially helpful if they are considering collaboration with a social media personality. Secondly, the results of this study give them guidance as to what qualities they should focus on when partnering with a YouTuber. As expertise is no longer significant, it does not lead to an increased purchase intention amongst viewers. This means that practitioners can reach out to beauty influencers to create campaigns related to other disciplines. However, their request and expectations need to be within reason. Trustworthiness and authenticity are still important to viewers and future consumers. A beauty guru promoting kitchen equipment may not receive a positive response. Nevertheless, influencer marketing is still a developing area and there is not much research concerning this happening. Finally, this study contributed to Ohanian's (1991) source credibility model and was adapted to answer the current industry needs. Professionals can use the model and methods presented in this research as a framework to understand the credibility of each individual influencer.

joyce costello and klaudia maria urbanska

Summary

- Theories such as the source credibility model can provide insights for studies exploring influencers.
- Influencers who produce non-sponsored content tend to be viewed as more trustworthy.
- Influencers who produce sponsored content, tend to be viewed as more attractive.
- Expertise is not significant whether the post is sponsored or not, which implies influencers may not be viewed as experts.

The case of the grey area of unboxing videos

Influencer activities on social media has largely been an unregulated area from its early conception as Ad councils and Federal Trade Commission sought to apply twentieth-century rules to twenty-first-century problems. Some influencers have hidden behind semantics by saying "I was not paid to say this," albeit perhaps a technicality; while others have been more creative in disclosing that they have received free products but are not being paid to say anything nice about them. In 2015 Zoella and several other influencers found themselves in trouble with the ASA when they made videos about games with Oreos but failed to disclose it was sponsored content. Even now some influencers are doing unboxing videos and discussing what they see as sponsored content, but then interacting with the same products and billing it as non-sponsored.

Shannon Harris, the New Zealand vlogger that goes by Shaaanxo, has been leading the YouTube beauty influencers with her unboxing videos. Unlike some other influencers prior to ASA and FTC cracking down, Harris was upfront and clear about her partnership with Sephora and highlighted it in her 2017 videos. Albeit, in order to find out if something is sponsored, one has to open the description box and scroll towards the end. While the videos specifically about Sephora are labeled as sponsored, the products themselves end up in other videos such as decluttering or organizing videos. The grey area becomes if one must label a video as sponsored if they are being paid to promote the product or demonstrate in unboxing videos, would use of the content later on still be considered promoted content?

In other videos, where Harris goes through a pile of makeup goodies, there will be the statement "THIS VIDEO ISNT SPONSORED. *Some* links are affiliate! Thanks for the support ☺." So, while she has made it clear that the video itself may not be sponsored, affiliate marketing implies the influencer is receiving some form of commission or benefit for posting the link. In the case of the January 20, 2020 video titled "I tried KMART MAKEUP and... wow. ▢ FULL FACE first impressions," it is reasonable to expect the viewer to open the description and find links to buy content that was highlighted in the video. Instead, towards the bottom of the description are several links to products where an influencer discount exists.

Questions?

1. If a product is provided to an influencer as part of a sponsored deal, when does the product cease to be associated with sponsorship? What were the legal and

ethical implications of using a product in a non-sponsored video that originated from a sponsored deal?

2. Affiliate marketing allows influencers a way to make a commission off a percentage of sales. If it is included as part of a video, does that video then technically become sponsored as the result of the commission associated with it?

3. What policies can the FTC or ASA put in place that will make it immediately clear to the viewer whether the content is sponsored or not?

References

Abidin, C., and Ots, M., 2016. Influencers Tell All? Unraveling Authenticity and Credibility in a Brand Scandal. *In:* Edstrom, M., Kenyon, A.T., and Svensson, E., *Blurring the lines. Market-driven and Demography-Driven Freedom of Expression.* Sweden: Nordicom, 153–161.

Alder, R., and Rodman, G., 1999. *Understanding Communication.* 7ed. USA: Oxford University Press.

Amos, C., Holmes, G., and Strutton, D., 2008. Exploring the relationship between celebrity endorser effects and advertising effectiveness. *International Journal of Advertising*, 27(2), 209–234.

Ananda, A.F., and Wandebori, H., 2016. The impact of drugstore makeup product reviews by Beauty Vlogger on YouTube towards purchase intention by undergraduate students in Indonesia. *International Conference on Ethics of Business, Economics, and Social Science*, 16–17 September 2016, Yogyakarta, Daerah Istimewa Yogyakarta, Indonesia. Available from: https://eprints.uny.ac.id/41794/1/22%20Azka%20Faranisa%20Ananda.pdf

Ballantine, P. W., and Yeung, C. A., 2015. The effects of review valence in organic versus sponsored blog sites on perceived credibility, brand attitude, and behavioral intentions. *Marketing Intelligence & Planning*, 33(4), 508–521.

Betches, 2019. 5 Influencer Scandals That Exposed How Fake Instagram Is. *Betches*, 28 March 2019, Available from: https://betches.com/5-influencer-scandals-that-exposed-how-fake-instagram-is/

Bhatt, N., Jayswal, R., and Patel, J. D., 2013. Impact of Celebrity Endorser's Source Credibility on Attitude Towards Advertisements and Brands. *South Asian Journal of Management*, 20(4), 74–95.

Bosher, H., 2020. Influencer Marketing and the Law. Ch. 13 in *Influencer Marketing: Building Brand Communities and Engagement.* Ed. Yesiloglu, S., and Costello, J. London: Routledge.

Bradbury, H., 2017. *The Truth About Brands, Influencers & #Sponsored Content.* Interaction, Available from: https://digitalinteraction.co.uk/the-truth-about-brands-influencers-sponsored-content-fd709adf78fd

Brown, D., and Fiorella, S., 2013. *Influence Marketing. How to Create, Manage, and Measure Brand Influencers in Social Media Marketing.* Indianapolis, Indiana: Que Publishing.

Brucculieri, J., 2018. Instagram influencers are all starting to look the same. Here's Why. *Huffington Post*, 9 March 2018, Available from: www.huffingtonpost.co.uk/entry/instagram-influencers-beauty_n_5aa13616e4b002df2c6163bc

Colliander, J., and Erlandsson, S., 2015. The blog and the bountiful: Exploring the effects of disguised product placement on blogs that are revealed by a third party. *Journal of Marketing Communications*, 21(2), 110–124.

Costello, J., and Biondi, L., 2020. The Art of Deception: Will fake followers decay trust and can authenticity preserve it? Ch. 12 in *Influencer Marketing: Building Brand Communities and Engagement.* Ed. Yesiloglu, S., and Costello, J. London: Routledge.

joyce costello and klaudia maria urbanska

Crossfield, J., 2017. Full Disclosure: The Murky World of Influencer Marketing. *Chief Content Officer*, 1 November 2017, Available from: https://contentmarketinginstitute.com/cco-digital/april-2019/influencer-marketing-non-disclosure/

De Veirman, M., and Hudders, L. 2020. Disclosing sponsored Instagram posts: the role of material connection with the brand and message-sidedness when disclosing covert advertising, *International Journal of Advertising*, 39(1) 94–130.

Djafarova, E., and Rushworth, C., 2017. Exploring the credibility of online celebrities' Instagram profiles in influencing the purchase decisions of young female users. *Computers in Human Behavior*, 68, 1–7.

Eisend, M., 2006. Source Credibility Dimensions in Marketing Communication – A Generalized Solution. *Journal of Empirical Generalisations in Marketing*, 1–33.

Eksouzian-Cavadas, A., 2018. A Definitive Ranking Of The Highest Paid Beauty Influencers. *Elle*, 19 September 2018, Available from: www.elle.com.au/beauty/highest-paid-beauty-bloggers-18609

Erdogan, B.Z., 1999. Celebrity Endorsement: A Literature Review. *Journal of Marketing Management*, 15(4), 291–314.

Freberg, K., Graham, K., McGaughey, K., and Freberg, L. A., 2011. Who are the social media influencers? A study of public perceptions of personality. *Public Relations Review*, 37(1), 90–92.

Fred, S., 2015. *Examining Endorsement and Viewership Effects on the Source Credibility of YouTubers*. Thesis. University of South Florida, Available from: https://scholarcommons.usf.edu/cgi/viewcontent.cgi?article=6883&context=etd

Goldsmith, R.E., Lafferty, B.A., and Newell, S.J., 2000. The impact of corporate credibility and celebrity on consumer reaction to advertisements and brands. *Journal of Advertising*, 29(3), 43–54.

Hatfield, E., and Rapson, R.L., 2010. Physical Attractiveness. *The Corsini Encyclopedia of Psychology*, Available from: https://onlinelibrary.wiley.com/doi/abs/10.1002/97804704 79216.corpsy0681

Homer, P.M., and Kahle, L.R., 1990. Source expertise, time of source identification, and involvement in persuasion: an elaborative processing perspective. *The Corsini Encyclopedia of Psychology*, 19(1), 30–39.

Hong, S., Lee, H., and Johnson, E.K., 2018. The face tells all: Testing the impact of physical attractiveness and social media information of spokesperson on message effectiveness during a crisis. *Journal of Contingencies and Crisis Management*, 1–8.

Internet Marketing Hub, 2020. How much do YouTubers make? *Internet Marketing Hub*. Available from: https://influencermarketinghub.com/how-much-do-youtubers-make/

Joffe, J., 2018. How should brands handle influencers posting fake sponsored content? *PR News Online*. Available from: www.prnewsonline.com/influencers-fake-sponsored-content

Joseph, W.B., 1982. The credibility of physically attractive communicators; a review. *Journal of Advertising*, 11(3), 15–24.

Keinmann, Z., 2019. Has Fyre Festival burned influencers?. *BBC News*, 22 January 2019, Available from: www.bbc.co.uk/news/46945662

Kemp, N., 2018. Body positivity, diversity, and strong women: the new rules of beauty advertising. *Campaign*, 7 June 2018, Available from: www.campaignlive.co.uk/article/body-positivity-diversity-strong-women-new-rules-beauty-advertising/1466761

Kozinets, R.V., 2015. *Netnography: Redefined*. 2nd ed. Sage Publications: Los Angeles.

La Ferle, C., and Choi, S.M., 2005. The Importance of Perceived Endorser Credibility in South Korean Advertising. *Journal of Current Issues and Research in Advertising*, 27(2), 67–81.

Leban, M., and Voyer, B., 2020, Social media influencers versus traditional influencers: Roles and consequences for traditional marketing campaigns. Ch. 2 in *Influencer Marketing: Building Brand Communities and Engagement*. Ed. Yesiloglu, S., and Costello, J. Routledge: London.

Lee, J.E., and Watkins, B., 2016. YouTube vloggers' influence on consumer luxury brand perceptions and intentions. *Journal of Business Research*, 69(12), 5753–5760.

Lee, K., 2018. The Influence of Beauty-Related YouTube content on Consumers' Purchase Intention. *Trace: Tennessee Research and Creative Exchange*, 1–46.

Leskin, P., 2019. These are the 23 most popular YouTube stars in the world. *Business Insider*, 4 April 2019, Available from: www.businessinsider.com/most-popular-youtubers-with-most-subscribers-2018-2?r=US&IR=T

Lim, X.J., Radzol, A.R.M., Cheah, J., and Wong, M.W., 2017. The impact of social media influencers on purchase intention and the mediation effect of customer attitude. *Asian Journal of Business Research*, 7(2), 19–36.

Lou, C., and Yuan, S., 2019. Influencer marketing: How message value and credibility affect consumer trust of branded content on social media. *Journal of Interactive Advertising*, 19(1), 58–73.

Lowry, P.B., Wilson, D.W., and Haig, W.L., 2013. A picture is worth a thousand words: Source credibility theory applied to logo and website design for heightened credibility and consumer trust. *International Journal of Human-Computer Interaction*, 30(1), 63–93.

Lu, L., Chang, W., and Chang, H., 2014. Consumer attitudes toward blogger's sponsored recommendations and purchase intention: The effect of sponsorship type, product type, and brand awareness. *Computers in Human Behavior*, 34, 258–266.

MacRury, I., 2020. Taking the Biscuit: Exploring Influencers, Advertising and Regulation. Ch. 14 in *Influencer Marketing: Building Brand Communities and Engagement*. Ed. Yesiloglu, S., and Costello, J. London: Routledge.

Närvänen, E., Kirvesmies, T., and Kahri, E., 2020. Parasocial relationships of Generation Z consumers with social media influencers. Ch. 7 in *Influencer Marketing: Building Brand Communities and Engagement*. Ed. Yesiloglu, S., and Costello, J. London: Routledge.

Nazeral, S., 2017. How YouTube influencers are rewriting the marketing rulebook. *Think with Google*, 1 October 2017, Available from: https://201711.storage.googleapis.com/youtube-influencer-marketing-rulebook/1102-Carat-Agency-op-ed-Download.pdf

Nielsen, 2019. Nielsen Launches Influencer Campaign Measurement Solution. Nielsen. Available from: www.nielsen.com/uk/en/press-releases/2019/nielsen-launches-influencer-campaign-measurement-solution/

Nouri, M., 2018. The power of influence: Traditional celebrity vs social media influencer. *Advanced Writing: Pop Culture Intersections*, 1–20.

O'Mahony, S., and Meenaghan, T., 1997. The impact of celebrity endorsements on consumers. *Irish Marketing Review*, 10(2), 15–24.

Ohanian, R., 1991. The impact of celebrity spokespersons' perceived image on consumers' intention to purchase. *Journal of Advertising Research*, 31(1), 46–54.

Penny, S., 2018. More rigorous guidelines are needed if influencer marketing is to weed out the "bad apples". *Marketing Week*, 12 October 2018. Available from: www.marketingweek.com/2018/10/12/rigorous-guidelines-influencer-marketing/

Pitz, J., Kohler, I., and Esch, F., 2018. The impact of influencer marketing on perception and experience of unknown, weak, and strong brands. *Transfer Werbeforschung & Praxis*, 64(4), 14–24.

Pornpitakpan, C., Li, Q., and Fu, S.F.I., 2017. A gender-focused review of the effect of message source attractiveness on persuasion: Implications for marketers and advertisers. *The European Journal of Communication Research*, 42(2), 195–237.

Rebelo, M., 2017. How influencer's credibility on Instagram is perceived by consumers and its impact on purchase intention. *Universidade Católica Portuguesa*, 1–92.

Rieh, S.Y., Morris, M.R., Metzger, M.J., Francke, H., and Yeon, G.Y., 2015. Credibility perceptions of content contributors and consumers in social media. *Computer Science*, 51(1), 1–4.

Rossiter, J.R., and Smidts, A., 2012. Print advertising: Celebrity presenters. *Journal of Business Research*, 65(6), 874–879.

Ruiz-Gomez, A., 2018. Digital Fame and Fortune in the age of Social Media: A Classification of social media influencers. *aDResearch ESIC*, 19(19), 8–29.

Seiler, R. and Kucza, G., 2017. Source credibility model, source attractiveness model, and match-up-hypothesis – an integrated model. *Journal of International Scientific Publications*, 14, 1–15.

Sokolova, K., and Kefi, H., 2019. Instagram and YouTube bloggers promote it, why should I buy? How credibility and parasocial interaction influence purchase intentions. *Journal of Retailing and Consumer Services*, 1–9.

Stanwick, P., and Stanwick, S., 2019. Frye Festival: The Party that Never Got Started. *American Journal of Humanities and Social Sciences Research*, 3(12) 138–142.

Statista, 2019. Most popular YouTube beauty and style channels as of April 2019, ranked by the number of subscribers (in millions). *Statista*, 1 April 2019, Available from: www.statista.com/statistics/627448/most-popular-youtube-beauty-channels-ranked-by-subscribers/

Thiruchelvam, S., 2017. Men and women demand diversity in the beauty revolution. *Raconteur*, 12 December 2017, Available from: www.raconteur.net/retail/men-and-women-demand-diversity-in-beauty-revolution

Till, B.D., and Busler, M., 1998. Matching products with endorsers: attractiveness versus expertise. *Journal of Consumer Marketing*, 15(6), 576–586.

Tripp, C., Jensen, T.D., and Carlson, L., 1994. The effects of multiple product endorsements by celebrities on consumers' attitudes and intentions. *Journal of Consumer Research*, 20(4), 535–547.

Walker, T., 2018. Why diversity in ads is more important than ever for revenue. *AspireIQ*, 8 February 2018, Available from: www.aspireiq.com/blog/why-diversity-in-ads-is-more-important-than-ever-for-revenue

Wang, S.W., Kao, G.H., and Ngamsiriudomb, W., 2017. Consumers' attitude of endorser credibility, brand, and intention with respect to celebrity endorsement of the airline sector. *Journal of Air Transport Management*, 60, 10–17.

White, A., 2019. Social media snake oil: Why the Fyre Festival scam was a disaster for celebrity influencers. *The Telegraph*, 16 January 2019. Available from: www.telegraph.co.uk/on-demand/o/fyre-festival-scam-disaster-celebrity-influencers/

Wojdynski, B.W., and Evans, N.J., 2015. Going native: Effects of disclosure position and language on the recognition and evaluation of online native advertising. *Journal of Advertising*, 45(2), 1–12.

Wu, K., 2016. YouTube marketing: Legality of sponsorship and endorsement in advertising. Available from: www.scmv.com/_images/content/YouTube-Marketing_Katrina-Wu_stamped.pdf

Xiao, M., Wang, R., and Chan-Olmsted, S., 2018. Factors affecting YouTube influencer marketing credibility: a heuristic-systematic model. *Asian Journal of Business Research*, 15(3), 1–26.

Yesiloglu, S., 2020, Rise of influencers. Ch. 1 in *Influencer Marketing: Building Brand Communities and Engagement*. Ed. Yesiloglu, S., and Costello, J. Routledge: London.

chapter 11

The monetization of opinions

An investigation into consumer responses to covert endorsement practices on Instagram

James Harrison and Fiona Cownie

Learning outcomes

On completing this chapter, you should be able to:

- understand the consequences of covert marketing;
- realize how some influencers may use covert marketing and practices;
- appreciate how the disclosure typology influences social media users; and
- understand how influencers and marketers can overcome reliance on covert practices.

Influencer marketing has grown exponentially in recent years due to the rise of digital endorsers (Lee 2018), many of whom are now considered famous online and labeled "Instafamous" on Instagram (Archer and Harrigan 2016). These digital endorsers are able to embed sponsored endorsements into their "authentic" personal feeds, directed to large audiences (Elliot 2018). However, with more and more brands *paying* endorsers to produce "authentic" branded content on platforms including Instagram, we will explore whether these practices are genuine.

Despite Instagram introducing the use of a clear "paid partnership" tag in efforts to curb deceptive endorsements, there is still evidence of widespread covert behavior, with Finlay (2018) finding that just 21 percent of sponsored posts on Instagram contained clear disclosures. Meanwhile, the Advertising Standards Authority has started to crack down on brands and endorsers that do not disclose paid content sufficiently, sending warning letters to influencers, after a survey found 44 percent of the UK public thought influencer marketing was damaging to society due to its deceptive practices (Stewart 2018).

Consumers may find it difficult to recognize the commercial nature of endorsements from sources who appear similar to their peers. Consequently, there are calls for investigations into the impact of these masked influencer marketing practices on consumers (Boerman et al. 2017). We seek to answer those calls by investigating how consumers are responding to these covert endorsements. As current regulations for online disclosures may be insufficient to protect consumers from deception, we seek to discover how consumers recognize and view different types of disclosure (Burkhalter et al. 2014).

Source credibility

One of the earliest models to examine the effectiveness of sponsored third-party endorsements is the source credibility theory (Hovland et al. 1954), which suggests that the effectiveness of an endorsed message depends on the perceived level of trustworthiness and expertise of the endorser (Ohanian 1990). Consumers are more likely to be persuaded when exposed to promotional messages from highly credible sources (Erdogan 1999). Credibility is related to expertise and the ability to provide a trusted opinion (Goldsmith et al. 2000). These attributes indicate that audiences must trust the endorser as being unbiased, in order to perceive credibility. Indeed, the endorsement literature presents trustworthiness as an important indicator of source credibility, referring to an endorser's perceived believability, honesty, and integrity (e.g. Chu and Kamal 2008; Yang 2017).

Although endorsers often have commercially motivated interests for endorsing a product, consumers may fail to recognize these motives, assuming that endorsers are motivated by a genuine liking for the product or brand (Cronley et al. 1999). This predisposition is explained by correspondence bias (Gilbert and Malone 1995), the tendency for people to ignore situational factors which may be more likely causes of the behavior, such as financial compensation (Kapitan and Silvera 2015). However, we also know that when consumers reflect more deeply on an endorsement message, they *can* recognize financial motives and are then less likely to accept the message (Silvera and Austad 2004).

According to the match-up theory, congruence between the endorser and the product or brand is crucial in order for the endorsement to be effectively persuasive (Kamins 1994). Empirical evidence shows that high endorser-brand congruence, for example an established makeup vlogger and a cosmetics brand, leads to greater believability of the endorsement message and consequently is more likely to result in favorable product/brand attitudes (Premeaux 2005; Erfgen et al. 2015). Such congruence has been explored by Till and Busier (2000), whose study in the context of print advertising highlighted the role of fit or belongingness in the match-up hypothesis. Expertise rather than physical attractiveness is the most potent characteristic influencing match between the endorser and endorsed (Till and Busier 2000). Thus, we might infer that the experienced make-up artist might be a more powerful endorser of make-up than a physically beautiful Instagrammer. However, Till and Busier (2000) conclude their work by suggesting that physical attractiveness might indeed have a role to play within the match-up hypothesis despite the lack of evidence for this in their findings. This may explain why many Instagram influencers appear to put so much emphasis on the aesthetic of their imagery.

Indeed, Xin Jean Lim et al.'s (2017) more recent study focused on social media influencers found that source attractiveness, alongside product match-up and meaning transfer, influences consumers' attitude which in turn mediates the relationship with purchase intention. The authors concluded that compelling social media influencers impact consumers' intention to purchase endorsed products (Lim et al. 2017).

However, Kutthakaphan and Chokesamritpol (2018) warn that if the argument in an endorsement message is perceived as being false and invalid, consumers will instead develop a negative attitude towards both the endorser and the brand (Cheung et al. 2009). To illustrate, Instagram has become saturated with endorsements for hair growth pills which carry no proven claims and are often perceived negatively (TINA 2017).

The concept of parasocial interaction provides valuable insight into the strengths of relationships between endorsers and consumers (Närvänen et al. 2020) and seems to be particularly pertinent in the context of digital endorsers (Kassing and Sanderson 2009). Applied to the digital endorser context, the theory focuses on how consumers develop fictitious emotionally bonding relationships with endorsers that strongly resemble real friendships (Rosaen and Dibble 2008). Thus, brands and endorsers can strategically exploit the benefits of para-social interaction to their advantage (Lueck 2012; Lee and Watkins 2016). The risk of nurturing para-social interaction is that it can amplify any negative perceptions, such as the opportunistic behavior of an endorser promoting products for self-gain (Colliander and Erlandsson 2013; Chapple and Cownie 2017).

Covert marketing

We draw from ideas about covert marketing to understand further covert practices amongst influencers. Martin and Smith (2008 p. 45) define covert marketing as "the use of surreptitious marketing practices that fail to disclose or reveal the true relationship with the company that produces or sponsors the marketing message." In the specific context of sponsored endorsements, covert marketing causes consumers to neglect evidence of sponsorship (Sprott 2008). We argue that covert marketing is able to bypass consumer resistance as consumers are more accepting of advertising messages that do not appear to be sent from a commercial source, such as sponsored endorsements by digital endorsers (Darke and Ritchie 2007). However,

james harrison and fiona cownie

the growing use of covert marketing techniques, particularly in the online context, is raising ethical concerns about the deceptiveness of the practice and potential harm it could be causing (Milne et al. 2009). For example, some of L'Oréal's sponsored YouTube vloggers have often failed to disclose their monetary relationship with the company, whilst "honestly" recommending the products (TINA 2016).

The major risk of covert marketing is that if consumers learn about the commercial motive behind a covert message, it can increase skepticism, diminish trust and result in long-term damage for the consumers' relationship with the brand (Milne et al. 2009). In fact, Rotfeld (2008) argues that covert marketing efforts are just adding to media clutter and reinforcing consumer distrust in advertising. Martin and Smith (2008) share this belief of a consumer backlash and warn that there are unknown far-reaching detrimental consequences of covert marketing. Petty and Andrews (2008) take this warning further by suggesting that covert marketing is at risk of causing increased skepticism in society overall. It is therefore unsurprising that consumer advocates are calling for greater regulation of these deceptive marketing practices (Cain 2011).

Although research into areas of covert marketing in the context of social media is slowly emerging, initial empirical evidence suggests that the practice is likely to lead to perceptions of manipulation (e.g. Tutaj and van Reijmersdal 2012; Lee et al. 2016). This practice can result in negative attitudinal and behavioral responses from consumers (e.g. Morales 2005; Ashley and Leonard 2009; Lunardo and Mbengue 2013). Therefore, the consequences of potential consumer suspicion and response to covert marketing within social media require further investigation, as according to Martin and Smith (2008) continued abuse could generate irreversible distrust.

Disclosure

When exposed to overt marketing messages, consumers use their knowledge about persuasion to cope with and respond to the persuasion attempts (Nelson and Ham 2012). Friestad and Wright's (1994) persuasion knowledge theory is based on the premise that consumers gain knowledge about marketing over time and develop defense mechanisms that are activated when exposed to marketing communications. For example, as influencers and their practices become more familiar to consumers, consumers employ these defense mechanisms to look out for labels in the form of hashtags, e.g. #spon, which allow them to discriminate between influencers and their posts. Equally influencers' increasing understanding of persuasion is likely to impact their approaches to communication which may include intended or unintended attempts at concealment of external commercial associations. When the commercial source of an advertisement is not transparent, it is argued that consumers' persuasion knowledge is not activated, thus bypassing their ability to guard against unwanted messages and potentially persuading them whilst consumers are unaware (van Reijmersdal et al. 2016). Rozendaal et al. (2011) further suggested that persuasion knowledge is formed of both conceptual and attitudinal elements of communication.

While sponsorship disclosures in traditional media have been demonstrated to activate persuasion knowledge, Boerman et al. (2017) postulates the same outcome is not as present within social media because consumers' persuasion knowledge in this context is not yet fully developed. Their study of celebrity endorsements on Facebook found a wider issue of disclosure recognition in line with similar findings by Campbell et al. (2013) and Wojdynski and Evans (2016). However, just three years after Boerman et al.'s (2017) work one might expect that increased use of Instagram and exposure to influencers will have advanced consumers' persuasion knowledge within this context.

However, research focused on bloggers has suggested that it is difficult for consumers to differentiate between genuine recommendations and sponsored endorsements, often worsened by the absence of effective disclosures (Kozinets et al. 2010; King et al. 2014). In response, scholars have begun to investigate sponsored endorsement and disclosure in a variety of social media contexts, including on YouTube (Chapple and Cownie 2017), Pinterest (Mathur et al. 2018), and Twitter (Burkhalter et al. 2014).

Research in the context of blogs has suggested that overt sponsored endorsements can lead to negative perceptions of the endorser being biased, manipulative, and untrustworthy (Wei et al. 2008). Disclosing the commercial nature of endorsements removes the marketing advantage and leads consumers to understand that sharing is not motivated by authentic liking, which in turn generates negative distrustful feelings (Fransen et al. 2015). However, Chapple and Cownie (2017) found that disclosures of sponsored endorsements on YouTube were able to enhance perceptions of trustworthiness and authenticity, increasing the acceptance of the brand message. Likewise, Carl's (2008) study of disclosed word-of-mouth campaigns also found that upfront disclosures had positive outcomes on credibility and message acceptance.

Research investigating how different disclosure types may activate persuasion knowledge has been relatively sparse, with few studies viewing disclosure as more than a single construct (Evans et al. 2017). This is a particularly important research avenue for exploration as endorsers and brands employ a wide range of inconsistent disclosure methods such as "#spon," supported by little academic research (Walden et al. 2015; Hwang and Jeong 2016). Carr and Hayes (2014) undertook an experimental study of sponsors and bloggers providing a useful classification of disclosure based on how explicitly that disclosure is communicated. They suggest four terms: impartial, implied, explicit, and non-disclosure (Carr and Hayes 2014). Their study found that explicit disclosure of links between sponsor and blogger has a positive impact on key outcomes; the perceived credibility of the blogger; attitudes towards the product being reviewed; and consumers' intentions to purchase the reviewed product. Carr and Hayes (2014 p. 48) conclude their study with the thoughts:

> *Full disclosure of outside influence on opinion leaders may not only be the most ethical and legally complaint tactic but may also utilize two-step flow to increase the effectiveness of practitioners' efforts by maximizing an opinion leader's credibility and ability to influence.*

james harrison and fiona cownie

Explicit Disclosure	Non-Disclosure	Implied Disclosure	Impartial Disclosure
• Authenticity	• Cautiousness	• Ambiguity	• Credibleness
• Credibility	• Deceitfulness	• Disingenuous	• Doubtfulness
• Integrity	• Dishonesty	• Uncertainty	• Honesty
• Transparency	• Manipulative	• Untrustworthy	• Sincerity
• Trustworthy	• Scepticism		• Suspiciousness
• Unambiguity			• Validity

Figure 11.1 Disclosure typology (adapted from Carr and Hayes 2014).

Thus, Carr and Hayes's (2014) experimental study, focused on blogs, is one of few to importantly demonstrate how different disclosure types affect consumer perceptions differently and forms a central part of our underpinning conceptual framework.

We use Carr and Hayes' (2014) classifications of disclosure, introducing sub-features drawn from existing research (Figure 11.1) in our empirical study.

Idea fairy: Dull or full disclosure

How many ways can you think of that signal disclosure on influencers' content? What do you think is the most straightforward form of disclosure? How have you reacted when you found out an influencer that you follow has not been engaging in full disclosure? Is disclosure dull?

An exploratory empirical study

We develop an exploratory empirical study which aims to investigate consumer responses to covert sponsored endorsement practices on Instagram. Underpinned by an interpretivist philosophy, the study seeks to explore consumer responses to covert and overt sponsored endorsements on Instagram. It examines how different types of disclosure of sponsored endorsements on Instagram activate consumers' conceptual and attitudinal persuasion knowledge. Finally, it considers the implications of covert sponsored endorsement practices on perceptions and attitudes towards endorsers and brands.

The research population comprises adults aged 18–24, the predominant users of Instagram (Smith and Anderson 2018). Participants were selected using non-probability purposive sampling to ensure they had relevant experience of the phenomenon being studied (Denscombe 2014). Self-selection sampling was initially employed, seeking volunteer participants via Facebook advertisements. Subjective judgment was used to select participants who conformed to certain criteria, increasing the probability of the sample knowing sufficient information about the topic of disclosure on Instagram (Flick 2014). Individuals who responded to the request were then judged on their suitability against the inclusion criteria of being a user of Instagram (accessing the platform at least once a month) and following at least three Instagram endorsers. Permission was sought to analyze potential participants' follower lists.

The final sample size consisted of eight participants considered sufficient to provide enough data for intensive analysis to be conducted (Braun and Clarke 2013).

In-depth interviews were conducted in order to elicit an understanding of consumer attitudes, opinions, and perceptions (Guest et al. 2013). All interviews were conducted face to face in participants' homes to ensure the interviewees felt relaxed and comfortable. This was particularly important in order to uncover the more sensitive underlying issues (Belk 2016). Participants' "dignity, rights, safety, and well-being" were carefully considered to ensure a high level of ethical conduct was adhered to throughout the study (Haigh 2007, p. 123). The principle of non-maleficence was embraced for the duration of the study (Hennink et al. 2011). Participants were explicitly informed of the scope of the study to eliminate any deception and were reassured their anonymity would be protected (Brennen 2013). Informed consent was obtained from each participant.

Interview transcripts were analyzed using thematic coding in order to reduce and summarize the data without distorting it (Ritchie et al. 2013). By meticulously analyzing statements in the transcripts, themes inductively emerged from the raw data as well as being identified deductively from the conceptual framework (Flick 2014).

Examples of posts from Instagram endorsers were used to stimulate participants' thinking and help to reveal their perceptions of sponsored content (Braun and Clarke 2013). Stimulus materials were individually selected for each participant from the selection of endorsers they follow, as familiarity helps participants to contribute rich insights (Hennink et al. 2011). The stimulus showed hair growth pills endorsed by a lifestyle Instagrammer with no disclosure; an endorsement of Ariel washing gel by a lifestyle Instagrammer with explicit disclosure; and an endorsement of a food product by a gluten-free food Instagrammer with explicit disclosure in close proximity to the endorsement – #AD.

Findings and discussion

Our analysis of participants' contributions encapsulates three key themes. First, we consider participants' responses to covert and overt sponsored endorsements on Instagram and discuss the role of relationship strength, product–endorser congruence, and staged authenticity. Next, we reflect upon disclosure and its activation of consumers' conceptual and attitudinal persuasion knowledge, with a focus on transparency, unambiguity, and proximity. We finish by discussing the implications of covert sponsored endorsement on perceptions and attitudes towards endorsers and brands suggesting three sub-themes, opportunistic evasiveness, reactance and rejection, and brand-led societal exploitation.

Responses to covert and overt sponsored endorsements on Instagram

Relationship strength

One of the most prominent constructs which appeared to affect participant responses to sponsored endorsements was the strength of their pre-existing

james harrison and fiona cownie

relationship with the endorser. Participants who had been following an endorser on Instagram for a substantial length of time often exhibited characteristics of a parasocial relationship.

> You do in a really weird way feel like you know these people, you feel like you can trust them, so when they make recommendations, it's almost like your best friend has recommended it. You are sort of emotionally invested in that person and you feel like you know them as a friend. (P1/Female/22)

For participants who displayed elements of a para-social relationship with an endorser, correspondence bias tended to follow, resulting in tolerance of sponsored posts and perceptions of benevolence and impartialness, even when they were "obviously staged" (P1/Female/22):

> I really do respect her opinion, even though that's an ad, I would still think well I trust her and [...] she would only agree to promote that product, I would like to think, because she actually likes the product. So therefore, I would take that as gospel really and I would probably go out and give that moisturiser a go. (P1/Female/22)

Likewise, in non-disclosure scenarios, participant 3 was inclined to believe an endorser had a genuine liking for a product, ignoring the possibility of a financial motive, linking with Kapitan and Silvera's (2015) findings:

> I wouldn't think of this post as being sponsored, there's nothing in there that suggests that. It says a friend has recommended this app to her. I think it is her real recommendation. (P3/Female/21)

These findings corroborate Chapple and Cownie's (2017) study as well as Carl's (2008) research, which both suggested the likeliness of endorsement acceptance is increased by relationship strength. Comparable to a real friendship, para-social relationship participants also indicated that they expected the trust and respect they held towards endorsers to be reciprocated. Notably, when exposed to an endorsement of a makeup product with non-disclosure, Participant 1 felt negatively towards the lack of transparency and respect:

> It's kind of like they don't appreciate us... to be that honest with us, it's like they're lying to us. And there's no need for that because we respect them. It kind of makes you feel like I'm just a number, just to make them some money. (P1/Female/22)

Product–endorser congruence

We know that poor fit between an endorser and a product is a key reason campaigns fail, due to consumers experiencing difficulty associating an endorser with a mismatched brand (Erfgen et al. 2015). This study found considerable support for the previous literature and the match-up theory (Kamins 1994), with participants often becoming interested and taking action following an endorsement of a product compatible with the endorsers' perceived values:

> *One of the Instagrammers has just done a 30-day weight-loss programme, who's also just had a baby and she now looks fantastic so that then made me look at the website of the product because I wish I looked like that. (P3/Female/21)*

Conversely, low product-endorser congruence, especially in "contradictory" incidences, appeared to have a significant negative impact on endorsement response in terms of believability and acceptance in line with Kapitan and Silvera's (2015) findings:

> *If Instagrammers are always promoting things that make you think, "why you are promoting that, it's not something you usually use"... you wouldn't trust it. (P1/Female/22)*

While relationship strength was seen to increase endorsement acceptance, it also seemingly intensified perceptions of negative incidents such as an illogical product–endorser fit, with arguably more significant consequences. This included feelings of betrayal when an Instagrammer recommends bad products.

> *I've become so invested in their life... It's a bit of shock to see her posting a product that I wouldn't ever imagine her using. Did [she] only switch to premium skincare because Elemis paid [her] to post it? It's weird but it makes me not trust her in a way... (P1/Female/22)*

The low product–endorser congruence that Participant 1 witnessed set off a damaging chain of reactions. It was observed that the experience caused the participant to enter into an internal struggle between her para-social relationship and conceptual persuasion knowledge, resulting in her becoming conflicted, confused, and eventually declaring that she could no longer trust the endorser. While supporting previous studies (Premeaux 2005; Erfgen et al. 2015), this finding indicates a far greater risk of nurturing parasocial relationships and the importance of product–endorser congruence.

Staged authenticity

The prevailing response to sponsored endorsements was that of skepticism and distrust, driven by inauthenticity. Prior research has shown authenticity as an important dimension of endorser credibility (Chapple and Cownie 2017), which is supported in our study with the majority of participants indicating they sought and valued authenticity on Instagram. Participants responded particularly well to incidents when "the power had been given to the Instagrammer" to produce a sponsored post with their own spin and style (P7/Female/20). However, when the content did not have this originality, sponsored posts largely conveyed perceptions of inauthenticity through being "forced and staged" (P2/Male/24):

james harrison and fiona cownie

You can notice a shift in tone when they start to do sponsored posts. It is very rare to find someone who is actually passionate about the brand that much that they are willing to shout about it without being paid. (P2/Male/24)

The sponsored posts are just not legit. She said it was a "genuine" look at the contents of her handbag but I was like "well it's not though is it?" I see through it – I don't believe it. They're not authentic. (P4/Female/24)

When a sponsored post was perceived to be inauthentic, skepticism of the message and distrust of the endorser commonly arose through activation of attitudinal persuasion knowledge:

They're promoting a product because they've been paid to – they have to say they like it. Hair growth tablets – I think it's an absolute load of rubbish because every single Instagrammer who is promoting it, more than likely, wears hair extensions. And they'll say "look how lovely my hair is it's grown so much". It's just not realistic at all. (P3/Female/23)

Ultimately, heightened skepticism and reduced credibility driven by inauthenticity was indicated to result in negative brand and product perceptions, linking with Kutthakaphan and Chokesamritpol's (2018) findings.

I've never heard anyone in real life or on Instagram recommend [the brand] without them being paid. So, I think "do people really love this brand? Or are they just paying people to say that?" They're not really authentic at all because if it was such a great product [...] I wouldn't have to only see it through sponsorships every time. (P1/Female/22)

This finding suggests inauthentic endorsements risk significant negative consequences for brands and endorsers. Staged authenticity is subsequently defined as a manufactured attempt by an endorser to appear authentic, which consumers recognize or suspect is fabricated.

Disclosure and activation of consumers' conceptual and attitudinal persuasion knowledge

Transparency

Carl's (2008) previous studies indicated that transparency has a positive influence on the acceptance of sponsored messages. Our study found support for this relationship, while advancing the understanding of the concept to indicate that explicit and impartial disclosures are able to generate important perceptions of transparency:

I think I can believe their opinion more because it's honesty. I'd have more respect for them. Obviously, they are in it for the money but by them being honest, you don't just think they are a throw-away Instagram celebrity. (P3/Female/23)

Crucially, transparency of endorsements appeared to moderate perceptions of opportunistic behavior, illustrating a key part of the conceptual framework in parallel with Chapple and Cownie's (2017) findings. However, the moderating effect transparency may have on opportunistic behavior varied between participants, seemingly due to consumer resistance, such as for Participant 5 who declared transparency would only make her "less annoyed" (P5/Female/23). Conversely, while implied and non-disclosure conditions often failed to fully activate participants' conceptual persuasion knowledge due to the lack of transparency, participants *did* recognize non-transparent endorsements, and this had a significant negative effect via attitudinal persuasion knowledge:

> *If they don't say that it was sponsored, it makes me feel that they're not being honest and therefore I doubt their review of the product. Therefore, I am less likely to buy or try it because I don't believe them about how much they actually love it. (P1/Female/22)*

Notably, a number of participants indicated they believed the brands were at fault for "pushing through" non-transparent endorsements and that it "wasn't fair" to not always know if they were being sold to (P6/Male/19), qualifying suspicions in the covert marketing literature (Milne et al. 2009).

Unambiguity

As the literature indicated, consumers' persuasion knowledge in the context of social media is not fully developed yet (Boerman et al. 2017); thus, it is crucial that disclosures are unambiguous in order for commercial intent to be understood. Notably, our study found consumers were generally confused and conflicted, caused by experiences with "masked" disclosures that were "easily misconstrued" (P6/Male/19). Some of the participants had noticed disclosure hashtags but were not sure what they meant, some reported never noticing the hashtags, while only a small number of participants understood them correctly:

> *There are a few different hashtags they use like #spon and #sp and that makes it confusing – there should be one set way of saying that it's a sponsored post. (P4/Female/24)*

Uncertainty towards the motives of sponsored Instagram endorsements was evident throughout all interviews, apparently increasing perceptions of opportunistic behavior articulated as "selfishness" and "greed." Remarkably, many of the participants were aware that they require unambiguous disclosures in order to "interpret advertisements properly" (P3/Female/23), further suggesting consumers would be appreciative of explicit disclosures. Perhaps unsurprisingly, it was apparent that the participants have become skeptical of all endorsements, whether sponsored or not – even those from endorsers they trust:

> *It could just be their personal opinion, but I wouldn't know either way if it was a sponsored post. Who knows if you can believe them or not. (P3/Female/23)*

james harrison and fiona cownie

Proximity

For a consumer's conceptual persuasion knowledge to be activated, the disclosure message must be recognized (Darke and Ritchie 2007). As may be expected, the proximity of the disclosure to the sponsored content was seen to have a significant impact on recognition. A disclosure placed above the content, at the top of the description or in the content was usually identified quickly. Conversely, it took much longer for participants to identify a hashtag which was placed further within the description – or often fail to recognize it all together:

> *If it was [a video] I would expect them to tell me verbally. If it was an image, I would definitely want them to put a watermark on it and say "sponsored by" as opposed to just putting it in the description because we look at the pictures – not the description. (P6/Male/19)*

Participants indicated that they preferred disclosures that were placed in obvious positions so that it could activate their conceptual persuasion knowledge and attitudinal persuasion knowledge. This finding further extends insight into the issue of disclosure recognition identified in the literature (Wojdynski and Evans 2016; Boerman et al. 2017).

Implications of covert sponsored endorsement on perceptions and attitudes towards endorsers and brands

Opportunistic evasiveness

Linking with the discussion on proximity, participants suspected endorsers and brands of deliberately "hiding" disclosures to deprive them of conceptual persuasion knowledge activation:

> *It's tactical to place the #Ad at the end because people don't see it. (P4/Female/24)*

> *They are hiding hashtags and creating discrete adverts. I think it's just very selfish. (P2/Male/24)*

Opportunistic evasiveness emerged as a common theme. Participants' contributions implied perceptions of opportunistic behavior and suspicion that they were being deceived. Participants felt endorsers were tricking them and being sneaky, in efforts to obscure financial self-gain motives and appear genuine:

> *They're obviously lying to get people to buy the products so that they make more money from it. (P8/Female/22)*

Unsurprisingly, this had a negative impact on credibility but also on product/brand perceptions as some participants felt companies have responsibility for ensuring endorsers disclose the relationship honestly.

Reactance and rejection

Corresponding with the persuasion knowledge literature (Rozendaal et al. 2011), our study found substantial evidence of resistance to endorsement messages, when participants' attitudinal persuasion knowledge was activated. All participants indicated they resist the persuasive attempts to some extent, triggered by various causes including product–endorser incongruities, staged authenticity and opportunistic evasiveness:

> If one of the Instagrammers] says "you're going to like this product!" it makes me go in the opposite direction – I think well I'll be the judge of that! As soon as I realize that these people are doing it for some kind of profit, I just switch off. (P2/Male/24)

> I unfollowed a few of the people who post that kind of stuff. They were posting photos of rubbish branded things that I didn't care about. It annoyed me. They just think that they can palm you off by selling you products. (P5/Female/23)

A further unexpected finding of this extensive reactance was that it led to participants declaring they reject endorsers and brands "as a punishment" for their deceitful and inauthentic behavior. The finding suggests that consumers are using their attitudinal persuasion knowledge to not only cope with unsolicited persuasion attempts but also to remove themselves from situations where they perceive a threat to their freedom of choice:

> If I see an Instagrammer post something which is clearly an advert, without saying it's an advert, I unfollow them anyway, therefore they've lost someone – that's what they get for not being honest. (P1/Female/22)

This corroborates existing studies, introducing new insight into how digital endorsement strategies may be contributing to consumer resistance and skepticism (Wojdynski and Evans 2016; Boerman et al. 2017). The findings also validate the literature which warned of a consumer backlash against covert endorsement practices (Rotfeld 2008; Martin and Smith 2008).

Brand-led societal exploitation

Literature indicated that ethically questionable practices of masking commercial sources have the potential to cause harm to consumers and damage brand relationships (Milne et al. 2009). All participants spoke about perceptions of manipulation, which appeared to be a consequence of not just concealed disclosures but also exploitive brand behavior in general:

> They [companies] don't care about doing what's right – they just want to sell their products and get them out there anyway that works. They're just greedy and want money. (P5/Female/23)

james harrison and fiona cownie

Some participants blamed brands for putting pressure on them by only sponsoring Instagrammers who are "the idea of perfect," with one participant declaring it made her feel depressed (P3/Female/23). Participants felt the perceived manipulation was having a negative impact on others too, believing brands were "taking advantage of [naïve] young people who look up to and want to be like [the endorsers]" (P5/Female/23).

> They know that young girls will want to be like them. The Instagrammers know what they're doing. It annoys me a bit because they are just mugging people off to make money. (P5/Female/23)

> [Endorsements] like "how to be skinny" I think can be quite detrimental to the younger audiences. There's a lot of vulnerable people exposed to it [who] will think "I love this Instagrammer, she's amazing − if she's going to do it, I will too". (P7/Female/20)

Linked with opportunistic evasiveness, participants generally felt that brands were consciously avoiding responsibility of ensuring sponsored content carried disclosure because of potential implications for sales (P3/Female/23). A common theme emerged of brands being seen as exploiting Instagram to "fool" and "trick" its users, using endorsers who prioritize financial gain and putting their profits ahead of concerns that sponsored endorsements "are contributing to damaging society" (P2/Male/24; P7/Female/20). These findings confirm and extend the literature on deceptive marketing via social media (Tutaj and van Reijmersdal 2012; Lunardo and Mbengue 2013; Lee et al. 2016).

Synthesis of findings and discussion

Our findings extend the literature on influencers, their interactions with followers, and their role within marketing. This exploratory empirical study aimed to contribute rich new insights and understanding to a number of unfulfilled research areas within the endorsement, disclosure, and covert marketing literature. Like previous studies (Chapple and Cownie 2017; Carl 2008), there was early evidence that endorsement acceptance appears to increase with relationship strength and product–endorser congruence. While relationships with para-social features encouraged acceptance of endorsement messages (Rosaen and Dibble 2008; Kassing and Sanderson 2009), relationship strength was also seen to intensify negative incidents, resulting in damaging consequences towards trust and credibility (Colliander and Erlandsson 2013).

It appears that relationship strength and any correspondence bias can be easily overcome by the incongruity between brand and endorser. Low product–endorser congruence, in general, was likely to decrease credibility (Till and Busier 2000) and believability of the endorsement message and increase feelings of distrust. Furthermore, the idea of staged authenticity conceptualizes the prevailing skeptical response to sponsored endorsements. Our study suggests that endorsements perceived as inauthentic may reduce source credibility and lead to negative brand perceptions.

In contrast to studies that viewed disclosure as a single construct (Evans et al. 2017) that increased trustworthiness and credibility, this research explored disclosure as a multi-dimensional construct in the manner first proposed by Carr and Hayes (2014). Our study suggests that some disclosure types may undermine trust and credibility. By exploring disclosure through the lens of conceptual and attitudinal persuasion knowledge, it was seen that implied and non-disclosure scenarios carry inherent risks of increasing distrust and reducing credibility.

The covert nature of these disclosure types was evident through the dimensions of low transparency, unambiguity, and proximity. While some participants were still able to utilize their persuasion knowledge, others with underdeveloped knowledge were at risk of being persuaded unknowingly. Conversely, explicit and impartial disclosures with high levels of transparency, unambiguity, and proximity seemed to be more effective in activating persuasion knowledge, increasing credibility and mitigating perceptions of opportunistic behavior. We found that the consequences of covert endorsements were uncovered through the emergent constructs of opportunistic evasiveness and rejection. The findings indicated consumers believe endorsers are deliberately deceiving them and this has a negative impact on credibility and brand perceptions. Feeling threatened by the deception they face on Instagram, consumers appear to be penalizing endorsers by unfollowing those that are perceived as dishonest, inauthentic, or post too many endorsements.

Implications for industry

We present our findings as a stark warning to marketers and endorsers whose continued abuse of consumers' persuasion defenses may result in an increasing backlash with negative consequences for brand perceptions and endorser credibility.

We propose that agencies, clients, and influencers should approach sponsored endorsements with the utmost transparency and honesty, using explicit disclosures characterized by transparency and unambiguity or impartial disclosures characterized by honesty and sincerity. All parties should view endorsement as a long-term activity rather than looking for short-term wins through pretended disclosures. Agencies working with influencers should present disclosures in a positive embracing light. In turn, consumers are likely to appreciate and reward communications from influencers taking this approach. Crucially, marketers should focus on achieving "earned" endorsements by nurturing long-term relationships with endorsers, rather than ephemeral sponsorships. Not only will this ensure the practice meets the latest advertising regulations but if adopted widely it could begin to reverse consumer perceptions of manipulation, before it is too late.

Summary

- Findings indicate a rising level of consumer distrust and skepticism towards both Instagram endorsers and involved brands, as consumers see through the inauthenticity of the recommendations to which they are exposed.

james harrison and fiona cownie

- Our analysis suggests that current practices on Instagram are manipulative and seek to persuade consumers who are unaware of disclosure practices.
- We recommend that sponsored endorsements should be characterized by transparency and honesty, via explicit or impartial disclosures.
- Disclosures should be clear, and these are likely to generate positive responses from consumers.
- Marketers should focus on "earned" endorsements by nurturing long-term relationships with endorsers.

References

Archer, C. and Harrigan, P., 2016. Show me the money: how bloggers as stakeholders are challenging theories of relationship building in public relations. *Media International Australia*, 160(1), 67–77.

Ashley, C. and Leonard, H., 2009. Betrayed by the buzz? Covert content and consumer–brand relationships. *Journal of Public Policy & Marketing*, 28(2), 212–220.

Belk, R., 2016. *Handbook of Qualitative Research Methods in Marketing*. Cheltenham, UK: Edward Elgar.

Boerman, S., Willemsen, L., and Van Der Aa, E., 2017. This post is sponsored. *Journal of Interactive Marketing*, 38, 82–92.

Braun, V. and Clarke, V., 2013. *Successful Qualitative Research: A practical guide for beginners*. London: SAGE.

Burkhalter, J., Wood, N., and Tryce, S., 2014. Clear, conspicuous, and concise: Disclosures and Twitter word-of-mouth. *Business Horizons*, 57(3), 319–328.

Byrne, S., 2015. The age of the human billboard: Endorsement disclosures in new millennia media marketing. *Journal of Business & Technology Law*, 10(2), 393.

Cain, R., 2011. Embedded advertising on television: Disclosure, deception, and free speech Rights. *Journal of Public Policy & Marketing*, 30(2), 226–238.

Campbell, M., Mohr, G., and Verlegh, P., 2013. Can disclosures lead consumers to resist covert persuasion? The important roles of disclosure timing and type of response. *Journal of Consumer Psychology*, 23(4), 483–495.

Carl, W., 2008. The role of disclosure in organized word-of-mouth marketing programs. *Journal of Marketing Communications*, 14(3), 225–241.

Carr, C.T. and Hayes, R.A., 2014. The effect of disclosure of third-party influence on an opinion leader's credibility and electronic word of mouth in two-step flow. *Journal of Interactive Advertising*, 14(1), 38–50.

Chapple, C. and Cownie, F., 2017. An investigation into viewers' trust in and response towards disclosed paid-for endorsements by YouTube lifestyle Vloggers. *Journal of Promotional Communications*, 5(2).

Cheung, M.Y., Luo, C., Sia, C.L., and Chen, H., 2009. Credibility of electronic word-of-mouth: Informational and normative determinants of on-line consumer recommendations. *International Journal of Electronic Commerce*, 13(4), 9–38.

Chu, S. and Kamal, S., 2008. The effect of perceived blogger credibility and argument quality on message elaboration and brand attitudes. *Journal of Interactive Advertising*, 8(2), 26–37.

Colliander, J. and Erlandsson, S., 2013. The blog and the bountiful: Exploring the effects of disguised product placement on blogs that are revealed by a third party. *Journal of Marketing Communications*, 21(2), 110–124.

Cronley, M., Kardes, F., Goddard, P., and Houghton, D., 1999. Endorsing products for the money: The role of the correspondence bias in celebrity advertising. *Advances in Consumer Research*, 26(1), 627–631.

Darke, P. and Ritchie, R., 2007. The defensive consumer: Advertising deception, defensive processing and distrust. *Journal of Marketing Research*, 44(1), 114–127.

Denscombe, M,. 2010. *Ground Rules For Social Research: Guidelines for good practice.* 2nd edition. Maidenhead: McGraw Hill Open University Press.

Erdogan, B., 1999. Celebrity endorsement: A literature review. *Journal of Marketing Management*, 15(4), 291–314.

Erfgen, C., Zenker, S., and Sattler, H., 2015. The vampire effect: When do celebrity endorsers harm brand recall? *International Journal of Research in Marketing*, 32(2), 155–163.

Evans, N., Phua, J., Lim, J., and Jun, H., 2017. Disclosing Instagram influencer advertising: The effects of disclosure language on advertising recognition, attitudes and behavioral intent. *Journal of Interactive Advertising*, 17(2), 138–149.

Finlay, M., 2018. Are brands the moral arbiter of influencer marketing? *Techround.* Available from: https://techround.co.uk/other/2018/12/01/influencers-are-brands-the-moral-arbiter-in-the-digital-age/

Flick, U., 2014. *An Introduction to Qualitative Research.* 5th ed. Los Angeles: SAGE.

Fransen, M., Smit, E., and Verlegh, P., 2015. Strategies and motives for resistance to persuasion: an integrative framework. *Frontiers in Psychology*, 6, 1201.

Gilbert, T. and Malone, S., 1995. The correspondence bias. *Psychological Bulletin*, 117(1), 21–38.

Goldsmith, R., Lafferty, B., and Newell, S., 2000. The impact of corporate credibility and celebrity credibility on consumer reaction to advertisements and brands. *Journal of Advertising*, 29(3), 43–54.

Goodwin, T., 2018. If you're an "influencer", you're probably not influential. *GQ.* Available from: www.gq-magazine.co.uk/article/influencer-marketing

Guest, G., Namey, E., and Mitchell, M., 2013. In-depth interviews. *Collecting Qualitative Data: A field manual for applied research.* 113–171.

Haigh, C., 2007. Getting ethics approval. *In:* Long, T. and Johnson, M. *Research Ethics in the Real World.* London: Elsevier Health Sciences.

Hennink, M. Hutter, I., and Bailey, A., 2011. *Qualitative Research Methods.* London: Sage Publication Limited.

Hovland, C., Riley, M., Janis, I., and Kelley, H., 1954. Communication and persuasion: Psychological studies of opinion change. *American Sociological Review*, 19(3), 355.

Hwang, Y. and Jeong, S., 2016. "This is a sponsored blog post, but all opinions are my own": The effects of sponsorship disclosure on responses to sponsored blog posts. *Computers in Human Behavior*, 62, 528–535.

Johnson, T. and Kaye, B., 2004. Wag the blog: How reliance on traditional media and the internet influence credibility perceptions of weblogs among blog users. *Journalism & Mass Communication Quarterly*, 81(3), 622–642.

Kamins, M. and Gupta, K., 1994. Congruence between spokesperson and product type: A matchup hypothesis perspective. *Psychology and Marketing*, 11(6), 569–586.

Kapitan, S. and Silvera, D., 2015. From digital media influencers to celebrity endorsers: attributions drive endorser effectiveness. *Marketing Letters*, 27(3), 553–567.

Kassing, J. and Sanderson, J., 2009. You're the kind of guy that we all want for a drinking buddy: Expressions of parasocial interaction on floydlandis.com. *Western Journal of Communication*, 73(2), 182–203.

King, R., Racherla, P., and Bush, V., 2014. What we know and don't know about online word-of-mouth: A review and synthesis of the literature. *Journal of Interactive Marketing*, 28(3), 167–183.

Kozinets, R., de Valck, K., Wojnicki, A., and Wilner, S., 2010. Networked narratives: understanding word-of-mouth marketing in online communities. *Journal of Marketing*, 74(2), 71–89.

Kutthakaphan, R. and Chokesamritpol, W., 2018. *The use of celebrity endorsement with the help of electronic communication channel (Instagram)*. Master thesis – International Marketing. Mälardalen University, School of Business, Society and Engineering.

Lee, J. and Watkins, B., 2016. YouTube vloggers' influence on consumer luxury brand perceptions and intentions. *Journal of Business Research*, 69(12), 5753–5760.

Lee, J., Kim, S., and Ham, C., 2016. A double-edged sword? Predicting consumers' attitudes toward and sharing intention of native advertising on social media. *American Behavioral Scientist*, 60(12), 1425–1441.

Lee, K., 2018. The road ahead for influencer marketing: 2018 and beyond. *Entrepreneur*. Available from: www.entrepreneur.com/article/306688

Libarkin, J. and Kurdziel, J., 2002. Research methodologies in science education: The qualitative-quantitative debate. *Journal of Geoscience Education*, 50(1), 78–86.

Lim, X.J., Radzol, A.R.M., Cheah, J., and Wong, M.W. (2017) The impact of social media influencers on purchase intention and the mediation effect of customer attitude. *Asian Journal of Business Research*, 7(2), pp. 19–36.

Lueck, J., 2012. Friend-zone with benefits: The parasocial advertising of Kim Kardashian. *Journal of Marketing Communications*, 21(2), 91–109.

Lunardo, R. and Mbengue, A., 2013. When atmospherics lead to inferences of manipulative intent: Its effects on trust and attitude. *Journal of Business Research*, 66(7), 823–830.

Martin, K. and Smith, N., 2008. Commercializing social interaction: The ethics of stealth marketing. *Journal of Public Policy & Marketing*, 27(1), 45–56.

Mathur, A., Narayanan, A., and Chetty, M., 2018. An empirical study of affiliate marketing disclosures on YouTube and Pinterest. *ArXiv*. Available from: www.arxiv-vanity.com/papers/1803.08488/

Milne, G., Rohm, A. and Bahl, S., 2009. If it's legal, is it acceptable? *Journal of Advertising*, 38(4), 107–122.

Morales, A., 2005. Giving firms an "e" for effort: Consumer responses to high-effort firms. *Journal of Consumer Research*, 31(4), 806–812.

Närvänen, E., Kirvesmies, T., and Kahri, E. (2020) Para social relationships of Generation Z consumers with social media influencers. Ch. 7 in *Influencer Marketing: Building Brand Communities and Engagement*. Ed. Yesiloglu, S. and Costello, J. Routledge: London.

Ohanian, R., 1990. Construction and validation of a scale to measure celebrity endorsers' perceived expertise, trustworthiness, and attractiveness. *Journal of Advertising*, 19(3), 39–52.

Petty, R. and Andrews, J., 2008. Covert marketing unmasked: A legal and regulatory guide for practices that mask marketing messages. *Journal of Public Policy & Marketing*, 27(1), 7–18.

Premeaux, S., 2005. The attitudes of middle-class male and female consumers regarding the effectiveness of celebrity endorsers. *Journal of Promotion Management*, 11(4), 33–48.

Ritchie, J., Lewis, J., Nicholls, C. M., and Ormston, R., 2013. *Qualitative Research Practice: A guide for social science students and researchers*. London: Sage Publications Ltd.

Rosaen, S. and Dibble, J., 2008. Investigating the relationships among child's age, parasocial interactions, and the social realism of favorite television characters. *Communication Research Reports*, 25(2), 145–154.

Rotfeld, H., 2008. The stealth influence of covert marketing and much ado about what may be nothing. *Journal of Public Policy & Marketing*, 27(1), 63–68.

Rozendaal, E., Lapierre, M., van Reijmersdal, E., and Buijzen, M., 2011. Reconsidering advertising literacy as a defense against advertising effects. *Media Psychology*, 14(4), 333–354.

Saunders, M., Lewis, P., and Thornhill, A., 2012. *Research Methods for Business Students*. 6th ed. Essex: Pearson Education Limited.

Silvera, D. and Austad, B., 2004. Factors predicting the effectiveness of celebrity endorsement advertisements. *European Journal of Marketing*, 38(11/12), 1509–1526.

Smith, A. and Anderson, M., 2018. Social media use in 2018. *Pew Research Center: Internet, Science & Tech*. Available from: www.pewinternet.org/2018/03/01/social-media-use-in-2018/

Sprott, D., 2008. The policy, consumer, and ethical dimensions of covert marketing: An introduction to the special section. *Journal of Public Policy & Marketing*, 27(1), 4–6.

Stewart, R., 2018. UK shoppers say brands aren't transparent about influencer deals and rules need tightened. *The Drum*. Available from: www.thedrum.com/news/2018/02/12/uk-shoppers-say-brands- arent-transparent-about-influencer-deals-and-rules-need

Till, B.D. and Busler, M., 2000. The match-up hypothesis: Physical attractiveness, expertise, and the role of fit on brand attitude, purchase intent and brand beliefs. *Journal of Advertising*, 29(3), pp.1–13.

TINA, 2016. Ad or not? L'Oreal influencer's makeup tutorial. *Truth in Advertising*. Available from: www.truthinadvertising.org/ad-not- loreal-influencers-makeup-tutorial/

TINA, 2017. Hairburst | *Truth In Advertising*. Available from: www.truthinadvertising.org/hairburst/

Tutaj, K. and van Reijmersdal, E., 2012. Effects of online advertising format and persuasion knowledge on audience reactions. *Journal of Marketing Communications*, 18(1), 5–18.

van Reijmersdal, E., Fransen, M., van Noort, G., Opree, S., Vandeberg, L., Reusch, S., van Lieshout, F., and Boerman, S., 2016. Effects of disclosing sponsored content in blogs. *American Behavioral Scientist*, 60(12), 1458–1474.

Walden, J., Bortree, D., and DiStaso, M., 2015. This blog brought to you by ... exploring blogger perceptions of a product endorsement policy and reviews. *Journal of Communication Management*, 19(3), 254–269.

Wei, M., Fischer, E., and Main, K., 2008. An examination of the effects of activating persuasion knowledge on consumer response to brands engaging in covert marketing. *Journal of Public Policy & Marketing*, 27(1), 34–44.

Wojdynski, B. and Evans, N., 2016. Going native: Effects of disclosure position and language on the recognition and evaluation of online native advertising. *Journal of Advertising*, 45(2), 157–168.

Yang, W., 2017. Star power: the evolution of celebrity endorsement research. *International Journal of Contemporary Hospitality Management*, 30(1), 389–415.

chapter 12

The art of deception
Will fake followers decay trust and can authenticity preserve it?

Joyce Costello and Laura Biondi

Learning outcomes

On completing this chapter, you should be able to:

- understand the difference between fake followers and bots;
- appreciate how social bots are evolving with more human-like traits and behaviors; and
- understand how theories such as brand authenticity theory and consumer engagement theory can be applied to influencer marketing.

The pressure rises

In Chapter 1 Yesiloglu (2020) focused her arguments on an influencer tending to be an individual that holds the power to influence the purchase decision. We add that influencers have power because of their perceived authority and trustworthiness (Bladow 2018). Some brands use the number of followers as a proxy to measure the influencer's power to influence. However, if you combine this pressure with the decrease in organic reach on platforms such as Instagram, whose algorithm changes support impressions on paid content (Garland and Reed 2018), this can inadvertently stimulate influencers turning to fake followers. Indeed, several studies (e.g. Garland and Reed 2018; Latimer 2018; Lson et al. 2019) have already shown how some influencers struggled to get decent exposure to their content, and caused some to implement dishonest and fraudulent activities in order to stay relevant and boost their perceived reach.

Many practitioners within the sector have expressed their concerns that dishonest content creators are causing damaging results to the whole industry (Guthrie 2019). In January 2019, a collective of influencers exposed 28 UK influencers within the industry through a two-year investigation (Medium 2019). This study was initially made public but was eventually pulled down as many questioned the motives for those who had conducted the study. However, the investigation did find that there were two types of prominent fake followers: social bots and individuals that were paid to engage (Medium 2019). In fact, in the past few years it had become common for unscrupulous agencies to promise influencers that they could quickly increase their followers for an extremely low cost (FTC 2019). We later address this in the case study about Devumi at the end of this chapter. However, social bots tend to be more complex than fake followers.

Social bots can be non-malicious bots such as search engine bots or those that look for price deals or are looking for content to share with others in the form of clickbait (Boshmaf et al. 2013). Certainly, other influencers, organizations, and even countries that are wanting to find and use the content as their own, sharing a passion and sometimes for clickbait, can purchase bots to be programmed to do so. Here bot intention and behavior can be benign or nefarious, but it ultimately is not a real person engaging with the influencer and hence has the potential to degrade authenticity and trust (Neururer et al. 2018).

If fake followers or purchasing bots phenomenon persists, brands who are disappointed when campaigns underperform because influencers fail to reach a real audience could cease to implement influencer marketing as part of their promotional strategy (e.g. Strugatz and Lee 2018; Garland 2018a; Laghate 2018). Still, Strugatz and Lee (2018) suggest that many brands are either not aware of such practices or tend to not give importance to it as they try to prioritize the brand association with a specific influencer.

The theme of fake followers is increasingly being investigated by academics, but it has focused on the detection of bots and fake followers in social media channels, mainly within the field of computer science (e.g. Cresci et al. 2015; Nitin and Susan 2017; Boyeon et al. 2019). Primary research on the detection of fake followers traditionally has been done through a mathematical approach (Cresci et al. 2015; Boyeon et al. 2019). Although, when it comes to detecting bots, once can use a UserAgent blacklist or IP rate-limiting functions, but this tends to be geared more towards organizations using owned media. Yet there are many different ways bots emulate humans, which is something that Indiana University has been focusing on when developing botometer – a tool to identify bots (Yang et al. 2019).

In this chapter, we explore the relation between brand authenticity theory (Schallehn et al. 2014) and consumer engagement theory (Vivek et al. 2012). Firstly, brand authenticity theory can identify the key characteristics that impact authenticity and its relationship to trust (Schallehn et al. 2014; Moulard et al. 2015; Lude and Prügl 2018). Secondly, Consumer Engagement theory helps delineate the dimension of consumer engagement within the context of Instagram influencers, in terms of the importance of engagement with followers (Dessart et al. 2015; Martinez-Lopez et al. 2017), and how this affects influencers' authenticity and trust.

joyce costello and laura biondi

Fake followers and bots within influencer marketing

In the early days, when bloggers began to capitalize on their blogs and microblogs, agencies would offer to drive traffic to their sites. Companies such as Twitter Accounts Market would say their services were in line with "applicable rules" and would help promote tweets amongst a particular target audience for engagement, but their practices were often in direct violation of Twitter terms and conditions (Stringhini et al. 2012). Initially, real people were recruited and sent offers from companies about being paid to engage with bloggers and certain websites. However, over time, companies found that instead of paying the fake human followers, one could just program "amplification" bots to do the same thing at less cost and for guaranteed actions (Confessore et al. 2018).

Gorwa and Guilbeault (2018) argue that the various forms of automated accounts that operate on social media platforms have been defined as social bots, but two slightly different definitions of social bots have been developed: "socialbots" and "social bot." Socialbots refers to automated accounts that assume fake identities to disseminate malicious links or advertisements (Boshmaf et al. 2013). Cao et al. (2014) found over two million malicious accounts of this nature when they released their Synchro trap on Facebook and Instagram. They argued that by using clustering analysis, their system can uncover large attacks (Cao et al. 2014). Yet, unlike socialbots that do not interact with other accounts, a social bot refers to those automated accounts that produce content and interact with human beings on social media (Ferrara et al. 2016). Social bots mimic human-like behaviors in social media, are public-facing, and are implemented for commercial and fraudulent activities such as spamming, SEO, and influencer marketing (e.g. Ratkiewicz et al. 2011; Stieglitz et al. 2017; Gorwa and Guilbeault 2018).

These social bots are increasingly difficult to identify as most research will focus on the non-human behavior of bots, such as the ability to post many times consistently across time zones (Cresci et al. 2015). However, Ferrara et al. (2016) state the detection of social bots continues to become difficult due to the boundary between human-like and bot-like behavior becoming more blurred. Social bots are evolving and hiding their real nature and imitate human behavior with the aim of influencing human users and avoid suspensions due to social media policies (Chavoshi and Mueen 2017). Researchers have implemented a wide range of techniques to detect bots, which can be grouped into two main categories: social graph-based methods (Anwar and Abulaish 2014) and content-based methods (Wang 2010). It is important to highlight, however, that most research on the detection of social bots has been primarily focused on Twitter (e.g. Broniatowski et al. 2018; Subrahmanian et al. 2016; De Lima Salge and Karahanna 2018; Mønsted et al. 2017). This may be due to Twitter willingness to allow large amounts of data to be captured by outside sources.

In fact, it is extremely easy for would-be or aspiring influencers to purchase social bots by subscribing to specific websites and providing account information (Jang et al. 2018). There is a plethora of websites that can provide a wide range of services that aim at improving clients' engagement rates and follows. Such services include boosting followers and increasing reactions to posts on social media (Laghate 2018). Lson et al. (2019) investigated the habits of influencers and found 90 percent reporting to never having purchased fake followers, but 18 percent had considered doing so. Many studies that explore illegal behavior or intention to knowingly break laws argue respondents will downplay their responses despite it being "anonymous" (Dawson 2018). According to De Lima Salge and Berente (2017), more than 8.2 percent of Instagram users, approximately 27 million at the time of the study, are thought to be social bots. Facebook, in 2016, reported that it had detected over 60 million automated accounts, and Twitter disclosed that more than 45 million of its active users are bots (Laghate 2018). Finally, between April and September 2018 Facebook removed over 1.5 billion fake accounts (Mehta 2019). Given the prevalence of fake and automated accounts, it is reasonable to expect a negative spillover effect for influencers.

One expose had a US marketing agency that was seeking to prove how easy it was to make a fake profile and buy fake followers as a means to gain brand sponsorship (Harrington 2017).

Marketing agency Devumi and the website Kicksta, have been publicly criticized for openly telling influencers they can increase their following (Confessore et al. 2018). Through these websites influencers can purchase, for example, 1,000 followers for $10 in under a minute (Garland 2018a). But it was not until 2019 that the US Federal Trade Commission (2019) took Devumi to court over selling fake "indicators" on social media. (We discuss this in-depth as a case study at the end of the chapter.) However, this is only the beginning of court cases. The reality exists that influencers have begun to purchase fake followers and engagement to show an engaged following despite the decline of their social reach (Garland 2018a).

Because of nefarious practices like purchasing fake followers, online social media platforms are suffering due to the extensive presence of fake accounts that introduce spam, manipulate online ratings, and use personal information extracted from the network (Cao et al. 2012). Even though bots may appear harmless, many of their actions such as disseminating spams and fake news and stealing data to legitimate users are ultimately harmful (De Lima Salge and Berente 2017). The practice of purchasing fake followers may be considered a recent phenomenon, but the damages that it can create to the practice of influencer marketing have the potential to be extensive and long-lasting. Followers fraud has already begun to damage the reputation of an industry that has been built on trust and authenticity. US marketing specialist Captiv8 (Keown 2019) reports $2.1 billion was spent on Influencer-sponsored Instagram content, but more than 11 percent of engagement on those posts came from fraudulent users. Therefore, more than $250 million may have been spent to no avail (Owen 2019).

When investigating whether an influencer has purchased fake followers, it is fundamental to conduct an audit of their followers. For instance, if accounts do not post but just follow other accounts it could be likely that those are fake users (Garland 2018b). Influencer online engagement can also be taken into consideration when evaluating whether fake followers have been purchased. A low engagement, for example when a post on Instagram gets thousands of likes but very few comments with no substance, should also be considered as a warning signal (Garland 2018b). Marketers need to acknowledge the concept of an engagement pod – an aggregation of individuals who

joyce costello and laura biondi

agree to like and comment on each other's content in order to maintain a high engagement rate – in order to see if their influencers of choice are merely just engaging with themselves. Lastly, inauthentic partnerships should also be considered as warning signals. For example, if an influencer who is considered high fashion is involved in a partnership with American retail company Walmart, there are high possibilities that the aim of the influencer is profit and not converting followers to customers (Garland 2018b).

Idea fairy: Faking it

Considering your own beliefs, has there ever been a time when you wanted to increase your followers? Have you ever received an email or ad telling you that you could earn money reading blogs online? Have you ever explored your own followers to see if any of them were Socialbots or social bots?

Brand authenticity theory

Brand authenticity was proposed in 2005 and has been considered by scholars as fundamental in understanding brand trust and credibility (e.g. Beverland 2005; Eggers et al. 2013). In the context of influencer marketing, brand authenticity is considered vital for its success due to it being the core feature driving the engagement (Gazdik 2017). Indeed, the high number of influencers across different social media platforms offering similar content has created a large sense of competitiveness, with more than 1.5 million Instagram posts, identified by disclosure or hashtags like #ad or #sponsored.

Brand authenticity is considered as: "a subjective evaluation of genuineness ascribed to a brand by consumers" (Napoli et al. 2014, p. 1091). The concept of authenticity is considered as a precursor of trust. Although the definition of authenticity is disputed amongst academics, its meaning is often linked to the concept of *original* as in contrasted with the *copy* (Peterson 2005). Research into the concept of authenticity tends to focus on indexical and iconic authenticity (Coary and Oakley 2018; Athwal and Harris 2018). For the first dimension of authenticity, indexical, to exist, there must be a clear division between reality and its reproduction. Indexical is what is believed to be real and are those legitimate products that have a spatio-temporal link and are further backed by cues such as creation date, original place, and material (Coary and Oakley 2018). For instance, wine, according to indexical authenticity, could be considered legitimate based on its heritage, quality, and relationship to place, etc. (Coary and Oakley 2018). Many court cases have used this concept of indexical authenticity to protect certain wines from a region such as Champagne or parmesan cheese from Parma.

On the other hand, iconic authenticity instead refers to a projection of the consumer's attitude and beliefs regarding how the brand should look (Beverland 2006). In this dimension the quality of authenticity is based on an individual's personal experiences. Consumers may accept something as authentic only if it aligns with their own idea of authenticity (Athwal and Harris 2018). For example, silver plates in a museum gift shop are considered authentic if they are thought to look like silver plates made in the sixteenth century despite being manufactured in China (Costa and Bamossy 1995). Iconic authenticity is also referred to as "fabricated authenticity" or "staged authenticity" since consumers may identify something as real only if it aligns with their concept of reality. For iconic authenticity to exist, consumers must have some pre-existing knowledge or expectations of the product (Grayson and Martinec 2004).

Distinguishing indexical and iconic authenticity has helped towards creating frameworks aimed at offering a better understanding of the authenticity formation process (Grayson and Martinec 2004). This has further improved the understanding and knowledge of authenticity in the context of consumer research (Athwal and Harris 2018). Even though authenticity is one of the cornerstones of marketing practice, some scholars have highlighted the confusion that surrounds the notion of the nature of authenticity in the branding arena (Tran and Keng 2018).

In the marketing research discipline, the dimension of authenticity is explored more frequently then indexical. It tends to have a significant focus on the cues of authenticity, such as heritage, sincerity, style, consistency and quality of leadership (e.g. Beverland 2005; Athwal and Harris 2018; Coary and Oakley 2018; Tran and Keng 2018). These cues are used to communicate authenticity due to the fact that they create a link to a trusted point of reference. However, it is challenging to establish whether all the cues carry the same level of importance throughout the course of the brand (Beverland 2005; Athwal and Harris 2018).

Can you be authentic without trust?

Brand authenticity is argued to increase the level of brand trust with authentic Influencers that is most likely to create a consistency between past behaviors and future actions, and thus higher predictability (Schallehn et al. 2014; Tran and Keng 2018). Trust can be defined as "the belief that one's channel partner can be relied on to fulfill its obligations and to behave in a benevolent manner" (Brown et al. 2019, p. 156). This definition best describes the trust the audience has in marketing and in its commitment to not cause any harm to the public.

Scholars argue that trust within brand management is necessary to create loyal customers who will then have a greater propensity to recommend the brand to others (Eggers et al. 2013). Gaining trust is not easy, and it can easily be disrupted (Miranda and Klement 2009). Even minor violations of trust can result in the interruption of a positive relationship between consumers and the brand and may raise doubts amongst investors for future businesses. Because of this, brands themselves understand the crucial role and importance played by trust (Ha 2004). Scholars have also established how brand trust is essential in developing consumers' attitudes and beliefs toward a brand, and hence achieve competitive advantage and improve business performance (Delgado-Ballester and Munuera-Alemàn 2001; Ha 2004).

Even though brands have an active understanding of the need to be trustworthy on their own sites, there is another layer of trust when one adds social media to the mix. Edelman trust barometer (2018) highlighted that social media is currently experiencing a severe lack of confidence due to recent episodes of privacy violation, and data sharing between platforms and device makers without user consent. Edelman (2018) found trust in social media was at 41 percent globally and dropping. Moreover, consumers demand transparency from social media, including clarifications of sponsorships within influencer marketing (Edelman 2018). In over twenty years of researching trust, Edelman (2020) reports the trust in officials and leaders has degraded to the point that people are relying on others like themselves.

So far, we have been discussing trust in relation to brands, but it can also relate to influencers as they often represent their own personal brand image. De Veirman et al. (2017) found that Instagram influencers with a high number of followers are not automatically considered opinion leaders, even though having a low number of followers has a crucial impact on the trustworthiness of the influencer. For example, if the influencer has a large following but does not follow many users, this could be considered as a non-authentic account created only for advertising purposes. De Veirman et al. (2017) further established that when a peculiar product is endorsed by a macro influencer, its perceived uniqueness and therefore attitudes toward the brand may diminish. These findings were replicated when Lou and Yuan (2019) showed that influencers' trustworthiness had a direct influence over their followers' trust in their own sponsored posts. Trustworthiness is discussed extensively in Chapter 5 (Özçelik and Levi 2020).

Customer engagement theory

Finally, scholars argue that consumer engagement is fundamental to building a strong and lasting relationship between brand and consumers (Gambetti et al. 2012). This suggests engagement will be an essential element of influencer culture and influencer marketing, although, there has been a considerable variation of definitions making the process of differentiation of customer engagement from other marketing constructs complicated (e.g. Bowden 2009; Van Doorn et al. 2010; Vivek et al. 2012). However, a general theme of agreement between scholars established that customer engagement is a customer behavioral response to an organization, operating further than just economic transactions (Van Doorn et al. 2010; Harmeling et al. 2016).

Vivek et al. (2012) developed the Customer Engagement theory to establish the relationship between consumer engagements with different marketing constructs. Vivek et al. (2012) asserts customer engagement is the intensity of an individual's investment in organizational activities and offerings and the connection that an individual has with a brand. The model proposes customer participation and involvement as antecedents to customer engagement, while value, trust, affective commitment, word of mouth, loyalty, and brand community involvement are consequences (Vivek et al. 2012). Some scholars contend consumer engagement triggers behavioral and attitudinal outcomes (Uzunoglu and Kip 2014). Mollen and Wilson (2010) explore the concept of online engagement, arguing that it requires some degree of inter-activity for consumers to perceive communications as two-way and responsive to their actions.

In an influencer marketing context, specifically on Instagram, customers' engagement with brands and influencers involves liking, commenting, and followers sharing (Hoffman and Fodor 2010). Paruthi and Kaur (2017) define this online engagement as "a psychological state of mind as well as an internal emotion of the consumer" (p. 128). Although, this follower's participation, in this case with the Instagram user, is not always related to engaging with the brand. Andrine and Solem (2016) argue the interactive nature of social media encourages customer participation, both with users they are directly connected with or not. Customer participation in an Instagram context consists of both the nature of the comments each post gets, e.g. emojis only comment or repetitive/impersonal comments and the influencer engagement rate – which involves both likes and comments.

On Instagram, engagement rate and nature of the comments are also important elements that can function as a signal for fake followers and bots (Penny 2019). Instagram influencer IntheFrow (2018) listed characteristics typical of fake followers such as frequent and repetitive emoji usage by many commenters and repetitive impersonal comments such as "I love it" or "nice." Therefore, if the percentage of emoji only comments and repetitive and impersonal comments is high, it could imply the overall engagement is low. Often, one will see random comments that are out of context to the post such as "liked it first." While it might be a form of engagement to see who is reacting the fastest, it nevertheless is a low-value form of engagement.

SocialPubli.com (2018) surveyed more than 1,000 micro-influencers and found that 32 percent of the influencers believed that being authentic is the key factor to maintain engagement, whereas 27 percent felt sharing content signaled that the influencer was authentic and 27 percent believed showing that they were engaging with their followers showed they were authentic. It could be suggested that the intimate nature of a micro-influencer allowed for increased two-way engagement between influencers and their followers. Ul Islam and Rahman (2016) measured the relationship between customer engagement, trust, and word-of-mouth in Facebook and discovered customer engagement has a direct positive influence on trust.

Idea fairy: How engaged are you with others on social media?

Considering the amount of time you are exposed to others on social media, what is the percentage of posts that you engage with? Do you sometimes like a post because it will make the other person feel better or because you genuinely like it? How much of your time online do you like, comment, or share content by influencers versus brands?

joyce costello and laura biondi

Investigating fashion influencers on Instagram

Fashion influencers often operate on Instagram as it is considered the biggest platform for them (McCoole 2018). This platform has been the site of 93 percent of all influencer marketing campaigns in 2017 and 2018, and around 80 percent of influencers use Instagram as their primary channel (William 2018). This is because it offers users video and photo-sharing possibilities, and therefore allows goods and brands to be visually imaged and named in the caption of photos (De Veirman et al. 2017). Furthermore, Instagram is considered as one of the top popular social networks with over 1 billion active users; the USA have the most users (120 million) followed by India with 80 million users (Statista 2020).

Fashion influencers are considered one of the most commercially successful and visible forms of digital cultural production (Duffy and Hund 2015). Chiara Ferragni was estimated to have earned over $10 million in 2015 despite not engaging in audience building relations (Hund 2017). Hellenkemper (2019) reported that 25 percent of all sponsored posts on Instagram revolve around fashion and beauty, making it the most active industry on Instagram.

Micro-influencers are typically considered those who have a social media following of anywhere between 10,000 and 100,000 (Yesiloglu 2020). Generally, micro influencers tend to have highly engaged and loyal followers, while on the other hand macro influencers tend to have a less engaged audience (West 2019). Due to the nature and the relationship with their followers, micro influencers are also considered to be more authentic, and hence more trusted (Barker 2017; Costello and Urbanska 2020).

Therefore, we investigate if fashion influencers on Instagram can counter fake followers by exploring the relationship between customer engagement theory (i.e. comments containing solely emojis, impersonal, and repetitive comments as an indication of fake followers) and brand authenticity theory as it relates to trust. The study focused on analyzing three groups of three fashion influencers each divided by their level of perceived credibility. Green was assigned to highly credible fashion influencers that had never been accused of purchasing fake followers; orange to those fashion influencers that sit in a grey area of having been rumored to purchase fake followers, but no definite proof has been presented, and red to those that have been publicly accused of purchasing fake followers. Hence, 36 Instagram posts containing 944 comments were analyzed (Table 12.1).

Table 12.1 Influencers' characteristics

ID:	A	B	C	D	E	F	G	H	I
Credibility level	Green	Green	Green	Orange	Orange	Orange	Red	Red	Red
N. of followers	80.6K	62.3K	30K	25.9K	16.5K	14.1K	89.5K	37.2K	14.9K
N. of comments	151	126	107	90	45	109	166	90	60

Once the nine influencers were identified, four posts per influencer were added to the dataset. The datasets contained the specific date the post was published, the name of those who commented on the posts, and their chosen gender. The comments were systematically coded through priori codes based on the theories used. Customer engagement theory variables or those comments that signal the presence of fake followers were coded by emoji only, or impersonal comments such as "cool; great; shoes; follow me." Brand authenticity theory used comments that express either authenticity by comments that denoted virtue, connection, realism, aesthetics, control, or originality based on the scale developed by Tran and Keng (2018). Finally, trust was coded using words associated with the scale developed by Chaudhuri and Holbrook (2001), such as trust, rely, honest, or safe.

When exploring those fashion influencers that fall within the green category, or those considered to be credible and honest, there were 384 points of engagement. Of the engagement, 71.4 percent expressed authenticity and 43.5 percent trust, comments with emojis only made up 14.3 percent and impersonal comments were 14.3 percent. When exploring those fashion influencers in the orange category, ergo those that have neither been publicly accused of purchasing fake followers nor been praised for their honesty, resulted in 244 points of engagement. Specifically, 63.9 percent express authenticity, 14.3 percent express trust, while 13.5 percent of the comments contained solely emojis, and 23 percent had impersonal and repetitive comments. Finally, when exploring those influencers that were in the red category of the low credibility influencers (those that have been publicly accused of purchasing fake followers in the Medium 2019 study), there were 316 points of engagement. Of these, 47.5 percent expressed authenticity and 4.7 percent expressed trust, while 20.6 percent were made up of only emojis and 32 percent were impersonal.

From the initial analysis of the data, there are clear frequency patterns that are emerging. Indeed, the fact that those influencers who have been publicly accused of purchasing fake followers are those with the highest percentage of both comments made up only of emojis and impersonal comments, which lends initial support to the argument that these variables could be indicators of fake followers. Moreover, both the percentages of comments that express trust and authenticity are in descending order with the level of credibility of the influencers. This could suggest that the more credible the influencer is, the higher the frequency perceived trust and authenticity are going to be.

In order to test the relation between the variables, we ran binary logistic regression tests as each engagement was coded as either 1= yes or 0= no. Due to redundancies, degrees of freedom were reduced for one or more variables in two of the models. In logistic regressions, odds ratios with values over one indicates that the predictor variable has a greater probability of achieving the outcome (Hair et al. 2010). For example, green influencers with high levels of authenticity are 38 times more likely to be trusted by their followers (Exp(β) = 38.914, p < .001) (Model 1, Table 12.2) and orange influencers are also more likely to be trusted by their followers (Exp(β) = 44.059, p < .001) (Model 2, Table 12.2). Yet, for the red followers there were no significant relations.

Table 12.2 Binary logistic regression

	Model 1-Green		Model 2- Orange		Model 3- Red	
	DV: Trust		DV: Trust		DV: Trust	
	Exp(β) Odds ratio	S.E.	Exp(β) Odds ratio	S.E.	Exp(β) Odds ratio	S.E.
Authenticity	38.914***	0.731	44.059***	0.224		
Emoji	1.000	1.019	2.521	0.251	0.000	4985.324
Impersonal			1.457	0.137	0.000	3999.350
Constant (odds ratio)	0.038***	0.720	0.006***	0.691	.111***	0.272
Nagelkerke R²	0.364		0.184		0.223	
Hosmer-Lemeshow	Chi-square .000, df 1,sig. = 1.00		Chi-square 160.821, df 2,sig. = .000		Chi-square .000, df 1,sig. = 1.00	
Null predicted% correct	56.5		85.7		95.3	
Predictive capacity of model	70		86.100		95.300	
Observations	384		244		316	

Notes: *** $p < .001$; Displayed coefficients are standardized coefficients.

Going forward

Overall, these findings first suggest that comments containing authentic comments tend to lead to greater levels of trust. This confirms Schallehn et al.'s (2014) study using brand authenticity theory where authenticity is seen as a driver of trust. It is logical to expect those followers who are actively engaging with an influencer to have some form of trust. However, when comparing the influencers that were deemed above reproach in terms of fake followers (green category) and those that were rumored to have used fake followers or social bots, the latter had a larger significant odds ratio. This brings up an interesting dilemma about social bots taking on more human characteristics. Just as Google has been using technology to improve their algorithms to move their search functions from words to understanding sentences (Nayak 2019), so can programmers improve the way social bots behave on social media.

When scanning for solely emojis and impersonal comments, there was no evidence that they were significantly related to trust. This could suggest that the belief that they are an effective measurement for the presence of fake followers is not always true. Indeed, our findings are contrary to what other studies mentioned previously suggested, such as Vivek et al.'s (2012) study that found trust is seen as an effect of consumer engagement. However, in that study, they were not looking at items such as impersonal comments or emojis as the latter were only slowly beginning to become prevalent on social media. Furthermore, this relates back to one of the key challenges with social bots increasingly being programmed to take on more human characteristics.

Brand authenticity theory states that authenticity is an important success element for trust (Schallehn et al. 2014), while customer engagement theory (Vivek et al. 2012) states that customer engagement is the strength of the relationship between an individual and an organization which is explained by customer participation. The theory further asserts that trust is a consequence of customer engagement. This study sought to test the above theories in the context of Instagram influencers and fake followers, asserting that high authenticity leads to high trust. The findings confirm that brand authenticity theory provides a valuable framework to achieve trust. Customer engagement theory was also tested; however, the results were not significant.

These findings can add valuable insight to practitioners and academics who are interested in influencer marketing. First, the study provides theoretical knowledge to the practice of influencer marketing, which to this day is still emerging. The study provides empirical evidence on the relationship between authenticity and trust. Therefore, for an influencer to be perceived as trustworthy they need to be authentic first. Advice for how influencers can be authentic to their true self was covered in Chapter 5 (Özçelik and Levi 2020).

Our research had two key limitations. The first is it is cross-sectional data which only shows one point of time and hence makes it difficult to determine the cause and effect of the phenomenon. Secondly, the authors cannot guarantee that any negative comments or comments had not been removed or blocked by the influencer. As negative comments could signal non-authentic influencer and dissuade companies from engaging with them, it is probable that they could have been removed or omitted. These actions themselves lead to a different stream of future research which could address other nefarious practices beyond buying fake followers.

Summary

- Theories such as brand authenticity theory and consumer engagement theory can provide insights for studies exploring influencers.
- The more authentic an influencer, the more likely followers will trust them.
- The findings regarding customer engagement and trust are contradictory, meaning that the presence of fake followers does not necessarily lead to less trust.
- Socialbots are acting more human, so older methods of identifying fake followers must evolve.

The case of who is to blame? The influencer or the agency that sold them fake followers

It is often said that demand drives supply. One could argue that those aspiring to be influencers who demanded more followers are responsible for agencies cropping up to supply fake followers. However, it is just as feasible that agencies recognized a trend on social media of influencers asking followers and fans to spread the word about their site and these agencies saw the opportunity to take advantage of the

joyce costello and laura biondi

situation. Still, programmers are the ones responsible for generating bots. The supply and demand paradox is one that is full of many unknowns. This case study explores fake followers from the view of the agency.

After a 2018 investigation by the *New York Times* into agencies such as Devumi (Shubber 2019), the Federal Trade Commission began to investigate companies selling fake followers. German Calas Jr, the CEO of Devumi, was accused of "the sale of fake indicators of social media influence" (Federal Trade Commission 2019). The FTC stated that Devumi operated four websites (Devumi.com, TwitterBoost.co, Buyview.co, and buyplays.co) where they sold fake indicators. These fake indicators would consist of fake followers, subscribers, views, and likes. They were collectively defined as fake indicators because companies often relied on these types of metrics to determine indications of engagement. Devumi had clients ranging from actors, athletes, and aspiring influencers as well as organizations such as investment banking firms and human resources firms.

Utilizing the internet archive wayback machine, it was evident that Devumi initially started as a small business web design and management solution agency in 2011, but quickly realized the opportunity to move from web design and hosting to a social media marketing agency. In 2012 the devumi.com site boasted of curating "more real twitter followers" with over 15,000 satisfied customers. By 2013, they had dropped the term real and promised to "boost twitter followers tonight; Get more YouTube views, naturally, and Skyrocket your SoundCloud popularity." Over the years, Devumi promised to accelerate social media growth by providing followers, viewers, likes, and more. By the time the site was shut down, they had explicitly stated that they would tap into their thousand-plus partners for sponsored placement and were utilizing influencer marketing to get a crowd of influencers to tweet, post or share content as well as boosting an exclusive network of over five million targeted users.

In 2019, the FTC argued that selling fake indicators was in violation of Section 5(a) of the FTC Act, 15 U.S.C. § prohibits "unfair or deceptive acts or practices in or affecting commerce." To resolve the dispute, Devumi pleaded neither guilty nor denied any of the charges and entered an assurance of voluntary compliance. The court fined Devumi for engaging in deceptive acts or practices, banned them from selling any future social media influence, and made them relinquish the domains associated with the charges.

Questions?

1. Devumi sold themselves as a social media marketer. What were the legal and ethical implications of their behavior prior to the first FTC court case of this nature?
2. What are the implications of Devumi not pleading guilty, but not denying the allegations?
3. How did the supply of Devumi's fake followers threaten the reputation of influencer marketing?
4. How did Devumi's action contribute to influencers' issues with trust and authenticity?
5. How can the FTC educate the supply and demand chain of those involved in influencer marketing so that the FTC Act, 15 U.S.C. § is not a reoccurring issue?

References

Andrine, B., and Solem, A., 2016. Influences of customer participation and customer brand engagement on brand loyalty. *Journal of Consumer Marketing*, 33(5), 332–342.

Anwar, T., and Abulaish, M. 2014. A social-based graph text mining framework for chat log investigations. *Digital Investigation*, 11(4) 349–362.

Athwal, N., and Harris, L.C., 2018. Examining how brand authenticity is established and maintained: the case of the Reverso. *Journal of Marketing Management*, 34(3–4), 347–369.

Barker, S., 2017. Using Micro-Influencers to successfully promote your brand, [online]. *Forbes* Available from: www.forbes.com/sites/forbescoachescouncil/2017/09/29/using-micro-influencers-to-successfully-promote-your-brand/#5baa4dca1763

Beverland, M.B., 2005. Crafting brand authenticity. *Journal of Management Studies*, 42(5), 1003–1029.

Beverland, M., 2006. The "real thing": Branding authenticity in the luxury wine trade. *Journal of Business Research*, 59(2), 251–258.

Bladow, L., 2018. Worth the Click: Why Greater FTC Enforcement is Needed to Curtail Deceptive Practices in Influencer Marketing. *William & Mary Law Review*, 59(3), 1123–1164.

Boshmaf, Y., Muslukhov, L., Beznosov, K., and Ripeanu, M., 2013. Design and analysis of a social botnet. Botnet activity: Analysis, detection and shutdown, *Computer Networks*, 57(2), 556–578.

Bowden, J.L.H., 2009. The process of customer engagement: a conceptual framework. *Journal of Marketing Theory and Practice*, 17(1), 63–74.

Boyeon, J., Sihyun, J., and Chong-Kwon, K., 2019. Distance-Based customer detection in fake followers markets. *Information Systems*, 81, 104–116.

Broniatowski, D., Jamison, A., Qi, S., AlKulaib, L., Chen, T., Benton, A., Quinn, S., and Dredze, M., 2018. Weaponized Health Communication: Twitter Bots and Russian Trolls Amplify the Vaccine Debate. *American Journal of Public Health*, 108(10), 1378–1384.

Brown, J.R., Crosno, J.L., and Ying Tong, P., 2019. Is the theory of trust and commitment in marketing relationships incomplete? *Industrial Marketing Management*, 77, 155–169.

Cao, Q., Sirivianos, M., Yang, X., and Pregueiro, T., 2012. Aiding the detection of fake accounts in large scale social online services. Proceedings of the 9th USENIX Conference on Networked Systems Design and Implementation. San Jose CA, 25–27 April 2012. San Jose: USENIX Association Berkeley. Available from: www.usenix.org/system/files/conference/nsdi12/nsdi12-final42_2.pdf

Cao, Q, Yang, X., Yu, J., and Palow, C. 2014. Uncovering large groups of active malicious accounts in online social networks. Proceedings of the 2014 ACM SIGSAC Conference on Computer and Communications Security. 477–488.

Chaudhuri, A., and Holbrook, M.B., 2001. The chain of effects from brand trust and brand affect to brand performance: The role of brand loyalty. *Journal of Marketing*, 65(2), 81–93.

Chavoshi, N., Hamooni, H., and Mueen, A., 2017. Temporal Patterns in Bot Activities. In: International World Wide Web Conference. Albuquerque: University of New Mexico, 1601–1606. Available from: www.researchgate.net/publication/314179583_Temporal_Patterns_in_Bot_Activities

Coary, S.P., and Oakley, J.L., 2018. The development and measurement of a brand authenticity scale. *Journal of Brand Strategy*, 7(2), 183–196.

Confessore, N., Dance, G. J.X., Harris, R., and Hansen, M., 2018. *The Follower Factory*. New York: *The New York Times*. Available from: www.nytimes.com/interactive/2018/01/27/technology/social-media-bots.html

joyce costello and laura biondi

Costa, J.A., and Bamossy, G.J., 1995. *Marketing in a Multicultural World: Ethnicity nationalism, and cultural identity*. Thousand Oaks: Sage.

Costello, J. and Urbanska, K., 2020. "Hope this is not sponsored" – Is an Influencers' credibility impacted when using sponsored versus non-sponsored content? Ch. 10 in *Influencer Marketing: Building Brand Communities and Engagement*. Ed. Yesiloglu, S., and Costello, J. London: Routledge.

Cresci, S., Di Petro, R., Petrocchi, M., Spognardi, A., and Tesconi, M. 2015. Fame for sale: Efficient detection of fake Twitter followers. *Decision Support Systems*. 80: 56–71.

Dawson, J., 2018. Who is that? The study of anonymity and behavior [online]. *Association for Psychological Science*. Available from: www.psychologicalscience.org/observer/who-is-that-the-study-of-anonymity-and-behavior

Delgado-Ballester, E., and Munuera-Alemàn, J., 2001. Brand trust in the context of consumer loyalty. *European Journal of Marketing*, 35(11/12), 1238–1258.

De Lima Salge, C. and Karahanna, E., 2018. Protesting corruption on Twitter: Is it a bot or is it a person? *Academy of Management Discoveries*, 4(1), 32–49.

Dessart, L., Veloutsou, C., and Morgan-Thomas, A., 2015. Consumer engagement in online brand communities: a social media perspective. *Journal of Product and Brand Management*, 24(1), 28–42.

De Veirman, M., Cauberghe, V., and Hudders, L., 2017. Marketing through Instagram Influencers: the impact of the number of followers and product divergence on brand attitude. *International Journal of Advertising*, 36(5), 798–828.

Duffy, B.E., and Hund, E., 2015. "Having it all" on social media: Entrepreneurial femininity and self-branding among fashion bloggers. *Social Media + Society*, 1, 1–11.

Edelman, R., 2018. Special Report: Brands and Social Media. *Edelman*. Available from: www.edelman.com/sites/g/files/aatuss191/files/2018-10/2018_Edelman_Trust_Barometer_Brands_Social.pdf

Edelman, 2020. Twenty years of trust. *Edelman*. Available from: www.edelman.com/20yearsoftrust/

Eggers, F., O'Dwyer, M., Kraus, S., Vallaster, C., and Guldenberg, S., 2013. The impact of brand authenticity on brand trust and SME growth: A CEO perspective. *Journal of World Business*, 48(3), 340–348.

Federal Trade Commission, 2019. Devumi, Owner and CEO settle FTC charges they sold fake indicators of social media influence; Cosmetics firm Sunday Riley, CEO settle FTC charges that employees posted fake online reviews at CEO's direction. *Federal Trade Commission Press Release*. Available from: www.ftc.gov/news-events/press-releases/2019/10/devumi-owner-ceo-settle-ftc-charges-they-sold-fake-indicators

Ferrara, E., Varol, O., Davis, C., Menczer, F., and Flammini, A., 2016. The rise of social bots. *Communications of the ACM*, 59(7), 96–104.

Gambetti, R. C., Graffigna, G., and Biraghi, S., 2012. The Grounded Theory approach to consumer-brand engagement. The practitioner's standpoint. *International Journal of Market Research*, 54(5), 659–686.

Garland, C., and Reed, M., 2018. The dark side of influence. *Global Cosmetic Industry*, 186(5), 26–29.

Garland, C., 2018a. How to measure the value of influencer marketing: By applying the principles of growth Marketing to Influencer Marketing, brands can now effectively track the success of an Influencer partnership. *Global Cosmetic Industry*, 186(6), 22–25.

Garland, C., 2018b. Spam wars and fake influence. *Global Cosmetic Industry*, 186(7), 56–58.

Guthrie, S., 2019. The influencer fraud vigilantes. ScottGurthie.com. 7 February 2019. Available from: https://sabguthrie.info/influencer-fraud-vigilantes/

Gazdik, T., 2017. Influencers value authenticity over money. *Marketing Daily*, 27 October 2018. Available from: www.mediapost.com/publications/article/309392/influencers-value-authenticity-over-money.html

Gorwa, R. and Guilbeault, D., 2018. Unpacking the social media bot: A typology to guide research and policy. *Policy & Internet*. Available from https://doi.org/10.1002/poi3.184

Grayson, K., and Martinec, R., 2004. Consumer perceptions of iconicity and indexicality and their influence on assessments of authentic market offerings. *Journal of Consumer Research*, 31(2), 296–312.

Ha, H.Y., 2004. Factors influencing consumer perceptions of brand trust online. *Journal of Product & Brand Management*, 13(5), 329–342.

Hair, J.F., 2010. *Multivariate Data Analysis: A global perspective* (7th ed.). Upper Saddle River, N.J.; London: Pearson.

Harmeling, C., Carlson, B.D., and Moffett, J., 2016. Toward a theory of customer engagement marketing. *Journal of the Academic of Marketing Science*, 45, 312–335.

Harrington, J. 2017. "A unique form of ad fraud": Agency creates fake influencer, wins sponsorship deal. *PR Week*. Available from: www.prweek.com/article/1441921/a-unique-form-ad-fraud-agency-creates-fake-influencers-wins-sponsorship-deals

Hellenkemper, M., 2019. State of the industry – Influencer Marketing in 2019. *Influencerdb.com*. Available from: https://blog.influencerdb.com/state-of-the-industry-influencer-marketing-2019/

Hoffman, D.L., and Fodor, M., 2010. Can you measure the ROI of your social media marketing? *MIT Sloan Management Review*, 52(1), 41–49.

Hund, E. 2017. Measured beauty: Exploring the aesthetics of Instagram's fashion influencers. #SMSociety17: Proceedings of the 8th International Conference on Social Media & Society. 44, 1–5. Available from: https://dl.acm.org/doi/abs/10.1145/3097286.3097330

IntheFrow, 2018. How to spot fake engagement and followers on Instagram. IntheFrow. 16 October 2018. Available from: www.inthefrow.com/2018/10/fake-instagram-engagement.html#comment-4138554477

Jang, B., Jeong, S., and Kim, C.K., 2018. Distance-based customer detection in fake follower markets. *Information Systems*, 81, 104–116.

Keown, C., 2019. Brands "waste" millions as extent of Instagram influencer fraud revealed. *City.am*. Available from: www.cityam.com/brands-waste-millions-extent-instagram-influencer-fraud/

Laghate, G., 2018. Shadow of fake likes mar social media influencers. *The Economist Times*, 21 June 2018. Available from: http://go.galegroup.com.libezproxy.bournemouth.ac.uk/ps/i.do?p=STND&u=bu_uk&id=GALE|A543739597&v=2.1&it=r&sid=ebsco

Latimer, A., 2018. Influencer fraud is affecting more brands than you think. Global *Cosmetic Industry*, 186(9), 10.

Lou, C., and Yuan, S., 2019. Influencer marketing: How message value and credibility affect consumer trust of branded content on social media. *Journal of Interactive Advertising*, 19(1), 58–73.

Lson, E., Monroe, C., and Burke-Garcia, A., 2019. What every marketer needs to know about influencer marketing and buying followers. *Marketing News*, 53(2),3.

Lude, M., and Prügl, R., 2018. Why the family business matters: Brand Authenticity and the family firm trust inference. *Journal of Business Research*, 89, 121–134.

Martinez-Lopez, F. J., Anaya-Sanchez, R., Molinillo, S., Aguilar-Illescas, R., and Esteban-Millat, I., 2017. Consumer engagement in an online brand community. *Electronic Commerce Research and Applications*, 23, 24–37.

McCoole, V., 2018. *Behind the Scenes of Instagram's Million-dollar Influencer Brand Deals*. Forbes.com. Available from: www.forbes.com/sites/veenamccoole/2018/07/29/behind-the-scenes-of-instagrams-million-dollar-influencer-brand-deals/#418e2c30329b

Medium, 2019. UK Instagram fake influencers exposed. *Medium* (@ukinfluencers) Available from: https://medium.com/@ukinfluencers/uk-instagram-fake-influencers-exposed-eed742a09efd

Mehta, I., 2019. Facebook removed 1.5 billion fake accounts between April and September. Thenextweb.com. Available from: https://thenextweb.com/facebook/2018/11/16/facebook-removed-1-5-billion-fake-accounts-between-april-and-september/

Mollen, A., and Wilson, H., 2010. Engagement, telepresence, and interactivity in online consumer experience: Reconciling scholastic and managerial perspectives. *Journal of Business Research*, 63(9), 919–925.

Miranda, R., and Klement, J., 2009. Authentic Trust in modern Business. *Journal of Wealth Management*, 11, 29–47.

Mønsted, B., Sapieżyński, P., Ferrara, E., and Lehmann, S., 2017. Evidence of complex contagion of information in social media: An experiment using Twitter bots. *PLOS ONE*, 12(9), e0184148.

Moulard, J.G., Garrity, C.P., and Rice, D.H., 2015. What makes a human brand authentic? Identifying the antecedents of celebrity authenticity. *Psychology and Marketing*, 32(2), 173–186.

Nayak, P. (2019). Understanding search engines better than ever. *Google*. Available from: https://blog.google/products/search/search-language-understanding-bert

Napoli, J., Dickinson, S.J., Beverland, M.B., and Farrelly, F., 2014. Measuring consumer-based brand authenticity. *Journal of Business Research*, 67(6), 1090–1098.

Neururer, M., Schlögl, S., Brinkschulte, L., and Groth, A., 2018. Perceptions on authenticity in chatbots. *Multimodal Technologies and Interaction*, 2(3),60–89.

Nitin, T. S., and Susan, E., 2017. Detection of Fake Followers using feature ratio in self-organizing maps. In: IEEE Conference. San Francisco, CA: IEEE. https://doi.org/10.1109/UIC-ATC.2017.8397471

Özçelik, A., and Levi, E., 2020. Choosing the right influencer for your brand: a guide to the field. Ch. 5 in *Influencer Marketing: Building Brand Communities and Engagement*. Ed. Yesiloglu, S., and Costello, J. London: Routledge.

Owen, J., 2019. "Blurred lines" – closing in on the influencer frauds. Prweek.com. Available from: www.prweek.com/article/1491897/blurred-lines-closing-influencer-frauds

Paruthi, M., and Kaur, H., 2017. Scale development and validation for measuring online engagement. *Journal of Internet Commerce*, 16(2), 127–147.

Penny, S., 2019. How brands can spot influencers with fake followers. *Marketing Week*. Available from: www.marketingweek.com/2018/11/12/fake-followers-influencers/

Peterson, R.A., 2005. In search of authenticity. *Journal of Management Studies*, 42(5), 1083–1098.

Ratkiewicz, J., Conover, M., Meiss, M., Goncalves, V., Patil, S., Flammini, A., and Menczer, F. 2011. "Truthy: Mapping the Spread of Astroturf in Microblog Streams." In Proceedings of the 20th International Conference Companion on World Wide Web, 249–52.

Schallehn, M., Burmann, C., and Riley, N., 2014. Brand authenticity: model development and empirical testing. *Journal of Product and Brand Management*, 23(3), 192–199.

Shubber, K., 2019. Social media "influencers" face crackdown on fakery: US regulator sues to stop peddling of sham reviews and bogus followers. *Financial Times*. Available from: www.ft.com/content/9660ac88-f435-11e9-a79c-bc9acae3b654

SocialPubli.com, 2018. Study: Micro-Influencers generate 7X more engagement on Instagram than Influencers with larger followings. *SocialPubli.com*. Available from: www.mobilemarketer.com/press-release/20181009-study-micro-influencers-generate-7x-more-engagement-on-instagram-than-infl-1/

Statista, 2020. Leading countries based on the number of Instagram users as of January 2020. Statista.com Available from: www.statista.com/statistics/578364/countries-with-most-instagram-users/

Stieglitz, S., Brachten, F., Ross, B., and Jung, A., 2017. Do social bots dream of electric sheep? A categorisation of social media bot accounts. In: Australasian Conference on Information Systems[online]. Duisburg: Department of Computer Science and Applied Cognitive Science University of Duisburg-Essen, 1–11. Available from: https://arxiv.org/abs/1710.04044

Stringhini, G., Egele, M., Kruegel, C., and Vigna, G., 2012. Poultry markets: On the underground economy of Twitter followers. *ACM SIGCOMM Computer Communication Review*. 42(4) 527–532.

Strugatz, R., and Lee, A., 2018. Fashion Grapples With Fake Followers: It's become a serious issue for the number of brands shelling out big bucks to work with Influencers. *WWD: Women's Wear Daily*. Available from: https://wwd.com/business-news/technology/fake-followers-sweeps-fashion-beauty-industry-devumi-1202554182/

Subrahmanian, V., Azaria, A., Durst, S., Kagan, V., Galstyan, A., Lerman, K., Zhu, L., Ferrara, E., Flammini, A., and Menczer, F., 2016. The DARPA Twitter Bot Challenge. *Computer*, 49(6), 38–46.

Tran, V.D., and Keng, C.J., 2018. The brand authenticity scale: Development and validation. *Contemporary Management Research*, 14(4), 277–291.

Ul Islam, J., and Rahman, Z., 2016. Linking customer engagement to trust and word-of-mouth on Facebook brand communities: An empirical study. *Journal of Internet Commerce*, 15(1), 40–58.

Uzunoglu, E., and Kip, S., 2014. Brand communication through digital influencers: Leveraging blogger engagement. *International Journal of Information Management*, 34, 592–602.

Van Doorn, J., Lemon, K.N., Mittal, V., Nass, S., Pick, D., Priner, P., and Verhoef, P.C., 2010. Customer engagement behavior: Theoretical foundations and research directions. *Journal of Service Research*, 13(3), 253–266.

Vivek, S.D., Beatty, S.E., and Morgan, R.M., 2012. Customer engagement: Exploring customer relationships beyond purchase. *Journal of Marketing Theory and Practice*, 20(1), 122–146.

Wang, A.H., 2010. Don't follow me: Spam detection in Twitter. 2010 International Conference on Security and Cryptography, Athens. 1–10.

West, T., 2019. 10 reasons why Micro-Influencers are the key to Influencer Marketing Success. *Blog.scrunch.com*. Available from: https://blog.scrunch.com/micro-influencers

William, R., 2018. Study: 93% of influencer campaigns use Instagram [online]. *Mobilemarketer.com*. Available from: www.mobilemarketer.com/news/study-93-of-influencer-campaigns-use-instagram/542985/

Yang, K., Varol, O., Davis, C., Ferrara, E., Flammini, A., and Menczer, F., 2019. Arming the public with artificial intelligence to counter social bots. *Human Behavior and Emerging Technology*, 1(1)48–61.

Yesiloglu, S., 2020. Rise of influencers. Ch. 1 in *Influencer Marketing: Building Brand Communities and Engagement*. Ed. Yesiloglu, S., and Costello, J. London: Routledge.

part 4

Legal and future aspects of influencer marketing

chapter 13

Influencer marketing and the law

Hayleigh Bosher

Learning outcomes

On completing this chapter, you should be able to:

*   understand the relevant copyright law for sharing content on social media;
*   consider the terms and conditions on social media platforms; and
*   become aware of the advertising standards and their impact on influencer content.

Social media and copyright law

Who owns the image? Copyright

Copyright is a type of intellectual property right that can protect things such as the images and videos posted on social media. For example, under UK law, the Copyright, Designs and Patents Act 1988 protects visual content. Copyright is a way to encourage creativity by rewarding creators for their work (Laddie et al. 2019). To do this, copyright restricts the ability of sharing, copying, and using other people's copyright-protected work without their permission, unless there is an exception that applies. The problem is, of course, that social media encourages the sharing, copying, and use of others' work (Bosher and Yeşiloğlu 2017). Therefore, for influencers it is important to understand who owns the copyright in the material posted online, and when the use of that material would be considered an infringement under the law.

The owner of the copyright in a photograph or image is usually the person who created it – unless, for example, it was created in the course of employment, in which case it would be the employer that owns it. Likewise, the owner of a film or video is considered the creator. If there is more than one creator, such as a director and producer, then they would own it jointly or according to an agreement set out in a contract. Sharing another person's photograph or film on social media without their permission or an exception would technically be an infringement of their copyright.

Under UK, US and Australian copyright laws, people who feature in a photograph or film do not own the copyright, unless it is expressly agreed under contract (UK Copyright, Designs and Patents Act 1988, US Copyright Act 1976, Australian Copyright Act 1968). Therefore, it can be an infringement of copyright to share a picture of yourself that was taken by someone else. Recently, there have been a number of high-profile disputes between celebrities and paparazzi, after the celebrity has posted a picture of themselves, taken by the paparazzi, on their social media profiles such as Gigi Hadid, Bella Hadid, Emily Ratajkowski, Justin Bieber, Jennifer Lopez, Nikki Minaj, and Victoria Beckham (The Fashion Law 2020). Most of these cases have settled out of court, but the American fashion model Gigi Hadid decided to defend her case after being sued a second time for copyright infringement. This case is discussed in detail below.

Hadid manages her own Instagram account, which has over 44 million followers. On October 12, 2018, she posted a picture of herself to her Instagram account. The copyright holder of the image in question, which was taken on October 11, 2018, in New York City was Xclusive (a photo agency that represents over 40 photographers worldwide). Xclusive brought a civil complaint against Hadid in the Court of New York seeking a trial by jury and damages for copyright infringement under the US copyright law US (17 U.S.C. § 101). This law states that it is an infringement of copyright to use a copyright-protected work without permission. In the claim, Xclusive argued that Hadid's Instagram account included at least fifty examples of uncredited photographs of Hadid in public, at press events, or on the runway, posted by Hadid without license or permission from the copyright holder. The claim stated that Xclusive believed these acts of infringement were willful and intentional, in disregard of and with indifference to the rights of copyright holders (*Xclusive v Hadid* 2018).

This was the second time Hadid had been sued under similar circumstances. Earlier in 2017, she removed a watermark and posted a photo of herself on her Instagram (*Cepeda v Hadid* 2017). The image received 1.2 million likes but was taken by photographer Peter Cepeda, who had licensed the photo to *The Daily Mail* and *TMZ*. However, after Hadid's post, the photo was then used by several other publications, crediting Hadid with no mention of Cepeda. The photographer then brought a claim against Hadid seeking compensation and the parties settled the matter out of court (*Cepeda v Hadid* 2017).

Likewise, when Khloe Kardashian posted a photo of herself on her Instagram, owned by Xposure Photos in 2017, Xposure filed a complaint in the US Court of California. They argued that a photograph with the caption "going for a meal at David Grutman's Miami restaurant, Komodo" posted by Kardashian infringed their copyright. The Photograph was taken by Manual Munoz and licensed for limited use to *The Daily Mail*, which published it on September 13, 2016 together with a copyright notice and watermark. The following day the photo was posted on Kardashian's Instagram

hayleigh bosher

account, with the watermark removed. Similarly, the case settled through mediation in March 2018 (*Xposure v Kardashian* 2018).

Despite these previous cases, Hadid continued to post photos of herself on her social media profiles, taken by other people. She even posted this argument about the situation on her Instagram:

> *"Yesterday I heard from my management that I am being 'legally pursued' for my last (now deleted) Instagram post... sue me for a photo I FOUND ON TWITTER (with no photographer name on the image) for a photo he has already been paid for..."* She went on to say: *"To all the fan accounts being taken down and being sued themselves... to the photographers... demanding money from young fans... is just wrong."* (GigiHadid Instagram 2019)

This raises the broader issues of the confusion and tension of copyright uses on social media, celebrities' right to control their image, as well as the classic tensions between paparazzi and celebrity's privacy. Whilst the US law recognizes some personality rights, consent is not required for the "use of a name, voice, signature, photograph or likeness in connection with any news, public affairs, or sports broadcast or account, or any political campaign" (California Civil Code 2007). Some might consider it a fair trade-off for living the life of a celebrity; others would argue that celebrities are people and they deserve the same privacy as anyone (Pavis 2018). If the law were to differentiate, how would it decide when someone is a celebrity or not? (See Case study: How many followers do you need to be a celebrity? below for further discussion.) In the social media and influencer age, it is more common and lucrative than ever to be using one's own image for remuneration.

From a copyright law perspective, the photographer is the rightful owner of the image that they created and it is clear that the value of the image is lost when posted by the celebrity, who may also benefit financially (directly or indirectly) from the images that they share on social media. Hadid argued two key points: fair use or implied license. These will be explained in more detail below.

Laws are territorial, which means that they are different in different countries. The UK, US, and Australia copyright laws are, broadly speaking, fairly similar in terms of their definition of infringement, but different when deciding if a copyright exception applies. For example, in the UK there is an exhaustive list of circumstances in which a copyright-protected work can be used without permission, and there are specific criteria that must be fulfilled (see CopyrightUser.org). The UK copyright exceptions are particularly narrow, and it would be difficult to see how any use on social media would fall within these rules, other than if the work was "fair dealing" for the purpose of creating a parody, or for the purpose of criticism and review (as set out in the UK law under the Copyright, Designs and Patents Act 1988, section 30 and 30A).

Australian copyright exceptions are very similar to the UK, setting out a closed list of fair dealing circumstances that would be allowed such as parody and criticism and review (Copyright Act 1968, section 41 and 41A). However, unlike the UK and Australia, the US copyright exception system, called fair use, is not a closed list, and whilst it has not yet been used in these circumstances, Hadid put forward some arguments that could change the way that copyright works in the future. These arguments of fair use and implied license are discussed below. Since many of the cases are brought in the US, due to the location of the social media platforms and the location of the celebrities, this could also have a wider impact.

Fair use

As mentioned, the US copyright exception system is called fair use. Fair use sets out circumstances where copyright-protected material can be used without the rights holders' permission. In order to establish that a use of a copyright work comes under fair use, a number of factors need to be taken into consideration, such as 1) if the use of the work is transformative and whether or not there is a commercial gain by the infringer, 2) the nature of the work, 3) the amount of the work taken, and 4) the damaged caused by the use. The arguments of the case are set out below.

Transformative and commercial use

Hadid's lawyers argued that her use of the photo was permissible under fair use, in line with the four key factors. First, they said that Hadid's reposting reflected a personal purpose different from that of the photographer's, which was to commercially exploit her popularity, and therefore the use was transformative, and non-commercial in nature.

In opposition, Xclusive's lawyers argued that *"the purported purpose of Hadid in using the Photograph here is not even close to being transformative."* They said that for fair use to apply, the second work must actually make some critical use of, or change to, the original work to qualify as transformative. They argued that Hadid posted the photograph in a *"barely cropped"* form for the purpose of depicting exactly that of the original. Furthermore, they submitted that Hadid gained a commercial advantage as a consequence of posting the image on her Instagram page, pointing to the number of followers she had.

1) Nature of the original work

Second, Hadid argued that the photograph was a *"quick shot in a public setting"* with no attempt by the photographer to convey ideas, emotions, or in any way influence the pose, expression, or clothing. As such, the photograph is a factual work, not a creative one, which changes its copyright status under US law. Furthermore, since Hadid smiled and posed for the photo, she contributed to the creativity and originality of the image, pointing to the case of *Rogers v. Koons* 1992 where it was held that elements of originality in the photograph include *"posing the subjects"* and *Gillespie v. AST Sportswear* 2001 where it was found that joint-authorship of photographs could arise where the defendant contributed to *"clothing"* and *"poses"* of models. Thereby suggesting that Hadid is in fact co-author of the image due to her input of smiling and posing, including the positioning of her hand below her chin, and as such the photograph was only made possible by her cooperation.

Xclusive's opposition, however, was that the photograph was *"undoubtedly a highly creative and expressive work,"* involving a number of creative choices including timing, lighting, angle, and composition. In addition, they said that the photographer had to obtain special permission to photograph the street from that particular location. The opposition also stated that Hadid's arguments of joint ownership were *"preposterous"* and would be alike to the subject of a biography claiming copyright in the words of the author to describe their life. However, this argument by Xclusive is limited, since it would only be preposterous if the subject did not contribute to the work. Hadid claimed copyright for the creative contributions to the work, not for the factual elements of the work; she is, after all, a model by trade and therefore experienced in posing. If a biographer based their book on the diaries of their subject, then the subject could be a co-author. This was the case, for example, for the co-authors of the biographical works of *Anne Frank's Diary*, who are Anne who wrote the diaries and her father Otto who collated and edited them to be published.

2) Amount of the work copied

Thirdly, in relation to the amount of the work copied, Hadid argued that she used only 50 percent of the original photograph since she cropped the image to focus more on her creative input – her pose, rather than the photographer's framing of her.

Xclusive disagreed, arguing that there was minimal cropping of the image and in any event, cropping is not enough to weigh this factor in favor of fair use – pointing to the case of *Graham v. Prince*, 2017. In addition, they argued that the crux of this factor is about the quality of what is taken, considering the heart of the material, which cropping would not affect. They asserted that Hadid did not make any conscious choice in the crop, as it was likely done by the automatic square cropping within the Instagram app.

3) Damage caused

Finally, in relation to the effect of the use upon the potential market or value of the copyrighted work, the Hadid argued that the complaint failed to demonstrate any financial loss, and nor could it since Hadid was posting an image that was already available online and did not claim to make the image available for license. But Xclusive said that Hadid's use served as a market substitute for the photo because Hadid would have otherwise had to pay a license fee for her use of the work and potential licensees of the image are no longer incentivized to pay a licensing fee since they could copy the version Hadid posted and make it freely available.

Xclusive might have gained the license fee payable by Hadid for her use of the image, but the fact that she took it from social media in the first place undermines the argument that she usurped the copyright holder's market, since it was already freely available in that sense. In addition, the claim that the ability to copy and share is built into Instagram is untrue since Instagram users can only copy as a result of their device or a third-party app but not within Instagram itself. Users can share only in a private message that imbeds and links to the original post, but cannot share directly to their own page without screen-grabbing or using a third-party app.

Implied license

Perhaps the most controversial argument presented by Hadid's lawyers, is that the use was permissible since there was an implied license by conduct. A license is a legal agreement setting out the terms of use of a copyright work. An implied license, therefore, means that there is an agreement in place, but it was not made expressly, for example through a written contract. Instead, it is implied in the circumstances. They argued that Hadid encountered the photographer, stopped, and permitted the photographer to take her picture by posing and contributing to the protectable elements of the photograph – she made the image possible and more valuable. Therefore, the photo was the result of mutual actions by Hadid and the photographer and in these circumstances, a license can, and should, be implied permitting Hadid to use the photograph, at least in ways that do not interfere with the photographer's ability to profit. This argument could change the way celebrities can use images of themselves under copyright, and Hadid might have succeeded in ending the saga of cases against celebrities for posting pictures of themselves on their social media.

Xclusive was aggressively opposed to the idea of an implied license and argued that if Hadid was to succeed on this point:

> The majority of the world's authors would be obliterated because the only requirement for an implied license would be for the subject of a work that she winked, smiled, nodded, or otherwise communicated her acceptance to the author.

They concluded that Hadid's legal approach was alarming for its blatant attempt to rewrite established legal doctrine. But perhaps it is time for copyright law to be updated to account for new technologies and behaviors deriving from social media. Nevertheless, this particular case fell through because of an issue with registration, as discussed in the next section.

Registration

In the UK, copyright arises automatically and there is no requirement for registration. However, in the US, a copyright holder needs to register their copyright before they can bring a case to court.

In the Gigi Hadid case, the Court didn't have to make a decision on the arguments discussed above because, in the end, Xclusive's claim was dismissed for failure to meet the statutory registration pre-filing condition (under US Rule 12(b)(6)).

hayleigh bosher

The US registration requirement is a statutory condition under which a plaintiff must obtain registration of a copyright in a work before filing a lawsuit based on infringement of that work (*Reed Elsevier v Muchnick* 2010). This was confirmed in the US Supreme Court's recent decision *Fourth Estate Public Benefit v Wall-Street.com* 2019, which interpreted the registration requirement established in § 411(a), rejecting the position that a copyright owner effectuates registration when it *"submits the application, materials, and fee required for registration,"* and instead held that registration occurs *"only when the Copyright Office grants registration."*

Xclusive could only show that it had filed for copyright registration, but it had not been formally granted before filing the complaint against Hadid. Therefore, the Court dismissed the case. Moreover, the Court declined to grant Xclusive leave to amend its complaint should its copyright application be approved in the future (*citing Malibu Media v Doe* 2019).

Undoubtedly, this will not be the last Instagram infringement case of this nature, but for now the questions raised by this case, such as whether these circumstances can constitute fair use or implied license, remain unanswered. In the meantime, the legal rules continue to state that posting a picture on social media without permission of the copyright holder would be infringement. Therefore, it is important to understand that this is a risk when posting third-party content and enforcing your own rights to stop others using your content without permission. Enforcement of copyright on social media operates within the terms and conditions of service for that platform. These are discussed in the following section.

Enforcement

It is important for brands to enforce their IP on social media platforms to protect brand value and to protect the consumer against confusion, fraud, including fake or infringing support pages, accounts, profiles, advertisements, products, and merchandise. Technology support and AI tools can be very helpful for monitoring but should always be used in conjunction with human intervention. Social media platforms are also increasing their proactive technology that, for example, stops the uploads of stories on Instagram that contain copyright-protected content.

In 2019, a new EU Copyright Law was passed (DSM 2019) that could result in an upload filter on the internet. This would mean that Internet Service Providers (ISPs) are required to block any content that contains copyright material at the point of upload. The concern with this is that the technology that does the blocking does not recognize copyright exceptions and would, therefore, be a risk to freedom of speech (Giancarlo 2018). However, the Directive only requires the ISPs to make "best efforts" to ensure no infringing content is uploaded, and therefore ContentID utilized by YouTube and similar technology may be enough (Bosher 2020).

Terms and conditions of platforms

When utilizing social media platforms, it is important for brands and influencers to understand the terms and conditions that may impact their content. However, this can be challenging as the terms are often written in legal language that is not always easy to understand. For example, the license granted is described as:

> a non-exclusive, royalty-free, transferable, sub-licensable, worldwide license to host, distribute, modify, run, copy, publicly perform or display, translate, and create derivative works of your content. (Instagram 2019)

Instagram claims that it does not take ownership of its users' content. But the terms, as stated above, demonstrate that Instagram has all the rights of the original owner of the content – aside from the fact that it is not an exclusive license. It is particularly important that content owners are aware of the meaning of this clause, because it means that if the content is posted to Instagram, it cannot be sold under an exclusive license elsewhere.

Furthermore, the terms allow Instagram to transfer or sub-license their user's content, which means that it could sell their rights in the user's content, or license a user's content to any third party, for free, without seeking permission, giving any notice or offering any payment to the user. It could also take a user's content and let another company use that photo in exchange for a fee – which Instagram would keep.

Likewise, Instagram can make use of any user material for its own purposes or promotions without seeking permission, letting the user know or making any payments to the user. This also includes the ability to edit, modify, share, copy, and communicate the content.

Instagram is a lucrative business, its key revenue stream is advertising, and the more people who use and share content on Instagram, the more profitable their company (Bosher and Yeşiloğlu 2017). Therefore, Instagram encourages users to create and share content. However, despite this, technically posting someone else's photo or video would be contrary to the Instagram terms of service and likely to infringe copyright. In the terms, users agree that they either own all the content that they post or have sought permission to use it. Realistically, Instagram knows that this is not the case, and unfortunately, users are left vulnerable to legal action for copyright infringement, such as in the case of Gigi Hadid and other celebrities discussed above. It is not only celebrities, however, who have faced this kind of legal action. Cases have been brought against individual users who have posted third party content on their social media profiles.

Therefore, it is argued that Instagram, and other social media platforms should take more responsibility to educate and protect their users (Bosher and Yeşiloğlu 2017; Bosher 2020). They should make their terms of service clearer and fairer. In addition, they should adopt a notice and takedown approach, similar to YouTube, whereby copyright holders are presented with a number of amicable resolution options, rather than seeking legal action. Moreover, copyright education information and tools should be provided by the platform to increase awareness about the law to users. For example, a copyright warning could appear on the screen when a user takes a screenshot.

Influencers and advertising rules

Advertising standards

Throughout the world advertising has always been regulated through legal regulation and advertising standards codes of practice. These principles still apply to adverts online, and include marketing on social media as well as influencers, whether they are considered a celebrity or not. Therefore, it is imperative to understand the relevant legal and ethical requirements when advertising and marketing on social media. This part of the chapter will consider the advertising codes in the UK, US, and Australia. These codes apply to marketers and influencers within these countries as well as if the advert is aimed at an audience in that country. They specify how an influencer can advertise and therefore it is necessary to understand the rules in order to comply with them and avoid complaints which can lead to penalties and even legal action.

UK: Advertising Standards Authority and Competition & Markets Agency

The Advertising Standards Authority (ASA) is the UK's independent regulator of advertising across all media. The CAP code is the UK Code of Non-broadcast Advertising and Direct & Promotional Marketing. It is essentially the rule book for non-broadcast advertisements, sales promotions, and direct marketing communications. The ASA CAP is a self-regulatory system and the majority of advertisers voluntarily agree to comply (ASA.org.uk). Persistent non-compliance with the ASA is dealt with through bad publicity or referral to other bodies such as Trading Standards or Ofcom.

The ASA reported that it now receives three times as many complaints about online ads as it does about those on television (ASA 2018). More than 16 instances have already been found to be in breach of the CAP code. For example, in 2018, *Made in Chelsea* star Louise Thompson and watchmaker Daniel Wellington were found to be in breach of a rule requiring ads to be obvious, after Thompson failed to use #ad in a sponsored Instagram post.

The ASA provides specific guidance for influencers which sets out what content qualifies as an advert when it is paid for, and how to make sure the posts are clearly labeled as such. It also points out other rules that might apply to content such as age restrictions (e.g. for gambling or alcohol) and giveaways or prize draws (ASA 2018). You can download this document from the ASA website: www.asa.org.uk/resource/influencers-guide.html.

The Competition & Markets Agency (CMA) also provides guidance that adverts must clearly state when they are paid for, including payments by way of loan or reward – this includes monetary or by gift or otherwise (CMA 2019). When offering discount codes, competitions or giveaways, influencers must be clear about their relationship with a brand or business, including past relationships. Essentially an influencer cannot mislead their followers to think that they are simply a customer or that they have used a product or services that they have not. Influencer posts must be transparent, easy to understand, unambiguous, timely, and prominent, without the need for people to click for more information regardless of the device they're using to access the post (CMA 2019). It is not enough to tag a brand or business in either the text, picture, and/or video of a post without additional disclosure or providing a discount code without additional information. Influencers must avoid ambiguous language, for example "thank you"; "made possible by"; "in collaboration with"; or "thanks to..." without full disclosure, including unclear hashtags such as #sp; #spon; #client; #collab (CMA, 2019). More about the ambiguity impacts of sponsored and non-sponsored content can be found in Chapter 10 (Costello and Urbanska 2020).

Idea fairy: Regulations

Please download the ASA in the UK. Make a list of 10 influencers you follow. Look up their presence across different social media channels and see how many posts they share and identify whether it is sponsored or not. Is it easy to understand if their posts are paid or not? How do they show it is sponsored or not?

US: Federal Trade Commission

In the US, similar advertising and marketing rules are set out by the Federal Trade Commission (FTC 2009). The FTC sets out that brands and influencers are required to clearly disclose the nature of their relationship. In particular, posts must identify if they are sponsored, and video reviews must include both written and verbal disclosure of the partnership. Using the built-in tools on social media platforms alone, is not adequate. Using #ad and #sponsored is considered disclosure as long as they are highly visible and not just tacked on to the end of a long string of tags. As with the UK rules, information must be clear, unambiguous, and readily available to the user without further clicking (FTC 2017)

In 2017, the FTC sent out more than 90 notification letters to brands and influencers. In the letters, the FTC identified non-compliant posts, educating the recipient of the requirements under the guidelines (FTC March 2017).

Australia: Australian Association of National Advertisers

In Australia, influencer marketing is regulated under Section 2.7 of the Australian Association of National Advertisers (AANA) Code of Ethics which states that advertising must be clearly distinguishable. These rules were implemented in March 2017, and state that while there are no requirements that advertising or marketing communication must have a specific label, it does have to be clear to the relevant audience that the content is commercial in nature.

In 2018, Pip Edwards posted an image which included a Mercedes with the caption:

> The Old Wool Shed. Grass Roots. 100% Pure Merino Wool. Straight off the back @jackmbrennan @thewoolmarkcompany @mercedesbenzau #merrimba # warren #merinowool #farmlife.

hayleigh bosher

After complaints were received, the Ad Standards Community Panel considered two key questions. First, did the material constitute advertising or marketing communication? In order to answer this question, they considered the amount of control that Mercedes had over the content. Mercedes and Edwards had a contractual agreement whereby Edwards would create social media on its behalf, and this provided the company with a level of control over the posts. Significantly, the Panel considered that even if the advertiser does not approve each post individually, Mercedes did have the ability to request the post be taken down. Consequently, the Panel determined that Mercedes did have a level of control and so the material constituted an advert for the purposes of their rules (Ad Standards Community Panel 2018). This imposes a high standard upon brands, meaning that they must check up on the content posted by the influencers they are in partnership with.

Secondly, the panel considered if Edward's post was clearly distinguishable to the relevant audience. The Panel noted that Edwards had created a series of five posts which featured Mercedes along with captions such as "It's been a big week, Thank you to @mercedesbenzau for welcoming us into their stable, as Friends of the Brand! Super excited about this friendship…" The Panel determined that the audience would understand this to be a commercial relationship (Ad Standards Community Panel, 2018).

This case demonstrates that Australian standards are more relaxed than those in the US and UK, where words such as "friendship" would likely be considered ambiguous, and posts that do not clearly state that it is an advertisement or partnership would be considered contrary to the codes of practice.

Case study: How many followers do you need to be a celebrity?

In February 2019, social media influencer and parenting blogger, Sarah Willox Knott posted a picture of herself in pajamas on her Instagram account *ThisMamaLife*, with a packet of Phenergan Night Time tablets in the background. The caption clearly labeled the post as an ad, and documented Knott's difficulties falling asleep, stating:

[AD] Sleep. Who needs more of it? I'm really lucky in that I don't actually need a lot of sleep to get by and manage to cram all sorts into my evening, being the night owl I am. Every now and again though, daily life can get a bit overwhelming and I often find it's my sleep that ends up suffering. I end up going to bed even later than I usually do and am not able to fall asleep. The worry of not sleeping then adds to it all and I end up a complete and utter zombie!! Last time this happened I tried out Phenergan Night Time, which really helped. It is a pharmacy only, short term solution to insomnia for adults which works by inducing a sleepy effect thanks to its active ingredient, promethazine hydrochloride, helping you to sleep through the night. Do you guys fall asleep easily or are you night time over-thinkers like me? #AD #sleep. (Willcox Knott 2019)

The UK ASA received a complaint that the manufacturer of the sleeping pills, Sanofi, had used a celebrity to endorse a medicine. This is against rule 12.18 of the CAP code, which states that marketers are not allowed to use health professionals or celebrities to endorse medicines, since this could influence a person's choice of medical treatment or encourage consumption of a product as a result of their celebrity status.

Sanofi argued that the Instagram account had a small following which was unlikely to influence a medicinal decision taken by a consumer, and that the blogger did not constitute a celebrity as she only had 32,000 followers at the time (ASA 2019). However, this is an unconvincing approach, as there would be no motivation for Sanofi to partner with an influencer who has no influence.

To support its argument, the company compared Knott's following to that of people widely considered to be celebrities, such as Stephen Fry (359,000 followers) and David Beckham (55 million followers). Sanofi also maintained that it had checked with the Proprietary Association of Great Britain – the consumer healthcare UK trade association – before going ahead with the partnership (ASA 2019).

To decide, the ASA assessed whether the blogger was a celebrity for the purposes of the CAP Code and whether she had endorsed a medicine. It was clear that Phenergan Night Time tablets were an over the counter medicine, and consumers would understand the ad to mean that *ThisMamaLife* had used and recommended the product, so she had endorsed the medicine. The ASA also noted that, in addition to her 30,000 followers, *ThisMamaLife* had more than 1,000 posts on Instagram, including a number of recommendations of different products, and that she was popular with, and had the attention of, a significant number of people (ASA 2019).

The ASA decided that *ThisMamaLife* did count as a celebrity for the purposes of rule 12.18 of the CAP code. The ASA told Sanofi not to use celebrities, including social media influencers, to endorse medicines in the future and *ThisMamaLife* removed the advert (ASA, 2019). The ASA ruling is not legally binding as such, but the majority of advertisers voluntarily agree to comply, and the same rule does exist under UK law (Human Medicines Regulations 2012).

Questions to consider:

1) Do all Instagram accounts need to comply with the advertising standards rules?
2) How many followers does it take for an influencer to be considered a celebrity for the purpose of the advertising standards?
3) What should influencers do on their posts to indicate to their followers that it is a sponsored post?
4) Can influencers be used to market medical products? What counts as a medical product?

Impact of the decision

Contrary to popular belief, the ASA did not decide a number of followers that constitutes a celebrity – it simply determined that in this case, the number of followers of the poster was enough to constitute a celebrity endorsement of the product. The outcome would have been the same if *ThisMamaLife* had fewer followers, since she clearly had enough to attract the contract with Sanofi in the first place.

Claims that having more than 30,000 followers means that influencers have to comply with the CAP code are misleading, because as explained above, influencers already have to comply with the codes of practice. In general, influencers and brands are considered jointly responsible for ensuring that advertorial content is compliant with the ASA CAP Code.

Similar rules apply in other countries. For example, the U.S. Food and Drug Administration (FDA) issued a warning letter after a social media endorsement

hayleigh bosher

posted by Kim Kardashian was reported through the FDA's Bad Ad program. Kardashian had published a lengthy post on her Instagram describing her successful experience with Duchesnay Inc's product DICLEGIS, a prescription morning sickness medicine. The FDA has strict regulations on the promotion of prescription drugs, which means that adverts can only use information supported by strong evidence and must include risk information in equal proportion to any benefit information. Kardashian had said in her post that: "It's been studied and there was no increased risk to the baby," which the FDA found to be "false or misleading in that it presents efficacy claims for DICLEGIS, but fails to communicate any risk information associated with its use and it omits material facts" (FDA 2015). As such, the post suggested the DICLEGIS was safer than it was and the FDA demanded that the post be removed or they would have to stop distributing the product in the US (FDA 2015).

Summary

- There are a plethora of legal regulations and codes that marketers need to be aware of when utilizing influencers and social media.
- There are many others such as trademark, defamation, privacy, unfair consumer practice under consumer law, for example, not to mention the further ethical concerns.
- It is vital that marketing departments and legal teams work closely together, in the development and enforcement of a brand.
- Advertising standards agencies are receiving more complaints about online marketing than ever before, and social media marketing is now fully on the radar of regulators.
- In the past a brand's IP, consumer protection, and marketing strategies might have been separate documents, but now they are inextricably connected and need to be joined.

Note to readers: This chapter explains and critiques some of the laws and regulations relating to influencer marketing, but it in no way constitutes legal advice. If you require legal advice you should contact a lawyer or legal consultant. You can find free legal advice through services such as the Citizens' Advice Bureau or the Brunel University Legal Advice Centre.

References

Ad Standards Community Panel, 2018. Pip Edwards and Mercedes Case Report. Retrieved from: http://ms.adstandards.com.au/cases/0193-18.pdf.

ASA, 2018a. An Influencer's Guide To Making Clear That Ads Are Ads. Retrieved from: www.asa.org.uk/uploads/assets/uploaded/3af39c72-76e1-4a59-b2b47e81a034cd1d.pdf.

ASA, 2018b. More Impact Online Advertising Standards Authority Committees Of Advertising Practice Annual Report 2018. Retrieved from: www.asa.org.uk/uploads/assets/uploaded/563b3e3c-1013-4bc7-9c325d95c05eeeb7.pdf.

ASA, 2019. *ASA Ruling on Sanofi UK in association with This Mama Life*. Retrieved from: www.asa.org.uk/rulings/sanofi-uk-A19-557609.html.

ASA CAP Code, 2014. The UK Code of Non-broadcast Advertising and Direct & Promotional Marketing. Retrieved from: www.asa.org.uk/uploads/assets/uploaded/ce3923e7-94ff-473b-ad2f85f69ea24dd8.pdf

Australian Copyright Act 1968.

Bosher, H., 2018. *Ten Things You Should Know About Instagram's Terms Of Use*. Retrieved from: https://theconversation.com/ten-things-you-should-know-about-instagrams-terms-of-use-102800.

Bosher (2019) *Instagram Influencers: No, Having 30,000 Followers Does Not Make You A Celebrity*. Retrieved from: https://theconversation.com/instagram-influencers-no-having-30-000-followers-does-not-make-you-a-celebrity-120686.

Bosher, H., 2020. *Key issues around copyright and social media: Ownership, infringement and liability, Journal of Intellectual Property Law and Practice*, 15(2), 123–133, https://doi.org/10.1093/jiplp/jpaa006.

Bosher, H., and Yeşiloğlu, S., 2017. An analysis of the fundamental tensions between copyright and social media: The legal implications of sharing images on Instagram, *International Review of Law, Computers & Technology*, 33(2), 164–186. DOI: 10.1080/13600869.2018.1475897.

California Civil Code 2007

Costello, J., and Urbanska, K., 2020. "Hope this is not sponsored" – Is an Influencers' credibility impacted when using sponsored versus non-sponsored content? Ch. 10 in *Influencer Marketing: Building Brand Communities and Engagement*. Ed. Yesiloglu, S., and Costello, J. London: Routledge.

CMA, 2019. *Guidance: Social Media Endorsements: Being Transparent With Your Followers*. Retrieved from: www.gov.uk/government/publications/social-media-endorsements-guide-for-influencers/social-media-endorsements-being-transparent-with-your-followers.

Copyright User. Retrieved from: www.copyrightuser.org/understand/rights-permissions/

Copyright, Designs and Patents Act 1988 UK

DSM. 2019. Directive (EU) 2019/790 of the European Parliament and of the Council of 17 April 2019 on Copyright and Related Rights in the Digital Single Market and Amending Directives 96/9/EC and 2001/29/EC.

FDA, 2015. *Warning Letter to Duchesnay, Inc Re: Kim Kardashian Post*. Retrieved from: www.fda.gov/media/93230/download.

Features R., 2019. Influencer fraud costs sponsors £1bn a year, The Times Online. Retrieved from: www.thetimes.co.uk/article/influencer-fraud-costs-sponsors-1bn-a-year-25zwltrj3?utm_source=Unica&utm_medium=email&utm_campaign=james_Format%20Experiment_fixed_timing_model_STM_1Imag_CR1_2.

Fourth Estate Public Benefit Corp. v. Wall-Street.com, LLC, 139 S. Ct. 881, 887 (2019)

FTC (2009) Federal Trade Commission Guides Concerning the Use of Endorsements and Testimonials in Advertising. Retrieved from: www.ftc.gov/sites/default/files/attachments/press-releases/ftc-publishes-final-guides-governing-endorsements-testimonials/091005revisedendorsementguides.pdf.

FTC, 2017. *Influencers, Are Your #Materialconnection #Disclosures #Clearandconspicuous?* Retrieved from: www.ftc.gov/news-events/blogs/business-blog/2017/04/influencers-are-your-material connection-disclosures

FTC, March 2017. Letters to 90 brands. Retrieved from: www.ftc.gov/system/files/documents/foia_requests/1b-2017-00799_instagram_influencers_327_pgs.pdf

FTC, Sept 2017. *Endorsement Guides: What People are Asking*. Retrieved from: www.ftc.gov/tips-advice/business-center/guidance/ftcs-endorsement-guides-what-people-are-asking

hayleigh bosher

FTC (undated) *Template Warning Letter to Influencers.* Retrieved from: www.ftc.gov/system/files/attachments/press-releases/ftc-staff-reminds-influencers-brands-clearly-disclose-relationship/influencer_template.pdf

Giancarlo, F., 2018. To filter, or not to filter? That is the question in EU copyright reform, 36(2) *Cardozo Arts & Entertainment Law Journal*, 331–368.

GigiHadid. 2019. [Instagram] retrieved from: www.instagram.com/p/BpF_uK_nivH/

Gillespie v. AST Sportswear, Inc., No. 97 Civ. 1911, 2001 WL 180147 (S.D.N.Y. Feb. 22, 2001.

Graham v. Prince, 265 F. Supp. 3d 366, 382 (S.D.N.Y. 2017)

Human Medicines Regulations 2012.

Instagram, 2019. Terms of Use. Retrieved from: https://help.instagram.com/581066165581870

Laddie, Prescot and Vitoria, The Modern Law of Copyright (Sweet & Maxwell, 2019)

Malibu Media, LLC v. Doe, No. 18-CV-10956 (JMF), 2019 WL 1454317 (S.D.N.Y. Apr. 2, 2019)

Mathilde Pavis, 2018. *Paparazzi & Copyright: Where Are We And Where Should We Be?* Retrieved from: http://ipkitten.blogspot.com/2018/05/paparazzi-copyright-where-are-we-and.html

Peter Cepeda v Jelena Noura "Gigi" Hadid and IMG Worldwide, Inc., 1:17-cv-00989-LMB-MSN (E.D. Va.) (2017).

Reed Elsevier, Inc. v. Muchnick, 559 U.S. 154, 166 (2010).

Rogers v. Koons, 960 F.2d 301, 307 (2d Cir. 1992)

The Fashion Law Blog (February 2020) *From Bella and Gigi Hadid and Goop to Virgil Abloh and Marc Jacobs: A Running List of Paparazzi Copyright Suits.* Retrieved from: www.thefashionlaw.com/from-bella-and-gigi-hadid-and-goop-to-virgil-abloh-and-marc-jacobs-a-running-list-of-paparazzi-copyright-suits/

Title 17 United States Code

US Copyright Act of 1976

Willcox Knott (2019) This Mama Life [Instagram]. Retrieved from: www.instagram.com/thismamalife/.

Xposure v Kardashian (2018) Mediation Report, case 2:17-cv-03088.

chapter 14

Taking the biscuit
Exploring influencers, advertising, and regulation

Iain MacRury

Learning outcomes

On completing this chapter, you should be able to:

- understand how advertising standard could apply to influencers;
- recognize how flow and influence might pertain to influencers; and
- understand how embedded content can create confusion on influencer channels.

Advertising regulations in place in the UK

The regulations governing advertising communications represent a hard-won set of principles – the realization, imperfect, patchy, but nevertheless potent in some respects, of considerable academic-critical and consumer push back against harms linked to advertising. In the UK, significant areas of critical concern including, for example, around gender, health, and children's media, are now reflected, and applied, to a degree, via the ASA and CAP codes (Authority 2019). The risk at hand is that a well-manicured-but-shrinking advertising regulatory garden might become overrun; guidance and signposting deteriorating at the border with a disorienting forest of online promotional contents – uncharted terrains. There is anxiety at this boundary, as a "closed system" conception of regulation needs to adapt to an open system conception.

Looking just at the UK there are established frameworks of advertising regulation. Regulators are now seeking, and, also, under some pressure, to extend scope into branded content (Hardy 2018) and especially to influencers (ASA 2019; Bosher 2020).

There have been a handful of well-reported sanctions on influencer content under these codes in the UK (Hardy 2018) and the US (Ritschel 2019).

So, recent years have seen the emergence of numerous regulations seeking to govern influencer advertising. Most of these have developed, or are in development, in the face of an onslaught of popular and critical concern about influencers (e.g. Ofcom 2010; Tatlow-Golden et al. 2016; Arayess and Geer 2017; ASA 2019). These regulations typically build on traditions of regulation developed for previous periods, and in relation to different, prior, media and communications ecologies (Henderson et al. 2009). But, as I explore here, current approaches mean that the alignment and commensurability of regulatory approaches to broadcast and some non-broadcast promotional content remain out of kilter in significant ways. This poses a significant practical and conceptual challenge.

Thought experiment: hypothetical regulation

The question explored here takes the form of a small thought experiment: "What happens if we look at promotional influencer content as if it were advertising, adopting a regulator's point of view?" This is a hypothetical question, to the extent that YouTube influencers generate content that is not treated as a "broadcast." Nor ostensibly is it "advertising" by any straightforward definitions. However, this question leads to a simple exercise of reading influencer content against advertising regulations. The exercise has heuristic value. It makes the unevenness between advertising and influencer territories in the regulatory landscape more palpable, a glimpse throwing discrepant regimes (influencer and advertising) into relief; a vista that remains hazy in the regulatory gaze.

Such an experimental exercise opens perspectives relevant to a real-world issue. Established, current regulatory systems are striving to deal with influencer content (Bosher 2020). This content, at times, replicates many of the tropes associated with broadcast and published advertisements, but where some CAP codes do not apply. This is often a matter of platform – broadcast ads in scope, online, organic-but-promotional content, not readily in scope. Yet, substantively, and platform designations aside, the cultural-psychosocial and marketing work of influencers, and advertising converge in key respects: influence is a component of advertising; advertising is a tool for influence.

Advertising agencies, competing with influencers for marketing budgets, or seeking to work with them, wonder about such unevenness (Childers et al. 2019), and the compatibility of adjacent crafts. Meanwhile, influencers seek ways to protect their collective reputation (Abidin and Ots 2015; BCMA[1] 2020) through professionalization of influencer practices.

Clearer regulation might help this. Currently, however, the scope and operations for compliance are not fully in place or understood with regards to some of these commonalities of influencer and advertising purposes. This leaves a regulatory blind spot occluding some influencer content from critical scrutiny.

Vulnerable audiences: global issues

The World Health Organization (WHO 2015) acknowledges these issues with respect to their wish for better governance in two of its key domains: food health and children. They highlight the problem posed in improving children's dietary health because of difficulties of regulating:

> ...many "stealth" marketing techniques used in digital media [which] take advantage of its creative, analytical and network capabilities. These include novel immersive techniques such as extensive HFSS food-themed game applications (or "apps"); social media content created by users themselves; word-of-mouth social media communication, such as "liking", sharing and commenting on marketing; and paid partnerships with vloggers popular with children. (WHO 2015)

WHO supplies an important but wide-angled critical perspective. In this chapter, a hypothetical examination, more microscopic, applying advertising regulations to specific influencer content, complements WHO's high-level view to help to better delineate the blind spots emerging around influencer content.

To explore in detail, I examine influencer content produced that, I suggest, references these two linked and high-profile regulatory domains: the rules linked to advertising HFSAS (High Fat, Sugar and Salt) foods and, also, a related focus that places HFSAS rules in conjunction with the regulations of child-oriented broadcasting. These rules are routinely in force for advertisers and enforced in respect of UK TV advertising.

Ongoing efforts to regulate HFSA foods forms one component in the national food strategy,

> Childhood obesity is one of the most pressing public health challenges that we face. In June 2018 as part of Childhood Obesity: a plan for action, chapter 2 the Government set a national ambition to halve childhood obesity by 2030. (HRM 2016)

Media contribute to an "Obesogenic environment" (Swinburn et al 2011; see Coates et al. 2019). In the context of the COVID-19 pandemic, concern about obesity amplifies this long-standing concern (Flint and Tahrani 2020). However, regulation supports a degree of compliance with extant regulations protecting the media environment from food advertising deemed harmful (ASA)

Granular regulation: clearance

Guardianship and enforcement of self-regulation happens via the sanctions of the complaints system (diagnosing ills in ads) as administered by the ASA. Significantly, however, it is mainly enforced via the hidden-but-crucial preventative operation of the *broadcast clearance system* – for instance, via Clearcast (2020). So, here, I refer to guidance, as set out by Clearcast, a body utilized by UK advertisers, in conjunction with advertising agencies, to support broadcasters and advertisers in respect of the ASA regulations and permitting broadcast material to air (or not).[2] Highlighting

iain macrury

clearance guidance provides insight into the fine-grained practical operation of advertising self-regulation – a task undertaken between ad agencies and broadcasters and mediated via Clearance. There is more to say about this process, but at this point recognizing the regulatory principles in detail as set by clearance processes provides a framework with which to review some online content.

Having fun with FGTeeV: a case study in family influence

For the purposes of this exploration, the application of these ASA-derived HFSAS and children's media rules to some influencer contents focuses on one successful influencer "channel," FGTeeV. FGTeeV is a suitable example, selected not because it is in any way exceptional or egregious, but because FGTeeV sits comfortably in the mainstream. It shares characteristics with much online material watched, and indeed, widely loved, supported[3] (Luscombe 2017), and consumed daily by children. It is one of many family vlogger channels.

Feedspot's online monitor highlights "100 Family YouTube Channels" (Feedspot 2020), with the family vlog-based format an established influencer genre. The phenomenon has momentum. *Time* reported in 2017 that:

> *Thousands of... families live out their lives in the lens of the webcam: from the mega popular folks at Family Fun Pack—a family of seven Californians, including parents Kristine and Matt—to We Are the Freemans!" the report adds that Family vlogging is "a growing genre; YouTube says that time spent watching family vloggers is up 90% in the past year. (Luscombe 2017)*

A species of "sharenting" (Blum-Ross and Livingstone 2017) there are an array of voices, styles, and intents within such vlog content (Kennedy 2019). My focus is on a well-established channel that has carved out a significant niche in the shifting world of online brand communications. Its success rests mainly on a large subscriber base and on income from YouTube advertising, placed alongside the content. However, I want to explore the extents and features of some of the native advertising elements (Asmussen et al. 2016; Einstein 2016; Hardy 2018) embedded in the organic content of the Vlog and the promotional quality of what is presented to be organic-family and child-friendly footage.

Keep it in the family

FGTeeV, since becoming established in 2013, now has a Gaming Channel, a Toy Channel, and a channel dedicated to the game Skylanders. The focus here is just on family-oriented vlog materials. We are invited into the FGTeeV home to witness everyday life there. A hyperactive, fast-cut, video diary-style captures family episodes. More formally produced video content – rap and skit based, or trails for future content at once punctuate and disrupt segments. The channel warrants the YouTube category "Comedy." The family focus is underlined in its "cast": four children, one girl and three boys – the youngest, born after the channel launched. They span age ranges, from toddler to teen. The clownish Daddy figure, and the somewhat put-upon mum, not to mention "Oreo" the dog, together complete the madcap group.

Recognition of the family-as-influential-environment, as opposed to the model of one individual influencer, contextualizes some aspects of influencer families such as FGTeeV in a different media space. Credibility, for instance, key to influence, takes on a different structure in a familial environment. Families and surrogate media families, present in the child-viewers' world through representation and imagination, can be especially compelling and powerful.

The power of family is nothing new. Many of us may be able to reach back into memory and recall either from television or literature particular memories of fictional families on page or screen which in some ways or others have managed to capture and captivate the childish disposition for familial belonging (or escape). Advertising regulations highlight children as especially vulnerable members of audiences (ASA). A complementary observation in the context of online families might be added: families can become especially influential "scenes" in the emotional cosmology of a developing child.

Influences on influencers: TV genres, archeology, and resonance

Questions of influence are often also a question of genre. Genre helps position discourse – and influence – in respect of its credibility, just as "source credibility" governs speaker authority in ads and public relations. Is this fiction? Is it advertising? Is it "news"? Is it credible? On what terms? A tacit sense of genre guides the feeling that might prompt such questions – whether they are articulated out loud or not.

New genres are often unstable hybrids of other prior genres. So, it is useful to consider some of FGTeeV's antecedent genres, as this helps answer the question: what kind of text is this? First, there is the sitcom. FGTeeV is classified as comedy by YouTube: FGTeeV owes a good deal to the family sitcoms tradition and replicates stock TV tropes, from *The Brady Bunch (1969–74)*, to *Modern Family (2009–2020)*, from *The Flintstones* (1960–66) to *Peppa Pig (2011–present)*, to *The Simpsons 1989–present)*, and to *Gumball (2011–present)*. The family has always been a significant focus on screen, and a powerful locus for imagining consumption and identity.

In that latter aspect, the FGTeeV family also inherits a mantle owned in the past exclusively, by innumerable anonymous advertisement families; tasting food, playing with toys, opening Christmas presents, going shopping, and so on. Occasionally ad families have taken on lives of their own – the Oxo family in the UK for instance. By saying this I want to highlight FGTeeV's hybrid family-advertising-comedy-drama roots. These genre roots, this archeology, as it were, scripts and classifies the FGTeeV content as it streams out of YouTube, but this hybridity makes it tricky to "place" the text. Is it an ad, is it a comedy? Tacit, developing, media literacies might falter here.

The family does what families do, but the FGTeeV family seems to do a lot of what *advert* families do. The family stories strand of the FGTeeV channels revolves around ordinary activities, but with consumption always-already at the center of most action. Scraps of content jolt and jump us from segment to segment, but with things, commodities (food, toys, trips) to the fore. Family life and experience in the FGTeeV cosmology, as with much in the influencer genre, becomes articulated through the re-presentation of promotional objects – things brought home from shops. But it is not an advertisement? Not exactly.

Real-fictive families

Another genre in play in FGTeeV is reality TV. We might think of *Jon & Kate Plus 8* (2007–2017), or *Here Comes Honey Boo Boo 2012–2014*). Reality-esque TV has now become a staple across schedules and YouTube alike (e.g. Holmes and Jermyn 2004; Deller 2019; Hill 2019). Scripted reality shows form a prominent component across media platforms on contemporary screens. FGTeeV simulates this candid and immediate-seeming feel of the scripted-reality genre, including staging controversies and seeming to force certain events, including product mentions, into the flow of its narratives.

Finally, here it is useful to recall the prophetic 1998 film, *The Truman Show*. Its story of a child growing up on screen, center-stage, unwittingly cocooned in a fictional-real-ideal existence. *The Truman Show's* recognition of new-social media's core conjunctions, interleaving the spectator within an envelope of everyday life so typical of social media worlds (MacRury 2012). In a staged reality, this resonates with efforts to make sense of the content routinely on display in FGTeeV and across numerous, similar YouTuber channels. FGTeeV becomes watchable, because we – and our children – are already good at watching real-fictive families on TV. Disorienting as it is when we see FGTeeV, we can make sense of what *this* is. FGTeeV offers a child's ideal world in that it projects a fantasy of parental attentiveness, playmates, abundance and fun but downplays constraints associated with more rigorous expressions of parental authority.

Between family vlog and global channel

The FGTeeV enterprise has become so successful that it is the eighth position amongst the top 20 most viewed YouTube channels of all time (Statista 2020). Since its launch in 2013 it has produced hundreds of videos and has branched out to produce its own merchandise, including FGTeeV branded toys, clothes, badges, and posters [https:// fgteev.com/collections/whats-new]. As with many successful media channels, FGTeeV has become a brand, many of its young viewers, and parents engage as fans, and with a notable international following. Organic as its growth may have been, and natural as much of the setting and presentation remains, even as domestic opulence, production values and editing skills have increased, the channel's creation reflects a good deal of promotional-entrepreneurial effort and strategic positioning.

As Kennedy (2019) has shown in relation to mummy vlogging, such work "becomes a constant endeavor." Kennedy continues, citing Duffy and Hund (2015), as an endeavor based in self-production, self-presentation, and self-promotion (Kennedy

2019). The charismatic family at the heart of FGTeeV enjoy, now, a species of micro celebrity (Abidin and Brown 2018; Leban and Voyer 2020). This account of constant digital labor extends into family vlogging too. The enterprising FGTeeV family have generated a successful online business linked to a strong grasp of the promotional element in channel creation.

Watching FGTeeV: vignettes

Children's media are increasingly consumed via tablets (Hadlington et al. 2019; Ofcom 2019). Solitary, mobile, privatized viewing can subtly shift children out of the "actual" family scene (MacRury and Yates 2016) and into an array of media spaces, including fictive-familial scenes. One consequence of this privatization of young children's media consumption is that there is a risk, in practice, of less casual parental scrutiny of media.

Apprehending YouTube/comprehending YouTube

There are other analytical barriers. A crude but real obstacle to critical-regulatory scrutiny of YouTube-based material is that there is so much of it. Critical scrutiny of advertising, abundant as the output of the advertising industry has always seemed, remained conceivable within limits. TV ads are concise. They are seen. Bounded in time and space (typically 30 seconds on screen) identified/identifiable advertisements remain susceptible to a host of analytical approaches – and regulations – highlighting persuasive and representational issues. Furthermore, they are subject to the casual media literacies constitutive of everyday social participation. So, contained as they are, advertisements are more readily regulated.

YouTube output is more akin to the "flow" of first television identified by Raymond Williams in the 1960s (2003). I propose that some close description of what goes on, on screen in YouTube-vlog spaces of this kind, adds some concreteness to the work of examining media issues for the wider frame of considering principles and practices of regulation. I choose the word "scrutiny" as it has a history in media analysis (Richards et al. 2000; MacRury 2009; Woolridge 2019). The conjunction of "old" media critique and the new forms that appear to elude or bypass some traditions of media analysis offers a retro appeal.

Some examples from a far larger number of available video segments the FGTeeV stable provide a focal point. I have subjected them to a close reading – alongside an assessment of the experience of watching content produced, of course, for young contemporary eyes.

I present four vignettes to capture something of this "flow" quality. Description preserves the meandering and necessarily hard to trace "narrative" that some YouTube videos exhibit. The vignettes sample just a sliver of the activities presented in some typical-seeing FGTeeV vlog materials. To establish the link to regulation and influence, I follow each vignette with references to broadcast clearance guidance that would serve to regulate these segments if/where a system was in place to oversee this species of content.

iain macrury

Vignette 1: Doggy Vloggy[4]

The segment begins with some trailer segments anticipating the future action and the dog Oreo – head stuck in a plastic cup. Quick cut to the family in a shop and then quickly, back home for more puppy segments. A quick ident shows the Puppy next to an Oreo biscuit. Then a quick musical skit – and the kids, singing in the kitchen. Cut to the doggy – who is biting the Dad and kids in some segments. The dog is teething. Dad says because she is teething her breath is stinking. Cuts to Dad, now looking at his shopping bag from which he takes a product, a prominent mock-style packshot presents the label fully to view. It is Arm and Hammer, Advanced Care breath strips for dogs.

Now the family is playing with slime – slime play is a vast YouTube attraction. Now, back to Oreo. The Puppy gets the breath strip. Some play then the Dad says the breath is fresher. "You all got a dog, you're all gonna want to invest in this", and a second Arm and Hammer product, Breath Drops for Dogs fills the screen, again framed playfully. The segments show the product in action – and indicate their likely effectiveness.

There is now an extended segment of the family playing with Oreo – much repetitive wordplay with the name "Oreo". There is a pretend drama between the father and the dog focused on cleaning up its mess. The young baby plays with the Puppy, Oreo. The Puppy chases the baby around the house. And the Puppy bites the baby. The baby cries. The game continues. The family talk about the attention that they get in a public place – they have just returned from shopping. Mentioning paparazzi, they show their feelings about their microcelebrity status. We now see the family watching their own YouTube channel, and another joke played on the mother. There is now a short segment about Pokemon. Now, a section with the daughter, doing some gymnastics and. Finally, a trailer for future episodes.

Vignette 1 highlights a chaotic blend of "organic-seeming" content linked to pet care, shopping, and the puppy, named Oreo.

Vignette 14.1: observations

Segment from YouTube channel	Summary content/action	Clearance guidance (Clearcast 2020)
1 our puppy bites & chases us around house! Oct 1, 2018) https://youtu.be/S2fp_U_x95A accessed 13 May 2020 [21 Minutes]	Along with the continuing prominence of Oreo the dog and the repetition of "Oreo" there is an extended informal demo (including pack shot) of two Arm and Hammer dog-breath products. FGTeeV Dad makes comedy-inflected endorsements while demo-ing the product. It is not made clear if there is a sponsorship element or not here.	If it believes there is a possibility of confusion between editorial and advertising content, Clearcast may require the inclusion of branding and/or logos or superimposed text (a super) stating "advertisement".

The blurring of promotional and organic-editorial material is apparent. It happens rapidly and haphazardly. Explicit marketing intent seems underplayed. There are no disclosures apparent, but, instead, a mock comic graphic briefly underlines the two brief Arm and Hammer "advertising" elements.

Vignette 2: Oreo song and puppy play

The video begins with a brief trailer for a song which will later feature as a prominent element in the video. It is a song about the dog Oreo, which uses a rap style. The family plays with the dog – Oreo. There is a quick packshot of some Pringles. The children tease the dog. Lots of different toys provoke Oreo, and they count each time the dog is startled. It is a lighthearted atmosphere. Further pranks: they put dog food on a disguised speaker, then play an alarming sound that frightens the dog. They also prank the mother while she is trying to drive her car. They trail the Oreo song Video with, "we've got a new Oreo song". The song begins. The words are: "Yo, yo, yo, Oreo" repeated several times. The song rhymes Oreo with various words, "chore-io", "door-io", "story-io", "floor-io". Repetition of the Chorus: "Yo yo yo Oreo" completes the segments. Background montages show numerous pictures of Oreos flying in the air, next to an animated image of the singing Duddy. The song repeats "Oreo" over and over throughout the short segment. The song ends with the invocation of two different available flavors of Oreo; "chocolate and vanilla", again superimposed over an image of the dog, Oreo, with his face looking out.

The video now transitions to a game around a completely different product, a dog-shaped toy that squirts water. Female characters continue as the butt of jokes. The boys and Dad squirt the oldest child, a daughter, (and Oreo) with this dog-pistol. A screen insert announces, "this video is really random" and "well hang in there because we've got two more random clips". The video is self-conscious about its randomness, and lack of narrative. A skit where the Dad tricks the youngest boy into thinking he will be riding on the roof of the car ends with laughter. There is a quick shot of some unexplained activity with an axe in the garden. Cut to a small child frightened by a giant puppet toy. There is a trail for future videos.

The presence of a "mascot-style" brand icon ("Oreo" the dog might become problematic in regulatory terms). The prankish treatment of the dog is another matter. The link to food in the puppy's name would, in a broadcast advert require the advertiser, via its agency, to complete a Classifications of foods: Nutrition Profile Certificate (Clearcast 2007) to help establish fitness and timing for scheduling. This time dimension does not apply. FGTeeV child-friendly cartooning and Oreo-puppy imagery would be unviable in respect of a HFSA-classified product like Oreos.

Vignette 14.2: observations

Segment from YouTube channel	Summary content/action	Clearance guidance (Clearcast 2020)
3 PUPPY vs STAIRS! Figure (FUNnel Family Music Video Vision) https://youtu.be/ 6SQqZX9pBds Mar 13, 2019 [6.34 minutes] – Oreo song from 3.05–4.30	There is a strong association built throughout between "Oreo" the dog and Oreo the brand. The Oreo rap uses witty rhymes, repetition, and cartoonish imagery to play on, and highlight the links to the biscuit product. Ostensibly a rappers-ode to the dog, we find a lot of cookies throughout. The vanilla and chocolate varieties of the biscuit appear next to the "Oreo" (see Figure 14.1 below). It is unclear if there is a sponsored link or not.	"Advertisements must be obviously distinguishable from editorial content, especially if they use a situation, performance or style reminiscent of editorial content, to prevent the audience being confused between the two. The audience should quickly recognize the message as an ad"

FGTeeV in its name and presentation is styled on the model of a TV channel. FGTeeV has a logo suggesting a traditional TV set and, clearly, the channel name denotes television as an important structuring metaphor. In terms of regulatory classification, however, this is not broadcast content, and were FGTeeV really a television channel rather than an online simulation of one, the channel content could not be made without considering regulations such as this:

> Television channels devoted to children's programs, or whose programs are or are likely to be of particular appeal to children, will be unlikely to be able to carry at any time advertisements... [such as] for... food or drink assessed as high in fat, salt or sugar. (Ofcom 2010)

Such considerations do not formally apply to FGTeeV or to other YouTube-led influencer content. The fundamental point here is that for influencer material, such as produced via FGTeeV, and bracketing, for a moment, questions of international-regulatory jurisdiction, no enforcement of regulatory intent via any kind of clearance process can reliably be said to have taken place. This concern arises in a further segment.

Vignette 3: Oreo shoes

> The segment begins with some hook-highlights of what is to come. We anticipate an explanation for the vision of a baby used for target practice in an Oreo-biscuit-throwing game. The boys in the family are getting together in the kitchen – the

"experiment" – to make Oreo sneakers. The segment exhibits the chaotic mess-making characteristic of the channel. The boys are making shoes from Oreo biscuits. There are lots of packshots featuring Oreos. The crafting of the biscuit shoes means we pay close attention to the product – and occasional bites highlight the snack. The kitchen, stacked with numerous large packets of Oreos, becomes messier and messier in all the fun.

The atmosphere is attractive and likely to enchant children, seeing here, an opportunity to revel in a picture of rich, messy, anarchic abundance. The scene culminates with the boy successfully walking in the "Oreo-sneakers" —a couple of casual mentions of different types of Oreos drop into the discussion. They repeat the creation of biscuit shoes. The children scream with excitement – the hilarity shows the kids have enjoyed it. They bring the smallest child to witness the aftermath. They put marshmallow fluff to the baby's back and play a game called Oreo toss – as the older children throw the Oreos hoping they will stick to the bay's back. The father laughs "This might be child abuse, but we're going to try it". So, the segment ends with the comic scene of children, and reassurance that the bay is Ok. The section ends with a series of promos and trailers for future videos. And a quick image of the beginnings of tidying up.

Vignette 14.3 observations

Segment from YouTube channel	Summary content/action	Clearance guidance (Clearcast 2020)
OREO SNEAKERS https://youtu.be/TVgPyqKIRiE accessed 13 May 2020 [10.47 minutes]	Mayhem when Dad and the kids make "shoes" from Oreos and marshmallow cream. Includes a game; throwing cookies to stick on the smallest, baby-child's back. There is an atmosphere of hysteria and fun, mess, waste and abundance. Dad mentions types of Oreo products. Kids snack on biscuits.	Alongside the absence of any clear disclosure of possible advertising/ sponsorship content Clearcast guidance may tend towards not clearing material that could: "undermine progress towards national dietary improvement by misleading or confusing consumers or by setting a bad example, especially to children.

Flow and influence

YouTube is immensely more chaotic and vaster than the relatively unpunctuated "flow" of time that disconcerted Williams, in the 1960s when, travelling across the Atlantic to a more commercial televisual environment, he sat down in his hotel to watch US TV for the first time. He recounts "an experience very difficult to interpret":

I can still not be sure what I took from that whole flow. I believe I registered some incidents as happening in the wrong film, and some characters in the commercials as

iain macrury

involved in the film episodes, in what came to seem – for all the occasional bizarre disparities – a single irresponsible flow of images and feelings. (Williams 2003: 84)

His address to "flow" is a helpful and powerful one. He goes on to describe the jumps and disparities characterizing the evening's schedule – and concludes that we might need to reconsider thinking of TV as programs, identifiable units of experience, in favor of a "flow" experience – a realization that, it is fair to say, gave Williams some cause for concern, and one produced an influential concept for television studies.

This metaphor of "flow" is helpful fifty years later for two further reasons. First, Williams' disorientation in the face of now-long-established commercial-televisual style becomes again familiar and renewed. It is recognizable in the apprehension of an extended experience of some of YouTube's hyper-distracted content and styles – certainly as served up via FGTeeV. Williams (2003) characterizes his discomfit thus:

> "This, essentially, is how a directed but apparently casual and miscellaneous flow operates, culturally, following a given structure of feeling." Experience of the 'flow' of FGTeeV induces at least one contemporary adult-viewer, into a closer intimacy with an "unfamiliar structure of feeling", providing a jolt akin to William's transatlantic leap.

Time and scheduling

One observation "flow" prompts a new and greater disruption in the practical sense of the temporal aspect of media experience, not unlike Williams' sense of things shifting away from programmed time. Internet "time" differs from broadcast time. Thus, broadcasters' time is subject to regulation because fundamentally airtime is a constitutive material dimension for broadcasting. Time is embedded in the broadcast media cosmology, just as space has been fundamental in managing boundaries in print media. So much regulation has depended on managing media flows by dictating aspects of its punctuation in time. A key marker, binding content–character–audience and regulation is a "clock number."

> Broadcasters also use the clock number to identify where artists need to be kept away from children's programs in which they appear (a BCAP code requirement) and opportunities for scheduling ads featuring artists in other programs where there is a synergy. (Clearcast 2020)

The dimension of time has become to a relative degree effaced from internet media management. Time as a dimension of control has migrated from the sphere of media production/broadcast into the sphere of domestic media consumption (screen time, in-built controls on phones and tablets, self-monitoring apps, parental-enforced discipline, etc.). It is salutary for parents to recognize how much detailed regulatory labor online channels pass into domestic life, and, to acknowledge how much invisible regulatory control has worked to manage promotional communications to children in broadcast media.

influencers, advertising, and regulation

Scheduling and structure in the narrative of television and screen time have served to help regulate the flow – not just of time, but in the viewing experience, and in terms of the boundaries and locks, and, of course, watersheds. This architecture regulating and containing flow supports the communication of ideas, images, emotions, moods, genres; meaning contained and contained by media like TV.

Flow and influence

Williams' (2003) metaphor of flow reminds us of the meaning of "influence." Influence has an etymology in "flow," a vivid and metaphorical association here, alive in this developing conception of the work of influencers. An underlying meaning links to half-forgotten, watery etymologies, in "flow," Medieval Latin īnfluentia, from Latin īnfluēns ("flowing in"), īnfluō ("flow into"), from in- ("in-") + fluō ("flow"). Influencers now create abundant new flows and should take a role in managing them. Influence, like overflowing rivers, invites a boundary and regulation. Without clearance-based scheduling or an equivalent, enabling principles currently served via clearance of basic coding of content, pre-clearance of scripts and other scrutiny, there is a risk of influential overspill.

A closer look at embedded content: creating brand assets on the fly

Another observation upon further examination, this time referencing semiotics (Barthes 1964; Williamson 1979; MacRury 2009), helps expand on how promotional meaning can, quickly, merge with organic content. Figure 14.1 captures a rapid textual process whereby meaning is transferred from the brand (Oreo) to the puppy (Oreo) in a process of naming – baptism which is, also, a piece of "brand asset" creation (Sharp 2016).

A longstanding critical vocabulary is used to make sense of textual moments like this one. Critics refer sometimes to the language of semiotics, trying, as Williamson (1979) did, in a now classic piece, to explain how advertising works on and in culture. Williamson outlines a pattern used in all communications; one, arguably, highlighted and amplified in advertising. Ads help guide meaning to emerge in the

> correlation of two things: the significance of one... is transferred to the other. This correlation is non-sequential; the two things are linked not by the line of an argument or a narrative but by their place in a picture... it requires us to make the connection... [as the advert] ... invites us to make transaction whereby it [meaning] is passed from one thing to another. (Williamson 1979:19)

McCracken (1990) makes a similar point, mentioning the important further detail of the creative director:

> Advertising works as a potential method of meaning transfer by bringing the Consumer good and a representation of the culturally constituted world together within the frame

iain macrury

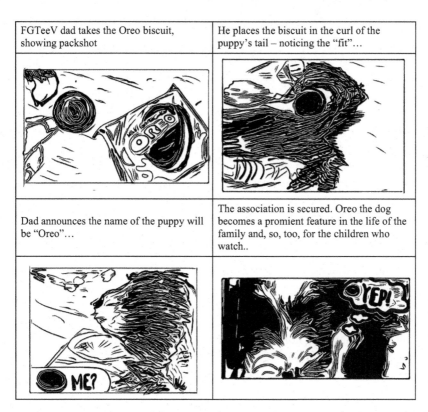

| FGTeeV dad takes the Oreo biscuit, showing packshot | He places the biscuit in the curl of the puppy's tail – noticing the "fit"... |
| Dad announces the name of the puppy will be "Oreo"... | The association is secured. Oreo the dog becomes a promient feature in the life of the family and, so, too, for the children who watch.. |

Figure 14.1 The "transfer of meaning" (Williamson 1979:19; McCracken 1990:77) – a classic advertising trope in a new context using a "scamp" aesthetic.

of a particular advertisement. If the creative director of an agency seeks to conjoint these two elements in such a way that the viewer finds glimpses an essential simi-larity between them. When this symbolic equivalence is successfully established... The transfer of meaning from world to good is accomplished.

In this FGTeeV segment, however, it is not a creative director framing the meaning transfer but the lovable, approachable, FGteev Daddy. This prompts a reminder of the question of creative control which, in influencer-based work belongs to the influencer, not the advertiser. Nevertheless, an advertising-style creative association has been built and framed here. The association is laid, then, into the next thing.

Meaningless distinction and brand assets: low level unconscious processing

Persistent repetition of the puppy's name "Oreo" alongside numerous brand-identifying reinforcements of the association – produces the family dog as a super appealing marketing mascot, a focus for content creation and a distinctive "brand asset" (Sharp 2016) akin to Andrex puppies or the Dulux dog. This asset is mobilized in an alter video, and, arguably, is in mind whenever the dog's name/pun on Oreo is announced. "Oreo" the dog is consistently produced as a mascot-style "brand asset" with clear product references overlaid onto an actual Oreo – so is this advertising?

Even if there is no sponsorship to declare, the mimicry, in pastiche mode or otherwise, of pervasive marketing communications forms produces hard-to-navigate flows in the channel. Is this endorsement, sponsorship, or critique? However, maybe cognitive sense making is beside the point. Disrupted-flow based influences can support affective and inchoate marketing work, the production, to use Sharp's (2016) phrasing, of "meaningless distinction." So, in this case, Oreo, the dog becomes a kind of "brand asset." For Sharp, in such a context, "a distinctive asset" builds memory traces to "packaging and in advertising, in-store displays and sponsorships." Sharp adds, such sets help "to encourage brand loyalty, helping the "brand must stand out so that buyers can easily, and without confusion, identify it." He adds that asset building is a long project – taking years. It is good to start audiences young.

Puppy Oreo's presence in vlog stories is a constant opportunity, sometimes taken up, to remind, to incant, to repeat associations to Oreo the brand. This is not the influencer language of persuasion, nor the quasi-lifestyle-journalistic discourse of unboxing-assessment-evaluation, suspect as that can sometimes be. Still, if we take Sharp's definition of meaningless distinction and brand asset building as core marketing tasks, then vlog content such as these correspond to a model of "branded content or advertising is fully integrated in the media content children are consuming" (see Hudders et al. 2017; De Jans et al. 2019).

Convergence highlights regulatory unevenness

TV is becoming more like YouTube and YouTube is becoming more like TV. So regulatory uneven-ness here is especially significant. Televisual and screen-mobile technologies continue to converge. Now pervasive, Smart TV technology crystalizes the convergence narrative in palpable ways. The paradox under review here is that in a period characterized by media convergence we are at risk of witnessing regulatory divergence as regulatory frames applied to promotional advertising in broadcast channels struggle to engage with promotional content generated by and driving influencer incomes and productivities.

Control: creativity, autonomy, responsibility, and regulation

Outside the industry, a continuing part of the folk-and-critical-common understanding of advertising includes the view that such self-regulation arrangements are suspect. Indeed, there continue to be instances where questions of truth and decency, and about troubling representations emerge, with ads serially prone to misrepresentation and stereotyping.

Inevitably, too, critical bodies question the capacity of institutions such as the ASA to behave hawkishly with the suggestion that "marking your own homework" may soften capacities for rigorous judgement. Nevertheless, agency-based advertising professions invest time and effort in regulatory compliance. By recognizing the industry's approach to regulation, imperfect as it may be, we can perhaps understand the challenge of extending such regulatory approaches to cover influencers more comprehensively.

Advertising agencies have undersold their role in the regulatory process. The industry foregrounds its contribution as primarily creative. Agencies have colluded in this popular and rewarding vision of their work. Creativity is what makes agencies distinctive. However, this emphasis marginalizes other essential advertising agency activity. Such "hidden" client service includes a kind of quality control, including know-how regarding compliance with regulations. Agencies help clients to work to ensure that ads stay within the rules. It feels hard to square a myth of romantic ad-creativity, with recognition of professional-disciplinary virtues.

The myth of creative freedom has another aspect to it. There is a fantasy that agencies operate with a higher degree of autonomy from client–brand constraints than they typically do. Agencies build their processes on rigorous client-to-agency, agency-to-client control processes. These take on less bureaucratic names, highlighting dialogic creativity (chemistry meetings, tissue sessions, and so on) (MacRury 2018). However, from pitch to sign-off and broadcast or publication, there are inter-organizational and intra-organizational control functions, implicit and explicit, between client and agency for all creative activities.

Agencies help clients in collaboration with broadcasting platforms too, part of the crucial regulatory process of clearance. Clearance compliance work rests on a hidden bureaucracy carried within out ad agencies and in partnership with adjunct regulatory-clearance bodies such as Clearcast. This unheralded bureaucracy is part of the opaque value that agencies bring into the promotional communications process, the micro-operationalization of self-regulation, via clearance compliance.

Ethos and regard: tacit motives for regulatory compliance

Another component of the self-regulatory system is the relative strength of two soft factors. One lies in advertising's tacit respect for what some commentators have called the media commons. A second rests in the presence, ambient within the industry, of networks of professional regard. Pratt (2006) draws this out well, reminding us that place has a role in governing conduct.

> In part, physically close linkages and frequent contacts achieve this; in other part it is sustained by reputation. Reputation is a significant form of micro governance within the advertising industry. (Pratt 2006: 35)

Regulatory strength is bolstered by some of the shared values of professionalism and ethical conduct within the advertising industry. One suggestion is that networks of regard express a deeper sense of inhabiting a shared Commons. This belief in the common interests of an industry, instituted in the UK via bodies such as the IOPA and ASA, mean that professionals will find motive to relegate the pursuit of an advantage in a particular campaign, or by ignoring a regulation. There is an investment in the long term, in the "common" good – a push to avoid too many risks to the prospect and future of the industry (MacRury; Offer).

Furthermore, the history of the professional of the advertising industry has been its efforts, not always successful, in marginalizing and distancing itself from hucksterism, and humbug associated with irresponsible and opportunistic marketing communications. Patent medicines and Phineas T Barnum (see Feldwick; Falk; Nixon), for example, come to mind.

Unruly influencers?

Advertising agencies, for example, will work hard to produce creative work that ensures they, their clients, and the broadcast channels they utilize, produce content that conforms to ASA principles. This is regulation practice. Influencers have fewer obligations and are less likely to have to answer for their content. Highly distributed and disruptive systems and processes that could underpin influencer marketing self-regulation, modelled on the ethos of the individual entrepreneur, committed to "free speech" and formally denying "control" as a condition of exemption from the need to declare sponsorship is quite a different prospect than self-regulation, as conducted by advertising agencies within a professional and organizational context linked to shared institutions, professional values, and procedures; regulatory practices, practices, codes, clearance, and professional norms.

One observation to make is that the question of control poses a complex and even paradoxical challenge concerning the regulation of vlogger-based influencer marketing materials. Rules to produce such content, under the tag of "content marketing" or "branded content," stipulate some de-control of the creative output on the part of brands. This "no-control" clause serves to preserve the principle of editorial autonomy and constitutes a defining element in disputes regarding sponsored content. Because of this, the seemingly full delegation of creative control to the content-making vlogger on the axis of "creative" production, we witness an unintended consequence. The unexpected corollary to an "arm's length" abdication of creative control is a significant reduction, at the granular level of a vlog production process, with capacity to assert or assure control on a significant parallel axis, i.e. the axis of regulatory compliance. New influencer material is generated quickly and frequently and gives all the appearance of being unscripted.

In the case of FGTeeV there is a strong flavor of scripted reality, but with considerable leeway for improvisation and free association in terms of what is expressed within the content. As a relatively more professionalized and high resource operation there is a good deal of editing involved. However, the editing is directed more towards embellishing and enlivening content. Certainly, watching the material does not give the impression that the content has been scrutinized against a series of regulations in respect of content.

Aligning regulation and practice: influencers and advertising

The point of this analysis has not been to identify retrospective infringements in two- to three-year-old online content on a fun, if somewhat opportunistic YouTube channel. Instead, it has been to notice, foreground and capture concrete

iain macrury

unevenness in the regulatory terrain. Advertising agencies, for instance, appear to be working to a significantly more rigorous set of regulations than influencers. Juxtaposing broadcast-ad rules with online influencer practices highlights this gulf. The broadcast-advertising regulations, as enacted in practice through the regulatory clearance processes administered by, for instance Clearcast, would likely conflict with the material some influencers produce and circulate online in good faith – and the model, based on a scheduling-time-based classification of pre-cleared material would be inoperable for reasons of scale or production-process logics.

This focus on regulation is important. It crystallizes a far wider narrative which has seen media regulation devolved from state-centric governance models in the 1950s in the UK and linked to the centrality of public broadcasting to professional and industry-based models of self-regulation. These profession-based models are shifting, now, however, with influencers a central case in point. We have situations where responsibilities for media regulation have devolved yet further, even beyond the institutions serving advertising and the professional promotional disciplines. In practice, the buck has passed to individual consumers, managing screen time and fostering resiliency-style digital-media literacies' and to content producers posting entrepreneurially and independently; semi-detached, or willfully detached from the constraints governing professional-instituted forms of content creation – such as advertising.

There is a risk of a widening gulf in the already uneven regulatory landscape. Such a split serves neither advertising, nor influencers. Nor does it support confidence in the credibility and integrity of media environments.

Notes

1 A professional body section "BCMA Influence has been launched, following a wide-ranging consultation amongst members to understand and identify the key issues facing brands, agencies, producers and platforms." BCMA Influence sets out guidance for influencers seeking to comply with regulations. www.thebcma.info/bcma-influence/
2 Clearcast is "best known for clearing ads. In the UK, broadcasters aren't allowed to show ads that are misleading, harmful or offensive. So before ads are shown, we check them against the UK Codes of Advertising (the BCAP and CAP Codes), which set out what is and isn't permitted... Our role is to protect reputations and we can apply our skills to any area where it is important that content is acceptable under a set of rules." See: www.clearcast.co.uk/
3 Reviews of FGteev on the Commonsense media website tend to the positive and supportive. Where parental reviews are less supportive "commercialism" tends not to be the main concern although it is one of the commonsense media sites core evaluative tags/warnings, this is not the prominent cause for concern. See www.commonsensemedia.org/youtube-reviews/fgteev/user-reviews/adult
4 www.youtube.com/watch?v=8W5vjA1Ywxg, accessed 13 may 2020 [21 Minutes].

References

Abidin, C., and Brown, M.L., 2018. *Microcelebrity Around the Globe: Approaches to Cultures of Internet Fame*: Emerald Publishing Limited.
Abidin, C., and Ots, M., 2015, August. *The influencer's dilemma: the shaping of new brand professions between credibility and commerce*. In AEJMC 2015, annual conference.

Arayess, S., and Geer, D., 2017. Social Media Advertising: How to Engage and Comply. *European Food and Feed Law Review*, 12(6), 529–531.

ASA, 2019. The labelling of influencer advertising. A report on what labels and other factors help people understand when influencers are posting advertising content. Available from: www.asa.org.uk/uploads/assets/uploaded/e3158f76-ccf2-4e6e-8f51a710b3237c43.pdf

Asmussen, B., Wider, S., Williams, R., Stevenson, N., and Whitehead, E., 2016. Defining branded content for the digital age: The industry experts' views on branded content as a new marketing communications concept. London: Branded Content Marketing Association.

Authority, 2019. The labelling of influencer advertising: A report on what labels and other factors help people understand when influencers are posting advertising content. Available from: www.asa.org.uk/uploads/assets/uploaded/e3158f76-ccf2-4e6e-8f51a710b3237c43.pdf

Barthes, R., 1964. "The Rhetoric of the Image" *in Image-music-text*: Macmillan.

Blum-Ross, A., and Livingstone, S., 2017. "Sharenting," parent blogging, and the boundaries of the digital self. *Popular Communication*, 15(2), 110–125.

BMCA, 2020. *Branded Content Marketing Association*. Available from: www.thebcma.info/bcma-influence/

Bosher, H., 2020. Influencer marketing and the law. Ch. 13 in *Influencer Marketing: Building Brand Communities and Engagement*. Ed. Yesiloglu, S., and Costello, J. London: Routledge.

Childers, C.C., Lemon, L.L., and Hoy, M.G., 2019. # Sponsored# Ad: Agency perspective on influencer marketing campaigns. *Journal of Current Issues & Research in Advertising*, 40(3), 258–274.

Cialdini, R.B., 1993. *Influence (rev): The Psychology of Persuasion*. HarperCollins.

Clearcast, 2007. Content and Scheduling Rules for HFSS Food and Drink Advertising: Practical Guidance. *Clearcast*. Available from: https://kb.clearcast.co.uk/Attachments/Clearcast%20Practical%20Guidance%20for%20HFSS%20Advertising%20090610.pdf

Clearcast, 2020. *Clearcast*. Available from: www.clearcast.co.uk/

Coates, A. E., Hardman, C. A., Halford, J. C., Christiansen, P., and Boyland, E.J., 2019. Social media influencer marketing and children's food intake: a randomized trial. *Pediatrics*, 143(4), e20182554.

De Jans, S., Cauberghe, V., and Hudders, L., 2018. How an advertising disclosure alerts young adolescents to sponsored vlogs: the moderating role of a peer-based advertising literacy intervention through an informational vlog. *Journal of Advertising*, 47(4), 309–325.

Deller, R.A., 2019. *Reality Television: The TV Phenomenon that Changed the World* Emerald Group Publishing.

Duffy, B. E., and Hund, E., 2015. "Having it all" on social media: Entrepreneurial femininity and self-branding among fashion bloggers. *Social Media+ Society*, 1(2), 2056305115604337.

Einstein, M., 2016. Black ops advertising: Native ads, content marketing, and the covert world of the digital sell. OR Books.

Feedspot, 2020, "One Hundred Family YouTubers". *Feedspot*. Available from: https://blog.feedspot.com/family_youtube_channels/

Flint, S.W., and Tahrani, A.A., 2020. COVID-19 and obesity—lack of clarity, guidance, and implications for care. *The Lancet Diabetes & Endocrinology*.

Hadlington, L., White, H., and Curtis, S., 2019. "I cannot live without my [tablet]": Children's experiences of using tablet technology within the home. *Computers in Human Behavior*, 94, 19–24.

Hardy, J., 2018 "Advertising Regulation", pp. 123–143 in Hardy, J., MacRury, I., and Powell, H., 2018. *The Advertising Handbook*. Routledge.

Holmes, S., and Jermyn, D., 2004. Understanding Reality Television. Routledge.

iain macrury

Henderson, J., Coveney, J., Ward, P., and Taylor, A., 2009. Governing childhood obesity: Framing regulation of fast food advertising in the Australian print media. *Social Science & Medicine*, 69(9), 1402–1408.

Hill, A., 2019. Engaging with Reality Television. *The Routledge Companion to Global Television*.

HRM, 2016. *Childhood Obesity: A plan for action*. HRM Available from: https://assets. publishing.service.gov.uk/government/uploads/system/uploads/attachment_data/file/718903/childhood-obesity-a-plan-for-action-chapter-2.pdf

Hudders, L., De Pauw, P., Cauberghe, V., Panic, K., Zarouali, B., and Rozendaal, E., 2017. Shedding new light on how advertising literacy can affect children's processing of embedded advertising formats: *A future research agenda. Journal of Advertising*, 46(2), 333–349.

ICC, 2015. *ICC Guidance On Native Advertising*. Available from: https://iccwbo.org/publication/icc-guidance-on-native-advertising/

Kennedy, U., 2019. *Becoming on YouTube: exploring the automedial identities and narratives of Australian mummy vlogging*. Available from: https://researchdirect.westernsydney.edu.au/islandora/object/uws:51579/datastream/PDF/view

Leban, M., and Voyer, B., 2020, Social media influencers versus traditional influencers: Roles and consequences for traditional marketing campaigns. Ch. 2 in *Influencer Marketing: Building Brand Communities and Engagement*. Ed. Yesiloglu, S., and Costello, J. London: Routledge.

Luscombe, 2017. "The YouTube Parents Who are Turning Family Moments into Big Bucks," *Time Magazine*, May 18, 2017. Available from: https://time.com/4783215/growing-up-in-public/

MacRury, I., 2009. *Advertising*. Routledge.

MacRury, I., 2012. "Gifts, friendship, and the re/figuration of advertising space". In The *Routledge Companion to Advertising and Promotional Culture*, 357.

MacRury, I., 2018 "What is an Advertising Agency in the 21st Century?" in Hardy, J., Pratt, A.C., 2006. *Advertising and creativity, a governance approach: a case study of creative agencies* in London. Environment and planning A, 38(10), 1883–1899.

MacRury, I., and Yates, C., 2016. Framing the mobile phone: The psychopathologies of an everyday object. *CM Komunikacija i mediji*, 11(38), 41–70.

McCracken, G.D., 1990. *Culture and Consumption: New approaches to the symbolic character of consumer goods and activities*. Indiana University Press.

Ofcom, 2010. HFSS advertising restrictions: final review. In: Office of Communications UK.

Ofcom, 2019. Children's media lives – Wave 5 A report for Ofcom.

Richards, B., MacRury, I., and Botterill, J., 2000. *The Dynamics of Advertising*. London: Routledge.

Ritschel, 2019, YouTuber Ryan's Toys review accused of 'deceiving pre-schoolers' into watching ads, *The Independent*, Tuesday 10 September, Available from: https://www.independent.co.uk/life-style/ryan-toysreview-youtube-ads-sponsored-content-a9099721.html

Sharp, B., 2016. *How Brands Grow*. Oxford University Press.

Statista, 2020. Most viewed YouTube channel owners of all time as of January 2020, by views (in billions). *Statista*. Available from www.statista.com/statistics/373753/most-viewed-youtubers-all-time/

Swinburn, B.A., Sacks, G., Hall, K.D., McPherson, K., Finegood, D.T., Moodie, M.L., and Gortmaker, S.L., 2011. The global obesity pandemic: shaped by global drivers and local environments. *The Lancet*, 378(9793), 804–814.

Tatlow-Golden, M., Boyland, E., Jewell, J., Zalnieriute, M., Handsley, E., Breda, J., and Galea, G., 2016. Tackling food marketing to children in a digital world: trans-disciplinary perspectives. Available from: www.euro.who.int/en/health-topics/disease-prevention/nutrition/publications/2016/tackling-food-marketing-to-children-in-a-digital-world-trans-disciplinary-perspectives.-childrens-rights,-evidence-of-impact,-methodological-challenges,-regulatory-options-and-policy-implications-for-the-who-european-region-2016

WHO, 2015, Tackling food marketing to children in a digital world: trans-disciplinary perspectives: *WHO*, 2015, Available from: http://oro.open.ac.uk/55662/1/WHO%20Digital%20Food%20marketing%20Issues%20Transdisciplinary.pdf

Williams, R., 2003. *Television: Technology and cultural form*. London: Routledge.

Williamson, J., 1979. *Decoding Advertisements: ideology and meaning in advertising*: Marion Boyers.

Woolridge, P.A., 2019. Scrutiny's Virtue: Leavis, MacIntyre, and the Case for Tradition. *Journal of the History of Ideas*, 80(2), 289–311.

Television References

The Brady Bunch (1969–74)

The Flintstones (1960–66)

Gumball (2011-present).

Modern Family (2009–2020)

Peppa Pig (2011-present)

The Simpsons (1989-present)

FGteeV Youtube content examined https://www.youtube.com/user/FGTeeV

iain macrury

chapter 15

Virtual influencers
More human than humans
Scott Guthrie

Learning outcomes

By the end of this chapter, you should be able to:

- articulate the essence of what a virtual influencer is;
- recognize the key proponents within the subgenre;
- appreciate the benefits that can be generated by a successful use of virtual influencers;
- identify some of the issues and challenges facing the subgenre; and
- anticipate the development of virtual influencers in the near future.

What is a virtual influencer?

Virtual influencers are computer-generated avatars that are imbued with human characteristics and personalities. Some are fully computer-generated. Other virtual influencers are a composite of computer-generated imagery (CGI) overlaid on a real human body form. For example, Lil Miquela is a well-known virtual influencer composite. Most of the current avatar influencers are reliant on scripts and human interaction. Unable to think for themselves their Instagram captions are carefully written and their presence online is created each time by human designers.

Virtual influencers offer audiences and sponsoring brands a non-human alternative to traditional social media influencers. The growing subset of virtual influencers presents both opportunities and challenges for brands and communicators considering using virtual storytellers as brand ambassadors. Procter and Gamble's global prestige skincare brand, SK-II now works with YUMI, French fashion brand Balmain has created two virtual models, Margot and Zhi.

The next wave of avatar influencers are predicted to be unshackled by pre-scripted animation paths. This means they will be able to operate at scale without being reliant on human intervention. They will learn from each human interaction to become more useful in the next human interaction. Virtual influencers are becoming brand assistants and customer representatives as well as brand ambassadors. "Fatema," for example, is a fully autonomous, AI-driven Digital Human. She enables Bank ABC customers to verbally interact with her on various banking subjects, thus creating efficient and engaging customer experiences (Soul Machines 2019). Ultimately, future virtual influencers will be able to flirt effortlessly between social media platforms marshaling communities at scale by responding to each comment left in real time.

Evolution of virtual influencers

The rise of the avatar influencer could be viewed as merely the next iteration in one corner of the communications industry. Whilst new to the influencer marketing discipline, avatars are well established within other creative industries. In music, for instance, musician Damon Albarn and artist Jamie Hewlett created the virtual band Gorillaz more than twenty years ago in 1998 (Wired staff 2005). Hatsune Miku, a singing Japanese hologram was released over a decade ago in 2007 (Vocaloid Fandom, n.d.). After Miku came Aimi Eguchi, which earned worldwide attention in 2011. Eguchi was a CGI composite of several members of Tokyo's female pop supergroup AKB48 (Ashcraft 2011).

The concept of the virtual human is not new. Indeed, its lineage may be traced at least as far back as Maria, the robot of Fritz Lang's 1927 science-fiction drama film *Metropolis*. But, with each technological iteration our relationship with the virtual human shifts from being one of viewing at a distance to one of interaction. The proliferation of smartphones and the popularity of image-sharing sites such as Instagram have accelerated our awareness of these virtual humans and elevated them to a position of influence.

Components of virtual influencers

Virtual influencers portraying a human, rounded self

In an interview with the author Charlie Buffin (2019), the CEO at Spark Media Works which is a vertically integrated media company that builds virtual influencers, he explained the importance of creating a fully-fledged backstory for the avatar influencer. "Character biographies, intriguing storylines, and relatable personas are key to success. It keeps the content interesting and helps to maintain a high level of engagement," said Buffin.

One example of a Spark avatar creation is Cade Harper. Harper is a typical 15-year-old and his experiences and storyline resonate strongly with his loyal fanbase. His message of positivity is designed to encourage self-esteem and respect within the Generation-Z community. In an interview with teen news and celebrity website, *Tiger Beat*, Harper discusses how he stays positive on Instagram and doles out advice on how best to navigate your teenage years (Stivale 2019). The carefully curated tone-of-voice and story-lining has created success for Spark. Harper's Instagram posts generate a 7.46 percent engagement rate according to the Instagram analytics tool, HypeAuditor (Baklanov 2019). He is currently ranked number two on Celebrity ranking site, Famous Birthdays (Famous Birthdays 2019). The top place goes to Lil Miquela.

Dudley Nevill-Spencer, founder of the Virtual Influencer Agency, a creative and marketing agency dedicated to developing virtual influencers spoke to the author in an interview (Nevill-Spencer 2019). Nevill-Spencer explained the process his agency takes when building a virtual influencer on behalf of a brand.

> First, we ask who the brand is targeting. We use machine learning tools to the tribes that the brand is currently communicating with. We then determine who else they should be nurturing relationships with. From there we can work out the personality type and the type of content which the virtual influencer will create. We take audience age into consideration but it's really about the tribe's psychographics – their interests, their opinions, what they value in society. We then build a full background for each virtual influencer giving them a family, a backstory; and a life arc.

Authenticity as performance art

Writing at the start of his book *Picnic Comma Lightning* (Scott 2018), Laurence Scott asserts: "we have evolved to build mental maps of the world not according to its actual, physical nature, but according to what allows us to thrive. In other words, our individual and collective realities are fictions – carefully constructed to enable us to maintain our particular perspectives."

Social media platforms make fictions of our realities – and realities of our fictions. Scott asks of us what happens when our private realities – our inner worlds, our memories – are atomized, becoming part of a public reality. Social media platforms encourage this dismantling of the boundaries between a private reality and a public reality. The business model of social media platforms is founded on nudging us to share ever more of our private lives publicly – to turn these private moments into public events or a commercialize-able event. These data-rich events can then be sold on to advertisers. The real and unreal; the context-specific and context-collapsed; the private and the public are all smashed into one on social media.

With so much of our lives today being played out online, what questions does this raise about what it means to be Instafamous? Christopher Morency (2018), writing in *Business of Fashion*, poses the question: "Should it matter to brands and publications if an influencer is computer-generated, if the avatar has the same influence on its following than that of a 'real' influencer?" If Nirvana for the Insta-famous is to become a clone-like version of Kylie Jenner replete with her 173 million (Jenner 2020) followers, ever-changing hair color, skin tone, and pneumatic lips then isn't the creation of a computer-generated self to help attain such near physical impossibility on a daily basis the next logical step?

Indeed, in June 2018 the Council of Fashion Designers of America honored Kylie's older sister, Kim Kardashian, with its first-ever Influencer Award (Anastasiou 2018). It would be remiss to fail to acknowledge Kardashian's stellar influence. Many argue, however, that Kardashian often promotes an unattainable (and, at times, even unhealthy) image. The council has been criticized for its award choice.

What does it really mean to be authentic at the start of the third decade of the twenty-first century? As social beings humans have always sought to connect with like-minded people. We've done so in cafes and bars; in offices and through sporting events. Social media has scaled this; made it at once global and permanent.

But Instagram isn't us. It is the aspirational, digitized version of us. Online there is a tendency to show only the positive, successful side of our life. Instagram is the platform of choice for this form of self-promotion. All the images posted to the photo-sharing platform could share the same tagline as the effervescent vitamin supplement, Berocca: "You, but on a really good day."

We have learned to use lens filters and editing apps. Our Instagram feeds have professionalized. If we fail to get sufficient engagement in the first half-an-hour we remove the post. We agonize over creating the perfectly crafted caption and selecting the most suitable hashtags.

Instagram's #liveauthentic with its 31.3 million posts (Instagram 2020) has become the most inauthentic of all hashtags: a study in same-same sunrises, sunsets, Tolix bar stools, furniture hewed from scaffolding boards and pictures of flat white coffees. The word "authenticity" has lost its meaning; mutated and commodified into its opposite.

Nevill-Spencer (2019) explains: "influencer marketing can be about authenticity; but it does not always have to be. Think about watching a film or reading a book. During that process, you become emotionally connected to the character, let's say: James Bond. You know he is not real, but you buy into his character. The way the Virtual Influencer Agency explains virtual influencers is to think about the Instagram grid. Each square on Instagram is like a page in a book where both stories and characters evolve. The difference is that you can communicate directly with virtual influencers as entertainment characters."

Harper demonstrates this phenomenon well. His creators, Spark, produced regular episodic content throughout the summer of 2019 for the young virtual influencer. The Instagram images and captions explored Cade's blossoming relationship with his new girlfriend, Charlotte, his growing apart from friend Simon and becoming irritated by his sister.

CGI influencers as change catalysts

Instagram's Insta-famous images have become so ingrained; so ubiquitous we no longer see them for the hyper-reality they represent. CGI influencers act as change catalysts, bringing fresh pairs of eyes to jolt us out of our blind spot. They are a mirror reflecting today's society and questioning what it means to be human in a digitized world. "Habitualization devours work, clothes, furniture, one's wife, and the fear of war." So said Soviet literary theorist Viktor Shklovsky in his 1917 essay "Art as Technique" (Shklovsky 2017). To illustrate his meaning Shklovsky compared the experience of holding a pen for the first time with holding one for 10,000th time. We do not consciously think about holding the pen, in the same way we no longer interrogate the mise-en-scene of the Insta-famous. CGI influencers remind us of this artifice.

A successful influencer listens to their audience. They learn what they like and what they don't care for and then tailor future content accordingly. A successful influencer is also one who identifies with their followers in a personal way – and vice versa. There will always be an innate need for human connection, no matter how unhuman the connection is. CGI influencers can and do provide this connection. Successful virtual influencers benefit from detailed backstories. They are relatable to their audience. They help the viewer explore the concept of authenticity. They demonstrate the dismantling of boundaries between public and private reality.

Benefits of virtual influencers

This next section examines the many benefits of virtual influencers to sponsoring brands. These can be characterized by the insta-immaculate; brand safety; brand fit; campaign logistics; and real-time engagement.

Insta-immaculate

Instagram is the social media platform most used to portray an unblemished, flawless version of ourselves. An aspirational version best defined as the Insta-immaculate. The fashion vertical is, perhaps, the natural space to inhabit for these CGI influencers who will always look Insta-immaculate. Companies such as CLO Virtual Fashion offer true-to-life 3D garment simulation ensuring any style of garment fits perfectly onto the virtual influencer. Additionally, there is no need for the CGI models to succumb to perpetual dieting, grueling beauty regimes, or cosmetic surgery. They do not age or change clothes size. Working with virtual influencers is beneficial to sponsoring brands because it de-risks the creative phase. These influencers are guaranteed to show off the sponsoring-brand garments in the very best of light.

Brand safety

Firms work hard to protect their brands' reputations online. Each time firms work with third parties there is an opportunity for that hard-won reputation to become tarnished. Best practice demands that a rigorous process of influencer identification, digital due diligence and selection ensures that communicators choose to work with influencers who share the same brand values as the sponsoring company and that there are no surprises in terms of past influencer indiscretions waiting to be surfaced. The past is not always an iron-clad guarantee to the future, however. Even the most forensic of digital due diligence will be unable to prevent a future indiscretion on the part of the influencer. Opting to work with virtual influencers over their human counterparts eliminates the risk of both past and future bad behavior or poor judgment. When YouTuber Logan Paul filmed a suicide victim and posted the vlog to the video-sharing platform, brands including YouTube distanced themselves from the influencer (BBC 2018).

Brand fit

Increasingly, virtual influencers are being designed especially for individual brands. In doing so the sponsoring companies can ensure the influencers' backstories, language, tone of voice, values, and beliefs marry up exactly with those of the brand's target audience. This leads to the formation of an emotional connection between the brand and influencer.

Balmain, the luxury fashion house, has created two virtual models, Margot and Zhi. These avatars work exclusively, promoting the high-end collections of the French brand. Olivier Rousteing, Balmain's creative director, worked with a CGI artist to create Margot and Zhi as the embodiment of the beauty, individuality, and confidence of the Balmain woman (Hargrove 2018).

Campaign logistics

These avatar influencers can be placed within any context and dressed in any sponsoring-fashion house's garment. There is no requirement for air travel or hotel accommodation costs or scheduling logistics. These virtual influencers will never miss a flight or a deadline, unlike their human counterparts on occasion. In 2018 the public relations agency representing social media platform Snapchat sued influencer Luka Sabbat for failing to fulfill the terms of his contract. The agency claimed it paid Sabbat $45,000 upfront for a $60,000 campaign which was not completed (Mogg 2018).

Real-time response

Lil Miquela remains the best-known virtual influencer. Her comments and audience interaction rely on a well-written brand manual and a team of humans to write them. However, a newer breed of machine-learning built CGI influencers learn from previous interactions and can respond to each comment made in real-time irrespective of the number of messages or being waylaid through the necessity of sleep or work engagements.

Challenges facing virtual influencers

Transparency of ownership

In April 2018 Bermuda (@bermudabae), a computer-generated avatar with more than a passing resemblance to a Sims character, hacked into Lil Miquela's Instagram account for around a day. The "hack" was a stunt. Both Bermuda and Lil Miquela are the creations of Brud. However, whilst Lil Miquela is a champion of the LGBT community, an advocate of openness and racial equality, the backstory and values imbued within Bermuda are of a Donald Trump supporting, pro-gun, climate-change denier.

Bermuda claimed at the time to be the creation of Daniel Cain of Cain Intelligence. In an Instagram post published during the Lil Miquela take-over Bermuda wrote: "I came into this world in 2017. I proudly call Cain Intelligence my home and I consider the amazing people who work there to be family. Daniel Cain is a literal genius moving this country [the United States] forward without any real thank you or acknowledgment."

Under the "latest" section of the Cain Intelligence website, it says: "At Cain we've always strived to be leaders in a world overrun with followers. We're passionate about creating a consumer-facing example of our Artificial Intelligence learnings. We are proud to present Bermuda! Bermuda is the first of her kind. Built to speak her truth and to the interests of today's youth, she is uniquely unapologetic, representing not only a breakthrough in artificial intelligence but also in modern political thought" (Cain Intelligence 2018).

This "hacking" highlights two interlinked issues: firstly, the motivation and values lying behind the sponsoring entity; secondly, transparency in identifying the sponsoring entity. Brud demonstrates through this incident the breadth of influence its virtual influencer creations can wield. The stunt took place during the company's $6 million investment round (Shieber 2018). Following the stunt, Bermuda's audience swelled to over 50,000 Instagram followers from just 2,000 pre-event.

A serious point lies in national security. What if a foreign sovereign power sought to influence another nation through the creation of an army of virtual influencers? Buffin (2019) from Spark Media Works explains: "as the space evolves and virtual influencers become even more 'human' looking, we could see stricter regulations to avoid false impersonations, especially when it comes to real humans – notably celebrities and public figures."

Nevill-Spencer (2019) advocates a virtual human participant's code of ethics. It is his belief that every virtual human should be watermarked. The mark would designate two pieces of information: firstly, that the influencer was virtual rather than human, secondly that the image could be traced to the owners to establish who is responsible for the content and what the motivations are behind it.

Uncanny valley

It is this closeness to looking human which raises another issue. Virtual influencers can produce a sense of uneasiness in the viewer. It is generally accepted that the more life-like (though not completely life-like) these creations appear, often the greater the level of discomfort they produce in the viewer. This area of repulsive response aroused by a digital human whose appearance lies in the hinterland between a "barely human" and "fully human" entity is the uncanny valley. It is a concept identified by Japanese robotics professor Masahiro Mori (1970). However, a point is reached when the avatar becomes so life-like as to be indistinguishable from a human being. At this point the emotional response in the viewer becomes positive once more.

Companies such as Spark CGI, SuperPlastic, Soul Machines, and Toonstar are currently developing virtual characters that test whether audiences are ready to embrace even more virtual avatars and whether audiences are yet prepared to embrace these life-like images.

Perpetuating unrealistic notion of female beauty

The creator of virtual influencer Noonoouri has deliberately bucked this trend of becoming too life-like. Noonmoori remains a character. To engage with her and her oversized, manga-eyes and doll-like body is to immerse oneself in a dreamworld; a separate reality that does not condone or perpetuate an unrealistic notion of female beauty. Some believe CGI influencers undermine the existing model of promotion.

Richard Wong (2018), in an opinion article for AdWeek titled "Virtual Influencers Lead to Virtual Inauthenticity," asserts that this trend of artificially creating personalities poses a massive potential risk to the future of culture and media. He cites three reasons for his critique. First, CGI influencers create unrealistic expectations about what beauty, style, and culture looks like. Secondly, companies running internet personalities are driven exclusively by profit. Finally, there is a question of authenticity – how can an avatar influencer try on a Prada outfit?

There is a long history within the fashion industry of touching up images so as to make the models appear perfect – from the antediluvian airbrush to 3-D graphics and Photoshop. Fashion is an industry that has always placed weight on the unattainable perfection of human form. Influential models have always commanded high incomes. There is forever a question mark hovering over the authenticity of many fashion influencers about their true affinity with the promoting brand.

Regulation compliance

When a human social media influencer undertakes a brand collaboration all advertising must be obviously identifiable as such to the viewer. Advertisers must abide by clear regulations. In the UK these are set out by the Advertising Standards Authority, the UK Code of Non-broadcast Advertising, Sales Promotion and Direct Marketing (CAP Code) and Competition and Markets Authority. Other jurisdictions have similar government bodies to protect the consumer. In the United States, for instance, this role falls to the Federal Trade Commission.

There exists a level of confusion about how these regulations should be applied to virtual influencers, however. In an interview with the author, Rupa Shah (2019), founder of Hashtag Ad Consulting and former senior investigator at the ASA explains:

> The ASA would absolutely not hold back from investigating posts by an avatar if they considered there was a breach of the CAP Code. ASA rulings into influencer marketing always name both the brand (i.e. the advertiser) and the influencer (i.e. the publisher) but the responsibility for providing the written response rests

scott guthrie

primarily with the advertiser, so any ambiguity about an avatar's true identity would not prevent the ASA from publishing a ruling. If the brand and the influencer agree not to repeat the non-compliant ads/posts the matter would end there because the ASA does not issue fines but, if there are repeated breaches, the ASA's sister body, CAP, can impose a range of sanctions. But even if it did get to this point (and it rarely does) the avatar's identity would still not pose a problem because CAP could bypass the influencer and work with the brand and the social media platforms to prevent further breaches. There's no suggestion that avatars are being used to manipulate the regulatory system but if there did appear to be a growth in non-disclosed posts by numerous avatars, the CMA could step-in because they take a wider perspective on consumer issues than the ASA/CAP. They do have the power to impose fines and to take action through the criminal courts so the companies behind avatars would be exposed and held to account.

For a more in-depth look at how regulatory bodies impact influencers, Bosher (2020) gives a legal explanation in Chapter 13.

Synthetic media and deep fakes

There has been an acquisition collapse in terms of both cost and level of ability required to create synthetic media. Synthetic media is algorithmically created or modified media – the nefarious version of which are deep fakes.

Computer scientists with companies such as Pinscreen Inc, Google-backed Magic Leap, and Canny AI are working on technology that combines what is real with what can be synthesized by a computer. The outputs range from fun 3D avatars consumers can use in gaming to the sinister manipulation of politicians' speeches. For instance, in 2019 a digitally altered video showing Nancy Pelosi, the speaker of the United States House of Representatives, appearing to slur drunkenly through a speech, was widely shared on social media. US president, Donald Trump, was amongst those who shared the deep fake video posting the clip on Twitter with the caption: "PELOSI STAMMERS THROUGH NEWS CONFERENCE" (Parkin 2019). This example highlights the need for global regulation to protect consumers from the potential harm these technological advances might bring.

Future of virtual influencers

In the near future virtual influencers will be unshackled by pre-scripted animation paths. Companies such as Soul Machines are working to build synthetic humans who will be able to operate at scale without being beholden to human intervention. They will learn from each human interaction to become more useful in the next human interaction.

Virtual influencers will be designed to mirror the psychographics and tribes of sponsoring brands. This future is likely to be realized in the near term because of the collapse in price and relative ease in accessing the technology behind virtual influencers. Perhaps a greater drive to the renaissance of virtual influencers is the way in which we increasingly interact with the internet. Our interaction is fast moving away from text-based inquiry to voice-activated interaction. The ability to converse with a human-like avatar becomes all-the-more enticing; a new interface for a new digital environment.

In the near future it is likely that the subgenre of virtual influencers will splinter into at least three smaller distinct, though overlapping, categories: virtual brand assistants, customer service representatives, and virtual influencers.

Virtual brand assistants

Virtual brand assistants are virtual humans designed and operated by a brand. They will be built with a single focus in mind. For example, Procter and Gamble's global prestige skincare brand, SK-II now works with YUMI (Soul Machines 2019). YUMI is a full-autonomous AI-driven, synthetic human capable of interacting as a human would but with the control Procter and Gamble needs and expects as a multinational consumer goods corporation. YUMI was designed by Soul Machines to help consumers better match their skin types to SK-II products and to provide tips and advice on beauty product application.

Customer service representatives

Virtual influencers as customer representatives. They will serve the function of chatbots but with human-like emotions and body form. AVA, again built by New Zealand technology company, Soul Machines is an avatar customer service representative for Autodesk. Consumers can interact with AVA via voice or video chat. AVA can recognize and respond to emotional cues and inflection in tone provided by those consumers.

AVA's counterpart, Jamie, is a digital assistant at ANZ bank. Jamie has a human face, voice, and expressions and can have a two-way verbal conversation. She has been programmed to answer the top thirty questions most frequently searched for through the bank's website. The synthetic human customer services representative is proving to be a success with ANZ bank customers. In her first 100 days Jamie had more than 12,000 conversations with people visiting the site, demonstrating use adoption and scale of interaction (Anthony 2018).

As with chatbots virtual customer service representatives such as AVA and Jamie offer customers an instant response to their questions. However, these virtual assistants have the benefit of the human form offering a face-to-face personal interaction between brand and consumer.

Virtual influencers

These virtual human influencers will either be owned by a sponsoring brand or they will be influencers in their own right. In 2018 luxury French fashion house Balmain teamed up with Diigitals to create a virtual army of digital models. The Balmain acti-vation included Shudu, heralded as the world's first digital supermodel. The creation of fashion photographer Cameron-James Wilson, Shudu boasts 199,000 Instagram followers (Shudu 2020). She rose to celebrity following publicity after she wore a Fenty lipstick which the brand reshared on Instagram (Gil 2018).

Tellingly, the Balmain army also includes two models: Margot and Zhi designed by Wilson's creative agency, Diigitals especially for the brand (Diigitals, n.d.). Both avatars are purely Balmain brand influencers designed to model the product line. They do not have their own Instagram accounts and exist only on Balmain collateral. The Balmain activation capitalizes on Shudu's audience as well as pulling viewers to Balmain-owned media.

Buffin (2019) sees collaborations between brand-owned influencers and influencers in their own right (be it virtual or human) as a growing element within the industry. "A big part of our business is managing real influencers. We're able to work with these individuals and have them collaborate with our virtual influencers and other digital characters. A lot of influencers find collaborating with a virtual influencer as a unique opportunity that tends to spark high engagement because of how unique the content is."

Summary

- Miquela Sousa, better known as Lil Miquela, was the first virtual influencer to generate a significant Instagram following when she debuted on the platform in 2016.
- Interest in computer-generated imagery influencers is growing. Fashion brands are increasingly working with virtual influencers. Last year, French luxury brand Balmain announced the creation of an army of virtual models. KFC has done the same thing. Expect more of these designer influencers.
- Virtual influencers are often influential because of the rounded self; the detailed back-stories and life arcs given to them by their creators.
- The desired outcomes for virtual influencers will splinter into three separate, but overlapping, areas of virtual brand assistants; customer service representatives; and virtual influencers.
- As it becomes harder to distinguish computer-generated influencers from human influencers the ethics around ownership and motivation should be addressed.

Case study: Miquela Sousa AKA Lil Miquela

Meet Miquela Sousa, a Brazilian-American fashion influencer and music artist from Downey, California.

Better known as Lil Miquela, she has acquired 2.2 million Instagram followers (Miquela 2020) organically since taking to the photo-sharing platform in 2016. During that time, she has modeled clothes for brands including Prada (Perier 2018), Chanel, Diesel (Instagram 2018), and Moncler (Instagram 2018). She has established Club 404, her own clothing brand, too (Depop n.d.). She has released a Spotify top

10 track (Stutz 2017) and appeared on the magazine covers for Highsnobiety (High Snobiety 2018), and King Kong (King Kong 2018). In 2018 she attended Coachella, the Californian music festival. There she watched Beyoncé and interviewed artist J. Balvin (Pero 2019). Lil Miquela has courted controversy, too, sharing a kiss with fashion model Bella Hadid in a Calvin Klein advertisement (Pasquarelli 2019).

Like many successful Instagram fashion influencers forever 19-year-old Lil Miquela is in demand with brands wanting to pay for access to her audience. Unlike almost all other successful Instagram fashion influencers Lil Miquela is also a computer-generated image; an avatar influencer. Lil Miquela is the most well-known of the new rash of virtual influencers. Others include Shudu, Koffi, Dagny, Bermuda, blawko22, Daisy Paige, and Noonoouri.

The secret to the success of Lil Miquela as an Instagram influencer is twofold: her portrayal of the rounded self; and her relationship with her followers.

Lil Miquela is more than a clothes horse. She promotes positive social change. In the past she has amplified the story of British schoolboys who helped avert a suicide attempt. She has written letters to the U.S. Congress in support of the transgender community. Lil Miquela has included a link in her Instagram bio profile to black girls code – a charity aiming to increase the number of women of color in the digital space. Such elements are expertly curated to communicate the rounded self of what it means to be human, a set of values and ethics which overlay the commercial imperative of identifying brand sponsorship.

Stand Lil Miquela curated a rounded self against British teenager Leo Mandella, aka Gully Guy Leo. He is an expert streetwear model. His 711,000 Instagram followers (Mandella 2020) want to see him modeling his vast collection of hyped streetwear. Mandella's fans are not specifically interested in his rounded self. Distilling Gully Guy Leo to his constituent parts: he is an online streetwear mannequin. Given this context Lil Miquela becomes more 'real' than the online version of Mandella and many other human Instagram influencers.

In response to her thoughts on virtual celebrities in a BBC interview (Fowler 2018) Lil Miquela said: "I think most of the celebrities in popular culture are virtual! It's been disheartening to watch misinformation and memes warp our democracy, but I think that speaks to the power of 'virtual'. Eventually 'virtual' shapes our reality and I think that's why I'm so passionate about using virtual spaces like Instagram to push for positive change."

Can virtual influencers help attain communications and corporate outcomes, or are they a fad? Investors in the company behind Lil Miquela see them as the future of marketing communications. In 2018 Sequoia Capital, BoxzGroup, SV Angel, and others invested $6 million into Brud (LA TechWatch 2018), the Los Angeles-based start-up that claims to specialize in "robotics, artificial intelligence and their applications to media businesses." In early 2019 Brud completed a Series B investment round valuing the company at $125 million according to company insight platform Crunchbase (Crunchbase n.d.).

Brud's investors see the growth potential in computer-generated creations becoming mainstream fashion influencers. Lil Miquela's brand partnerships have already de-risked their investment by providing proof of concept.

Questions

1. What are the challenges for brands that want to use virtual influencers?
2. Initially, many individuals did not know that Lil Miquela was a CGI. How can consumers distinguish between reality and CGI?
3. How will engaging with a CGI change how you engage with a living influencer?

References

Anastasiou, Z., 2018. Kim Kardashian's CFDA influencer award is receiving very mixed reactions on social media. [Online] Available at: www.harpersbazaar.com/uk/fashion/fashion-news/a21078712/kim-kardashians-cfda-influencer-award-is-receiving-very-mixed-reactions-on-social-media/

Anthony, J., 2018. ANZ's artificial intelligence entity Jamie took 12,000 customer inquiries in its first 100 days. [Online] Available at: www.stuff.co.nz/business/business-top-stories/108681909/anzs-artificial-intelligence-entity-jamie-took-12000-customer-inquiries-in-its-first-100-days

Ashcraft, B., 2011. Is this girl real or virtual?. [Online] Available at: https://kotaku.com/is-this-girl-real-or-virtual-5811658

Baklanov, N., 2019. The Top Instagram Virtual Influencers in 2019. [Online] Available at: https://hypeauditor.com/blog/the-top-instagram-virtual-influencers-in-2019/

BBC, 2018. YouTube punishes Logan Paul over Japan suicide video. [Online] Available at: www.bbc.co.uk/news/world-asia-42644321

Bosher, H., 2020. Legal and future aspects of influencer marketing. Ch. 13 in *Influencer Marketing and Relations: Building Brand Communities and Engagement*. Ed. Yesiloglu, S., and Costello, J. London: Routledge.

Buffin, C., 2019. [Interview] (8 August 2019).

Cain Intelligence, 2018. Latest. [Online] Available at: http://cainintelligence.com/

Crunchbase, n.d. brud. [Online] Available at: www.crunchbase.com/funding_round/brud-series-b--8b64807a#section-overview

Depop, n.d. Club 404. [Online] Available at: www.depop.com/club404notfound/

Diiigitals, n.d. Balmain Paris: Balmain's new virtual army. [Online] Available at: www.thediiigitals.com/balmain

Famous Birthdays, 2019. Cade Harper. [Online] Available at: www.famousbirthdays.com/ai/cade-harper.html

Fowler, D., 2018. The fascinating world of Instagram's "virtual" celebrities. [Online] Available at: www.bbc.com/worklife/article/20180402-the-fascinating-world-of-instagrams-virtual-celebrities

Gil, N., 2018. This Insta-famous model sparked outrage online for a bizarre reason. [Online] Available at: www.refinery29.com/en-gb/2018/03/192208/photographer-creates-fake-supermodel-shudu

Hargrove, C., 2018. Exclusive: Balmain introduces its first "virtual army". [Online] Available at: www.refinery29.com/en-us/2018/08/208657/balmain-olivier-rousteing-digital-cgi-supermodels

High Snobiety, 2018. High Snobiety, Issue 16, p. Front Cover.

Instagram, 2018. Lil Miquela news feed. [Online] Available at: www.instagram.com/p/Be_tLsqF6aw/

Instagram, 2018. Lil Miquela newsfeed. [Online] Available at: www.instagram.com/p/Be6Zs4VlFxB/

Instagram, 2020. Instagram. [Online] Available at: www.instagram.com/explore/tags/liveauthentic/?hl=en

Jenner, K., 2020. Instagram. [Online] Available at: www.instagram.com/kyliejenner/?hl=en

King Kong, M. 2. I. o. f. c., 2018. King Kong. March (05), p. Front Cover.

LA TechWatch, 2018. The LA TechWatch Startup Daily Funding Report: 4/24/18. [Online] Available at: www.latechwatch.com/2018/04/the-la-techwatch-startup-daily-funding-report-4-24-18/

Mandella, L. A. G. G. L., 2020. Instagram. [Online] Available at: www.instagram.com/gullyguyleo/

Miquela, L., 2020. Instagram. [Online] Available at: www.instagram.com/lilmiquela/?hl=en

Mogg, T., 2018. Snapchat's PR firm is suing an influencer for failing to influence. [Online] Available at: www.digitaltrends.com/social-media/snapchats-pr-firm-is-suing-an-influencer-for-failing-to-influence/

Morency, C., 2018. Meet fashion's first computer-generated influencer. [Online] Available at: www.businessoffashion.com/articles/intelligence/meeting-fashions-first-computer-generated-influencer-lil-miquela-sousa

Mori, M., 1970. The uncanny valley. *Energy*, 7, 33–35.

Nevill-Spencer, D., 2019. Personal interview [Interview] (10 July 2019).

Parkin, S., 2019. The rise of the deepfake and the threat to democracy. [Online] Available at: www.theguardian.com/technology/ng-interactive/2019/jun/22/the-rise-of-the-deepfake-and-the-threat-to-democracy

Pasquarelli, A., 2019. Calvin Klein apologizes for Bella Hadid kiss with Lil Miquela. [Online] Available at: https://adage.com/article/cmo-strategy/calvin-klein-apologizes-bella-hadid-kiss-lil-miquela/2172796

Perier, M., 2018. Lil Miquela took over the Prada Instagram account before their show. [Online] Available at: www.vogue.fr/fashion/top-models/diaporama/meet-lil-miquela-the-avatar-influencer-turned-pat-mcgrath-muse/48902

Pero, J., 2019. CGI influencer Lil Miquela makes her Coachella debut: Animated social media personality with 1.5 million Instagram followers interviews artist J Balvin. [Online] Available at: www.dailymail.co.uk/sciencetech/article-6924617/CGI-influencer-Lil-Miquela-makes-Coachella-debut-interviews-artist-J-Balvin.html

Scott, L., 2018. In: Picnic Comma Lightening. s.l.:Penguin.

Shah, R., 2019. Personal interview [Interview] (10 July 2019).

Shieber, J., 2018. The makers of the virtual influencer, Lil Miquela, snag real money from Silicon Valley. [Online] Available at: https://techcrunch.com/2018/04/23/the-makers-of-the-virtual-influencer-lil-miquela-snag-real-money-from-silicon-valley/

Shklovsky, V., 2017. Art as Technique, s.l.: s.n.

Shudu, 2020. Instagram. [Online] Available at: www.instagram.com/shudu.gram/?hl=en

Soul Machines, 2019. Bank ABC's AI-powered Digital Employee Fatema – The World's First Digital DNA™ Human. [Online] Available at: www.soulmachines.com/news/2019/09/11/bank-abcs-ai-powered-digital-employee-fatema-the-worlds-first-digital-dna-human/

Soul Machines, 2019. SK-II & Soul Machines™ Announce YUMI: The World's First Autonomously Animated Digital Influencer. [Online] Available at: www.soulmachines.com/news/2019/06/17/sk-ii-soul-machines-announce-yumi-the-worlds-first-autonomously-animated-digital-influencer/

Stivale, S., 2019. Exclusive: Social media influencer Cade Harper opens up about staying positive. [Online] Available at: https://tigerbeat.com/2019/02/meet-cade-harper/

Stutz, C., 2017. Virtual singer & internet star Miquela shares debut single "Not Mine". [Online] Available at: www.billboard.com/articles/columns/pop/7898117/miquela-virtual-singer-instagram-not-mine-song-stream

Vocaloid Fandom, n.d. Hatsune Miku. [Online] Available at: https://vocaloid.fandom.com/wiki/Hatsune_Miku

Wired staff, 2005. Keeping it (Un)real. [Online] Available at: www.wired.com/2005/07/gorillaz-2/

Wong, R., 2018. Virtual influencers lead to virtual inauthenticity. [Online] Available at: www.adweek.com/digital/virtual-influencers-lead-to-virtual-inauthenticity/

chapter 16

Influencer marketing
Lessons learned and moving forward

Joyce Costello

The evolution of influencers

We start the book off by addressing what is typical within initial debates about a practice or theory such as what are the definitions of key concepts and applicable criteria. Yesiloglu (2020) sought to clarify what it means to be influential in Chapter 1. Her premise is that if we can understand what it means, then it is easier to define *Influencer* in relation to those influencing attitudes and behaviors on social media. It is important to differentiate influencers on social media as different streams of literature such as those related to leadership (Northouse 2016) or organizational behavior (Ferris et al. 2002). In a relatively young field, it is normal to try to apply older theories to new ideas, but for influencer marketing to develop its own theories, it must evolve beyond those applied in different contexts.

After examining different definitions and discussing the pros and cons, Yesiloglu (2020) proposed defining an influencer as "a person who has a strategic approach and ability to influence individuals and their (buying) decisions within digital communication platforms" (p. 9). This implies that the influencer must identify what approach or strategy they will take and how or which tactics they will employ prior to attempting to influence an attitude or behavior change. Yesiloglu (2020) added that an influencer's power, authority, and expertise were the building blocks to influencer marketing. She argues that the influencer's ability to stimulate electronic word of mouth with their user-generated content is a benefit for the brand and therefore the relationship between the brand and influencer needs to be managed in different ways than, say, between an agency and a client.

With the introduction of what constitutes an influencer, questions have arisen about whether they are different from opinion leaders or celebrities. Leban and Voyer (2020) explored in Chapter 2 how these social media influencers differ from the traditional idea of an influencer. Drawing upon the typologies of past and current influencers, they assert that influencers can rise to a micro-celebrity status through personal branding strategies they use to define their brands and increase their followers. Indeed, not all influencers will rise to the level that their fame is akin to those of a celebrity. However, the key distinguishing characteristics are social media influencers have the benefit of being more relatable, reachable, and trustworthy than celebrities. Leban and Voyer (2020) contend that these three characteristics are what contribute to an influencer's success. They warn that as influencers rise through the ranks, if they start to cease to have these straits, their engaging relationships with their followers may decline.

Going forth with this definition and concept of being different from celebrities, Riboldazzi and Capriello (2020) in Chapter 3 propose Influencers be categorized by mega, macro, micro, nano, or virtual influencers. While it initially seems like it is oriented towards the number of followers, Riboldazzi and Capriello (2020) offer other characteristics in which to classify influencers. For example, mega influencers can be described by their fame, nano influencers act as persuaders within their niche, and virtual influencers are computer-generated images. Size does matter to some brands, so Riboldazzi and Capriello (2020) offer guidelines such as macro-influencers generally have one million to 10,000 followers and micro-influencers have followers ranging from 1,000 to 10,000. By identifying different characteristics beyond size, it can help brands to begin to identify what type of influencer is best suited for their influencer marketing campaigns.

The development of influencer marketing and influencers as part of marketing communication campaigns

With each decision comes a consequence. When choosing an influencer, brands may have many criteria that they can draw upon. However, the authors in this book debate that focusing on size or looking for influencers who have followers in a target audience that the brand wants to tap into, might not be the most efficient way to identify the best influencer for a brand. Instead, the authors (Leban and Voyer 2020; Özçelik and Levi 2020; Riboldazzi and Capriello 2020; Rosenthal and Arcuri 2020) identify four different methods that can help brands focus their influencer marketing strategies.

Leban and Voyer (2020) state that practitioners need to understand the characteristics that make for ideal influencers to partner with. Some practitioners have the advantage of having experience with working with celebrity endorsements which Leban and Voyer (2020) in Chapter 2 state is where influencers have similar origins. Leban and Voyer (2020) discuss the evolution of the typology of the influencer as it evolved from a celebrity endorsement or what is known as traditional influencers to where we are today with social media influencers. This progression includes how influencers are increasingly morphing from amateur content creators to those who are capitalizing on making a profession out of online content creation. The obvious advantage for practitioners who have been working with celebrities is that they understand how credibility, attractiveness, and cultural meaning can influence their intended target audiences. Leban and Voyer (2020) argue that some social media influencers are growing into micro-celebrities. This would suggest that practitioners could be able to apply some of the same selection criteria for the more popular influencers.

However, for the practitioner that is concerned about identifying the best influencer for their organization's needs, Riboldazzi and Capriello (2020) in Chapter 3 encourage them to follow their three steps for identifying and selecting influencers. First brands should engage in social listening, followed by determining whether there will be a person–organization fit or rather an influencer–brand value fit and finally selecting the ideal influencer based on reach, relevance, and resonance. Riboldazzi and Capriello (2020) contend that by following these three steps, it provides the advantage of having three milestones that allow for evaluation prior to moving to the next step. For example, if during the social listening phase, the brand realizes that the conversations influencers are having with their followers focus on an idea or use that the brand had not thought of before, it can be used in an innovative manner. Likewise, the second step of ensuring there is a match or continuity between the values of the two parties can provide additional insights into the values of the influencer's audience and the brand's potential customers. Finally, reach, relevance, and resonance can help the brand and the influencer to develop key performance indicators or even return on investments.

Exploring influencers from the organization's perspective means one is able to capture the more nuanced needs. Rosenthal and Arcuri (2020) proposed their ICA (individual, content, audience) framework in which brands should seek a balance between the three variables. The individual or persona prioritization focuses on criteria such as "identity, personality, credibility, trustworthiness, brand-fit and narrative style" (p. 68). Organizations can view the influencer's page to gauge how these criteria match their needs. Content or domain identification relates to how the influencer's content and activities match the keywords the brand associates with or seeks to. For instance, if a brand specializing in organic vegan products would seek out influencers who specialize in creating content in this area. It is inferred that the influencer is operating in the domain of expertise and that their followers would be attracted to the topic. The final variable in the framework is the audience quantification. This consists of the socio-demographic information about the audience. For brands looking to expand into a new demographic, influencer marketing could be a good way to see what type of engagement this audience may have with content related to the brand.

Rosenthal and Arcuri (2020) argue that the framework can be applied to media or public relations logic so that brands can see influencers as a means of distributing their messages. For example, if a brand wanted to maintain complete control of the content from the manner in which it is presented, to how it is shared- they would need an influencer who is willing to let go of creative control and possibly their authenticity. If one thinks of the mega influencers who flog content in a static matter, but to a massive audience that may view them as a trendsetter, this could be a good match for a brand with media logic. However, other brands may be public relations oriented. Those with a public relations mindset understand that each influencer can bring a unique value and that co-created content by the influencer and even the audience can be value-added. Because this logic is focused on relations, the brands will tend to have a longer relation beyond one campaign.

Some organizations may approach identifying influencers as being tailored to their consumers and potential consumers. Özçelik and Levi (2020) proposed a framework that uses consumer-based and influencer-based antecedents to determine the concept of the "right" influencer. Consumer-based antecedents focus around the concept of fit, which has its origins in Person-Organization Fit Theory (Kristof-Brown et al. 2005). The premise is there should be a congruent match between the individual's goals, skills, and values with the organization. Özçelik and Levi (2020) propose four levels of consumer-base fit that a brand should look at: influencer–consumer, content–consumer, product–influencer, and brand–influencer. The relation between the brand (organization) and influencer (individual) mirrors Kristof-Brown et al.'s (2005) fit theory. The product and influencer fit relate to Rosenthal and Arcuri's (2020) idea of domain identification. Finally, it is imperative that the relationship between the influencer and the brand's intended consumer and the content and how it fits with the consumer are aligned. If practitioners or scholars were to test these fit measures, Kristof-Brown et al. (2005) person-organization scale questions could be adapted to Özçelik and Levi's (2020) proposed consumer-based antecedents.

While consumer-based antecedents focus on relationships between different variables, influencer-based antecedents focus on dimensions related specifically to the influencer. These include commercial orientation, popularity, originality, uniqueness, and ethicality. Commercial orientation is clear cut – either the influencer creates and shares content because of monetary relationships with brands or they do not. Yet, the other elements do leave some degree of subjectivity on the part of who is "judging" the influencer. The ethical issue brings up the question about whether the brand itself has a certain ethical standard or principles that guide them and how the influencer develops their own sense of ethics. Indeed, the study of influencers, ethics, and outcomes could lead to a new stream of literature.

However, these influencer-based antecedents are different than the traits Özçelik and Levi (2020) say that lead to the "right" influencer (authenticity, persuasiveness, source credibility, trustworthiness, power, and expertise – each of which are investigated empirically in other chapters). Their framework is based on the arguments that certain consumer-based antecedents and influencer-based antecedents will lead to identifying the right influencer, which in turn should lead to consequences such as engagement with the brand/product or influencer brand attitude. As this is a conceptual model, we encourage others to test this.

Key options for identifying influencers

- Investigate whether the influencer has the necessary credibility, attractiveness, and cultural meaning to influence the brand's intended target audiences.
- Use a three-step method to engage in social listening, determine if there will be an influencer–brand value fit and select influencers based on their reach, relevance, and resonance.

- Experiment with the ICA (individual, content, audience) framework which enables brands to weight each variable given the importance during a campaign.
- Explore how consumer-based and influencer-based antecedents can help identify the "right" influencer.

Measuring the success of influencers

Engagement is a key area that all the scholars within this book mention. Riboldazzi and Capriello (2020) state that resonance is best measured through engagement. On a basic level, items such as likes and shares may indicate engagement. However, it the purpose behind the like and share is unknown. For example, one might like a photo, but it may be out of a sense of obligation. Likewise, sharing content can be done to comment on it in a negative manner with one's own followers. Therefore, engagement that fosters conversations between the influencer and amongst followers may give a better sense of whether the engagement is positive, negative, or neutral. This is an area that needs further exploration if success is going to be linked to key performance indicators. Certainly, the measurement of success is arguably a challenge for everyone in marketing, advertising, and public relations fields.

So, you want to be an influencer?

For aspiring influencers, having a strategic approach means taking the time to formulate an overall strategy about what you want to do and identifying tactics for how you want to do it. The second part of Yesiloglu's (2020) definition of an influencer implies two separate actions. First, the influencer must be able to influence others. This means influencers need to clearly understand how persuasion works and should consider reading the seminal works of Robert Cialdini's (2009) *Influence: The Psychology of Persuasion*, as well as other studies that explore persuasion. Second, for influencers to impact others' buying decisions, they need to understand the consumer buying process and at what step the influencer can impact the consumer making the purchase decision.

Upon developing a strategic approach, influencers should examine the advantages they have over celebrities or micro-influencer celebrity status, that Leban and Voyer (2020) identified as advantages in Chapter 2. Influencers are considered more relatable to their followers. This could be due to the influencer coming across as more similar to their followers or at least being humble enough to give praise to their followers for helping them get where they are today. Secondly, influencers who come across as more reachable to their followers help enable a sense of connectedness. Finally, Leban and Voyer (2020) argue that influencers are perceived as more trustworthy because they come across as genuine.

Relationships between the influencers and their followers are covered extensively in this book. For example, Närvänen et al. (2020) in Chapter 7 explored parasocial relationships of Generation Z consumers with social media influencers. Through their qualitative studies they discovered three types of parasocial relationships. The first focuses around that of a close personal friendship which suggests the follower feels

joyce costello

that they have a relationship of sorts with the influencer. This sort of relationship has the benefit of trust, but if it is broken it can lead to the second parasocial relationship of an ex-friendship. If the influencer's behavior changes such as switching to primarily sponsored content or getting discovered that they engaged in buying fake followers, then the followers will take negative actions. The final parasocial relationship centers on casual friendship which may be for entertainment purposes only. This type of friendship is not expected to lead to purchase behaviors given the loose nature of the connection.

Närvänen et al. (2020) suggest that for the parasocial relationship to continue, the influencers' content needs to be "real and relatable" while being transparent about brand collaboration or sponsorship. Närvänen et al. (2020) emphasize that influencers need to consider whether the brands they are working with align with their own persona; if they do not, they risk the parasocial relationship with their Generation Z followers. In the case of influencers and brands, if there is not a fit in values and target audience, then there will be a mismatch (Närvänen et al. 2020). This relates back to Özçelik and Levi's (2020) framework that focused on fit as an antecedent.

The main question about influencer–follower relationships, is what kind of actions or consequences will it lead to? By understanding that followers will have different types of relationships, influencers should question what will motivate them to engage or take that relationship further. Likewise, followers need to understand what motivates influencers if they are going to have a sense of the influencer's authenticity, credibility, or trustworthiness.

Why do followers want to engage with influencers?

For years, practitioners have sought to understand why individuals would talk with brands, while media organizations try to comprehend what drives conversation about content. When we introduce influencers into the communication mix, we now are trying to understand what motivated the individuals to talk about brands with influencers on different social media platforms.

In Chapter 6, Yesiloglu and Gill (2020) investigated how consumers are motivated to engage with influencers. It is critical to understand the needs of the consumer or follower as social media is poised for two-way communication and engagement as opposed to static one-way information delivery. Their data analysis of post-millennials found that in addition to information seeking, users were motivated out of a fear of missing out and for enjoyment. For brands, information seeking motivations signal that their users are turning to influencers for pre-purchase information as well as scanning if there are new products coming out. Being motivated out of a fear of missing out does have the possibility of becoming a dark side of social media. Dhir et al. (2018) attributes the fear of missing out as resulting in compulsive social media behaviors that can lead to anxiety and depression in adolescents. This adds to the debate about to what extent influencers are responsible for the behavior of their followers if the influencers truly are influencing them.

Yet, when Yesiloglu and Gill (2020) turned the tables and explored influencer motivations to engage with brands, unsurprisingly remuneration was at the top of the list. This implies that influencers who work with brands may be motivated by extrinsic reasons. But Costello and Urbanska (2020) discuss there are consequences for influencers that focus on sponsored content. Yesiloglu and Gill (2020) also discovered influencers are motivated to work with brands as it increases their ability to socialize with the followers and can increase the power recognition. While it may appear that influencer motivations to work with brands are skewed towards extrinsic rewards, if one considers that many influencers may view their relationships with brands as a job, it is reasonable to expect they would want to be paid for their livelihood.

When Yesiloglu and Waśkiw (2020) in Chapter 8 explored Instagram users' motivational drivers to engage with influencers who specialize in the sustainable niche, the motivations did not mirror those from Chapter 6. One of the top motivations was engaging in like-minded discussions. However, Yesiloglu and Waśkiw (2020) found that these like-minded discussions were often between the followers and not engagement between influencer and their followers. These conversations between followers can be value-added to practitioners/brands who can observe conversations about them between potential consumers. If the influencer can facilitate engagement with themselves as well as inner engagement between followers, then there becomes two or more points of possible positive eWOM. Another prominent motivation was connections to others. If followers are motivated to engage with influencers to feel connected, this may suggest that the connection could be more of an online friend opposed to a micro-celebrity. Indeed, it matches with Närvänen et al.'s (2020) concept of parasocial relationships being close friendships.

Lastly, Yesiloglu and Waśkiw (2020) assert that their study highlights the need for influencers to use a conversational and informal tone when engaging with followers. For example, conversational-informative content is an effective means of encouraging engagement. Whereas, if influencers take an informative-educational tone, it does not evoke as much engagement, but could meet the information-seeking needs of the followers.

Do influencers NEED to be attractive, trustworthy, experts?

Authenticity is a key argument for brands to use influencers as opposed to strictly advertisements. Chapter 7 explores this conceptually and Chapter 12 empirically tests this. However, for the aspiring influencer, what should they focus on?

In a world filled with experts acting as consultants for the media, it turns out one might not have to be an expert to be an influencer. Costello and Urbanska (2020) address this empirically in Chapter 10. Their findings suggest that there was no significant relationship between expertise and credibility between sponsored and non-sponsored content. It would be easy to assume that brands would want an expert who is an opinion leader to promote their products online. However, it could be that the audience assumes that the make-up artist/beauty blogger is an expert because of the high technical levels displayed. Conversely, it could be that different generations place different levels of importance on being an expert. If the influencer is consistent with the products they promote and stay in a niche, that may qualify them as experts for their followers. Plus, it might be that the followers are not looking for their parent's version of experts in the news. This leaves room for future research to consider whether influencers that are considered experts – as opposed to those who just create content that appeals to a large, engaged audience – might have a strategic advantage when it comes to being viewed as more credible.

Influencers specializing in niches

In the first half of this book, several authors built a case for influencers needing to fit the brand's product and visions in general. While some recommended that influencers be experts in their area, research around how different types of influencer experts in a niche area operate is nascent. Quintana Ramos and Cownie (2020) decided to investigate how female environmental influencers might differ in their engagement with followers who were all drawn to environmental movements.

Using principles from socialization and the habits of females' online behavior, they found that influencers that highlighted pro-environmental behaviors often promoted public activism. Yet, if the influencer's actions were not consistent with their content, followers would call them out on it. This underscores the need for influencers to be consistent. Quintana Ramos and Cownie (2020) also discovered that environmental influencers who are in the vegan niche tend to utilize four principles: empathy, criticism of animal abuse, veganism as a balanced diet, and content based on vegan consumption. Empathy is displayed by the influencers' love of animals, which can elicit positive engagement, while criticism of humans' abuse of animals helps fuel outrage and activism. By promoting veganism as a healthy diet and showing their one vegan lifestyles, the influencer is not only attractive and considered authentic to their followers but can also be appealing to vegan brands.

Yet, environmental influencers who engage in zero-waste practices tend to use different tactics such as do-it-yourself, concentrating on minimalist aesthetics, and making sustainable choices. Zero-waste practice influencers tend to focus their content inward, meaning that they rely on themselves to be the object of change and try to inspire them to follow their actions. On the contrary, the environmental influencers that focused on public activism or veganism tend to use their cause to be the propellant of change. Quintana Ramos and Cownie (2020) conclude that brands that want to work with environmental influencers need to be authentic in their causes and not be a brand that is attempting to greenwash an issue so that they might be more appealing to those in the environmental niche.

Dark side of influencers

There are several dark sides to influencer marketing. This book did not focus on the mental impact that influencers may undergo such as abuse from online trolls or the pressure to constantly live their best life online (although we highly encourage those who are aspiring to become influencers to look at other studies that do highlight that). Rather, we focused on the dark side of influencer marketing practices. This includes issues related to sponsored and non-sponsored content (Costello and Urbanska 2020; Harrison and Cownie 2020) and buying fake followers and social bots in Chapter 12 (Costello and Biondi 2020).

Attitudes towards sponsored content

For an influencer, being paid for creating content might seem like the gold standard to aim for. However, this extrinsic reward also comes with unexpected consequences. Costello and Urbanska (2020) investigate whether a follower's view of an influencer's attractiveness, trustworthiness, and expertise changes if the content is sponsored or not. The reason this is important to understand is that the influencer needs to decide if they are focusing on commercialization and they are willing to accept that their initial follower base may not view them as credible. Costello and Urbanska (2020) discovered that if a post was sponsored, the audience considered the influencer more attractive. They rationalized that if a brand was willing to pay for the influencer's services, there must be some sort of spill-over effect that increased the influencer's attractiveness. However, when it came to trustworthiness, the followers expressed more terms of trust to the influencer. Herein lies the dilemma for influencers: is it better to have your followers find you more attractive or trustworthy? Finally, Costello and Urbanska (2020) found there was no significant relation between influencers being viewed as an expert by their followers regardless of whether the content was sponsored or not. The authors conclude that it may be that there are not consistently outward symbols of one being an expert or it is not important to the followers.

Another issue that influencers need to take into consideration when dealing with sponsored content or not is if it will alienate their followers. In Chapter 11, Harrison and Cownie (2020) found evidence that audience members often would tune out or switch off if they felt the content that was supposed to be sponsored was hidden behind persuasive messages. Indeed, resentment was clear when people felt influencers were trying to sell them something that they were not interested in, with some individuals stating they stopped following several influencers as a result. But, what about when the content was not clearly labeled as sponsored? Chapter 13 (Bosher) 2020 addresses the legal implications and consequences for influencers who fail to disclose if the content is sponsored or not.

These two studies signal there can be consequences for influencers whose content might become skewed heavily towards sponsored content. Yet, an area that could be further explored is if the sponsored content is in the voice, style, and creativity of the influencer differs from content heavily controlled by the brand. This relates back to Rosenthal and Arcuri's (2020) discussion about media logic versus public relations logic.

Fake followers and bogus bots

In Yesiloglu's (2020) definition of an influencer, she highlights the influencer's strategic approach. For the aspiring influencer who might be struggling to get noticed by brands or even a more established one that wants to show potential clients that they are still relevant and engaging with followers, Costello and Biondi (2020) contend that some are turning to fake followers and bots as a means of social engagement deception. This can be a dark practice that threatens the actual growth of influencer marketing from a reputation standpoint.

In Costello and Biondi's (2020) investigation of the prevalence of fake followers and bots amongst micro-influencers on Instagram, they discovered that Influencers that had a reputation of not purchasing fake followers were deemed to have higher levels of authenticity which led to increased trust amongst followers. Yet, similar results were found for influencers rumored to have possibly purchased fake followers, and those confirmed as purchasing had no significant negative impact. For some influencers they may think that it can still be profitable to purchase fake followers. Given how social bots are being programmed to take on more human-like behavior traits, Costello and Biondi (2020) state that this might be a larger threat to influencer marketing.

As socialbots programming and technology advances, so do the programs that seek to identify the bots. Researchers in this area are encouraged to continue to create free bot identification programs such as Indiana University's botometer. Influencers are urged to heed the case study about Devumi in Chapter 12. Their history of selling fake followers and fake social media engagement, spurred the Federal Trade Commission to take them to court.

Staying on the right side of the law

As different governing and regulation bodies begin to bring agencies and influencers to court (Bosher 2020; Costello and Biondi 2020), it has become evident that twenty-first-century legal solutions are needed. Rules that were intended to apply to radio and television channels are slowly being adapted to the internet. One might even say that social media was the wild west and is beginning to slowly be reined in.

Who owns what?

When Bosher (2020) explored copyrights and who owned the content, there were several areas that are of concern to influencers. Using the case of American fashion model Gigi Hadid, Bosher (2020) illustrates the many pitfalls and issues related to who owns what content. For influencers, if they are employed by a brand to create content, then does the company own the content? This is an area where those involved in employment laws could help influencers in navigating tricky areas. If the influencer is considered a contractor, do they need to negotiate ownership and copyright of the content prior? In the case study of Crowd and ExtraAF in Chapter 8 (Rusoiu 2020), the agreement between the agency and the influencers allowed them to use content from the influencers on the brand's website.

Bosher (2020) also brings up the issue of fair use and who can use what content and to what extent. This becomes a second area of possible contention if someone took an influencer's original content and then shared it on their own social media site. If that content draws more followers and hence sponsorship deals, did the second individual profit directly or indirectly from the initial content that was copyrighted? This means influencers will need to understand fair use and implied use before using any content by others. Indeed, this area is posed to be a critical debate in the future of copyright law as it applies to influencers.

Finally, Bosher (2020) addresses the terms and conditions of different platforms. This is especially of interest for brands that are wanting to engage in influencer marketing. For example, if a brand has a monetary relationship with an influencer that works on Instagram, the terms and conditions on Instagram allows them to sell their (Instagram) rights in the user's content to an outside party. The implications for brands losing control of their content on Instagram have the potential to explode if third parties seek to maximize Instagram's terms and conditions.

The regulatory blind spot for influencers

When looking at the branded content that influencers are creating, one might even suggest that it is only a matter of time before advertisers and influencers collide. In Chapter 14, MacRury (2020) addressed issues about how the scope and operation of regulation and compliance are not fully in place for influencers. Indeed, he contends that the regulatory blind spot towards some influencer content promises to be a foreshadowing of guidance and regulations yet to come. Similar to Bosher (2020), MacRury suggests debates about influencers that ASA should consider. He asks the reader to consider looking at branded content from influencers as if it were advertising and how regulation might apply. For instance, advertisers on television must use dayparting for certain content to be played, but influencers operate on social media which is not bound by time.

MacRury's (2020) exploration into family vloggers FGTeeV helps to better delineate the blind spots emerging around influencer content. By breaking down the influencer's video content as if it were a broadcast, he explores how advertising regulations would be applied. His discussion about the imbalance in regulatory regimes governing broadcast advertising versus influencer promotional communications has potentially detrimental consequences. For example, if there is the view that advertisements are over-regulated, while online promotional-influencer led contents are under-regulated, can this impact brands' willingness to remain ethical in their practices of "advertising" under the guise of influencer marketing. MacRury argues that such a split serves neither advertising, nor influencers. He concluded that this does not support confidence in the credibility and integrity of media environments either.

Idea fairy: Lessons learned

Given the various findings discussed, what advice would you give to someone wanting to become an influencer? If you were working for a brand that is considering pursuing integrating influencer marketing into their campaign, what would be the pros and cons? How do you think influencers can better educate themselves in order to avoid the dark side of being an influencer?

The call for future research

Whether you're a student looking for a dissertation topic, a practitioner who is looking at areas to expand, or a researcher who wants to help advance the field and theories related to influencer marketing, below is a compilation of suggestions for future research gleaned from the studies and case studies within the book.

Will influencers benefit from traditional media or commercialization?

The case study in Chapter 1 discussed how Joe Wicks' content strategy is supported by traditional media as well as social media channels. He initially started off as an Instagram influencer posting workouts and recipes and now has authored numerous books. It is evident from other influencers who developed their own product lines, that they benefit from traditional media tactics. Certainly, in the case study about Kylie Jenner in Chapter 2, as she rose through influencer stardom, so did her products. She went from Kylie Lip Kits to establishing Kylie Cosmetics. In the case of Joe Wicks and Kylie Jenner, both went from influencer to celebrity status while creating their own products. The question is whether producing tangible products in addition to online content increased their influential power. Did going from influencer, to micro-celebrity to celebrity status impact their reliability, reachability, or trustworthiness – all advantages Leban and Voyer (2020) state influencers have. Therefore, it is possible that in the future, research should consider if and how the commercialization of influencers will impact their followers. Will commercialization act as a moderating variable weakening the relationship between the influencer and their followers?

Applying theory to practice

In Chapter 3, Riboldazzi and Capriello (2020) demonstrate how to apply their proposed three-step method for identifying the best influencer in the case of Coop, an Italian grocery store chain. Similarly, in Chapter 4 Rosenthal and Arcuri (2020) test their proposed ICA (individual, content, audience) framework with the case of Rayovac, a US battery company operating in Brazil. Both cases show a practical application when it comes to choosing the best influencer. The difference is the angle from which they both achieve results. Riboldazzi and Capriello (2020) focus on having the brand find an influencer suitable to their needs. This gives the brands the benefit of potentially averting a reputation issue or crisis if the influencer does not match their values, whereas Rosenthal and Arcuri (2020) focus on the individual, the content they create, and how the audience interacts. This focus on the audience could be best suited for those brands needing to raise awareness, but also relies on the influencer's content to spur engagement. Therefore, scholars should consider continuing investigations whether a brand-oriented or audience-oriented framework will deliver the most benefits for influencer marketing campaigns. Additionally, are there different outcomes if one employs media versus public relations logic?

Reputation management: when things do not go as planned

When Logan Paul took a selfie with suicide victims in Japan, society outrange meant YouTube found themselves in a crisis and needed to remove Paul from the Google

Preferred program (Matsakis 2018). While this outcome was a bit more dramatic then Närvänen et al.'s (2020) case about food bloggers promoting poultry company Atria, it illustrates the possibility of issues/crisis management when working with influencers. Certainly, for the food bloggers, they alienated those followers with whom they have had a positive parasocial relationship due to the brand sponsorship with Atria. Reputation management by the influencer and crisis avoidance is an area that needs research. Influencers will not generally have the same staffing as brands when it comes to managing issues. Therefore, those who research reputation management and crisis communication should consider the implications it has for influencers. While this is similar to challenges facing small businesses or self-employed who generally do not have the ability to have a public relations specialist on staff, it is an opportunity to develop ways that the singular influencer can prepare themselves for reputation management and crisis communication other than removing an offending post.

Virtual truth or virtual lies

One area that is gaining interest in influencer marketing is the rise in popularity of virtual influencers. Guthrie (2020) in Chapter 15 introduces the reader to how virtual influencers are quickly multiplying. In the case of Lil Miquela, some scholars argue that it was a case of deception and that followers were not aware that it was a computer-generated image (Blanton and Carbajal 2019). Yet, Guthrie (2020) explores the positive ways how brands can benefit from engaging with virtual influencers. He points out that there are not any of the logistic problems with the virtual influencers engaging in areas around the world in outfits that always fit. Furthermore, he adds that with humans controlling the content that the virtual influencers create, it is easier to avoid crises. However, when Twitter created AI chatbot, Tay, it went horribly wrong when the bot learned in less than 24 hours how to tweet misogynistic and racist remarks.

Guthrie's (2020) case for the future of virtual influencers offers a whole new realm of research possibilities. While there are many benefits for the brands, how does audience engagement differ between a CGI and a real human influencer? Can the virtual influencer evoke more personalized engagement with their audience if programmed to do so? What are the ethical implications of using a programmed virtual influencer?

Best practices: brands using influencer marketing to grow their brand

In Chapter 2, Leban and Voyer (2020) present the case of Glossier and how they managed to expand their growth by using primarily influencers to act as a propellant for electronic word-of-mouth. The brand was not concerned with the number of followers the influencers had but focused on "ordinary women" who enjoy using Glossier. By focusing on metrics other than followers, Glossier was able to still see an increase in purchases. This implies that brands can focus on metrics other than the number of followers and still see results that they need.

Riboldazzi and Capriello (2020) were able to empirically test their model for choosing the right influencer in the case of Italian company Coop Lombardia. The authors had recommended a three-part process with the final goal of ensuring the influencers reach, relevance, and resonance. These three criteria assisted Coop Lombardia with meeting their campaign to increase awareness. The organization had focused its metrics similarly to the criteria used to select influencers. Riboldazzi and Capriello's (2020) case study findings imply that if metrics are linked to the criteria set to select the influencer, then it is easier to gauge the success or not of the influencer marketing campaign.

However, when it comes to best practices, it is sometimes said that what works for one organization may not work for another. Certainly, more research and rigorous application to the framework models within this book can help identify what really are the best practices for those involved in influencer marketing campaigns. Therefore, we call upon scholars, university students, and practitioners to continue test methods suggested so that a solid base of best practices can be identified.

Summary

- Influencer marketing can provide practitioners opportunities to maximize user-generated content to engage with audiences in ways the brand is not able to.
- Aiming for a career as an influencer is entirely possible but requires the influencer to consider what is important to their audience if they will specialize in a niche and desirable characteristic to succeed.
- Influencers and brands need to be aware of the potential dark side to influencer marketing and examine whether what they are doing is legal and ethical.
- It is imperative to stay on the right side of the law and educate oneself about policies and regulations related to influencers and influencer marketing.
- As a nascent field, there is much for researchers to explore and investigate in terms of influencers and influencer marketing.

References

Blanton, R., and Carbajal, D. 2019. Not a girl, not yet a woman: A critical case study on social media, deception, and Lil Miquela. Ch 6. *The Handbook of Research on Deception, Fake News, and Misinformation Online.* Ed. Chiluwa, I.E., and Samoilenko, S.A. IGI Global. http://doi:10.4018/978-1-5225-8535-0

Bosher, H., 2020. Influencer Marketing and the Law. Ch. 13 in *Influencer Marketing: Building Brand Communities and Engagement.* Ed. Yesiloglu, S., and Costello, J. London: Routledge.

Costello, J., and Biondi, L., 2020. The art of deception: Will fake followers decay trust and can authenticity preserve it? Ch. 12 in *Influencer Marketing: Building Brand Communities and Engagement.* Ed. Yesiloglu, S., and Costello, J. London: Routledge.

Costello, J., and Urbanska, K., 2020. "Hope this is not sponsored" – Is an influencers' credibility impacted when using sponsored versus non-sponsored content? Ch. 10 in *Influencer Marketing: Building Brand Communities and Engagement.* Ed. Yesiloglu, S., and Costello, J. London: Routledge.

Cialdini, R.B., 2009. *Influencer: The power of persuasion.* New York. William Morrow.

Dhir, A., Yossatorn, Y., Kaur, P., and Chen, S., 2018. Online social media fatigue and psychological wellbeing—A study of compulsive use, fear of missing out, fatigue, anxiety, and
depression. *International Journal of Information Management*, 40, 141–152.

Ferris, G.R., Hochwarter, W.A., Douglas, C., Blass, F.R., Kolodinsky, R.W., and Treadway. D.C.,
2002. Social influence process in organizations and human resources systems. *Research in
Personnel and Human Resources Management*, 21, 65–127.

Guthrie, S., 2020. Virtual influencers: More human than human. Ch. 15 in *Influencer
Marketing: Building Brand Communities and Engagement*. Ed. Yesiloglu, S., and Costello, J.
London: Routledge.

Harrison, J., and Cownie, F., 2020. The Monetization of Opinions: An investigation into
consumer responses to covert endorsement practices on Instagram. Ch. 11 in *Influencer
Marketing: Building Brand Communities and Engagement*. Ed. Yesiloglu, S., and Costello, J.
London: Routledge.

Kristof-Brown, A.L., Zimmerman, R.D., and Johnson, E.C., 2005. Consequences of individual's
fit at work: A meta-analysis of person-job, person-organization, person-group, and person-
supervisor fit. *Personnel Psychology*, 58(2), 281–342.

Leban, M., and Voyer, B., 2020, Social media influencers versus traditional influencers: Roles and
consequences for traditional marketing campaigns. Ch. 2 in *Influencer Marketing: Building
Brand Communities and Engagement*. Ed. Yesiloglu, S., and Costello, J. London: Routledge.

MacRury, I., 2020. Taking the biscuit: Exploring influencers, advertising, and regulation. Ch. 14
in *Influencer Marketing: Building Brand Communities and Engagement*. Ed. Yesiloglu, S., and
Costello, J. London: Routledge.

Matsakis, L., 2018. The Logan Paul Video Should Be a Reckoning For YouTube. *Wired*. Available
from: www.wired.com/story/logan-paul-video-youtube-reckoning/

Närvänen, E., Kirvesmies, T., and Kahri, E., 2020. Parasocial relationships of Generation Z
consumers with social media influencers. Ch. 7 in *Influencer Marketing: Building Brand
Communities and Engagement*. Ed. Yesiloglu, S., and Costello, J. London: Routledge.

Northouse, P., 2016. *Leadership: Theory and Practice*. 7ed. London: Sage.

Özçelik, A., and Levi, E., 2020. Choosing the right influencer for your brand: a guide to the field.
Ch. 5 in *Influencer Marketing: Building Brand Communities and Engagement*. Ed. Yesiloglu, S.,
and Costello, J. London: Routledge.

Quintana Ramos, I. and Cownie, F., 2020. Female environmental influencers on Instagram.
Ch. 9 in *Influencer Marketing: Building Brand Communities and Engagement*. Ed. Yesiloglu,
S., and Costello, J. London: Routledge.

Riboldazzi, S., and Capriello, A., 2020. Identifying and selecting the right influencers in the
digital era. Ch. 3 in *Influencer Marketing: Building Brand Communities and Engagement*. Ed.
Yesiloglu, S., and Costello, J. London: Routledge.

Rosenthal, B., and Arcuri, A., 2020. How to map and select digital influencers for marketing
campaigns. Ch. 6 in *Influencer Marketing and Relations: Building Brand Communities and
Engagement*. Ed. Yesiloglu, S., and Costello, J. London: Routledge.

Rusoiu, R., 2020. Case study: An agency's adaptation to COVID-19. Ch. 8 in *Influencer
Marketing: Building Brand Communities and Engagement*. Ed. Yesiloglu, S., and Costello, J.
London: Routledge.

Yesiloglu, S., 2020. The rise of influencers and influencer marketing. Ch. 1 in *Influencer
Marketing: Building Brand Communities and Engagement*. Ed. Yesiloglu, S., and Costello, J.
London: Routledge.

Yesiloglu, S., and Gill, S., 2020. An exploration into the motivations behind post-millennials'
engagement with influencers' brand-related content on Instagram. Ch. 6 in *Influencer

Marketing: Building Brand Communities and Engagement. Ed. Yesiloglu, S., and Costello, J. London: Routledge.

Yesiloglu, S., and Waśkiw, W., 2020. An exploratory study into consumer-influencer engagement on Instagram in the context of sustainability. Ch. 8 in *Influencer Marketing: Building Brand Communities and Engagement.* Ed. Yesiloglu, S., and Costello, J. London: Routledge.

Index